GOD'S MOST EARNEST PURPOSE

Praise for *God's Most Earnest Purpose*

Dennis Ngien brings his detailed knowledge of Luther's theology to bear on the issue, rather neglected in English-speaking study, of the content of Luther's catechetical instruction from the late 1520s. This reading is informed by understanding the Reformer's soteriological emphases as being ultimately Trinitarian, personalist, and relational, such that soteriology is no "mere doctrine" but an invitation to a life of trust and communion with the Lord of life, who is Father, Son, and Spirit. This includes the work of the Holy Spirit in believers' sanctification: "the Third Article is most important" (Luther). This is a carefully and deeply researched book that seeks to communicate something of the realities that Luther, the famous professor of biblical theology, sought to convey.

—**Mark W. Elliott**, professorial fellow, Wycliffe College, University of Toronto

In attending to Luther's Trinitarian grammar of faith, Ngien draws out the neglected riches of Luther's account of the self-giving of God and its centrality to our identity as those loved by God, accepted by Christ, and renewed by the Spirit. Characterized by deep learning, remarkably fresh insights, and pastoral sensitivity, *God's Most Earnest Purpose* will reward all who want to love God above all else with the love that God deposits in us by the Spirit, who is himself love.

—**Christopher R. J. Holmes**, professor of systematic theology, University of Otago

In *God's Most Earnest Purpose*, Dennis Ngien masterfully brings together a panoply of Luther scholarship and contemporary systematic theology. Against those, like Karl Holl and Adolf von Harnack, who claimed that the Trinity was only marginal to Luther's thinking, Ngien is able to successfully show the centrality of the Trinity to Luther's concepts of salvation and the Christian life.

—**Jack D. Kilcrease**, professor of historical and systematic theology, Christ School of Theology

Systematic theologians have bemoaned the fact that Luther produced no comprehensive dogmatics. However, echoing the heart of Luther's teachings, Ngien gives us a succinct outline of the Reformer's faith, flowing from the Trinitarian dynamics implicit in Luther's understanding of the gospel, mirroring and fleshing out his catechisms. Readers will find that Ngien provides an insightful and nuanced approach to Luther's doctrine of God and how it bears upon daily life.

—**Mark Mattes**, Lutheran Bible Institute chair and professor of theology, Grand View University

A fine achievement, representing the culmination of a career immersed in Reformation theology. Ngien illuminates the deep Trinitarian foundations of Luther's soteriology, offering a compelling interpretation of the great Reformer's doctrine of God. This is a book of careful scholarship, but it also radiates with the same passion and spiritual urgency that one finds in Luther's proclamation of the gospel.

—**James E. Pedlar**, Bastian Chair of Wesley Studies, Tyndale Seminary

Ngien's succinct interpretation of Luther's catechisms according to a "Trinitarian grammar of faith" allows the reader to appreciate the magisterial Reformer as precisely the theologian he aspired to be: not an "innovator," but a faithful exegete of the church's biblically grounded doctrinal tradition.

—**Bernd Wannenwetsch**, honorary professor of systematic theology and ethics, Freie Theologische Hochschule, Geissen

An excellent account of Luther's "Trinitarian grammar of salvation" which brings out clearly the internal consistency of Luther's approach to the work of God in the world and in believers, and especially its implications for the life of faith. This book both advances our scholarly understanding of Luther and our pastoral understanding of his contemporary significance.

—**Alister McGrath**, senior research fellow, Ian Ramsey Centre for Science and Religion, emeritus Andreas Idreos Professor of Science and Religion, and emeritus fellow, Harris Manchester College, University of Oxford

God's Most Earnest Purpose

Luther on Fearing, Trusting, and Loving God

Dennis Ngien

Foreword by Graham Tomlin

FORTRESS PRESS
Minneapolis

GOD'S MOST EARNEST PURPOSE
Luther on Fearing, Trusting, and Loving God

Copyright © 2026 Fortress Press. All rights reserved. Except for brief quotations in critical articles or reviews, no part of this book may be reproduced in any manner without prior written permission from the publisher. Email copyright@fortresspress.com or write to Permissions, Fortress Press, PO Box 1209, Minneapolis, MN 55440-1209.

Library of Congress Control Number: 2025022916 (print)

Cover design: Brittany Becker

Print ISBN: 978-1-5064-9817-1
eBook ISBN: 978-1-5064-9818-8

To my late brother Daniel Ngieng Kiong Ann,
a kindling fire, in faith, hope, and love.

CONTENTS

	Foreword by Graham Tomlin	ix
	Acknowledgments	xi
	Abbreviations	xiii
	Introduction *God's Most Earnest Purpose and the Grammar of Faith in Luther*	1
1.	Rooted in Tradition *Luther's Doctrine of the Trinity*	21
2.	God's Most Earnest Purpose in the Ten Commandments	47
3.	God's Most Earnest Purpose in Creation	77
4	God's Most Earnest Purpose in Redemption	111
5.	God's Most Earnest Purpose in Sanctification	151
6.	God's Most Earnest Purpose in the Lord's Prayer	189
	Conclusion *Let the Gospel Lead the Way*	217
	Afterword by Jeffrey G. Silcock	231
	Bibliography	235
	Index	247

FOREWORD

The doctrine of justification by faith, Luther famously taught, was the "article by which the church stands or falls."[1] So, not surprisingly, his theology has normally been thought of centering upon this very doctrine. Luther, we have been told, is a theologian of the word, of faith, of grace, of Scripture and of Christ. After all, the great *solas*—*sola fide, sola gratia, sola Scriptura, solus Christus*—were meant to be the great calls of the Lutheran Reformation.

As a result, the image that most of us have in our minds of Luther's gospel is of an understanding of the Christian faith focused around themes such as imputed righteousness, faith and works, law and gospel, the two kingdoms, and Christology. Most of the secondary literature about Luther, over the years, has explored countless aspects and perspectives on these themes. Of course, this is not an inaccurate description of Luther's theology. He dwelled on these notions a great deal in sermons, treatises, commentaries, and controversies.

Yet for many in the church, both in his time and since—from his catholic opponents at the time, such as Eck or Erasmus, to critics in more recent times such as John Henry Newman, to the devotees of the new perspective on Paul in our day—Luther's whole approach has felt like an exaggeration. Luther, for them, was guilty of twisting the Christian faith out of shape by an overstated focus on *sola fide* as the heart of the gospel. Luther has often been presented as a lopsided theologian, obsessed with marginal elements of the mainstream Christian tradition, and uninterested in some of its key themes.

However, there is another way of looking at this. Perhaps the reason why Luther emphasized such doctrines as justification by faith, the priority of divine grace, and the centrality of the word of promise in Christ was precisely because these were the points at which God's gracious heart and movement toward us were under attack. Luther's theology, like all theology, is contextual in that it focuses on the matters that were particularly at stake at the time.

In this carefully researched, widely read and theologically astute book, Dennis Ngien has done us a great favor. He has shown Luther as a fully fledged theologian of the Trinity and of the Holy Spirit. Through close analysis of Luther's treatment on the three great texts at the heart of Christian faith and worship—the Ten Commandments, the Creed, and the Lord's Prayer—he shows

---

1. See introduction, note 18.

Luther to stand within the great tradition of Trinitarian theology that reaches from the early fathers, through the Cappadocians, to Augustine, and beyond into more recent times. His focus may have been on God's gracious movement toward us in Christ through the Spirit, yet for him, as for the great tradition of faith, the works of the economic Trinity and the nature of the immanent Trinity are in complete harmony with one another.

This shift of emphasis is one that has been growing in recent times, through Luther scholars such as Dennis Bielfeldt, Paul Hinlicky, and Simeon Zahl. Ngien joins this number and offers a full account of these themes through the lens of the great texts of Christian faith. The gifts of God in the gospel expressed in the Creed become ours though faith, expressed in prayer (especially the Lord's Prayer), which enables us, in turn, to delight in and fulfill the commandments.

At the same time, this is a theology that characteristically does not deny the darkness. Luther knew, of his own experience, the absence of God, the lure of temptation, the terrors of conscience—how could he not when standing against the might of the Catholic Church of his time? Ngien shows how Luther's Trinitarian soteriological grammar helps faith cling onto the work of the God revealed in Christ through the Spirit, rather than the accusing voice of the hidden God that is indistinguishable from the voice of Satan.

This book manages to focus on Luther's pneumatologic and Trinitarian logic in a way that does not deny the centrality of justification by faith but sets that doctrine within a Trinitarian context—what Ngien calls the "Trinitarian grammar of salvation." He does the same with key Lutheran distinctions such as the two kingdoms or the law and the gospel, showing how this latter distinction refers to the Holy Spirit, who gives us the gift of faith to see past the divinity hidden in terrifying majesty to the true God revealed in Christ. The Father sends the precious gift of his Son, born into the world by the Holy Spirit, to work our salvation, and the Spirit enables us, through the gift of faith, to confess the Son who obtains salvation for us by enabling us to assume his righteousness, so that all God's goodness becomes ours in Christ.

This, however, is more than a mere academic game. This is a book that breathes the delight of God's work in Christ and through the Spirit, for us and in us, that brings the delights of a clear conscience and a sure faith anchored in the divine movement toward us in Christ. This book offers a rounded, energizing, and ultimately hope-filled picture of the salvation in which Luther, and his readers over the centuries, have found such joy.

Bishop Graham Tomlin

ACKNOWLEDGMENTS

The impetus behind this book comes from a common desire to allow the gospel to be heard again through the voice of the Magisterial Reformer Martin Luther. Several scholars, among whom I must mention Alister E. McGrath, Graham Tomlin, Jeffrey Silcock, and Terry J. Wright for special regard, have read and supported my work; each in his unique way helps me to read Luther accurately and fruitfully. This book also enjoys an ecumenical reception from notable scholars such as Christopher R. J. Holmes, Bernd Wannenwetsch, James E. Pedlar, Jack D. Kilcrease, Mark W. Elliott, and Mark C. Mattes. Gratitude must be extended to my dear students Brenden Bott and Geoffrey Butler, and to several anonymous thinkers, for their diligent reading of the manuscript, to the library team at Tyndale University for tirelessly checking citations, acquiring books and articles for me, and to many prayer warriors for standing with me faithfully. The timely completion of the book is credited to Ceceilia, my "Dearest," and Hansel, our son, a handy and perceptive editor, for their unfailing support and understanding.

My late brother Daniel, to whom this book is dedicated, has inspired in many an illustrious life of self-giving. Why the Lord did not extend his service longer on earth is hidden from us, a mystery indeed, but hidden in God, whose face he now beholds with joy and satisfaction. His sudden departure is a powerful witness of our struggle, that we frown upon God's purpose and doing, and of God's true disposition toward us, that his face ever shines upon us. We are at times like this more grateful than ever for the promise and hope of the resurrection (John 11:25) and truly feel the power of the gospel by which we live unto God against all odds of life.

ABBREVIATIONS

BC	*The Book of Concord: The Confessions of the Evangelical Lutheran Church.* Edited by Robert Kolb and Timothy J. Wengert. Fortress, 2000.
BC (Tappert)	*The Book of Concord: The Confessions of the Evangelical Lutheran Church.* Translated and edited by Theodore G. Tappert. Fortress, 1959.
LW	*Luther's Works: American Edition.* Vols. 1–30. Edited by Jaroslav Pelikan. Concordia, 1955–73. *Luther's Works: American Edition.* Vols. 31–55. Edited by Helmut T. Lehman. Fortress, 1957–86. *Luther's Works: American Edition*, n.s., vols. 56–82. Edited by Christopher Boyd Brown, Benjamin T. G. Mayes, and James L. Langebartels. Concordia, 2009–.
WA	*D. Martin Luthers Werke: Kritische Gesamtausgabe.* 65 vols. in 127. Weimar: Hermann Böhlau, 1883–1929. Abteilung 1: Schriften vols. 1–56.
WA TR	*D. Martin Luthers Werke: Kritische Gesamtausgabe.* 65 vols. in 127. Weimar: Hermann Böhlau, 1883–1929. Abteilung 2: Tischreden vols. 1–6.

Introduction

*God's Most Earnest Purpose and the Grammar
of Faith in Luther*

IN THE *PREFACE to the Large Catechism*, Luther asks rhetorically, "Moreover, what is the whole Psalter, but meditation and exercises based on the First Commandment?"[1] The first commandment teaches us "to have the Lord as our God." Hidden in his exposition of the first commandment is Luther's fiduciary claim on who God is in relation to his people; in his own words, "God's most earnest purpose is to be our God."[2] This phrase is Luther's ingenious original insight into the first commandment. To describe God's purpose thus underscores the character of God, that he is not impassively indifferent but immanently belonging to us in creation, redemption, and sanctification. The God whose "most earnest purpose is to be our God" is nothing other than the triune God of the Creed. The Creed offers a Trinitarian grammar of faith in which God is confessed as one God who relates to human beings *ad extra* in three distinct actions as Father, Son, and Holy Spirit. God's creating, justifying, and sanctifying actions all fall under a common rubric, *ex nihilo*; it is solely God's gift, received by faith and not achieved by works. As Luther contends, "God's work *ex nihilo* thus characterizes all of his work in all three articles of the Creed."[3] The triune God is simply and solely the God who gives himself in creation and redemption, and who constitutes human response to him definitively in Jesus Christ through the sanctifying agency of the Holy Spirit. The triune God does not dwell in his transcendent solitariness and aloofness but inhabits his created world, assumes the human plight to redeem it, and continues to work among us until we are fully God's, adorned with eternal righteousness, innocence, and everlasting life.

---

1. "The Large Catechism," in *BC*, 382.
2. *LW* 43:200. Though in the late modern period the word "fiduciary" has taken on a second, economic meaning, often in association with the management of property and/or monetary assets, it still bears its original meaning and conveys existential trust, that is, the confidence a person places in another to keep their word or fulfill a promise or duty.
3. See Charles P. Arand, "Introduction to the First Article," in *Luther's Large Catechism with Annotations and Contemporary Applications*, ed. John T. Pless and Larry M. Vogel (Concordia Publishing House, 2022), 317.

God's purpose to belong to us is accomplished through the material characteristics of the tripartite structure, "the three chief parts"[4] that govern Luther's exposition of his *Small* and *Large Catechisms*: the Ten Commandments, the Creed, and the Lord's Prayer. Albrecht Peters discerns in Luther a double ring as God's way of being God "for us": "[Luther] develops the external and internal relationships with respect to both context and content. He develops simultaneously both an outer ring (the relationship of the Creed to the Decalogue and the Lord's Prayer) and an inner ring (the relationship among the three articles of faith) as he interprets the three articles."[5] The tripartite structure sums up the entire substance of the Bible from which we are acquainted with the three things that are necessary for divine belonging—"that I may be his":[6] the knowledge of our illness under the law, the provision of medicine in the Creed, and the appropriation of the cure which faith grasps by the Lord's Prayer.[7] In God's economy of salvation—in Luther's phrase, "God's particular ordering of things"[8]—God seizes us and draws us into the orbit of divine-human intimacy. Luther conceives of the way God encounters sinners in this order: first by locating them under the Decalogue (law), then the gospel (Creed), and finally the Lord's Prayer (reception of the credal benefits). Luther's rationale behind this order is that we must first be crushed by the Ten Commandments with their stern demands that we, by ourselves, cannot fulfill. The Creed provides pure grace, by which we keep the commandments. The Lord's Prayer teaches us to receive the credal benefits acquired by the triune God for the fulfillment of the Ten Commandments.[9]

This book addresses three major themes—distance, belonging, and isolation—and interprets them in light of the interaction and interpenetration of the "outer ring" of the tripartite structure and the "inner ring" of the Trinity. This tripartite structure forms a template for the presentation of this book. Chapter 1 locates Luther's doctrine of the Trinity in early church tradition, in which he affirms the unity and distinction of the immanent Trinity and the economic Trinity. Chapter 2 focuses on God's purpose in the giving of the Ten Commandments (law) for the shape and practice of humanity. Chapters 3–5 flesh out God's external relation to us in Three Articles of the Creed as a fulfillment of the law's demands. Luther, like Christians throughout history (including us) upholds the Apostles' Creed as a cornerstone exposition of biblical faith. However the Creed is not identical to the Bible; rather it is a concise summary

---

4. "The Large Catechism," in *BC*, 456.

5. Albrecht Peters, *Commentary on Luther's Catechisms: Creed*, trans. Thomas H. Trapp (Concordia Publishing House, 2011), 3.

6. "The Small Catechism," in *BC* (Tappert), 345.

7. *LW* 43:13–14.

8. *LW* 43:13.

9. See James Arne Nestingen and Gerhard O. Forde, *Martin Luther: A Life*, rev. ed. (Augsburg Books, 2003), 76.

of classical orthodoxy. As Jaroslav Pelikan writes, "A creed is a concise, formal, and authorized statement of important points of Christian doctrine."[10] Chapter 6 focuses on prayer, especially the Lord's Prayer, by which we receive the gifts the triune God has bestowed on us.

The Ten Commandments (law) expose sin, that which creates, to use Berndt Hamm's phrase, "a cognitive and affective"[11] distance between God and humanity; the Creed (gospel) conquers the distance between them and confers on us God's immanence. The fall creates a breach between God and humanity, resulting in the tragic movement from life to death; grace bridges between them, effecting a radical reversal of that movement from death to life. The distance between God and sinners is conquered by the mediation of Christ so that we might be restored to the garden of Eden from which we fell. The discontinuity with the original creation's objective, that we may be God's, caused by sin is abolished by grace. Sinners cannot see this discontinuity unless by divine revelation, nor can it be healed unless by divine aid. The law causes us to acknowledge our inner vacuity so that everything we possess is God's gift. We expect nothing from, to use a scholastic phrase, "what lies in us"[12] but everything from God's promise. The Creed satisfies the law's stern demands and draws us into the triune life of sheer grace. The Creed, Luther writes, "sets forth all that we must expect and receive from God."[13] God alone is a storehouse of infinite abundance from which we, by prayer, can draw for our good; to seek security elsewhere is idolatry. Our identity is not self-created but received from the triune God who gives out of the surplus of God's being. God is the ultimate reason for and almighty mystery of everything that is. In consequence, our heart does not base itself upon anything creaturely, such as power, pedigree, piety, achievements, or the things of this world, but upon the triune God who is most glorious or godlike in all aspects of our lives: the source of our identity, the sustenance of our well-being, the luminosity of our reason, the quickening of our willing, and the power of our doing. God is the active giver of his manifold blessings to us without remainder; we are the passive recipients of God's bountiful gifts without cessation. As John W. Kleinig states, "The life of faith is the *vita passiva*, the receptive life. In it we do not make something of ourselves, God fashions and forms us."[14] The life we live before God is a gift for which we are obliged to thank, praise, and love him in passive reciprocity.

---

10. Jaroslav Pelikan, *Credo: Historical and Theological Guide to Creeds and Confessions of Faith in the Christian Tradition* (Yale University Press, 2003), 3.

11. Berndt Hamm, *The Early Luther: Stages in a Reformation Reorientation*, trans. Martin J. Lohrmann (Eerdmans, 2014), 79.

12. See *LW* 31:10.

13. "The Large Catechism," in *BC*, 431.

14. John W. Kleinig, "*Oratio, Meditatio, Tentatio*: What Makes a Theologian?," *Concordia Theological Quarterly* 66, no. 3 (2002): 265.

The phrase "analogy of faith" (*analogia fidei*) in Romans 12:6 governs Luther's reading and interpretation of Scripture. Luther writes, "Thus one may prophesy new things. But not things that go beyond the bounds of faith, that is, what a person prophesies may not have experiential proof of things but may be only the signs of the things that are in no way apparent."[15] This verse constitutes Luther's hermeneutical principle. Of this, G. Sujin Pak notes, "He employed the *analogia fidei* not only to demarcate right readings of Scripture from wrong according to whether they foster a right understanding of faith that leads to Christ, trust in God's promises, and an affirmation of justification by faith alone, he also increasingly implemented the *analogia fidei* as a tool to assert the prime authority of Scripture."[16] Luther uses the equivalent "the rule of faith" (*regula fidei*) as the rule of justification by faith, although he prefers the biblical phrase *analogia fidei*.[17] Justification by faith is, for Luther, "the central article";[18] it "preserves and guides all churchly teaching."[19] The doctrine of justification is "'the article by which the church stands or falls' (*articulus stantis et cadentis ecclesiae*)."[20] In his Galatians lectures, Luther expressly teaches, "For if we lose the doctrine of justification, we lose simply everything."[21] The same sentiment occurs in the *Smalcald Articles*: "Nothing in this article [justification] can be conceded or given up, even if heaven and earth or whatever is transitory passed away."[22] The heart of Scripture is the doctrine of justification, the very subject of theology's duty. Luther writes, "The proper subject of theology is man guilty of sin and condemned, and God the justifier and saviour of man the sinner. Whatever is asked or discussed in theology outside this subject is error and poison."[23] The first sentence refers to the "basis," the second the "boundary" of the theological task. The two sentences, Mark C. Mattes stresses, sum up Luther's task as a theologian: as "basis," the content of theological discourse comprises

---

15. *LW* 25:446; *WA* 56:456.

16. G. Sujin Pak, "The Protestant Reformers and the *Analogia Fidei*," in *The Medieval Luther*, ed. Christine Helmer (Mohr Siebeck, 2020), 234.

17. See *LW* 17:114; *LW* 10:462–63; *LW* 11:14 for the phrase "rule of faith." Pak rightly observes, "Notably, the early Luther employed the terminology of *regula fidei* in his First Lectures on the Psalms. From his 1515–1516 lectures on Romans forward, however, he switched to the more precisely biblical phrase *analogia fidei*. In the two most significant instances of his use of *regula fidei* in his First Lectures on the Psalms, Luther applied it as a generous hermeneutical principle stipulating that one should not reject a reading of Scripture so long as it does not conflict with the rule of faith." Pak, "The Protestant Reformers," 231.

18. *WA* 40.3:335.5–10.

19. *WA* 39.1:205.2–5.

20. The phrase "the article by which the church stands or falls" is Valentin Löscher's (1673–1749), not Luther's, although he teaches it. See Mark C. Mattes, *The Role of Justification in Contemporary Theology* (Fortress, 2004), 7.

21. *LW* 26:26; *WA* 40.1:72.

22. "The Smalcald Articles," in *BC*, 301:5.

23. *LW* 12:311.

"Jesus Christ as *sacramentum* to those oppressed by the law, living under divine wrath, or being made uncertain by the hidden God (*deus absconditus*)"; and as "boundary," it "sets limits to all attempts to subordinate this activity to any other comprehensive task."[24] Theological undertaking must be done in such a way that it does not lose its "proper subject." However, this in no way reduces theology to an exposition of justification only, nor does it so narrow the discourse that it bears no connection to or undercuts other basic theological themes. Positively, the rule of justification illuminates other theological themes; negatively, it eliminates what cannot be spoken of theologically.

This book does not try to trace the historical development and entirety of Luther's Trinitarian theology, which Reiner Jansen and Christine Helmer have done so masterfully,[25] but discusses how Luther applies Trinitarian discourse to other theological themes such as creation, redemption, and sanctification. Governed by soteriology, Luther's emphasis is placed on God's economic actions toward us *ad extra* as God's way of bringing us to himself. Luther's emphasis on the economic Trinity—God as he is toward us—does not exclude the immanent Trinity, or God as he is in himself. A distinction between things as they are revealed to us (the "epistemic" aspect) and things as they are in themselves (the "ontic" aspect) helps, Alister E. McGrath notes, in constructing an ontological foundation for the Christian experience of God.[26] This distinction provides a conceptual framework for a distinction between the economic Trinity, or the economic actions in history, and the immanent Trinity, or the relationship of the three persons in the immanent being in eternity. With Augustine, Luther affirms the unity and the distinction between the economic Trinity and the immanent Trinity, but with an emphasis on the former as the starting point for comprehension of the latter. The revelation of God in time does not constitute God as triune but corresponds to the reality of God who is triune in eternity; the subsequent disclosure corresponds to the antecedent reality.

John Thompson usage of the distinction between "the order of being (*ordo essendi*)" and "the order of knowing (*ordo cognoscendi*)" also helps elucidate Luther's Trinitarian theology.[27] The former speaks of the ontic reality of the Trinity itself—namely, God as he is in himself, the antecedent reality that exists prior to subsequent human recognition of it; the latter speaks of the epistemic conceptualization of God as he appears to us in his "two movements"

---

24. Mattes, *The Role of Justification*, 5.
25. See Reiner Jansen, *Studien zu Luthers Trinitätslehre* (Lang, 1976); Christine Helmer, *The Trinity and Martin Luther: A Study on the Relationship Between Genre, Language and the Trinity in Luther's Works, 1523–1546* (von Zabern, 1999; rev. ed., Lexham, 2017); Helmer, "Luther's Trinitarian Hermeneutic and the Old Testament," *Modern Theology* 18, no. 1 (2002): 49–73.
26. See Alister E. McGrath, *The Nature of Christian Doctrine: Its Origins, Development, and Function* (Oxford University Press, 2024), 134–35. I am indebted to McGrath's insight on this distinction.
27. John Thompson, *Modern Trinitarian Perspectives* (Oxford University Press, 1994), 100.

toward us.[28] First, God's gracious turn toward us is from the Father through the Son in the Holy Spirit, and second, our return to God is by the Holy Spirit through the Son to the Father. The former is the "descending" movement from God to us, the latter the "ascending" movement from us to God.[29] As Luther writes, "Christ's ascending and descending pertain not only to Him; no, they are significant especially for us."[30] Faith lays hold of the economic self-humiliation and ascension of God's Son that ultimately lead to the glorification of humanity. No one ascends into heaven apart from Christ who descends from there, and Christ takes with him those whom he has purchased and adorned with his righteousness to where he resides. As Luther writes, "In his skin and on his back we too must ascend."[31] This double movement of grace corresponds to Helmer's formulation of the "inside-out" and the "outside-in" movement.[32] Grace initiates the inside-out movement of the immanent Trinity from the Father through the Son by the Spirit; grace also effects the outside-in movement of the economic Trinity by the Holy Spirit through the Son to the Father. Both directions—downward and upward, inside out and outside in—correspond to each other, and are of one God, the triune God. Grace that flows inside out from the Father through the Son in the Holy Spirit is that by which we are drawn outside-in to the Father through the Son in the Holy Spirit. The direction from below to above, external to internal, from us to God through the incarnate Son, is attributed to the pneumatologic grace of the Third Article. We ascend to God by what Timothy J. Wengert calls "the reversed Trinity"—by the Holy Spirit who preaches to us the justifying action of Christ, a ladder to the Father. Wengert elaborates, "The theology of the reversed Trinity is literally 'theo-logy' (God word), where God speaks to us and by speaking declares the old new, the sinner a saint, the unbeliever a believer—God's service to us, not ours to God."[33] By the Holy Spirit, we are brought back to where we originally were, a pristine state of blissful intoxication and loving conversation with God.

Luther develops pneumatologic and Trinitarian logic so that the article of justification by faith remains central. The logic of justification *ex nihilo* permeates Luther's exposition of the Creed. The triune God we meet in Luther's exposition of the Creed is self-giving. For Luther, as Oswald Bayer rightly discerns, "'giving' binds together all three articles."[34] Creation is subject to vanity through no fault of its own save unbelief, which results in discontinuity with a blissful communion

---

28. Thompson, *Modern Trinitarian Perspectives*, 100.
29. *LW* 22:332, where the category of "ascending and descending" occurs.
30. *LW* 22:332.
31. *LW* 42:23.
32. Helmer, *The Trinity and Martin Luther*, 216.
33. See Timothy J. Wengert, *Martin Luther's Catechisms: Forming the Faith* (Fortress, 2009), 46.
34. Oswald Bayer, "The Ethics of Gift," trans. Mark A. Seifrid, *Lutheran Quarterly* 24, no. 4 (2010): 455.

with God, his objective in creating it. The Father's gifts in creation have been made "obscured and useless" through sinful abuse of them and are restored "subsequently" by the Son's giving of himself in redemption so that we might "have the Father and his gift."[35] Finally, the Holy Spirit gave himself "wholly" to impart into our hearts Christ's restoration of creatures to his original creational objective. All three persons act *ad extra* as one God "who has given himself to us all wholly and completely, with all that he is and has."[36] The self-giving of the triune God re-creates our identity as God's beloved, effecting communion with God for us. In Christoph Schwöbel's formulation:

> Because creation is the self-giving of God the Father, no one else is to be trusted in this unconditional sense: everything other than God is, first of all, the gift of God. Because our salvation is achieved by the self-giving of God the Son, one person in two natures, there can be no other ground of salvation, and therefore the salvation achieved in Christ includes the whole of created existence. Because the Spirit appropriates the whole work of God the Father and the Son to us by constituting faith, there is no other way in which humans can appropriately relate to God.[37]

The Creed reveals who we are before the triune God: before the Father, we are his noble creatures; before the Son, we are his beloved children; and before the Spirit, we are a redeemed member of Christ's body. Just as out of the nothingness of our sin, God re-creates a new person in Christ, so is the work of creation; both are a consequence of God's gracious will, with no condition attached. Niels Henrik Gregersen contends, "Luther depicts God's work of creation after the model of God's work of salvation, so that the first article of faith (about creation) is permeated by the insights that flow out of the gospel message of the second and third articles of faith (about the works of Christ and the Holy Spirit)."[38] However, the opposite movement is possible, as creation language *ex nihilo*, Jonathan A. Linebaugh argues, is also applied to the re-creation language of the Second Article.[39] The creative love of God in the First Article bestows goods upon the unlovely, making them lovely; likewise, the justifying grace of the Second Article bestows righteousness, making a saint out of a sinner. Creation

---

35. *LW* 37:366.
36. *LW* 37:366.
37. Christoph Schwöbel, "Martin Luther and the Trinity," in *Oxford Research Encyclopedia of Religion*, published March 29, 2017, https://doi.org/10.1093/acrefore/9780199340378.013.326.
38. Niels Henrik Gregersen, "Grace in Nature and History: Luther's Doctrine of Creation Revisited," *Dialog: A Journal of Theology* 44, no. 1 (2005): 20.
39. Jonathan A. Linebaugh, "Incongruous and Creative Gift: Reading *Paul and the Gift* with Martin Luther," *International Journal of Systematic Theology* 22, no. 1 (2020): 55, doi:10.1111/ijst.12388.

and re-creation interpret each other, just as *ex nihilo* and *sola gratia* mutually imply and constitute each other. In creation, we are nothing, just as we have been re-created *ex nihilo*, without any merits of our own. The reverse is true, too: in justification, we are nothing, just as we have been created *ex nihilo*, without any human contributions. Both the created and re-created identity are God's gifts; they are not of our own making. Through faith, bestowed by the Spirit of the Third Article, the gift of our identity is communicated to our hearts. The unmerited gift of our identity is Trinitarian in shape: loved by God's creative grace, accepted by Christ's justifying grace, and renewed by the Holy Spirit's sanctifying grace. With Augustine, the Reformer holds that all three persons act in full unity with himself externally, drawing us away from every creaturely thing to the God of the first commandment, the very reason for all that exists outside the Godhead.

Justification discloses the opposite of who we are, sinners before God. Gerhard Sauter writes, "The presence of God in God's promise eliminates self-certainty and its autonomy, because justification is the promise of participation in God's righteousness. Human beings cannot know in themselves who they are, especially when they stand before God. One's existence as a sinner comes to light before God. It is not a result of self-evaluation, but rather, it belongs to a confession of faith."[40] Knowledge of sin is not naturally derived but flows from Christ. The cross names the thing as it is,[41] revealing sin as a mighty tyrant whom only God can absolve. Christ comes to us not only as a sin revealer who acquaints us with the disease of sin, but also as a sin bearer who assuages it through his cross and resurrection. God hides his saving work in his Son's becoming not only "sin" but "a sinner"[42] in our place, suffering and dying the death of God-forsakenness on the cross. Vítor Westhelle says, "God's hidden work is a way of naming in a radical way our experience of being abandoned by God as Jesus himself experienced."[43] Faith lays hold of the atoning efficacy Christ achieves for us. As a result, believers receive the "highest comfort" hidden in the "fortunate exchange"[44] in which all sin, death, curses, and God's wrath are vanquished, and Christ's grace, life, blessing, and mercy are credited to us.

In his *Meditation on Christ's Passion*, Luther reflects on his personal dimension of faith, saying, "Of what help is it to you that God is God, if he is not God to you?"[45] Likewise, of what benefit is God as creator, redeemer, and sanctifier if he is not all these to us? That God is creator, redeemer, and sanctifier is, *in*

---

40. Gerhard Sauter, "God Creating Faith: The Doctrine of Justification from the Reformation to the Present," *Lutheran Quarterly* 11, no. 1 (1997): 19.

41. *LW* 31:53.

42. *LW* 42:12.

43. Vítor Westhelle, *The Scandalous God: The Use and Abuse of the Cross* (Fortress, 2006), 56.

44. *LW* 26.284; *WA* 40.1:443.

45. *LW* 42:8.

itself, a fact that does not impact us. But the credal announcement that God is creator, redeemer, and sanctifier *to me* has personal relevance. The meaning of the gospel resides in the personal pronoun "me." So Luther adds a personal "for us" after every clause of the Apostles' Creed. He recognizes the significance of this little pronoun "me," or "us"; he writes, "If you leave out 'for us,' then the entire sermon is for nothing."[46] Whoever applies this pronoun "me" to themself in faith knows for sure that they belong to God and God belongs to them. The "for us" phrase identifies us as the passive recipient of God's action, a gift of grace; it accentuates the relevance of God "*to us*," not in three different gifts from God, but rather in his threefold giving of himself in creation, redemption, and sanctification. God's being corresponds to God's acts; God is most Godself in these acts he performs "for us." To borrow a salient phrase of Robert Kolb, "God is truly God at his most Godly"[47] when he shows himself to be God for us.

The relevance of God to us is found in the links among the first commandment, the First Article, the introduction of the Lord's Prayer ("Our Father"), and the fourth petition ("Give us this day our daily bread"). The God of the first commandment is the creator God, our heavenly Father, who provides all creaturely gifts for us. Luther confines the usage of "daily bread" to a physical function. In doing so, Luther highlights the significance of civil authority, God's "left hand" rule to provide physically.[48] The ongoing activity of God in creation is affirmed in Luther's view of the vocation as the "mask"[49] by means of which God's creative giving is achieved. Mark D. Tranvik writes, "When we view the world through the eyes of vocation, it becomes difficult to talk about God's 'absence.' God is anything but distant and aloof. Nor is God a spectator, content to watch the action from afar. The lens of vocation provides a far different perspective, one that captures the spirit of Psalm 24:1: 'The earth is the Lord's and all that is in it; the world and all that live in it.'"[50] Our creatureliness is not expressed in some nebulous, spiritualistic sphere, isolated or separated from this earthly world in which God dwells, and through which he provides manifold goods. We are created along with other creatures, which Luther calls "masks" behind which God hides his creative activity to accomplish his purpose. God's gifts hidden in creation ground our vocation: we are called not out of creation but into it, to labor to receive, not achieve, God's blessings. Only faith perceives God as invisibly present in creation and ceaselessly active in providing goods for

---

46. See *WA* 27:493.7–8, as quoted in Todd R. Hains, *Martin Luther and the Rule of Faith: Reading God's Word for God's People* (IVP Academic, 2022), 68n88.
47. Robert Kolb, *Bound Choice, Election, and Wittenberg Theological Method: From Martin Luther to the Formula of Concord* (Fortress, 2017), 34.
48. See Kim A. Truebenbach, "Luther's Two Kingdoms in the Third and Fourth Petitions," *Lutheran Quarterly* 24, no. 4 (2010): 471–72.
49. *LW* 14:114.
50. Mark D. Tranvik, *Martin Luther and the Called Life* (Fortress, 2016), 160.

us through social orders or institutions, which remain good despite our sinful neglect of them.

God's hidden work in the created order does not exclude human agency but incorporates it so that divine acts and human acts coalesce in bringing about a result. While God alone creates, we cooperate with him as his instrument. Human industry is God's ordained means to receive, not earn. Creatureliness remains, even after the fall; sinners continue to stand before God as a creature, totally dependent on God's will and action. This creaturely relation with God is not that of an active creator, one who creates out of his natural endowments, but of a passive recipient of bountiful gifts that come from God's omnipotent acts in creation. Luther indicates three orders through which God mediates his rule: the ecclesial, the political, and the household.[51] The victory of any order is to be attributed to the abundance of God's blessings hidden in it, not our labor. The various roles and specific duties are not a means of acquiring our righteous identity but the expression of it. Whether at home, in the workplace or politics, or in the church, vocational obedience to God's command is exercised so that the performance of various good works may abound, although human achievements do not count as a measure of our worth. Luther's exposition of Genesis 17:1, where God commands Abraham to be blameless, is an instance of "a twofold righteousness: the perfect righteousness [passive] through which we are righteous before God through faith, and the imperfect righteousness [active] through which we are righteous before God and other human beings insofar as our conduct and reputation are concerned";[52] in Kolb's words, "both the human trust, the human side of passive righteousness, and human performance, the human side of active righteousness,"[53] find their source in God. The two kinds of righteousness reflect two distinct ways of living: before God by the gift of "passive righteousness" through faith, and before one's neighbors by the works of "active righteousness" through love. Through God's gracious action, sinners regain their trust in God, and on that basis do works that God accepts as good, as they are done in faith (cf. Rom 14:23).

Luther cites Romans 3:25–26 to teach that God justifies himself by going to the cross for us. Propitiation of God's wrath through Christ's blood is God's way of reconciling sinners to God's mercy. Christ was made "the place of propitiation" for sins, but only for believers; through unbelief, "the place of propitiation" is converted to "the place of judgment."[54] "Our place of propitiation," says Luther, "is not won by our merits, but in His, Christ's blood, that is, in His suffering,

---

51. *LW* 41:177.
52. *LW* 3:79; *WA* 42:604.29–32, quoted in Robert Kolb, *Luther and the Stories of God: Biblical Narratives as a Foundation for Christian Living* (Baker Academic, 2012), 88, brackets added.
53. Kolb, *Stories of God*, 88.
54. *LW* 25:32; *WA* 46:38.

whereby He made satisfaction and merited propitiation for those who believe in Him. This was to show His righteousness, to show that His righteousness alone makes men righteous."⁵⁵ The redemption wrought by Christ is costly, as it cost the loss of God's Son, his "dearest Son," to liberate us from the curse of the law. Luther writes, "He is the heavenly image, the one who was forsaken by God as damned, yet he conquered hell through his omnipotent love, who gives this to us all if we but believe."⁵⁶ God's "omnipotent love" is revealed in its opposite, in the weakness and suffering of God's Son through which God's wrath is conquered, and with this, we are transferred from the kingdom of perdition to the kingdom of God's mercy. God's "omnipotent love" forms the etiology of Luther's soteriology, creating through the act of the incarnate Christ *sub contraria* "the object of his love" as the teleology of his soteriology.⁵⁷ The beauty of God's mercy has made us attractive and lovely despite the uncomeliness of our depravity. In Luther's words, "Therefore, sinners are attractive because they are loved; they are not loved because they are attractive."⁵⁸

Against Gabriel Biel's proposition "the human will of the pilgrim is able by its natural power to love God above all,"⁵⁹ Luther states in Thesis 18 of his *Disputation Against Scholasticism*, "To love God above all things by nature is a fictitious term, a chimera, as it were."⁶⁰ Thesis 20 states, "An act of friendship is done, not according to nature, but according to prevenient grace."⁶¹ "God's most earnest purpose," that we should love him above all else, is achieved not by a preexistent love that we do not have, but by God's love that is deposited in us by the Holy Spirit, who himself is love. Just as we cannot believe in Christ unless by a faith given to us by the Holy Spirit, so too we cannot love God unless by a love given to us by the Holy Spirit. The antinomy between God's wrath and God's mercy is revealed in Christ but most crucially resolved for those whom the Holy Spirit establishes as the object of God's fatherly love in his Son. Luther confesses, "That I love God is the work of God alone."⁶² We love God by, to borrow Simeon Zahl's phrase, "the affective experience of the Holy Spirit"⁶³—that is, by "the love

---

55. *LW* 25:32; *WA* 46:37.
56. *LW* 42:107.
57. *LW* 31:57.
58. *LW* 31:57.
59. Gabriel Biel, *Collectorium circa quattuor libros Sententiarum*, vol. 3, ed. Wilfrid Werbeck and Udo Hofmann (Mohr Siebeck, 1979), 504, as quoted in Theodor Dieter, "Martin Luther and Scholasticism," in *Remembering the Reformation: Martin Luther and Catholic Theology*, ed. Declan Marmion, Salvador Ryan, and Gesa E. Thiessen Fortress, 2017), 59.
60. *LW* 31:10.
61. *LW* 31:10.
62. *LW* 34:160.
63. Simeon Zahl, "The Bondage of the Affections: Willing, Feeling, and Desiring in Luther's Theology, 1513–1525," in *The Spirit, the Affections, and the Christian Tradition*, ed. Dale M. Coulter and Amos Yong (University of Notre Dame Press, 2016), 197. This article argues for the "affective"

of God which lives" in us, making alive the dead, a son out of a slave, and a righteous person out of a sinner.⁶⁴ We grasp God by the Spirit's affective power that grasps us first. God's affective turn toward those who are deserving of nothing but damnation effects in them a reversal, a turn from loving the self to loving God, from servile fear to filial fear, from trusting in our own powers to trusting in God alone. Peters, for one, sees in the Trinitarian economy of salvation the significance Luther places on the Third Article; he explains, "Just as we do not have the ability to know God the Father as a well-meaning creator and merciful preserver apart from Jesus Christ through the Holy Spirit, it is thus only in the Son through the Spirit one can fulfill the commandments of the Father and thus love and praise God thereby, without hesitation, thank Him, and serve Him."⁶⁵ In God's economy of salvation, Christology and pneumatology are one; christological grace is realized in us by pneumatologic grace, or else the benefits of the cross of Christ are of no use to us. The Spirit "inculcate[s] the sufferings of Christ for the benefit of our salvation."⁶⁶ Trinitarian grace—that in Christ, God's blessing, which the Spirit imparts to our hearts, has prevailed over God's curse—is the condition of the possibility of loving God above all else, thereby fulfilling the demand of the first commandment. The "epistemic" appropriation of the sublime knowledge of God's gracious turn toward us in Christ to restore us to God's favor is the gift of the Holy Spirit *extra nos*.

God does not will that we have anything to do with God as he hides in himself, the terrifying, ungraspable deity, but rather God as he hides in the efficacious activities of his incarnate Son, the revealed God graspable by faith. The content of the Spirit's sermon is, to borrow Mattes's phrase, "a graspable God,"⁶⁷ one who has stepped out of his own concealment and meets us as a friendly God. For our sake, Hermann Sasse says, "God really entered humanity and the infinite has actually come down into the finite."⁶⁸ The Almighty God is no apathetic deity, aloof and far away from us; he has entered our world that is riddled with sin, suffering, and vices in order to redeem it, but in no other form than, as Carl E. Braaten puts it, "the form of the passionate and passible love in a kenotic vision of ultimate reality."⁶⁹ The Spirit leads us away from God

---

Luther, who considers "imputation-based soteriology as resulting in some real sense in embodied affections and desires" (198).

64. *LW* 31:57.
65. Peters, *Creed*, 100.
66. *LW* 37:366.
67. Mark C. Mattes, *Martin Luther's Theology of Beauty: A Reappraisal* (Baker Academic, 2017), 102.
68. Hermann Sasse, *Here We Stand: Nature and Character of the Lutheran Faith*, trans. Theodore G. Tappert (Lutheran Publishing House, 1979), 153.
69. Carl E. Braaten, "The Problem of God-Language Today," in *Our Naming of God: Problems and Prospects of God-Talk Today*, ed. Carl E. Braaten (Fortress, 1989), 31.

as he hides in his naked majesty and toward the God who hides in the cross of Christ in order to effect, to borrow Gerhard O. Forde's phrase, "a reversal of direction":[70] from sin to righteousness, death to life, and hell to heaven.[71] The "terrifying" images of evil—sin, death, and hell—are conquered by the "glowing" images of Christ—righteousness, life, and heaven.[72] The Holy Spirit confirms in our hearts the gospel, that Christ's victory is given to us as a remedy to our sin. This accounts for Luther's superlative language of the Spirit, whom he regards as "most important";[73] as Bayer puts it, "The Spirit finally is nothing other than the opener and distributor of this self-giving of Christ—and thereby that of the Father as well. We recognize and love God the Father through Christ in the Holy Spirit."[74] Both the Son and the Spirit act together as mediators: As the Son mediates between God and us, by acquiring for us God's reconciliation with us, so the Spirit mediates between Christ and us, by applying to us Christ's accomplishment of our salvation.

Luther conceives of justification as a one-time act of God through the initial delivery of the promise of new life in Christ. That act of God sets in motion a movement of daily repentance—that is, a movement from the discontinuity or death of the old self into the daily renewal of the promise that raises a person to a life lived in Christ. Justification is conceived as God's call for the ungodly person to leave themselves behind and cleave solely to Christ alone for the reconstitution of a new self. "Self-leaving"[75] and Christ cleaving exist as "coincidental opposites,"[76] as do sinner and saint. The movement from the former to the latter occurs by faith, resulting in a new identity. The new identity is beyond depiction; it rests on God's judgment that faith grasps. Justification is effective, just as God's word declares. This newfound identity needs no rational defense or empirical demonstrability. The more we try to subject it to human verification, the more we foster the old self that deserves nothing but God's judgment, and therefore remains in captivity to self-incurvature; the new self does not aim at proving its own identity by looking for signs of change within through introspection, or without through good deeds. No, the new person has left themselves behind; they want nothing but God's judgment by which they now live, and therefore they

---

70. Gerhard O. Forde, "Luther's Theology of the Cross," in *Christian Dogmatics*, vol. 2, ed. Carl E. Braaten and Robert W. Jenson (Fortress, 1984), 49.
71. "The Large Catechism," *BC*, 434.
72. *LW* 42:106.
73. *LW* 43:24.
74. Oswald Bayer, *Martin Luther's Theology: A Contemporary Interpretation*, trans. Thomas H. Trapp (Eerdmans, 2008), 254.
75. The term "self-leaving" appears in Sauter, "God Creating Faith," 28..
76. The term "coincidental opposites" (*coincidentia oppositorum*) appears in Oswald Bayer, "Luther's 'Simul Iustus et Peccator,'" in Robert Kolb et al., *Simul: Inquiries into Luther's Experience of the Christian Life* (Vandenhoeck and Ruprecht, 2021), 35.

are rescued from self-imprisonment. The event of justification lies beyond empirical verification (seeing or depicting); the timing or moment of being grasped by God's justifying action is beyond human assessment or predictability. Yet the new identity created by God's word is not beyond epistemic perception, the subjective awareness of it. As Sauter explains, "Justification is the judgment of God in which the perception of a new person is formed in two senses: God perceives humanity anew; and through justification, the individual recognizes himself or herself totally and completely new. One knows in general that one stands before God and that this, which is given to one to know about oneself, is completely sufficient."[77]

Sauter's salient phrase "God perceives humanity anew" amounts to what Luther means by "imputation." Being divinely perceived anew leads to being humanly perceived anew; the former confers its validity to the latter. Justification places us "in Christ," a new reality from which we acquire a twofold knowledge of self and God. God's perception of us changes; he radically distinguishes we miserable, damnable sinners as God's beloved, no longer under his wrath. Conversely, our perception of God changes: He ceases to be against us, no longer a wrathful, but rather a merciful God. The epistemic perception of the new self and Godself is not the result of rational discourse or self-analysis. Rather it is made possible by the economic action of the Trinity; more precisely, by the *gratis extra nos* of the Holy Spirit. The Holy Spirit renews in those who are in Christ a twofold "epistemic" appropriation despite what we feel or see, despite appearances—knowledge of God's identity as ours, and knowledge of our identity as God's beloved. This new reality of double knowledge flows from God's judgment, which the Holy Spirit impresses on believers, making them the agents of self-accusation as miserable sinners, unworthy in themselves, but deemed objects of the suffering love of the cross.

Human beings "justify God"—that is, they acquiesce in the word's verdict through which they come to a cognition of themselves as "vile, nothing, abominable and damnable"[78] so that they cling to Christ's "alien righteousness" in order to stand before a righteous God. God's judgment never lies, and it discloses things as they are in themselves. God's judgment is complete and completely effective, not in need of any supplementation or revision. Luther's audacious phrase "justify God" refers to our consent to God's judgment on us. We "justify God" by accepting God's disclosure of us via the law, followed by an appropriate act of self-accusation out of reverence for God. Just as God makes us a sinner before he makes us a saint, so too he makes us the agents of self-accusation before he makes us the objects of God's acceptance. God works in us accusation via the law to then work in us affirmation via the gospel. To "justify God" is to accept God's

---

77. Sauter, "God Creating Faith," 28.
78. *LW* 10:404.

Introduction

verdict, including his accusation of us; to accept God's verdict is to self-accuse of that which God's word discloses about us before we are made ready to accept God's justification of us.

By nature, the Trinitarian God relates to himself in speech *ad intra* in which no one has any share; it is hidden from creatures. By grace, the same God opens himself, moves outside of himself, and speaks with us. God comes to us in speech *ad extra* and confers on believers a privilege to participate in the inner circle of divine speech. The God who speaks the world into being continues to speak with us through his Son in the Holy Spirit. The cry for help for unbelief will surely be heard, simply because it is "God's most earnest purpose" to include us as his conversation partner. Luther writes, "It is a glorious privilege that the Sublime Majesty in heaven condescends to let us poor worms open our mouths in conversation with Him and gladly listens to us."[79] Grace fosters in us "a twofold conversation: the one which we carry on with God and the one which God carries on with us."[80] Filiation, a peculiar property of the Son, is shared with believers as God's gift. Sonship is the Son's by nature; it is ours by adoption. His Father is our Father, to whom we pray with the Son, in the Spirit. The Lord's Prayer is Christ's prayer for us with his Father; it is also our prayer to the Father with Jesus our mediator, with whose prayer our prayer is united and made just as efficacious. God grants us the privilege, intrinsic to the Son, of speaking with him to the Father through the "Spirit of supplication"; he also speaks with us through "the Spirit of grace" (Zech 12:10) so that we may hear him.[81] The latter is "a far more precious privilege."[82]

Faith is effective in its opposite—that is, where there is nothing to see. Likewise, prayer is operative in its opposite—that is, when it flows from the nothingness of a beggarly heart. The law's deconstruction of all contraries of justification is the basis of an effective prayer. Not until we are reduced to nothing is the cry for help heard. The *ex nihilo* doctrine shapes Luther's understanding of the Three Articles of faith; likewise, the fulfillment of prayer presupposes nothingness. God removes from us all that hinders prayer without removing himself from us; he vacates our heart to make it ready for the reception of God's gifts. This is God's creation, and it finds fulfillment outside itself and in the surplus of God's being. Faith, expressed in prayer, receives the benefits that are already achieved for us by the economic action of the triune God (outlined in the Creed). What is invoked in prayer is not the preexistent soteriological resources in us, which we do not have, but the preexistent boundless gifts of the triune God, which are conveyed to us through his word. Prayer has validity not on account of "our person," but

---

79. *LW* 24:419; *WA* 41:108.
80. *LW* 24:419; *WA* 46:108.
81. *LW* 24:419; *WA* 46:108.
82. *LW* 24:419; *WA* 46:108.

on account of the performative nature of "God's Word and the obedience" to it.[83] Prayer flows from Luther's doctrine of justification; we do not earn God's hearing, just as we do not merit God's acceptance. Both are grounded in the theological character of God's effective word. In justification, God's word declares us righteous, effecting a reality that corresponds to itself; so too in prayer, God's promise to hear us never fails, effecting a reality just as it says.

The telos of the triune God's merciful descent into history is to make us God's, filled with purity and holiness, and adorned with new, immortal, and glorified bodies. Justification and eschatology are juxtaposed. What the Son has accomplished in justification is continued by the Holy Spirit in sanctification, working daily in us until we become fully holy and righteous at the end. Sanctification is not about moral transformation, a second step as fruit following justification in the economy of salvation. It is not to be, Wengert notes, "so divorced from justification as to define a separate part of the Christian life."[84] Ian D. Kingston Siggins captures Luther's point accurately:

> Now, if Christ is our righteousness alone, He is also our Holiness and sanctification by faith alone. Christ's righteousness is constantly defined in opposition to all so-called human righteousness; and in the same way, the only true holiness stands over and against every self-styled sanctity of man. Sanctification for Luther normally does not mean the process of moral purification in virtue, which is its chief connotation in post-Reformation theology. Rather, in the biblically strict sense, that is holy which is set apart for the worship and service of God.[85]

God's word is addressed to the spiritually deaf, and it opens their ears to create faith. The word does not borrow authority from elsewhere but bears self-authority to create its own adherents. Luther's doctrine of the word as inherently causative and re-creative has far-reaching ramifications for the Reformation understanding of justification. Justification is neither forensic nor effective; it is both—and, because in his understanding of the word as "action-word,"[86] the word, when declared, performs what it says. Whatever God speaks will occur, for what God says he does. The same word that spoke the world into being now says, "You are justified." Creation and re-creation are God's gifts, freely bestowed by

---

83. "The Large Catechism," *BC* (Tappert), 422.
84. Wengert, *Martin Luther's Catechisms*, 63.
85. Ian D. Kingston Siggins, *Martin Luther's Doctrine of Christ* (Yale University Press, 1970), 154.
86. See *LW* 37:180n32; David C. Steinmetz, *Luther in Context*, 2nd ed. (Baker Academic, 2002), 115.

God's "speech-act."[87] The forensic-effective character of justification appears in Luther's *Small Catechism*: "Where there is forgiveness of sin [forensic], there is also life and salvation [effective]."[88] Hence justification, Forde rightly concludes, is "'not only' forensic, but that is the case only because the more forensic it is, the more effective it is."[89] The creative power of God's word repudiates any opposition between the declared righteousness and the effective righteousness. There is no "'as if declared righteousness'" without "an effective 'made righteousness.'"[90]

Luther's pneumatology grounds his ecclesiology. This is reflected in the order in which the Third Article is arranged, beginning with the Spirit, followed by the church, not vice versa. The Holy Spirit sanctifies the church through the external means of the word, "holy sacraments and absolution as well as all the comforting words of the entire gospel."[91] The power to justify resides not in these creaturely forms but in "the Word," in Luther's term, "the principal item," which contains all of God's treasures and accomplishes its own purpose.[92] What is crucial, says Michael Richard Laffin, is "that the Word is mediated, not by our own interpretations or hermeneutical methodology, but rather by the Word Himself."[93] Sacraments themselves have no inherent power to confer grace; they are instruments of God's presence. Just as God is bound to real humanity to reach us, so too the word is bound to materials such as baptism and the Lord's Supper to meet us. Kirsi I. Stjerna clarifies, "The Word needed a tangible element, an element that God can make God's own and thereby reach us in a way most fitting to our being."[94] God's purpose that he is ours and we are his is linked to his word, the source of self-constitution and growth in our newfound identity. The delivery of God's gifts is by the Spirit, who acts together with the word, the vehicle of his graces. Kimlyn J. Bender writes, "For Luther, Christ himself spoke with efficacy through his Word, a Word that the Church could proclaim but not claim to

---

87. Bayer, *Martin Luther's Theology*, 102.

88. "The Small Catechism," *BC*, 362. Also quoted in Mark C. Mattes, "Luther on Justification as Forensic and Effective," in *The Oxford Handbook of Martin Luther's Theology*, ed. Robert Kolb, Irene Dingel, and L'ubomír Batka (Oxford University Press, 2014), 266.

89. Gerhard O. Forde, *Justification by Faith: A Matter of Death and Life* (Sigler, 1990), 36. See also Mattes, "Luther on Justification," 264–73. I am indebted to Mattes's observation.

90. See Sauter, "God Creating Faith," 33. As with Luther, Melanchthon holds the same view; Sauter notes, "This *imputatio* is not understood 'as if declared righteousness' as opposed to an effective 'made righteous.' Such an opposition is a misunderstanding of the righteousness of God. This is the righteousness by which God justifies and accepts.... God announces God's righteousness. God creates what he promises by announcing it."

91. cf. *LW* 39:75, where Luther mentions the external signs by which the true church may be identified.

92. *LW* 22:304.

93. Michael Richard Laffin, *The Promise of Martin Luther's Political Theology: Freeing Luther from the Modern Political Narrative* (Bloomsbury T&T Clark, 2018), 73.

94. Kirsi I. Stjerna, *No Greater Jewel: Thinking about Baptism with Luther* (Augsburg, 2009), 45.

control it. It was through this Word of Christ enlivened by the Spirit that faith is awakened."[95] God is omnipresent, but only in the word where we know for sure he is present "for us." The Spirit engenders faith, enabling us to receive his gifts offered in the word and the forms that the word assumes. The church is the matrix in which the sanctifying work of the Holy Spirit occurs. Peters phrases it Trinitarianly: "By the means of His sanctifying work, the Spirit prepares us to be the dwelling place for the Son and the Father. . . . God is the carpenter and is at work in His dwelling place every day in order to make it sturdy for the Day of judgment."[96] Through the Spirit-empowered response to the external word we hear, we submit our lives in gratitude to God's fatherly remaking.

The dialectical distinction between law and gospel is the Spirit's daily way of shaping us into the image of God or Christ. God is actively making us anew, crushing the old you and its vices so that the new you could fear, trust, and love him above all else. The law is never life giving, even though it remains life informing for people of faith. The Spirit strips us of all "active capacity" or righteousness of our own so that all of life is lived by "passive capacity," or God's work of grace.[97] The new life we now live is no longer ours but Christ's, as Paul taught in Galatians 2:20 ("It is no longer I who live, but Christ who lives in me"). The old life living in and for itself dies so that the new life living in and for Christ rises in power. All forms of allegiance vacate the heart so that "Christ can be formed and alone" in us (cf. Gal 4:19).[98] Christ is formed in us, but not so that the old Adam is revitalized to better perform the law. That would be to embrace Christ as a moral example, not as gift. Forde says, "The Word comes not to coddle but to kill old beings, to put them out of their misery, to make way for a life-giving spirit."[99] God's word does its alien work through the law to strip us of all preexistent materials so that it might perform its proper work through the gospel to implant Christ's image in us. The external word preached in the power of the Holy Spirit enters through the ears to the heart where it begins to live and shape us. As Luther affirms, "There the Holy Spirit is present and impresses that Word on the heart, so that it is heard. In this way, every preacher is a parent, who produces and forms the true shape of the Christian mind through the ministry of the Word."[100]

For Luther, doctrine and life form a seamless garment, not to be separated. Timothy George rightly captures the Reformation primarily as "a movement

---

95. Kimlyn J. Bender, *Reflections on Reformational Theology: Studies in the Theology of the Reformation, Karl Barth, and the Evangelical Tradition* (T&T Clark, 2021), 14–15.

96. Peters, *Creed*, 256–57.

97. *LW* 31:49.

98. *LW* 27:308; *WA* 40.2:548.

99. Gerhard O. Forde, *The Essential Forde: Distinguishing Law and Gospel*, ed. Nicholas Hopman et al. (Fortress, 2019), 250–51.

100. *LW* 26:431; *WA* 40.1:650.

of applied theology and lived Christianity. It is not anti-intellectual, but it was antiabstractionist."[101] The crucial thing, as this book demonstrates, is not so much what we know of God doctrinally as it is what that knowledge does in, to, and through us. Hence no doctrine of God is ever complete unless it shows its relevance to practical life and action. Luther's theology is basically practical, though it is so not by attempting to establish infallible techniques, but instead by showing how the gospel leads the way to the triune God, whose goodness pursues us without exhaustion despite our residual sins, and whose purpose remains firm despite appearances to the contrary. The emphasis is not so much on our actions but on the economic actions of the triune God that faith grasps. Instead of placing human agency at the center of our lives, the triune God of the first commandment calls for a radical reversal, placing himself at the center so that the human self is taken out of itself to live in correspondence to God's purpose. The sublime knowledge of God's most earnest belonging to us, to borrow Karl Barth's phrases, "engenders a desire to act," which in turn "engenders a new seeking of God."[102]

---

101. Timothy George, *Reading Scripture with the Reformers* (IVP Academic, 2011), 228.
102. Karl Barth, *The Theology of John Calvin*, trans. Geoffrey W. Bromiley (Eerdmans, 1995), 388.

CHAPTER ONE

Rooted in Tradition

Luther's Doctrine of the Trinity

LUTHER'S PERSONAL CONFESSION of the Trinity as the grammar of faith occurs when he is battling sickness, awaiting an impending death. With solemnity, the confession assumes the form of "a last will and testament."[1] He sums it up in his *Confession Concerning Christ's Supper* (1528):

> First, I believe with my whole heart the sublime article of the majesty of God, that the Father, Son, and Holy Spirit, three distinct persons, are by nature one true and genuine God, the Maker of heaven and earth; in complete opposition to the Arians, Macedonians, Sabellians, and similar heretics, Genesis 1[:1]. All this has been maintained up to this time both in the Roman Church and among Christian churches throughout the whole world.[2]

This confession includes three major historical heresies that the early church repudiated, indicating that Luther's theology of the Trinity sits comfortably within the catholic tradition of the church. They are the Macedonians, who rejected the deity of the Holy Spirit but affirmed the created nature of the Holy Spirit; the Arians, who professed a temporal beginning for Christ, that he is the first creature, and is ontologically subordinate to the Father; and the Sabellians, who collapsed the distinction of three persons into one and argued for a modalist conception of the one God appearing in three modes.

The philosophical context in which theological discourse such as the Arian controversy took place was partially Neoplatonic. Arthur Repp rightly notes, "A key construct of Neoplatonism was understanding God's activity as procession and return. God's activity in Jesus was seen as a procession into the world of which humans are a part in order to return to God with a redeemed humanity in tow, as it were."[3] The effective return to God is not of human origin but of God. Hence Nicene theologians argued that the Son was God, "of the same being"

---

1. *LW* 37:361; *WA* 26:500.27–32.
2. *LW* 37:361; *WA* 26:500. 27–32.
3. Arthur (Chris) Repp, "The Trinity as Gospel," in *Gift and Promise: The Augsburg Confession and the Heart of Christian Theology*, Edward H. Schroeder, ed. Ronald Neustadt and Stephen Hitchcock (Fortress, 2016), 64.

(*homoousios*) with the Father, a definition that entered the Nicene Creed in 325 CE and was later adopted as definitive at the Council of Constantinople in 381 CE. By the same logic, Athanasius reasoned, the Holy Spirit was God, of the same being (*homoousios*) with the Father and the Son.[4]

Unity and Distinction
The Immanent and Economic Trinity

Luther remains, as Marc Lienhard notes, faithful to the thought of Augustine in that the three persons must be distinguished in God's immanent life *ad intra*, while at the same time the persons must not be separated in their economic action toward his creature *ad extra*.[5] God's temporal revelation in three persons mirrors God in his eternal being. God is eternally triune, antecedent to his economic actions in history. From this concept, Christine Helmer gives two propositions: first, that "the Trinity has an 'inner' side, a side 'outside' the creature's grasp"; and second, that "the Trinity has an 'outer' side at which the Creator is situated in relation to the creature."[6] To use Eberhard Jüngel's phrase, "God corresponds to himself"[7] in this distinction between the inner and outer being of God. Karl Barth maintains the unity of this distinction that "as Father, Son, and Holy Spirit God is, so to speak, ours in advance."[8] The triune God is ours, in Luther's terms, "beforehand in eternity."[9] The ontic account of God—that in the order of being, God is triune—and the epistemic account of God—that in the order of knowing, God is revealed to be triune—correspond to each other. We know the immanent Trinity only because we see God acting in Jesus Christ and the Holy Spirit (the economic Trinity). Of this, Alister McGrath writes:

> The economic Trinity is *epistemically prior* to the immanent Trinity, in the sense that the biblical witness to God's actions is both the immediate ground and precipitant for the process of reflection that leads *initially* to the human recognition of the epistemically coordinated account of God

---

4. See Athanasius and Didymus, *Works on the Spirit: Athanasius the Great and Didymus the Blind*, ed. Mark DelCogliano et al. (St. Vladimir's Seminary Press, 2011), Letter 1.

5. Marc Lienhard, *Luther: Witness to Jesus Christ*, trans. Edwin H. Robertson (Augsburg Publishing House, 1982), 322.

6. Christine Helmer, *The Trinity and Martin Luther: A Study on the Relationship Between Genre, Language and the Trinity in Luther's Works, 1523–1546* (von Zabern, 1999; rev. ed., Lexham, 2017), 68.

7. Eberhard Jüngel, *God as the Mystery of the World: On the Foundation of the Theology of the Crucified One in the Dispute between Theism and Atheism*, trans. Darrell L. Guder (Eerdmans, 1983), 346.

8. Karl Barth, *Church Dogmatics*, trans. G. W. Bromiley, ed. G. W. Bromiley and T. F. Torrance, vol. 1.1, *The Doctrine of the Word of God*, 2nd ed. (T&T Clark, 1975), 383.

9. *LW* 34:218.

that constitutes the *economic* Trinity and *subsequently* to the ontological account of God that constitutes the *immanent* Trinity. The acts of God within the "economy of salvation" are clearly laden with ontological implications, which it is the task of theology to unfold and correlate. This does not mean that the ontic reality of God is secondary to its historical disclosure; it is rather a comment on the process of theological reflection that leads into deeper and enhanced understandings of the nature of God. The epistemic coordination of observations leads to the recognition of the ontic reality that undergirds them—and was there before the human processes of observations and reflection.[10]

In the academic theses for the promotion of Erasmus Alber, Luther affirms the unity of the divine essence. Each person is wholly God, yet not alone God because there are three persons. All three persons together are God, yet one God, because there is no partition of essence in the same Godhead. Luther clarifies this by means of three statements:

1. Holy Scriptures teach that God is in the most simple way and that there are three persons (as they say) who are truly distinct.
2. Of these persons, it is true that each is the whole (*totus*) God, and apart from him there is no (*nullus*) other God.
3. Nevertheless, one cannot say each person alone (*personam solam*) is God.[11]

In his *Three Symbols*, we find Luther's teaching of the immanent Trinity. He distinguishes the three persons through the "relations of origin":[12] "The Father is of no one, neither born nor made nor created. The Son is of the Father, not made or created, but born. The Holy Spirit is of the Father and the Son, not born or created but proceeding."[13] The differentiation of persons in the same Godhead finds support in Scripture; Luther cites Psalm 2:7, "The Lord said to me, 'You are my Son, today I have begotten you,'" and John 15:26, "When the

---

10. Alister E. McGrath, *The Nature of Christian Doctrine: Its Origins, Development, and Function* (Oxford University Press, 2024), 135, McGrath's italics.
11. Christoph Schwöbel, "Martin Luther and the Trinity," in *Oxford Research Encyclopedia of Religion*, published March 29, 2017, https://doi.org/10.1093/acrefore/9780199340378.013.326: "*Scriptura sancta docet esse Deum simplicissime unum, et tres (ut vocant) personas verissime distinctas. 2. Harum personarum qualibet totus est Deus, extra quam nullus est alius Deus. 3. Nec tamen dici potest, quamlibet personam solum esse Deum.*" WA 39.2:253.2–6. I follow Schwöbel's translation. For the translation of Luther's academic discussions, see "Appendix: Three Disputations of the Late Luther with Explanatory Notes," in Dennis Bielfeldt et al., *The Substance of the Faith: Luther's Doctrinal Theology for Today*, ed. Paul R. Hinlicky (Fortress, 2008), 191–209.
12. Scott R. Swain, *The Trinity: An Introduction* (Crossway, 2020), 32.
13. *LW* 34:216–17.

Comforter comes, whom I shall send to you from the Father, the Spirit of truth, who proceeds from the Father, he will testify of me." Luther identifies "to be sent" with "proceed from," thus affirming the double procession of the Holy Spirit, known as the *filioque* doctrine.[14] Luther elaborates:

> The Holy Spirit proceeds from the Father and is sent by the Son. One who is sent, however, is also said to "proceed from." Just as the Son is born of the Father and yet does not depart from the Godhead, but on the contrary remains in the same Godhead with the Father and is one God with him, so also the Holy Spirit proceeds from the Father and is sent by the Son, and does not depart from the Godhead, and is one God with both.[15]

Luther explains the Son's "eternal birth" and the Spirit's "eternal procession" by way of analogy. Analogy has nothing to do with identity but with the likeness of the things in view. In Luther's words, "The Son shows his eternal birth through his physical birth, and the Spirit shows his eternal proceeding through his physical proceeding. Each of them has an external likeness or image of his internal essence."[16] The eternal birth of the Son is not identical to the physical birth of the Son; similarly, divine proceeding differs from human proceeding. A human person separates himself from his father from whom he is born. Not only is he "a separate individual person" but also "a separate individual substance."[17] He remains outside his father's substance, just as the father remains outside the son's substance. "But here the Son is born as another Person and nevertheless remains within his Father's substance, and the Father within the Son's substance. They are accordingly distinct as to Person, but remain in one single, undivided, and unseparated substance."[18] The same procedure applies to the Holy Spirit who proceeds from the Father and the Son. Just as the Son does not separate into another person, so it is with the Holy Spirit who "remains nevertheless within the Father's and the Son's substance, and the Father and the Son within the Holy Spirit's substance, that is, all three Persons in one Godhead."[19] The Son's birth from "the Father alone" is called an "immanent birth" and remains within the Godhead; the Spirit's proceeding is called an "immanent proceeding" from "the Father and the Son alone," which does not depart from the one Godhead.[20]

---

14. For a historical study of the *filioque* doctrine, see A. Edward Siecienski, *The Filioque: History of a Doctrinal Controversy* (Oxford University Press, 2010).
15. *LW* 34:217.
16. *LW* 34:218.
17. *LW* 34:217.
18. *LW* 34:217.
19. *LW* 34:216.
20. *LW* 34:217–18.

The Son's two births mean Jesus is not only the Son of the Father in eternity but also the son of Mary in time. The incarnate Son and the eternal Son are one. "The middle Person was physically born and became a son, the same who was born beforehand in eternity and is Son."[21] Likewise, the Holy Spirit proceeds physically in the form of a dove (Matt 3:16), "the same who proceeds in eternity."[22] Neither the Father nor the Spirit have physical birth, which is exclusive to the Son; proceeding is declared only of the Holy Spirit and not attributed to the Father or the Son. Luther endorses the Trinitarian distinction of persons in the one Godhead: "All three Persons are in majesty, and yet in a manner that the Son has his Godhead from the Father through his eternal immanent birth (and not the other way around), and that the Holy Spirit has his Godhead from the Father and the Son through his eternal immanent proceeding."[23] The early church fathers resorted to external, creaturely images, comparing the Father to the sun, the Son to its brilliance, and the Holy Spirit to its heat to capture the three distinct realities of the one thing. For Philo, the Logos is "the most brilliant and radiant light of the invisible and almighty God." For Origen, the Son's "generation as eternal [is] as the radiance which is produced from the sun." For Tertullian, the Holy Spirit is "a third from God and the Son, just . . . as the apex of the ray is third from the sun."[24]

In his *Treatise on the Last Words of David*, Luther turns to a discussion of the economic Trinity. Commenting on 2 Samuel 23:3, "The God of Israel has talked to me, the Rock of Israel has spoken; He who rules justly over men, He who rules in the fear of God," Luther discerns an exchange of three persons but only one speaker:

> Now we have three speakers. Above, David remarks that the Spirit of the Lord has spoken through his tongue. There the Person of the Holy Spirit is clearly indicated to us Christians. . . . Thus, we have heard that Scripture and our Creed ascribes to the Holy Spirit the external working, as He physically speaks to us, baptizes us, and reigns over us through the prophets, apostles, and ministers of the church. Therefore, these words of David are also those of the Holy Spirit, which He speaks with David's tongue regarding two other Speakers. What does He say of these? First of all, He speaks of the God of Israel and says that He has spoken to David, that is, has given him a promise. Which Person of the Godhead this Speaker is we Christians know from the Gospel

---

21. *LW* 34:218.
22. *LW* 34:218.
23. *LW* 34:218.
24. Henry A. Wolfson, *The Philosophy of the Church Fathers*, vol. 1, *Faith, Trinity, Incarnation* (Harvard University Press, 1956), 300–303, 359–60, 301n25.

of John. It is the Father who said in the beginning (Genesis 1:3): "Let there be light." And His Word is the Person of the Son, through which Word "all things were made" (John 1:3). The same Son the Spirit by the mouth of David here calls צור, *"Rock" of Israel* and just Ruler among mankind. He, too, speaks, that is, the Holy Spirit introduces the Rock of Israel to let Him speak, too. Thus, all three Persons speak, and yet there is but one Speaker, one Promiser, one Promise, just as there is but one God.[25]

As further proof, Luther cites Psalm 33:6: "By the Word of the Lord the heavens were made, and all their host by the Breath of His mouth." There, three persons are named: the Lord, his word, and his Spirit; yet David acknowledges no more than one creator. With Athanasius, Luther neither separates the one Godhead as in tritheism nor mingles the three persons as in modalism. In Luther's words: "For if I ascribe to each Person a distinct external work in creation and exclude the other two Persons from this, then I have divided the one Godhead and have fashioned three gods or creators. And this is wrong. Again, if I do not ascribe to each Person within the Godhead, or outside and beyond creation, a special distinction not appropriate to the other two, then I have mingled the Persons into one Person. And that is also wrong."[26] Luther follows Augustine's rule *"opera trinitatis ad extra sunt indivisa"* to affirm that all three persons are one creator.[27] The works of the Trinity in relation to all that is outside the Trinity remain inseparably one. God is indivisibly one without distinction, thus what one person does is attributable to the other two. "The Lord does not do His own work separately, the Word does not do His own work separately, and the Breath does not do His work separately."[28] Against Arius, who divides the one essence, Luther holds that there is one God and creator of all: "The Father is my God and Creator and yours, who created you and me. This same work, your creation and mine, was also performed by the Son, who is also my God and Creator and yours, just as the Father is. Likewise, the Holy Spirit created the self-same work, that is, you and me, and He is my God and Creator and yours as well as the Father and the Son."[29] In God's own life, the persons are distinguished but not separated. So, too, in God's action with us the persons are distinguished but not separated. Such a perspective enables Luther to counteract the modalistic collapse of the distinct of persons:

---

25. *LW* 15:276. Also cited in Schwöbel, "Luther and the Trinity," 9.
26. *LW* 15:302.
27. See Augustine, *De Trinitate*, in *Patrologiae Cursus Completus: Series Latina*, ed. J. P. Migne, 221 vols. (Paris, 1844–64), 2:5:9, 42:850, as cited in *LW* 15.302.n31
28. *LW* 15:302.
29. *LW* 15:303.

> When I go beyond and outside of creation or the creature and move into the internal, incomprehensible essence of divine nature, I find that Holy Scripture teaches me... that the Father is a different and distinct nature from the Son in the one indivisible and eternal Godhead. The difference is that He is the Father and does not derive His Godhead from the Son or anyone else. The Son is a Person distinct from the Father in the same, one paternal Godhead. The difference is that He is the Son and that He does not have the Godhead from Himself, nor from anyone else but the Father, since He was born of the Father from eternity. The Holy Spirit is a Person distinct from the Father and the Son in the same one Godhead. The difference is that He is the Holy Spirit, who eternally proceeds from both the Father and the Son, and who does not have the Godhead from Himself nor from anyone else but from both the Father and the Son, and all of this from eternity to eternity.[30]

God's Being as Self-Conversation
Ad Intra and Ad Extra

With Augustine, Luther employs the human word as an analogy for the inner-Trinitarian word.[31] In Luther's exegesis of the Gospel of John, he uses the image of "word," or "conversation" or "speech," to shed light on the inner life of the Trinity. The word (John 1:1) the Father speaks does not depart from the Godhead, but is in himself—unlike a human word, which when spoken, remains outside the speaker; and the Spirit listens in and remains within the same divine nature. The Father preaches the word which he identifies as the Son; the Son hears his Father; and the Holy Spirit listens in; this occurs in the one Godhead. All three are coeternal and coequal, yet one God.

> Thus, these are two distinct Persons: He who speaks and the Word that is spoken, that is, the Father and the Son. Here, however, we find the third Person following these two, namely, the One who hears both the Speaker and the spoken Word. For it stands to reason that there must also be a listener where a speaker and a word are found. But all this speaking, being spoken, and listening takes place within the divine nature and also remains there, where no creature is or can be. All three—Speaker, Word, and Listener—must be God Himself; all

---

30. *LW* 15:303.
31. Augustine, *De Trinitate*, in Migne, *Patrologiae Cursus Completus,* 18:15, 42:1077–79, as cited in Helmer, *The Trinity and Martin Luther*, 236n188.

three must be coeternal and in a single undivided majesty. For there is no difference or inequality in the divine essence, neither a beginning nor an end. Therefore, one cannot say that the Listener is something outside God, or that there was a time when He began to be a Listener; but just as the Father is a Speaker from eternity, and just as the Son is spoken from eternity, so the Holy Spirit is the Listener from eternity.[32]

The analogy of speech in John's Gospel characterizes the inner-Trinitarian relationship and its outer relationship to believers. Luther elaborates, "God ... in His majesty and nature, is pregnant with a Word or conversation in which he engages with Himself in His divine essence and which reflects the thoughts of his heart. This is as complete and excellent and perfect as God Himself. No one but God alone sees, hears, or comprehends this conversation. ... God is so absorbed in this Word, thought, or conversation that he pays no attention to anything else."[33] His speech is God's by right and nature; it is not derived or received from anything other than himself; in Luther's terms, "No one has given Him His speech, His Word, or His conversation. ... He alone has everything from Himself."[34] Concerning divine ontology, Robert Jenson muses that "the being of God is conversation,"[35] and Jeffrey Silcock proposes that "God is not simply love but ... speech or speech-event."[36] More precisely, it is persons in an ontic conversation within the one identical Godhead. God's speech is his own being; God is, in Jaroslav Pelikan's term, "never speech-less":

> It was characteristic of the God of the Bible that He not only created by His power and redeemed by His love, but that both His creating power and His redeeming love proceeded from Him through His speaking. Luther frequently warned against a picture of God that would paint Him in remote and self-contained isolation. It was in the very nature of God to want to speak and to be able to speak, and therefore by definition God was never speech-less. The Speech of God was as eternal as God Himself, and was God Himself. The God of the Christian faith was one who had a voice, an eternal Speech. This voice and eternal Speech of God was the cosmic sense of the term "Word of God."[37]

---

32. *LW* 24:364–65; *WA* 46:59.26–60, 6.
33. *LW* 22:9–10.
34. *LW* 22:9.
35. Robert W. Jenson, *Systematic Theology*, vol 2, *The Works of God* (Oxford University Press, 1999), 270.
36. Jeffrey G. Silcock, "The Role of the Spirit in Creation," *Lutheran Theological Journal* 44, no. 1 (2010): 8.
37. Jaroslav Pelikan, *Luther the Expositor: Introduction to the Reformer's Exegetical Writings*, companion volume to *Luther's Works* (Concordia, 1959), 50.

Underlying the speech-event is a fundamental difference between the true God and idols. The true God cannot be seen but can only be heard, for he never falls silent; idols can be seen but never heard, for they cannot speak. In God's relation to us, he remains the subject who refuses to be objectified or controlled by anything external to himself. Jenson differentiates between audible and visible means of communication, but with an emphasis on passive hearing, and the ear as the receptive organ of divine speech through which divine-human intimacy is created. God's speech places us under him, in the passive position of receiving what that word might do to us. In seeing, we are in control; in hearing, God is. The true God wills that he be orally proclaimed so that we might hear him and receive his "speech-act" rather than visibly objectify him to see and control him. Jenson captures this matter well:

> We have efficient flaps on our eyes but not on our ears, and can aim our eyes but not our ears: we are in control of what we see but hear what we must. We use our eyes instantly to locate what we apprehend; only inefficiently and with effort can we locate by hearing. Sight is thus the chief medium of *objectifying* consciousness: consciousness that intends realities as located in that world out there which I am not, and seeks to control my relation to them, to handle them indeed as the "objects" of my subjectivity. The God of Israel willed to be spoken for you, but refused to be visibly depicted.[38]

The analogy of people in love who engage in an intimate conversation, Silcock contends, helps illustrate "the mutual love of the three persons of the immanent Trinity" who engage in "an eternal conversation that begins *ad intra* and then *ad extra* (to the world), embodied in Jesus Christ, God's definitive Word to us. But long before he began speaking to Israel, he spoke the world into existence."[39] The ontic conversation between the Father and the Son is something which no angel or creature knows of, only the incarnate Son. Luther writes, "God . . . from all eternity has a Word, a speech, a thought, or a conversation with Himself in His divine heart. . . . This is called His Word. From eternity He was within God's paternal heart, and through Him God resolved to create heaven and earth. But no man was aware of such a resolve until the Word became flesh and proclaimed this to us."[40] Out of God's mercy, God discloses his inner speech through his incarnate Son, who is the same in eternity; the Spirit, whom the Father and the Son send, communicates God's inner thought to us. Like the

---

38. Robert W. Jenson, *Visible Words: The Interpretation and Practice of Christian Sacraments* (Fortress, 1978), 12–13, Jenson's italics.
39. Silcock, "Role of the Spirit," 8.
40. *LW* 22:9.

Son, the Spirit is the same in eternity. The Spirit is "a Listener," who hears the conversation between the Father and the Son and preaches their mutual thought or heart to us. The conversation between the Father and the Son, to which only the Holy Spirit has access, is not closed but is openly shared with us; by the Holy Spirit, we are drawn into the inner intimacy that the Son has with his Father. Schwöbel notes, "The communication from the Father to Jesus is thus continued through the Holy Spirit who communicates to believers what he hears in the eternal conversation between the Father and the Son."[41] Quoting Luther:

> But Christ points in particular to the distinctive Person of the Holy Spirit or His attribute, also to His divine essence together with the Father and the Son, when He says: "Whatever He hears He will speak." For here Christ refers to a conversation carried on in the Godhead, a conversation in which no creatures participate. He sets up a pulpit both for the speaker and for the listener. He makes the Father the Preacher and the Holy Spirit the Listener. It is really beyond human intelligence to grasp how this takes place, but since we cannot explain it with human words or intelligence, we must believe it. Here, faith must disregard all creatures and must not concentrate on physical preaching and listening; it must conceive of this as preaching, speaking, and listening inherent in the essence of the Godhead.[42]

The Spirit's Sermon
Incarnation and Cross

God's inner life is constituted by, to use Wolfhart Pannenberg's term, "a differentiated unity"[43] of three poles: The Father's is that of bestowing, giving the Son to death; the Son's is that of receiving, willingly giving himself as a fulfillment of the eternal plan of God; and the Holy Spirit's is that of reciprocity, bringing to completion God's eternal resolve in redeeming us in his Son. The intra-Trinitarian relational dynamism marked by bestowing (Father), receiving (Son), and reciprocity (Holy Spirit) is most expressly taught in *Treatise on the Last Words of David*:

> For the Person who gives must be distinct from the Person who *receives*. Thus the Father *bestows* the eternal dominion on the Son, and the Son

---

41. Schwöbel, "Luther and the Trinity," 12.
42. *LW* 24:364; *WA* 46:59. Also quoted in Schwöbel, "Luther and the Trinity," 12.
43. Wolfhart Pannenberg, "God of the Philosophers," *First Things*, June 1, 2007, 33.

receives it from the Father, and this is from eternity; otherwise this could not be an eternal dominion. And the Holy Spirit is present, inasmuch as He speaks these words through Daniel [Chap. 7:13–14]. For such sublime and mysterious things no one could know if the Holy Spirit would not *reveal* them through the prophets.[44]

Inscribed in the eternal heart of God, Helmer notes, "is the word of death"[45]—namely, the death of God's Son, whom God offers as "the price of our redemption." God's self-humiliation in history is an event of continuity in the life of God. It mirrors God's inner life in which there is sending and obeying, a giving and a receiving. Because the Son comes, suffers, and dies, there must be in God's inner life the form of receptivity that makes incarnation and Calvary possible. This is evident in Luther's *Meditation on Christ's Passion*: "Christ would not have shown this love for you if God in his eternal love had not wanted this, for Christ's love for you is due to obedience to God."[46]

The Spirit does not derive his divine essence from himself; he receives it from both the Father and the Son. This is based on Luther's interpretation of John 16:15: "All that the Father has is mine; therefore I said that he will take what is mine and declare it to you." The phrase "all that the Father has is mine" means Christ's deity is his by virtue of his consubstantiality with his Father from whom he takes his essence. From this, Luther concludes that the Holy Spirit is truly God, since he derives his essence from Christ who said, "[The Spirit] will take what is mine." Luther avers, "Here the circle is completely closed, and all three—the Father, the Son, and the Holy Spirit—are embraced in one divine essence."[47] Commenting on John 16:13, "For he will not speak on his authority, but whatever he hears he will speak," Luther asserts, "Christ makes the Holy Spirit a Preacher."[48] The consubstantiality of the Spirit with the Father and the Son ensures that the Spirit, who is God and comes from God, can speak with authority to us concerning the inner-Trinitarian essence. Helmer comments, "Luther's understanding of the Spirit as the person who, in its outer-trinitarian role, reveals the inner-Trinity to Christians."[49] Luther notes that "what God speaks concerning his nature must be believed."[50] This has its roots in Hilary's *De Trinitate*, to which Luther often alludes: "Hilary says: 'Who can speak better of himself than God himself?' [*Sic Hilarius: Quis potest, inquit, melius*

---

44. *LW* 15:291; *WA* 54:48, italics added.
45. Helmer, *The Trinity and Martin Luther*, 237.
46. *LW* 42:13.
47. *LW* 24:373; *WA* 45:68.
48. *LW* 24:362; *WA* 46:57.
49. Helmer, *The Trinity and Martin Luther*, 215.
50. *WA* 45:182.10, as cited in Helmer, *The Trinity and Martin Luther*, 220n131.

de se loqui quam deus ipse?]."⁵¹ Such a perspective reinforces the Spirit's role in the revelation of the inner-Trinity; conversely, Helmer notes, the knowledge of God's intra-Trinitarian life is not derived from "any *a posteriori* inference from the data of the world to the unity of God."⁵² The Spirit is one being with the Father and the Son, and thus knows the inner-Trinitarian discourse. Luther holds that "only the Holy Spirit from heaven above can create listeners and pupils to accept this doctrine."⁵³ Christ receives from his Father the word, which forms the very content of the Holy Spirit's office of preaching through which we are led into all truth. The Spirit wants us to adhere to Christ's word alone, through which he governs the church to the end. The Spirit preaches nothing except what he receives from Christ, and from his Father, as they are one. Luther expands on this:

> His message will have substance; it will be the certain and absolute truth, for He will preach what He receives from the Father and from Me. And you will be able to recognize Him by the fact that He does not speak on His own authority—as the spirit of lies, the devil, and his mobs do—but will preach about what He will hear. Thus He will speak exclusively of Me and will glorify Me, so that the people will believe in Me.⁵⁴

Helmer observes that, when commenting on Genesis 1:26, "Let us make man according to our image," Luther digresses to speak of "the inner-trinitarian conversation in view of the incarnation. The divine counsel decides, 'Let us make the human' [*faciamus hominem*], and already its intention is formulated, 'so that the Son might become a human and that all might believe in him' [*utque filius fiat homo, ut omnes credentes in eum*]."⁵⁵ The substance of God's self-conversation between the Father and the Son is the incarnation and cross, which the Spirit preaches to us so that we know where to find God. The Son's incarnation is already in the mind of the triune God. The Father's sermon is the cross of Christ, which occurs at a particular time in history but already exists as "promise" in eternity. This is taught in Revelation 13:8: "Christ was not in reality slain from the foundation of the world, except in promise."⁵⁶ As Althaus writes, "Thus all men

---

51. *WA* 34.1:500.9–10, as cited in Helmer, *The Trinity and Martin Luther*, 220–21. For a discussion of Hilary's Trinitarian theology in relation to Luther's doctrine of ubiquity, see Robert Mayes, "St. Hilary's Trinitarian Theology and Luther's Theology of Incarnate Omnipresence," *Logia: A Journal of Lutheran Theology* 14, no. 4 (Reformation 2005): 31–40.
52. Helmer, *The Trinity and Martin Luther*, 228.
53. *LW* 22:8; *WA* 46:543.
54. *LW* 24:363; *WA* 46:58.
55. *WA* 45:93.7–10, as cited in Helmer, *The Trinity and Martin Luther*, 237; cf. *LW* 1:53; *WA* 42:43.
56. *LW* 34:313; *WA* 39.2:197.

of all times who believe the promise, and thereby are blessed, live from the work of Christ – even though this actually first took place on Golgotha."⁵⁷ Unlike modalism's rejection of the three distinct persons in God, the inner-Trinitarian distinction that Luther affirms allows him to hold that the second person is destined to become one of us, to suffer and die to redeem us. The Son's incarnation is eternally preordained, and it is the abiding presupposition of the Son's temporal mission: "Because the Son of God must die, neither the Father nor the Holy Spirit became human [*Weil dei filius sol sterben, non pater, nec spiritus sanctus, sey mensch worden*]."⁵⁸ Though only the Son is attired with our humanity, all three persons are involved in the one indivisible act of clothing the Son. The Trinity is the subject of the incarnation, even if only the Son is incarnate. Luther illustrates incarnation by way of a crude analogy, borrowed from the scholastic theologian Bonaventure: "If, for example, three young women would take a dress and clothe one of them with this dress, then one could say that all three were dressing her; and yet only one is being attired in the dress and not the other two."⁵⁹ The whole Trinity is thus involved in an indivisible act of salvation. Soteriology springs from God's eternal resolve to redeem through the incarnate Son in history; and this bears a timeless significance as believers of all ages live because of the lamb that was slain "in promise" from eternity.

The "communicative relation"⁶⁰ with God is wrought in us by the Holy Spirit who comes to us as *donum dei* (a gift of God) but never departs from the Godhead. Luther asserts, "He himself is called 'gift' because he makes us holy and gives us life. Without this 'gift' of the Holy Spirit himself, the law condemns our sin, because the law is never 'gift.'"⁶¹ Luther endorses Augustine's distinction between the Spirit as a divine person and the Spirit as a divine gift while remaining inseparably one being. In his *First Disputation against the Antinomians* (1537), Luther asserts, "We distinguish the Holy Spirit as God in His divine nature and substance [immanent] from the Holy Spirit as he is given to us [economic]."⁶² The Holy Spirit is "a living, eternal, divine gift and grace";⁶³ he adorns believers with faith and other spiritual gifts, including resurrection from the dead, forgiveness of sins, and the subjective assurance that God wishes to be

---

57. Paul Althaus, *The Theology of Martin Luther*, trans. Robert C. Schultz (Fortress, 1966), 211.
58. *WA* 45:91.10–11, as cited in Helmer, *The Trinity and Martin Luther*, 237.
59. *LW* 15:306; *WA* 54:60.
60. Michael Richard Laffin, *The Promise of Martin Luther's Political Theology: Freeing Luther from the Modern Political Narrative* (T&T Clark, 2018), 63. The phrase "communicative relation" is Laffin's.
61. See *WA* 39.1:370–71, as quoted in Bernhard Lohse, *Martin Luther's Theology: Its Historical and Systematic Development*, trans. and ed. Roy A. Harrisville (Fortress, 1999), 170.
62. *WA* 39.1:370.12–13, as quoted in Jeffrey G. Silcock, "Luther on the Holy Spirit and His Use of God's Word," in *The Oxford Handbook of Martin Luther's Theology*, ed. Robert Kolb, Irene Dingel, and L'ubomír Batka (Oxford University Press, 2014), 307.
63. *LW* 37:366.

our Father in Christ. Economically, the Spirit appears as God in his distinctive manner as gift, as he "who has been given to us," as Paul said in Romans 5:5. Immanently, the triune God exists in self-relatedness as paternity (Father), filiation (Son), and gift (Spirit). Luther seeks the scriptural foundation for Augustine's account of the *filioque* doctrine, that the Spirit proceeds from the Son. If the New Testament reveals to us that Jesus sends to us as his own the Holy Spirit from the Father, as Augustine held, then in the immanent Trinity the Holy Spirit must proceed from the Father and the Son as from one single source. Since the Holy Spirit proceeds as a person from the Father and the Son, he must be in his person the "communion" of love that exists between them. Augustine writes:

> So the Holy Spirit is a kind of inexpressible communion or fellowship of Father and Son, and perhaps he is given this name just because the same name can be applied to the Father and the Son. He is properly called what they are called in common, seeing that both Father and Son are holy and both Father and Son are spirit. So to signify the communion of them both by a name which applies to them both, the gift of both is called the Holy Spirit.[64]

The Spirit, the "common gift" of both the Father and the Son, is "love" and thus, Augustine reasons, "he suggests to us the common charity by which the Father and the Son mutually love each other."[65] The ideas of mutual love and communion become for Augustine practically interchangeable: "And if the love by which the Father loves the Son and the Son loves the Father ineffably demonstrates the communion of both, what is more suitable than that He should properly be called love who is Spirit common to both."[66] The mutual love between the Father and the Son is known only to the Holy Spirit; it is bestowed on us by the Spirit, who himself is the unity of love between them. This is borne out in Luther's exegesis of Romans 5:5, where he asserts that the love of God is God's gift, poured into us by the Holy Spirit who himself is eternally a gift and "has been given to us."[67] Quoting Augustine:

> So the love which is from God and is God is distinctively the Holy Spirit; through him the charity of God is poured out in our hearts, and through it the whole triad dwells in us. This is the reason why it is most

---

64. Augustine, *The Works of Saint Augustine: A Translation for the 21st Century*, ed. John E. Rotelle, trans. Edmund Hill, vol 5, *The Trinity* (New City, 1991), 15:5:3, 197.

65. Augustine, *The Trinity* 15:5:27, 418.

66. Augustine, *On the Holy Trinity* in *Augustine: On the Holy Trinity, Doctrinal Treatises, Moral Treatises*, ed. Philip Schaff, vol. 3, *The Nicene and Post-Nicene Fathers*, 1st ser., repr. (Hendrickson, 1995), 15:19:37, 219.

67. *LW* 25:292; *WA* 56:306.

apposite that the Holy Spirit, while being God, should also be called the gift of God. And this gift, surely, is distinctively to be understood as being the charity which brings us through to God, without which no other gift of God at all can bring us through to God.[68]

To Be God Is to Be Related
God's Speech Ad Intra and Ad Extra

By the Holy Spirit, believers are given a glorious privilege to participate in the Son's love-communion with the Father, or in Hinlicky's terms, in the one God who "more than exists as self-identical; He ever *lives as internally related in love.*"[69] Differentiation of persons in the one undivided God gives rise to the very being of God as relational; as Jenson puts it, "to be God is to be related,"[70] the opposite of the static nature of Hellenic deity from which relational dynamism, movement, and love are excluded. Hinlicky expands on the dynamic nature of God's relatedness to himself and to the world: "God is not the still silence before the world began—and for that matter ever since. God is the ever-abundant eternal love that called the world into being, speaks the world along its way, and will bring it to fulfillment in His company at the victory shout, 'Behold, I make all things new!'"[71] The God who exists in relation to himself as speech is not separated from his relation to creatures external to himself, for he has spoken. Humans cannot create "a communicative relation" with God; they do not "lay the first stone," Luther insists. "God alone—without any entreaty or desire of man—must come first and give him a promise."[72] Unless God opens up to creatures, his self-conversation or intra-Trinitarian conversation remains hidden from us in himself. God has spoken generally in creation, and definitively in Christ, making it possible for us to gain access to him and his inner word. As Thomas Torrance asserts, "[God] has opened up himself to our knowledge of his own being as Father, Son, and Holy Spirit for what he has revealed himself to us through Christ and in the Spirit he is in himself."[73] God's immanent speech in himself is his by nature, and is beyond our grasp; his economic speech to us is God's gift, and is within our reach. God's inner speech corresponds to his outer speech. The outer

---

68. Augustine, *The Trinity* 15:5:32, 421.
69. See Paul R. Hinlicky, *Divine Complexity: The Rise of Creedal Christianity* (Fortress, 2011), 222, Hinlicky's italics.
70. Robert W. Jenson, *The Triune Identity: God According to the Gospel* (Fortress, 1982), 85.
71. Hinlicky, *Divine Complexity*, 225.
72. *LW* 35:82.
73. Thomas F. Torrance, *The Trinitarian Faith: The Evangelical Theology of the Ancient Catholic Church*, 2nd ed. (Bloomsbury T&T Clark, 2016), 67–68.

speech places us in a passive position of receiving from God the knowledge of the Father's heart through the Son in the Spirit. As Luther states, "Whatever we are, we received from Him and not from ourselves."[74] The immanent God initiates the "inside-out" movement of speech from the Father through the Son by the Holy Spirit to us so that we might be drawn into his inner life of communion via the "outside-in" movement of the "reversed Trinity"—that is, by the Holy Spirit through the Son to the Father. Faith participates in the fullness of these two movements of the Trinity. God's immanent relation to himself as speech *ad intra* is prior to and the ground of his economic relation to us as speech *ad extra*. His coming to us in speech in a free act of grace effects in his sinful creatures a reciprocal engagement with him in speech. Grace, not works, admits us to his inner circle of divine discourse. The wonder of the gospel is that God speaks with us, and we hear his voice. He addresses us personally in his speech, and we miserable sinners are thereby summoned into conversation with the supreme majesty in heaven. Hinlicky puts it thus: "In the Spirit, the Trinity's own discourse here and now freely turns outward to the creation, including creatures *in spite of sinfulness* in eternally loving discourse of divine life."[75] Luther exults, "It is a glorious privilege that the sublime Majesty in heaven condescends to let us poor worms open our mouths in conversation with him and gladly listens to us."[76] But he continues, "it is a far more precious privilege that He speaks with us and that we listen to him. Both are good and great benefits conferred by God."[77] Nothing is more effective than God's speech—not human speech, nor any other power on earth—only the speech of "the Man who is God Himself" is so efficacious that it produces a peaceful and joyful heart, as is borne out in Psalm 85:8, "Let me hear what God the Lord will speak, for He will speak peace to His people."[78]

The Economy of Gift in the Creed
The Trinitarian Grammar of Faith

Luther scholarship has largely focused on the christological grammar of justification,[79] overlooking the Trinitarian grammar of justification. But Pelikan reasons that the christological grammar makes sense "only if [the doctrine of

---

74. *LW* 22:9.

75. Paul R. Hinlicky, "Luther's New Language of the Spirit: Trinitarian Theology as Critical Dogmatics," in Bielfeldt et al., *Substance of the Faith*, 139, Hinlicky's italics.

76. *LW* 24:419; *WA* 46:108.

77. *LW* 24:419; *WA* 46:108.

78. *LW* 24:419; *WA* 46:108.

79. Siggins and Lienhard focus on Christological basis of justification. See Ian D. Kingston Siggins, *Martin Luther's Doctrine of Christ* (Yale University Press, 1970); Lienhard, *Luther*. For a major historical study of the doctrine of justification, see Alister E. McGrath, *Iustitia Dei: A History of the Christian Doctrine of Justification*, 4th ed. (Cambridge University Press, 2020).

justification is] seen as a development not only from Augustinian anthropology, but [also] from the dogma of the Trinity."[80] Risto Saarinen contends that Luther's doctrine of the Trinity generally falls between two viewpoints: "On the one hand, it cannot be concluded that Luther's concentration on the doctrine of justification would lead to the neglect of Trinitarian theology as futile speculation; on the other hand, however, it is also true that he develops his explicit Trinitarian theology only in so far as it serves his Reformatory programme and acute controversies related to it."[81] Luther's theological method does not begin with the knowledge of God's being *in se*, which is inaccessible to us, but rather with experience; more specifically, the experience of the gospel. What God is in himself is for God, hidden in himself and from creatures outside himself; what God is to us is for us, accommodated to our limited understanding. Such perspective has its root in Augustine, who distinguishes between what God is to himself and what he is to us, but with an emphasis on the latter, on God's actions for us. Commenting on the name of God, Augustine writes, "The name I AM WHO AM is suitable to me [God], but the name *The God of Abraham, the God of Isaac, and the God of Jacob* is adjusted to your comprehension. If you fall back from what I am to myself, understand what I am for you."[82] The economic Trinity, for Luther, is the self-disclosure of the immanent Trinity. God's being in eternity corresponds to God's revelation in temporality. The redemptive act of God in history is in continuity with what God is from all eternity; it merely enacts what has been ordained from eternity—namely, the interactive action of the three persons for our salvation. As Lienhard rightly assesses, "Everything depends on the fact that the accomplishment of salvation by the Father, the Son, and the Spirit is determined in the very eternity of God."[83] The God who saves is indeed the God who is in himself, and any division between them would put the assurance of salvation in jeopardy. Lienhard further explains, "And that is where modalism ultimately leads, wherein the Father, the Son, and the Holy Spirit are reduced to different modes by which the divinity is manifest in history."[84]

The gospel, that God is for us, is so strong in its efficacy that it informs our understanding of other areas of theology and life—creation, redemption, and

---

80. Jaroslav Pelikan, *The Christian Tradition: A History of the Development of Doctrine*, vol. 4, *Reformation of Church and Dogma (1300–1700)* (University of Chicago Press, 1984), 157.

81. Risto Saarinen, "*In sinu Patris*: The Merciful Trinity in Luther's Exposition of John 1:18," in *Trinitarian Theology in the Medieval West*, ed. Pekka Kärkkäinen (Luther-Agricola-Seura, 2007), 294.

82. Augustine, *Expositions of the Psalms*, trans. Maria Boulding, vol. 1, *Expositions of the Psalms 1–32*, ed. John E. Rotelle (New City, 2000), 196, as cited in Christopher R. J. Holmes, The Lord is Good: Seeking the God of the Psalter (IVP Academic, 2018), 53; Augustine, *Expositions of the Psalms*, trans Maria Boulding, vol. 6, *Expositions of the Psalms 121–150*, ed. Boniface Ramsay (New City, 2004), 214, as cited in Holmes, *The Lord is Good*, 53.

83. Lienhard, *Luther*, 319.

84. Lienhard, *Luther*, 319.

sanctification—as this book bears out. All these areas where the gospel extends are concrete proof of the manifold gifts of the triune God before whom we can only respond passively with gratitude and love. Because of the Father of the First Article, creation is possible; because of the Son of the Second Article, re-creation is possible; and because of the Holy Spirit of the Third Article, the certainty of belonging to God through the Son is made epistemically real in us. God's creating, justifying, and sanctifying actions fall under a common rubric, *ex nihilo*; it is solely God's gift, received by faith and not achieved by works. "Following the movement of the creed," Jonathan Linebaugh notes, "Luther describes the action of the economic Trinity as an economy of gift."[85] The gift-character of the whole Godhead serves us. As Saarinen argues, "The gift-character of creation is seen in the fact that creatures 'serve and benefit' us. It is not the perspective of man's domination over creation, but the perspective of us receiving this gift."[86] This gift-character of creation flows into the Second Article, that God's fatherly gifts are hidden in the Son, our sole mediator, and into the Third Article, that the gifts Christ has acquired belong to us in the power of the Holy Spirit, the completion of God's Trinitarian action. The Creed offers, in Scott Swain's phrase, a "grammar of divine agency"[87] in which all three persons are present and work *ad extra* indivisibly as one God, achieving his "most earnest purpose" to attach himself to us, or to fulfill his promise to be our God. The Trinitarian grammar of faith by which we live is summed up at the conclusion of Luther's *Large Catechism*: "We see here in the Creed how God gives himself completely to us, with all his gifts and power, to help us keep the Ten Commandments: the Father gives us all creation, Christ all his works, and the Holy Spirit all his gifts."[88] The entire Godhead bestows "wholly and completely"[89] the gift, not of objects, but of himself as Father, Son, and Holy Spirit.

> These are the three persons and one God, who has given himself to us all wholly and completely, with all that he is and has. The Father gives himself to us, with heaven and earth and all the creatures, in order that they may serve us and benefit us. But this gift has become obscured and useless through Adam's fall. Therefore the Son subsequently gave himself and bestowed all his works, sufferings, wisdom, and righteousness, and

---

85. Jonathan A. Linebaugh, "Incongruous and Creative Gift: Reading *Paul and the Gift* with Martin Luther," *International Journal of Systematic Theology* 22, no. 1 (2020): 54, doi:10.1111/ijst.12388.

86. Risto Saarinen, *God and the Gift: An Ecumenical Theology of Giving* (Liturgical Press, 2005), 46.

87. Scott R. Swain, *The Trinity and the Bible: On Theological Interpretation* (Lexham Academic, 2021), 262.

88. "The Large Catechism," *BC*, 440.

89. See Steven D. Paulson, *Luther's Outlaw God*, vol. 3, *Sacraments and God's Attack on the Promise* (Fortress, 2021), 336–37.

reconciled us to the Father, in order that we, restored to life and righteousness, might also know and have the Father and his gift.

But because this grace would benefit no one if it remained so profoundly hidden and could not come to us, the Holy Spirit comes and gives himself to us also, wholly and completely. He teaches us to understand this deed of Christ which has been manifested to us, helps us receive and preserve it, use it to our advantage and impart it to others, increase and extend it.[90]

Luther provides an exquisite articulation of the threefold self-giving of God—Father, Son, and Holy Spirit—to the world of creation. The divine self-giving originates with the Father, the fountainhead of all gifts that are already woven into the creaturely world. The Father gives himself "wholly and completely" to all of creation; but the divine gifts are made "useless" due to human disdain of God's grace. As a remedy, the Son gave himself "subsequently" in order that we may be restored to "the Father," and all his gifts, which were lost due to Adam's fall, may be reinstated. Finally, the Holy Spirit gave himself "wholly" to impart into our hearts Christ's restoration of creation and joyous exchange of Christ's righteousness for our sins.

The Holy Spirit's office is to fill our hearts with no other glory than the glory of the cross. "The Holy Spirit," says Bertrand de Margerie, "is a real and divine sphere of revelation in which the risen Christ alone is present as redemptive reality, . . . [not as] an idea."[91] The Holy Spirit is not a separate deity, disclosing some new or different revelation than the word Christ receives from his Father. The God who appeared in Christ is identical to God who appears as the Holy Spirit. A theologian of the cross grasps God as he is hidden in the human form of Jesus who died on the cross. On the other hand, a theologian of glory affirms that in the Holy Spirit we meet God unmediated, no longer veiled and hidden in human form. However, as William Hordern rightly argues, "the theology of the cross applies just as completely to God the Holy Spirit as it does to God the Son."[92] For the Holy Spirit kindles and preserves faith, whose object is not the unmediated, naked majesty with whom we have nothing to do, but the incarnate, crucified Christ, the God "with whom we have to do" (cf. Heb 4:13).

Luther's articulation of the Trinity focuses on the interactive roles the Father, Son, and Holy Spirit play in restoring our image, lost in Adam's fall. As

---

90. *LW* 37:366; also cited in Oswald Bayer, *Living by Faith: Justification and Sanctification*, trans. Geoffrey W. Bromiley (Eerdmans, 2003), 53; Saarinen, *God and the Gift*, 46.
91. Bertrand de Margerie, *The Christian Trinity in History*, trans. Edmund J. Fortman (St. Bede's Publications, 1982), 201.
92. William Hordern, *Experience and Faith: The Significance of Luther for Understanding Today's Experiential Religion* (Augsburg Publishing House, 1983), 96.

the grammar of faith, to use Saarinen's phrase, "the merciful Trinity"[93] is the subject of God's saving actions for us. Timothy Wengert provides a succinct summary of the economic actions of the triune God as the content of the Creed: "God created 'out of pure, fatherly, and divine goodness and mercy, without any merit or worthiness of mine at all'; God the Son ransomed humanity from the evil 'kidnappers' of sin, death, and the devil by his suffering, death, and resurrection; God the Holy Spirit bestows faith and makes us holy through forgiveness proclaimed in the Christian assembly."[94] The justified identity lives by, to use Pannenberg's phrase, "a differentiated unity"[95] of God's "incongruous" grace; we are loved by God's creative grace, accepted by Christ's justifying grace, and renewed by the Holy Spirit's sanctifying grace. The three actions are distinctive to each person, but not exclusive to that person. With Augustine, the Reformer holds that all three persons act in full unity with himself externally, drawing us away from every creaturely thing to the God of the first commandment, the very reason for all that exists outside the Godhead. In keeping with the primacy of the soteriological "for us," Luther dwells on the economic Trinity, on how the triune God operates in three distinct ways in his people to draw them to his bosom of "pure, unutterable love."

However, the immanent Trinity is not unaccounted for. In his exposition of John 1:18, Luther explores the concept of mediation between the Father and the Son. The Son's eternal relationship with his Father is the epistemological ground of God's merciful action on us. The Son, "who is in the bosom of the Father," reveals the merciful heart of God. Christ and his Father are one; yet Christ directs our gaze from himself to his Father, opening to us "the Father's love for us which is just as strong and profound as His own, which is reflected in His sacrificial death."[96] Luther imagines Christ saying, "'Whoever beholds the Father's love also beholds Mine; for Our love is identical. I love you with a love that redeems you from sin and death. And the Father's love, which gave you His only Son, is just as miraculous.'"[97] The love the Father has initiated for us is accomplished in his Son's passive obedience to death on the cross. Luther writes, "Christ is the only one whom the Father loves; and this Son has nothing but love for us, because he died for us. Therefore it must be our concern to come and look here, for this is the only place where you will find anything."[98] As God's beloved children, we are included in the identical love between the Father and the Son and are eternally loved by the Father as is the Son. The paternal heart is identical

---

93. Saarinen, "*In sinu Patris*."

94. Timothy J. Wengert, "The Small Catechism, 1529," in *The Annotated Luther*, vol. 4, *Pastoral Writings*, ed. Mary Jane Haemig (Fortress, 2016), 207.

95. Pannenberg, "God of the Philosophers," 33.

96. *LW* 22:355.

97. *LW* 22:355.

98. *LW* 22:500.

to the filial heart; the Father and the Son are one being and share one identical love. Unless the incarnate Son reveals this to us, we will never know of God's paternal heart; and unless the Holy Spirit communicates it to our hearts, we will not grasp the eternal heart of God. Our identity as God's children is known to the Father and to the Son—but we know this, too, because the Holy Spirit preaches it to our hearts. Christ's obedient response to the Father's initiatory love becomes effectual in us, not through any prior worth or work of ours but solely through a "trusting apprehension" in the Holy Spirit of the gospel. "Becoming the temporal object of the Father's eternal love for the Son," Hinlicky states, "she therewith becomes a new subject in the Spirit of its trusting apprehension."[99] We are thereby drawn into the Trinitarian dynamic of God's purposive love: love that flows from God as Father through God as Son and in God as the Holy Spirit, finally transforming us to be perfectly holy, and restoring us to the hope of eternal life. The Spirit's sanctifying work of conforming us to Christ as the object of the Father's love has reached the end when sin, death, and all misfortunes are terminated, thereby making us whole. In Hinlicky's apt assessment:

> The Father's love for the sinful world initiates the Son's coming into the flesh and our inclusion of Him by the Spirit in a free act of grace. The Son's response to the Father's love in the Spirit works out the inclusion of the godless by His way to the God-forsaken death on Golgotha. Consequently, as the crucified and risen Lord, He bestows His own Spirit to bring the Father's love to fulfillment in the gathering of the church, the resurrection of the dead, and the life everlasting.[100]

Christology and pneumatology are one, as both the Son and the Spirit act together as mediators. While the Son mediates between God and us by attaining for us God's reconciliation with us, the Spirit mediates between Christ and us by applying to us Christ's accomplishment of our salvation. The grace of the triune God effects a return to the state of innocence where Adam was, in Luther's words, "intoxicated with rejoicing toward God and was delighted also with all the other creatures."[101] Lois Malcolm summarizes Luther's position well, which takes as his starting point the triune God's economic actions *ad extra* as God's way of restoring us to his immanent being *ad intra*:

> In the work of these three persons (the so-called economic Trinity), we have the "the entire essence, will, and work of God" (that is, the so-called

---

99. Hinlicky, "Luther's New Language," 143.
100. Hinlicky, "Luther's New Language," 143. See also Timothy J. Wengert, *Martin Luther's Catechisms: Forming the Faith* (Fortress, 2009), 44.
101. *LW* 1:94; *WA* 42:71.

immanent Trinity). Through it, God opens to us "the most profound depths of his fatherly heart and his pure, unutterable love," showing us how he has not only created us to redeem us and make us holy but has also given us "his Son and his Holy Spirit, through whom he brings us to himself"—since we would not be able to recognize "the Father's favor and grace" were it not for Christ, the "mirror of the Father's heart," and the Holy Spirit, who reveals Christ to us.[102]

"The Creed is a dear little letter, as it were," for Luther, and is "the entire gospel" in brief.[103] All benefits secured by the Creed would not avail us unless faith, created by promise, was added. Every Article of the Creed concludes with faith, the fiduciary expression: "This is most certainly true."[104] With the tradition, Luther distinguishes between the content, "the faith that is believed" (*fides quae creditur*), and the means, "the faith by which it is believed" (*fides qua creditur*). The first is "I believe *that*," referring to believing what is propositionally true about God; second is "I believe *in*," referring not only to the fact that I believe or know that these things (for example, that God is real and that he loves me) are true about God, but also to the fact that I believe *in* him, putting my personal "trust in him," regarding him as the basis of everything in life and death, as is taught by the Scriptures.[105] Both are necessary to be a Christian, but the second, Todd Hains suggests, "is an especially Christian act" through which we receive from God all his gifts.[106] Luther stresses, "So that little word '*in*' is well chosen and should be noted carefully; we do not say, I believe God the Father, or I believe about the Father, but rather, I believe *in* God the Father, *in* Jesus Christ, and *in* the Holy Spirit. And this faith is given only by God himself."[107] To believe *that* God exists is purely historical knowledge, which even the devil believes without placing his trust in him. To believe *in* God is to trust in him, with a certainty that he relates to me as truly as Scripture teaches.

The fiduciary language of trusting, praising, and loving God, Oswald Bayer notes, is itself a "counter-gift";[108] the creature is enabled to respond to God, not to earn grace, but because of creative grace. The new life we possess is bestowed

---

102. Lois Malcolm, "Martin Luther and the Holy Spirit," in *Oxford Research Encyclopedia of Religion*, published March 29, 2017, https://doi.org/10.1093/acrefore/9780199340378.013.328. This is based on "The Large Catechism," *BC*, 439–40.

103. See *WA* 11:48.24–26, as cited in Todd R. Hains, *Martin Luther and the Rule of Faith: Reading God's Word for God's People* (IVP Academic, 2022), 68n86.

104. "The Small Catechism," *BC*, 354–55.

105. *LW* 43:24.

106. Hains, *Luther Rule of Faith*, 67.

107. *LW* 43:25.

108. Oswald Bayer, "The Ethics of Gift," trans. Mark A. Seifrid, *Lutheran Quarterly* 24, no. 4 (2010): 458. Also quoted in John M. G. Barclay, *Paul and the Gift* (Eerdmans, 2017), 114n89.

by, to borrow Barclay's phrase, "the incongruity of a gift,"[109] totally without any prior action or worth of the beneficiaries. This life is an alien life, lived not in us (*in nobis*) but outside us (*extra nos*), in Christ. The image of Christ is formed in us by the Holy Spirit through the proclamation in the Christian assembly around God's effective word and its created forms. Philip Watson captures Luther's emphasis: "The creaturely words whether written or spoken, are for him rather the vehicle or media of the Divine creative Word, by which God addresses Himself directly and personally to us."[110] These material forms of God's word are the accommodated means through which God has condescended into our lives to persuade us to seek what we need from him. To implement the first commandment is to avail ourselves of the infinite riches of the triune God hidden in ecclesial community, the locus where the Holy Spirit begins to make us holy and renew us until we become fully righteous in Christ. The Spirit is the power of contemporaneity with God, placing us in the horizon of the creative power of the Father and the redemptive activity of the Son, and moving us toward the end where brokenness gives way to perfection. As Schwöbel sums up:

> The work of the Holy Spirit is therefore the form of God's trinitarian work.... The Spirit makes us co-present with God's acts in the past and in the future in memory and hope. We are thereby located in the horizon of the totality of God's activity as the creator of everything there is, as a redeemer of his alienated creation and as the one who brings us to the sanctified perfection of eternal life.[111]

The triune God that Scripture reveals is not an isolated, self-enclosed deity but an open, self-disclosed deity, who goes out of Godself and enters communion with us through the three distinct, economic activities of the Father as creator, the Son as redeemer, and of the Holy Spirit in whom the operations of the former two find their consummation in us. In Luther's own words: "Working through the Holy Spirit, Father and Son stir, awaken, call, and beget new life in me and in all who are his. Thus the Spirit in and through Christ quickens, sanctifies, awakens the spirit in us and brings us to the Father, by whom the Spirit is active and life-giving everywhere."[112] Hence the Third Article, for Luther, is "most important,"[113] as it brings the whole of God's Trinitarian activities to unity in us. The Holy Spirit effects the communication of properties between Christ

---

109. Barclay, *Paul and the Gift*, 73.
110. Philip S. Watson, *Let God be God: An Interpretation of the Theology of Martin Luther* (Fortress, 1947), 152.
111. Christoph Schwöbel, "The Triune God of Grace: Trinitarian Thinking in the Theology of the Reformers," in *The Christian Understanding of God Today*, ed. James M. Byrne (Columba, 1993), 55.
112. *LW* 43:28.
113. *LW* 43:24.

and sinners. Justification is framed within the context of "joyous exchange": Christ's righteousness is transferred to us, and our sins are transferred to him. Christ's righteous identity is ours in exchange for our sinful identity, assuring us of our justified status before God. Christ's Sonship by nature is credited to us, so that we truly become God's Son by grace, loved as dearly as God's Son by the Father; this is made real in our hearts by the "convincing Spirit."[114] The Spirit is the effector in whom the Father, through and with the Son, brings to fulfillment God's Trinitarian purpose to be ours so that we may be his. In the order of knowing, Luther considers the Third Article as "most important"[115] on which the others are based. This is not so in the order of being, because all three persons are essentially coequal and coeternal. To highlight the Spirit as "most important" is not to undermine his consubstantiality and coequality with the other two persons. Luther's language of the Spirit is not to be taken literally but rhetorically to underscore the Spirit's unique function of applying to us the work of the Father and the Son within the unity of the same Godhead.

God's "downward movement" to us in grace, Berndt Hamm recognizes, is the dynamism of our "upward movement" to him by faith.[116] God's gracious descent to us causes our faith in Christ's ascent to the Father by the Holy Spirit. Without the Holy Spirit, what God has accomplished in his Son remains a historical fact to be discussed in academic schools, devoid of relevance for us. In Niels Henrik Gregersen's phrase, "The Holy Spirit thus works *in us* by making real *for us* what is already realized in Christ."[117] Sinners of themselves cannot generate a reversal of movement from sin to righteousness, death to life, unbelief to faith except by the Holy Spirit, the effector. Luther stresses, "But the ungodly does not come even when he hears the Word, unless the Father draws and teaches him inwardly, which He does by pouring out the Spirit."[118] Luther's pneumatology, Wengert rightly declares, "holds the key" to his Trinity:

> His descriptions of the Trinity grew out of his understanding of the Holy Spirit's work. . . . It is the Holy Spirit who turned Luther's (and turns our) understanding of the Trinity on its head. Luther captured this reversal when he wrote for the Small Catechism the shocking first words for his paraphrase of the third article: "I believe that I cannot

---

114. *LW* 33:286.
115. *LW* 43:24.
116. Berndt Hamm, *The Early Luther: Stages in a Reformation Reorientation*, trans. Martin J. Lohrmann (Eerdmans, 2014), 218.
117. Niels Henrik. Gregersen, "Grace in Nature and History: Luther's Doctrine of Creation Revisited," *Dialog: A Journal of Theology* 44, no. 1 (2005): 22, Gregersen's italics.
118. *LW* 33:286.

believe." . . . Because the Holy Spirit makes us believers, it stands to reason that we experience the Trinity backward.[119]

The economic action of the Holy Spirit "backward" is the key to an apprehension of Luther's doctrine of the Trinity. The whole of Luther's outlook on life, his theology, and his vocation as a Reformer, Kirsi I Stjerna rightly observes, is wrapped up with the Third Article. She asserts, "What he experienced in his faith journey makes no sense without recognizing the involvement of the Holy Spirit. His theology of grace and justification would not work if the essential role of the Spirit was out of the equation."[120] Luther has been primarily labeled as a theologian of faith or grace, but he is also a theologian of the Trinity—and more specifically, of the Holy Spirit.[121]

---

119. Wengert, *Martin Luther's Catechisms*, 44–45.
120. Kirsi I. Stjerna, *Lutheran Theology: A Grammar of Faith* (T&T Clark, 2021), 104.
121. See Regin Prenter, *Spiritus Creator: Luther's Concept of the Holy Spirit* (Fortress, 1953).

CHAPTER TWO

God's Most Earnest Purpose in the Ten Commandments

LUTHER USES THE Decalogue for his method of catechesis. He employs the Exodus 20 / Deuteronomy 5 text as a call for repentance, introducing children to a law-gospel rhythm for the Christian life. He later returns to using these commands implicitly for instruction in Christian living when it comes to the Table of Christian Callings at the end of the *Small Catechism*.[1] Unlike Calvin, who followed the Hebrew Bible, in which the second commandment is "Thou shall not have any graven images," Luther continues to number the Ten Commandments according to the medieval system, in which the second commandment is "You are not to take the name of God in vain." Luther incorporates the image prohibition of the second commandment of the Hebrew Bible into the first commandment and separates the last commandment into two: "Thou shall not covet your neighbor's house," and "Thou shall not covet your neighbor's wife, or whatever is his." While the first tablet—the first through the third commandments—is directed to God, the second tablet—the other seven—relates to our neighbor.

Luther's exposition of the Ten Commandments does not begin with the prologue from Exodus 20:1 ("I am the LORD your God, who brought you out of Egypt, out of the house of bondage"), but with the prohibition of idols as the first commandment in Exodus 20:3, "You shall have no other gods." The rationale for this change is found in his 1525 treatise *How Christians Should Regard Moses*: "This text makes it clear that even the Ten Commandments do not pertain to us. For God never led us out of Egypt, but only the Jews . . . We will just skip that. We will regard Moses as a teacher, but we will not regard him as our law giver—unless he agrees with both the New Testament and the natural law."[2] The Ten Commandments reflect the law written into creation. As James Nestingen and Gerhard Forde write, "The Ten Commandments, in that sense, are not Christian or even religious teachings: they summarize what life requires of everyone."[3] They demand that human beings recognize themselves as contingent upon and accountable to the creator. Luther explains, "Nature also has these laws.

---

1. "The Small Catechism," *BC*, 365–67.
2. *LW* 35:165.
3. James Arne Nestingen and Gerhard O. Forde, *Free to Be: A Handbook to Luther's Small Catechism* (Augsburg Publishing House, 1975), 76.

Nature provides that we should call upon God. The Gentiles attest to this fact. For there never was a Gentile who did not call upon his idols, even though they were not the true God."[4] Humans are imbued with the propensity to call upon whomever and whatever they might have as their deity. Those who do not have the true God will inevitably fabricate a god in their image to meet their need.

The First Commandment
"The Most Important"

By incorporating the image prohibition into the first commandment, "You shall have no other gods," the solemnity of God's lordship over all creatures is declared. God alone is the one who is to be "feared, loved, and trusted" above all things. The first commandment, Paul Hinlicky rightly notes, functions as a demand ("Have no other gods"); but it could also serve as a promise ("I am the Lord, your God").[5] Luther discovers in the first commandment the best news, that "God's most earnest purpose" is to be ours, and that we are his. God's purpose, that he belongs to us, and our trust, that very posture by which we belong to him, coincide. This coincidence constitutes the force of the first commandment; in Luther's own words, "[God] wishes to turn us away from everything else apart from him, and to draw us to himself, because he is the one, eternal good."[6] The first commandment proclaims God's promise: "I, I myself will give you what you need and help you out of every danger." Corresponding to this promise is God's claim: "Only do not let your heart cling or rest in anyone else."[7] Luther expands further:

> Here I earnestly consider that God expects and teaches me to *trust* him sincerely in all things and that it is his *most earnest purpose to be my God*. I must think of him in this way at the risk of losing eternal salvation. My heart must not build upon anything else or *trust* in any other thing, be it wealth, prestige, wisdom, might, piety, or anything else.[8]

The first commandment, Luther argues, is "most important" because it helps "to illuminate and impart its splendor to all the others."[9] The recurring phrase "thus we are to fear, love, and trust in God" attaches to all the commandments "like a clasp or hoop of a wreath that binds the end to the beginning and

---

4. *LW* 35:168.
5. Paul R. Hinlicky, *Luther for Evangelicals: A Reintroduction* (Baker Academic, 2018), 129.
6. "The Large Catechism," *BC*, 388.
7. "The Large Catechism," *BC*, 387.
8. *LW* 43:200, italics added.
9. "The Large Catechism," *BC*, 430.

holds everything together."[10] Every subsequent commandment teaches us the proper and improper way of fearing, loving, and trusting in God alone. The first commandment opens up the subsequent commandments, showing how God's purpose is to be lived out in this world.[11] The exposition of fearing, loving, and trusting in God above everything else extols the superlative character of God; in Anselmian fashion, God is the divine superlative, "that than which nothing greater can be conceived."[12] The first commandment is the foundation of the rest of the commandments; all others are an outflow from this. Whoever fears, loves, and trusts in God above all else fulfills this commandment and all the others; whoever does otherwise violates it and the rest.

Law and Gospel
Opposition in Unity

The paradoxical distinction between law and gospel governs Luther's theological task. "Dealing with any doctrine in a formally correct manner is never enough," Bernhard Lohse asserts, "unless we also express the proper distinction between Law and Gospel in the double nature of God's activity as well as the twofold relationship to God as people who are both judged and who have experienced mercy. Precisely here we become most clearly aware of the powerful dynamic that flows through Luther's theological work."[13] God's dual activity of judging via the law and saving through the gospel constitutes the twofold relationship of humanity to God. Paul Althaus writes, "Law and gospel are not only contrary to each other but are, in this opposition, related to each other. They are to be sharply distinguished but not to be separated from each other."[14] Justification is framed within the distinction between law and gospel. As law, God threatens to punish those who disobey his commandments; as gospel, God promises grace to those who keep them.[15] The law is life annihilating; the gospel is life constituting. The "true and proper" function of the law is to humble us and create in us a desire for grace.[16] The law "is a minister and a preparation for grace";[17] "it is a most useful servant impelling us to Christ."[18] The truth about God and self is

---

10. "The Large Catechism," *BC*, 430.
11. Nestingen and Forde, *Free to Be*, 69.
12. Benedicta Ward, *The Prayers and Meditations of St. Anselm with the Proslogion* (Penguin Books, 1973), 245.
13. Bernhard Lohse, *Martin Luther's Theology: Its Historical and Systematic Development*, trans. and ed. Roy A. Harrisville (Fortress, 1999), 158.
14. Paul Althaus, *The Theology of Martin Luther*, trans. Robert C. Schultz (Fortress, 1966), 257.
15. "The Large Catechism," *BC*, 390.
16. *LW* 26:328; *WA* 40.1:508.
17. *LW* 26:314; *WA* 40.1:488.
18. *LW* 26:315; *WA* 40.1:490.

not immediate; it originates not from within or without but from the story of Christ's passion. Luther notes, "The main benefit of Christ's passion is that man sees into his own true self and that he be terrified and crushed for help."[19] The law causes despair of ourselves so that we do not turn inward to ourselves for aid but turn outward to the gospel, our sole hope. Those whom the law strips of all things and casts down would find the word of promise a powerful consolation. The law leads to the gospel; its salutary function is, in Hans Iwand's assessment, "to wrap the truth of the person and the truth of God together into one so that no one can despair of himself without at the same time believing in God and no one can believe in God without despairing of himself."[20] Despair of self is not healed unless it cleaves to God; conversely, God is not embraced unless pride is conquered.

The knowledge of self and God exists as "a differentiated unity." In his exposition of Psalm 18:13, Luther quotes Bernard of Clairvaux favorably, speaking of the interplay of the twofold knowledge and its relation to pride and despair: "For just as, according to Bernard, knowledge of self without the knowledge of God leads to despair, so knowledge of God without the knowledge of self leads to presumption."[21] Bernardine spirituality of self-abasement, Franz Posset discerns, has its root in St. Augustine. Bernard quotes Augustine's sermon on *Humility and Pride*: "What else is pride but, as a saint [St. Augustine] has defined it, the love of one's own excellence. We may define humility in the opposite, the contempt of one's own excellence."[22] God blesses the humble, those who "justify God" by showing contempt of self out of reverence for God's word. God condemns the proud, those who show contempt of God's judgment, and live by self-judgment on divine things. God's word assigns the power of judging to its recipient, making it the agent of self-accusation that forms the basis of divine acceptance. To justify God is to self-accuse, an act that brings the self under God's impeccable judgment, which ultimately leads to the recognition of the sinful self. Not only does God's judgment result in the epistemic act of self-accusation, a sign of humility and fear of God, but it also acquaints us with the epistemic perception of the bound self, which cannot free itself unless by a power external to it. Such knowledge is salvific, as it leads one away from presumption to dependence upon God's grace. However, self-accusation and the

---

19. *LW* 42:10.

20. Hans Joachim Iwand, "The Preaching of the Law," in *Hans Joachim Iwand on Church and Society: Opened by the Kingdom of God*, ed. Benjamin Haupt et al., trans. Christian Einertson (T&T Clark, 2023), 21.

21. See *WA* 5:508.23–26, as cited in Franz Posset, *Pater Bernhardus: Martin Luther and Bernard of Clairvaux* (Cistercian Publications, 1999), 225–26.

22. See Augustine: "*Quia qui confitetur peccata sua et accusat peccata sua, iam cum Deo facit.*" *Johannis Evangelium*, in *Patrologiae Cursus Completus: Series Latina*, ed. J. P. Migne, 221 vols. (Paris, 1844–64), 12:13, 35:1491, as cited in Posset, *Pater Bernhardus*, 226.

misery of self-captivity may cause utter despair if we allow them to remain in us, or unless we hide them beneath God's mercy for relief.

Human beings justify God—that is, they agree with the word's verdict through which they become aware of themselves as "vile, nothing, abominable and damnable" before a righteous God.[23] The negative knowledge of the self through the law causes despair of the self that can only be healed by leaving the self and cleaving to the delight of God's comfort. Those who fortify themselves with "active righteousness" are presumptuous and are no candidates of God's justifying work. Whoever has suffered under the illusory efficacy of active righteousness comes to a recognition that justification is anchored solely on the "passive righteousness" bestowed by Jesus Christ. All self-righteousness must perish through law in order that God's righteousness might arise through gospel. Luther expands:

> Therefore as long as we do not condemn, excommunicate, and loathe ourselves before God, so long we do not "rise" [cf. Ps 1:5] and are justified.... There will not be, nor arise in us, the righteousness of God, unless our own righteousness falls and perishes utterly. We do not rise unless we who are standing badly have first fallen. Thus altogether the being, holiness, truth, goodness, life of God, etc., are not in us, unless in the presence of God we first become nothing, profane, lying, evil, dead. Otherwise the righteousness of God would be mocked, and Christ would have died in vain.[24]

By consistently using these two words (law and gospel), God is determined to remain the God who works within the contraries of "alien work" and "proper work," of wrath and mercy—all are constitutive of Luther's "theology of the cross" as laid out in his *Heidelberg Disputation* (1518). The paradoxical action of God "under the appearance of the opposite,"[25] for Luther, consists in this: that in order to achieve his proper work of saving, God performs an alien work of judging. Just as the law precedes the gospel, so God's alien work precedes his proper work. The former leads to the latter. The alien work God performs appears to be "unattractive" and "evil,"[26] but hidden in it is the proper work God does to restore and heal. The law exposes the ugliness of total depravity, not so that we remain in it, but so that we may seek and receive the beauty of God's grace.

---

23. *LW* 10:404, 406.
24. *LW* 10:33–34.
25. To capture the paradox, Luther uses the phrases "under the appearance of the opposite," "hidden under the alien appearance," and "hidden under the opposite appearance." See *LW* 2:229–332; *LW* 12:208.
26. *LW* 31:44.

Luther holds, "Thus an action which is alien to God's nature results in a deed belonging to his very nature: he makes a person a sinner so that he may make him righteous."[27] The law serves the gospel. So what is most unpleasant by means of the law and its alien work becomes most appealing by means of the gospel and its proper work. Luther concludes that "in this way, consequently, the unattractive works which God does in us, that is, those which are humble and devout, are really eternal, for humility and fear of God are our entire merit."[28]

The law in its civil use restrains evil, but the law in its spiritual use supports the gospel.[29] Luther argues, "On this score, it [spiritual use] is not only a powerful and rich element but omnipotent and extremely wealthy, in fact, an invincible omnipotence and wealth."[30] But when used improperly as a means for justification, the law is "a weak and beggarly" element, as it is ineffectual in making us strong and secure (Gal 4:9). Luther expands his rhetoric, offering three ways to speak of the inefficacy of the law: "Actively," the law weakens us and deprives us of all riches; "passively," of itself it has no power to confer righteousness; and "neutrally," it is "weakness and poverty," which further weakens the weak and makes the poor increasingly beggarly.[31] The law's proper function is negative but invincibly omnipotent and wealthy in what it intends to achieve: that it terrifies us to lead to the consolation of the gospel. When the law is given the power of justifying, which only the gospel does, its omnipotent function ceases. Instead of leading us to the sweetness of God's promise, it leads us away from it and sinks us in despair from which there is no recovery. It no longer serves the gospel but contradicts it, in which case God's abundant riches remain outside us. "God corresponds to himself"[32] in the antithetical unity of God's double actions: that negatively, the Spirit crushes the obstinate people with the law so that positively, he might create in them a willful reception of the gospel. The latter is his ultimate end.

In his *Large Catechism*, Luther attaches Exodus 20:5–6 as the appendix to the first commandment: "I am the LORD your God, the strong, jealous God, visiting the iniquities of the fathers upon the children to the third and fourth generation of those who hate me, and showing mercy to many thousands who love me and keep my commandments." The appendix ought to be applied to all commandments, though it was primarily linked to the first. To highlight the importance of keeping this commandment, God has added to it a terrible threat

---

27. *LW* 31:44.
28. *LW* 31:44.
29. *LW* 26:308–09; *WA* 40.1:479–81.
30. *LW* 26:402–3; *WA* 40.1:612.
31. *LW* 26:403; *WA* 40.1:614.
32. Eberhard Jüngel, *God as the Mystery of the World: On the Foundation of the Theology of the Crucified One in the Dispute between Theism and Atheism*, trans. Darrell L. Guder (Eerdmans, 1983), 346. The phrase is Jüngel's.

under the law, followed by a comforting promise under the gospel.[33] Luther reckons the paradoxical work of God as part of God's gracious design in which his comfort is hidden in its contrary. Luther states, "All God's chastisements are graciously designed to be a blessed comfort.... God hides and imparts his goodness and mercy under wrath and chastisement."[34] God's design, that his attitude toward his people is hidden in its opposite, governs Luther's understanding of the appendix, where he sees God's mercy hidden under his wrath. While God executes his wrath against wrongdoers, though only for a brief period, he extends his mercy to many thousands of generations, simply because God is "sheer goodness."[35] God's threats and promises are two distinct ways in which the command comes to us. If only the negative aspect of the commandment is preached, we would never encounter a God whom we could love, but only a terrifying God whom we would hate. But when the negative aspect is heard alongside the positive aspect, it impels us to seek grace by our prayers. Nestingen rightly comments, "God makes both the threat and the promise for the same reason—out of love, in the determination to make you his own."[36]

Luther's dialectic of law and gospel helps steer him away from two errors: One is legalism, with its emphasis on the law as the basis for righteousness; the other is antinomianism, denying the law a role in repentance. John Pless summarizes it well: "It is only when this distinction [between law and gospel] is rightly made that the Decalogue can be embraced not as a path to salvation but as a path that the disciple walks within this fallen creation, fearing, loving, and trusting the triune God above all things and serving the neighbor in love according to the will of the Creator."[37] Althaus argued that Luther did not use the term "third function of the law (*tertius usus legis*).... But in substance, however, it [does occur] in Luther."[38] As law, the Ten Commandments play a positive role for the person of faith. Though Luther mostly stresses the punitive function of law, he does not deny the positive role that the law has in the justified life, guiding us in fearing, loving, and trusting in God above all else. He explains:

> Here, then, we have the Ten Commandments, a summary of divine teaching on what we are to do to make our whole life pleasing to God. They are the true foundation from which all good works must spring, the true channel through which all good works must flow. Apart from these Ten Commandments no action or life can be good

---

33. "The Large Catechism," *BC*, 390.
34. *LW* 14:142; *WA* 18:481.
35. "The Large Catechism," *BC*, 388; cf. 391.
36. Nestingen and Forde, *Free to Be*, 66.
37. John T. Pless, *Luther's Small Catechism: A Manual for Discipleship* (Concordia Publishing House, 2013), 45–46.
38. Althaus, *Theology of Martin Luther*, 273.

or pleasing to God, no matter how great or precious it may be in the eyes of the world.[39]

The Ten Commandments liberate us from the captivity of righteousness by works; they give us freedom from being bound to God's creatures instead of God himself. They encompass God's agenda for the practice of humanity, the performance of active righteousness, and the fundamental attitude for human living and actions, the consequence of passive righteousness. Robert Kolb discerns in Luther the law's instructional function, both positive and negative:

> [Luther] did put the law to use to enforce civil order and outward discipline, to accuse and crush sinners, and to instruct believers in God's expectations for their lives, in positive as well as negative instruction. He did not use the phrase "uses of the law" because it had been rare in the scholastic theology he learned and did not function as a dogmatic category for his instructors. He used the word "law" as a fundamental concept in his understanding of God's plan and design for human living, the parental expectation for those whom he created to be his children and whom he re-created so that they might be returned to that status, to enjoy fellowship with him, and therefore put his will into practice.[40]

The law itself does not motivate good works but they are done by the power of the Spirit working through faith in the gospel. "True and living faith," Luther affirms, "arouses and motivates good works through love."[41] Good works done apart from faith are futile. "Doing good works," Ruth Whiteford notes, is "only good insofar as the doer has faith and confidence in God; the works are never good in themselves."[42] God-approved services proceed from faith alone but are instructed or shaped by the law. Luther extols not the law but faith as the causative agency of good works. Only when we are justified as doers could we ever begin to do the law. A "true doer of the law" (Rom 2:13) is thus predicated upon faith, the root of good works, its fruit. The passive righteousness of faith transforms the person, making him into "a tree," and the active righteousness of work becomes "fruit."[43] Kolb clarifies, "The bestowal of righteousness in God's sight so alters a person's self-perception that from faith in God's promise flow

---

39. "The Large Catechism," *BC*, 428.
40. Robert Kolb, "Wittenberg Uses of Law and Gospel," *Lutheran Quarterly* 37, no. 3 (2023): 249, https://doi.org/10.1353/lut.2023.a905030.
41. *LW* 27:30; *WA* 40.2:37.
42. Ruth Ang-Onn Whiteford, "The Second Commandment: Contemporary Christians and Honoring the Name of God," in *Luther's Large Catechism with Annotations and Contemporary Applications*, ed. John T. Pless and Larry M. Vogel (Concordia Publishing House, 2022), 202.
43. *LW* 26:255; *WA* 40.1:402.

good works. The gospel gives birth to a view of self that seeks to demonstrate actively its passively received righteousness."[44] With Erasmus, Luther conceives of faith as power or energy, transforming our existence, with love as its outcome: "[It] is powerfully active, not one that snores once it has been 'acquired.'... It is powerfully active through love."[45]

God Is He Whom Our Hearts Trust
The Creative Function of Faith

As law, the first commandment prohibits every rival deity. But hidden in such prohibition is the gospel that God alone is God.[46] The meaning of "You are to have no other gods" is "We are to fear, love, and trust God above all things."[47] In connection with that brief statement, Luther offers a definition of who God is: "God is that in which we are to look for all good and in which we are to find refuge in all need. Therefore, to have a god is nothing else than to trust and believe in that one with your whole heart."[48] Simply put, God is that on which our heart rests completely. The God we meet in the *Large Catechism*, Kirsi I Stjerna comments, is "the infinite source of life and sustenance, the real God, who wants to be reckoned from who God is and furthermore, who wants to be desired and loved. God emerges to the human being in a personal and communal relationship between the Creator and the created."[49] Human being proceeds from the creator's word, and is characterized essentially by, in Kolb's rendering, "trust in him as the ultimate source of 'all good' and the 'refuge in all need' that human action presupposes."[50] The knowledge of who we are is not self-defined but defined by faith in God, the basis of our identity and security. Luther's explication of who we are is intrinsically bound up with trust, whose object is the creator God of the First Article, not his created things. Creatures are "only the hands, channels, and means" through which God provides for us;[51] they do not constitute our identity. As part of God's design, our identity is founded and forged in his word. His human creatures place true faith and confidence in their Maker, the one true God to whom they fly and cling. Luther's intensely personal understanding of God shines when he has God say:

---

44. Kolb, "Wittenberg Uses of Law," 274.
45. *LW* 27:226; *WA* 2:567.
46. Oswald Bayer, *Theology the Lutheran Way*, ed. and trans. Jeffrey G. Silcock and Mark C. Mattes (Eerdmans, 2007), 62.
47. "The Small Catechism," *BC*, 351.
48. "The Large Catechism," *BC*, 386.
49. Kirsi I. Stjerna, *Lutheran Theology: A Grammar of Faith* (T&T Clark, 2021), 100.
50. Robert Kolb, *Luther and the Stories of God: Biblical Narratives as a Foundation for Christian Living* (Baker Academic, 2012), 66.
51. "The Large Catechism," *BC* (Tappert), 368.

> See to it that you let me alone be your God, and never seek another....
> Whatever good thing you lack, look to me for it and seek it from me,
> and whenever you suffer misfortune and distress, come and cling to me.
> I am the one who will satisfy you and help you out of every need. Only
> let your heart cling to no one else.[52]

Faith alone, Luther contends, "make[s] both God and an idol." Where your faith is right, there you have the true God; if otherwise, you have an idol.[53] God's essence, Michael Lockwood clarifies, is not at the whim of our feelings toward him.[54] What is changed is not God himself, but our relationship with him. Through faith, God is born in us; otherwise, an idol takes his place. Martin Brecht explains, "Everything depended on the relationship between God and faith in such a way that it almost seemed as if faith makes God."[55] In his *Commentary on Galatians*, Luther asserts that "faith creates the deity."[56] Such an assertion would fall prey to Feuerbach's critique of religion as a projection of our wish. Thus, Luther immediately qualifies it with "not in [God's] person but in us."[57] Faith, B. A. Gerrish says, "by believing,"[58] acknowledges God as God, and in so doing, creates God in us, not in himself.

> The believer does not earn the divine imputation with his faith, neither
> is there any legal fiction: God counts the confidence of the heart as
> "right" because that is what it is. Its rightness lives in the fact that faith,
> for its part, does not make God an idol but takes him for exactly what
> *he* is: the author and giver of every good, the precise counterpart of the
> believer's confidence. In a sense faith, by believing, is the "creator of
> divinity" in us: it lets God be God.[59]

God's deity is independent of, and prior to, human experience of him. But God is God "in us" only by faith. The trust of the heart indeed constitutes reality; as Luther famously states: "As you believe, so it will happen to you, because this faith is not taken from human judgement but drawn from the

---

52. "The Large Catechism," *BC* (Tappert), 365.
53. "The Large Catechism," *BC* (Tappert), 365.
54. See Michael A. Lockwood, *The Unholy Trinity: Martin Luther against the Idol of Me, Myself, and I* (Concordia Publishing House, 2016), 36.
55. Martin Brecht, *Martin Luther: Shaping and Refining the Reformation 1521–1532*, trans. James L. Schaaf (Fortress, 1990), 278.
56. *LW* 26:227; *WA* 40.1:360.
57. *LW* 26:227; *WA* 40.1:360.
58. B. A. Gerrish, "By Faith Alone: Medium and Message in Luther's Gospel," in *The Old Protestantism and the New: Essays on the Reformation Heritage* (T&T Clark, 1982), 86.
59. Gerrish, "By Faith Alone," 86.

Word of God."⁶⁰ Faith, begotten by God's effective word, possesses its own creative function of making God real in the hearts of the believers. It enables us to perceive that God is merciful to the humble, and that we are wrapped in the bosom of grace. Unbelief causes us to negate God and make him a liar, not worthy of trust. To unbelief, God and the pile of blessings are futile. Luther affirms a close and causal relationship between the God we believe in and the God we behold. He explains, "The thought of God's wrath is false even of itself, because God promises mercy; yet this false thought becomes true because you believe it to be true."⁶¹ Likewise, the thought of God's mercy for sinners who have felt the burden of the law is true and remains so. Yet we "should not suppose that it will be this way because you believe this way. Rather be assured that a thing which is sure and true of itself becomes more sure and true when you believe."⁶²

Idolatry
Word and Image

Whoever lives by the first commandment engages himself in the battle of one God against many gods; as Pless puts it, "To meditate on the First Commandment and to pray from it is to let God be God, but for the flesh, the world, and the devil, such meditation is a declaration of war."⁶³ The first commandment reaches the heart and demands its undivided allegiance so that God alone is worshipped. Idolatry does not necessarily consist in erecting images as the objects of our worship. It is primarily an inclination of the heart that trusts wholly in creaturely things rather than in the God of the first commandment. The more dangerous idols are not in material forms but those we foster or create in our hearts, such as the greed for power or money. Ricardo Rieth rightly points out that for Luther, "the question about God and idols cannot be separated from the question about faith."⁶⁴ Luther regards greed as idolatry, and this worship of wealth is set opposite the true worship of God. He posits greed as unbelief, the opposite of faith in God's provision. Luther cites as an example a wealthy man, who did not construct images of God, but who made money and property, to which his heart was inclined, into gods.⁶⁵ Such a heart, says Luther, "neither cares

---

60. *LW* 12:322.
61. *LW* 12:322.
62. *LW* 12:322.
63. John T. Pless, "Luther's *Oratio, Meditatio,* and *Tentatio* as the Shape of Pastoral Care for Pastors," *Concordia Theological Quarterly* 80, no. 1 (2016): 45.
64. Ricardo Willy Rieth, "Luther on Greed," in *Harvesting Martin Luther's Reflections on Theology, Ethics, and the Church,* ed. Timothy J. Wengert (Eerdmans, 2004), 163.
65. "The Large Catechism," *BC,* 387.

for God nor expects good things from him sufficiently to trust that he wants to help, nor does it believe that whatever good it encounters comes from God."[66] Trust elicits gratitude and contentment in believers, for they will have enough for their bodily needs; conversely, those who do not believe will always be in want and crave for more, by which they fall into all kinds of vice. The depraved affection and lustful desire of the discontented heart inevitably leads to misery because it cleaves to these things—wealth, prestige, reason, wisdom, might, piety, or any creaturely beings—for the security God alone can give. John Maxfield expands the scope of idolatry, writing, "For Luther idolatry is the self-enslaving false worship of a heart turned in on itself, of religious piety shaped by self-will and thus works-righteousness in any number of ways, of substituting human reason for the revelation of God in the divine Word."[67] Victory is assured, but only for those to whom God is their stronghold and generous provider, an assertion of his faithful character in the First Article, and for those whom God cannot forsake, a consequence of God's efficacious promise in the first commandment: "God's most earnest purpose is to be [their] God" who "will give [them] what [they] need and help [them] out of every danger."[68] God's promise never becomes God's own prison. The God who is free in making promises remains free in fulfilling them.

For Luther, "the Word alone," is, David Steinmetz notes, the basis of true freedom "from idolatry."[69] The graven images in the heart, Luther argues, cannot be removed by external reforms such as the destruction of images spearheaded by Karlstadt.

> But Dr. Karlstadt, who pays no attention to matters of the heart, has reversed the order by removing them from sight and leaving them in the heart. For he does not preach faith, nor can he preach it.... For where the heart is instructed that one pleases God alone through faith, and that in the matter of images nothing that is pleasing to him takes place, but is a fruitless service and effort, the people themselves drop it, despise images, and have none made.[70]

Real liberty comes not by the external abrogation of images but by the word of God that instructs "the conscience that it is idolatry to worship them, or to trust

---

66. "The Large Catechism," *BC*, 388.

67. John A. Maxfield, "Martin Luther and Idolatry," in *The Reformation as Christianization: Essays on Scott Hendrix's Christianization Thesis*, ed. Anna Marie Johnson and John A. Maxfield (Mohr Siebeck, 2012), 168.

68. "The Large Catechism," *BC*, 387.

69. David C. Steinmetz, *Calvin in Context* (Oxford University Press, 1995), 56. See *WA* 18:62–125, 134–214 (*Against the Heavenly Prophets*) for Luther's long response to Karlstadt.

70. *LW* 40:84. For an elaboration of the events and discussion between Karlstadt and Luther, see Mark U. Edwards Jr., *Luther and the False Brethren* (Stanford University Press, 1975), 7–59.

in them, since one is to trust alone in Christ. Beyond this, let externals take their course."[71] The tenor of the *Invocavit* sermons Luther preaches in response to the aggressive and riotous reform of the radicals of his time is not coercive or hasty reform; G. Sujin Pak sums it up well when she says, "The Word of God alone and not human works is the agent of any true reform."[72]

"Have no other gods" (Exod 20:3) simply means "do not make yourself a graven image" (Exod 20:4). The "making" in the first commandment means nothing else than "to worship."[73] Luther finds supports for this in the subsequent words in Exodus 20:23, "You shall not make gods of silver to be with me, nor shall you make for yourselves gods of gold."[74] The little word "make" refers to the divine service of such gods. Luther augments his arguments: "So also in Deut. 4:15ff, where he forbids the making of images, the passage speaks clearly of worship."[75] This text does not mean a complete removal of images. Luther cites a few examples: the image of a cairn set up at Shechem under an oak in Joshua 24:26 is not strictly forbidden, because it was rendered as "a stone of testimony, and not for worship."[76] Likewise, in 1 Samuel 7:12, when Samuel set up a stone between Mizpah and Shen as "a stone of help," he did not violate the law because "no worship but only remembrance was intended."[77]

"An imageless faith," Jeffrey Silcock argues, is impossible for Luther.[78] "The sense of seeing," Gesa Thiessen writes, "is constitutive of the human being just as much as hearing. Thus being reminded of, and learning about, God through seeing shall not be denied to the believer as it is a fundamental reality in the human being to perceive and create mental and material images."[79] Thiessen's formulation coincides with Luther's own words against the image breakers:

> It is impossible for me to hear and bear it [the passion of the Lord] without forming mental images of it in my heart. For whether I will or not, when I hear of Christ, an image of a man hanging on the cross takes form in my heart, just as the reflection of my face naturally appears in the water when I look into it. If it is not a sin but good to have the image

---

71. *LW* 40:91.
72. G. Sujin Pak, *The Reformation of Prophecy: Early Modern Interpretations of the Prophet and Old Testament Prophecy* (Oxford University Press, 2018), 66. See also *LW* 51:76–78.
73. *LW* 40:87.
74. *LW* 40:86.
75. *LW* 40:87.
76. *LW* 40:87.
77. *LW* 40:87.
78. Jeffrey G. Silcock, "Hearing and Seeing (Eye & Ear): Word and Image in the Bible, Luther, and the Lutheran Tradition," in *Promising Faith for a Ruptured Age: An English-Speaking Appreciation of Oswald Bayer*, ed. John T. Pless et al. (Pickwick, 2019), 220.
79. Gesa E. Thiessen, "Luther and the Role of Images," in *Remembering the Reformation: Martin Luther and Catholic Theology*, ed. Declan Marmion et al. (Fortress, 2017), 174.

of Christ in my heart, why should it be a sin to have it in my eyes? This is especially true since the heart is more important than the eyes, and should be less stained by sin because it is the true abode and dwelling place of God.[80]

A mental image we form in our heart through hearing or seeing is not an idol, but it becomes an idol if it is venerated as an object of worship. The word forbids no other images, Luther argues against the radicals, "but an image of God which one worships. A crucifix, on the other hand, or any other holy image is not forbidden. Heigh now! You breakers of images, I defy you to prove the opposite."[81] Images and statues that are not used for worship are not forbidden. The faithful could make use of the material images as pedagogical tool, teaching people to know God and the biblical stories. Luther wishes that the whole Bible be painted everywhere so that everyone can see it. "Pictures contained in these books (especially in the Revelation of John and in Moses and Joshua) we would paint on walls for the sake of remembrance and better understanding, since they do no more harm on walls than in books."[82] Pictures painted on walls of God's creation story, Noah's ark, and other good stories are better by far than paintings of shameless worldly things. Images provide visual aids for the affective dynamism of the gospel.

The Second Commandment
You Shall Not Misuse the Name of Your God

The proper usage of God's name is a practical exercise of the first commandment. The God of the first commandment is almighty, before whom all the "heathens" are reduced to naught. The second commandment teaches us the proper usage of human language and tongues. The right use of God's holy name occurs not only in our discourse about God but also in our conversation with him; as Althaus writes, "Speech about God must be born of prayer, out of speaking with God."[83] The command to pray is embedded in the second commandment, as it deals with the language through which we converse with God. The second commandment is fulfilled when we honor God with our tongues. Luther writes, "First the heart honors God by faith and then the lips by confession."[84] Luther advises us to use

---

80. *LW* 40:99–100. For more discussion, see Mark C. Mattes, *Martin Luther's Theology of Beauty: A Reappraisal* (Baker Academic, 2017), 147–51.
81. *LW* 40:86.
82. *LW* 40:99.
83. Paul Althaus, *Thou Shalt! Sermons on the Ten Commandments*, trans. John W. Rilling (Chantry Music Press, 1971), 13.
84. "The Large Catechism," *BC*, 395.

our language reverently in our relationship with God, as it lays bare before him our hearts: "For the first things that burst forth and emerge from the heart are words."[85] The words we express to God mirror the hearts from which they proceed. Our hearts are disclosed to God in prayers, just as the psalmists in their earnest prayers and cries lay bare their hearts before God. "And that [the psalmists] speak these [earnest] words to God and with God," Luther opines, "is the best thing of all," because "the depths of the heart" are "open," and "whatever is in it . . . come[s] out."[86]

The name of the Lord is effective when we call upon him, as borne out in Psalm 50:15, "Call on me in the day of trouble; I will deliver you, and you will glorify me." Even when we fail to revere his name, it remains effective. Those who disdain his name will reap no benefit or significance from it; rather they fall under the judgment of God. Luther writes, "He punished the heathen, even though this brings no deliverance to the faithful, as the Romans destroyed one another and thereby carried out his sentence."[87] Just as nothing is more precious to us than hearing our name called out by our beloved, so nothing is more endearing to God than hearing his name called upon by his beloved. Calling upon his name touches the fatherly heart of God, moving him to come to our aid; as Albrecht Peters writes, "God's saving activity is concentrated in His Name; in fact, God has 'deposited' his name here on earth so that we would have a place to find refuge."[88] The proper way to hallow God's name is to cleave to it for all good and therefore to call upon it. Failure to pray places us under the crushing power of the law, from which the distressed conscience finds no relief unless it seeks the delightful comfort of the gospel. Many grievous and unexpected misfortunes would have crushed us had we not come under the canopy of God's name upon which we call. Luther exhorts us to inculcate in children a "blessed and useful habit" of reverently using God's name at all times.[89] Luther considers it a very effective way to combat the devil, for he disdains God's name and cannot bear to hear it invoked. The devil seeks many ways to tempt us into sin, misery, and chaos, but fails precisely because we keep the holy name upon our lips. Hallowing God's name is the ground of victory for the faithful and of the devil's defeat. Luther adds an autobiographical note: "I have tried it myself and have indeed experienced that often a sudden, great calamity was averted and vanished in the very moment I called upon God."[90]

---

85. "The Large Catechism," *BC*, 392.
86. *LW* 35:256.
87. *LW* 14:67–68; *WA* 31.1:112–13.
88. Albrecht Peters, *Commentary on Luther's Catechisms: Ten Commandments*, trans. Holger K. Sonntag (Concordia Publishing House, 2009), 155.
89. "The Large Catechism," *BC*, 396.
90. "The Large Catechism," *BC*, 395.

Luther suggests using "baby talk" when teaching children evening and morning blessings.[91] With kind and winsome methods, we are to instruct them in the commandment so that they end up fearing God more than the discipline itself. Fruitful training is not by means of harsh and rigorous discipline but by a simple and fun means such as making the sign of the cross when something dreadful appears and saying, "Lord God, save me!," or "God be praised!" when something good happens.[92] This playful practice is a confession of faith, which for Luther is more pleasing to God than other forms of religious duties.[93] It places us under the power of the gospel through which the devil and all his agents lose their grip on our children.

By a proper use of God's name, children are restrained from lying and using God's name to assert something false. The commandment forbids us to appeal to God's name when our hearts know that the facts are otherwise. Luther enumerates some instances of willful contempt of God's name, where people lie under oath in court, in the marketplace, and in business.[94] The improper use of God's name occurs also in marriage when two people secretly betroth themselves to each other, but later renege on it with an oath.[95] "The greatest abuse," for Luther, occurs spiritually, when false preachers arise and proclaim messages that are contrary to God's word.[96] Lying and deceiving are grievous sins; they stir up God's displeasure much more, especially when we try to camouflage them under God's name. It is the natural tendency of human nature to self-justify, so God has imposed judgment on disobedience: "For the Lord will not acquit anyone who misuses his name." (Exod 20:7).[97] When violation occurs, we should confront offenders with this commandment, or else nothing good will come of it.

Related to the proper use of God's name is the swearing of oaths, which should not be done to support vices and falsehood, but to support the common good of our neighbor. This is what Christ, St. Paul, and other saints often did (cf. Matt 5:33–37; Gal 1:20; 2 Cor 1:23).[98] We are commanded to use God's name in the service of truth and justice, thereby hallowing it, as we pray in the Lord's Prayer. In due course, the ungodly will face the disastrous consequences of every false oath and will not escape their just deserts. Misery and calamity will be their portion, not joy and peace.[99]

---

91. "The Large Catechism," *BC*, 396.
92. "The Large Catechism," *BC*, 396.
93. "The Large Catechism," *BC*, 396.
94. "The Large Catechism," *BC*, 393.
95. For the subject of secret engagements, see Luther's *On Marriage Matters* (1530), in *LW* 46:259–320; *WA* 30.3:205–48.
96. "The Large Catechism," *BC*, 393.
97. "The Large Catechism," *BC*, 393.
98. See Luther's *Sermon on the Mount* (1532), in *LW* 21:99–104; *WA* 32:381.23–238.
99. "The Large Catechism," *BC*, 395.

The Third Commandment
You Shall Keep the Sabbath

The Sabbath falls on the seventh day (Gen 2:3). The Hebrew "sabbath" means "rest." The Old Testament renders the Sabbath as the day of rest. The Jewish observance of Saturday is not in view here. Luther wants to demonstrate that natural law is in accord with but also distinct from its specific Mosaic form. This commandment was originally given only to Israel to serve an outward purpose—namely, physical rest from labor. But in Christ, all ceremonial rites of the old covenant find their fulfillment and are obsolete. This commandment thus does not refer to an "outward meaning,"[100] viewing Sabbath merely as an external matter. The focus is not on a specific day for worship but God's word, "the true holy object"[101] that hallows us and guards us against the devil. Hans Wiersma argues that by putting the emphasis on God's word, "Luther in a sense *expanded* the commandment to cover *all* days which the Word can be heard."[102] The new life we have is a life of perpetual Sabbath, as it is lived not in ourselves but in Christ, whose words are spirit and life.

We fear and love God above all things when we have high regard for the word, gladly hearing and learning it. God's word is "not idle or dead, but effective and living."[103] As Carl Trueman says, it "not only defined reality but also in a very real sense made reality."[104] It does not merely describe things as they are but actually brings about what it says. It proclaims God in action paradoxically: it crucifies the old creature with its false security through the law, and it enlivens the new creature through faith in the gospel. Keeping the Sabbath holy simply means diligently hearing God's word, allowing it to regulate our thoughts, hearts, and tongues. The day itself is holy, as it was created as such. But God intends it to be holy "for us."[105] The sanctifying occurs, not when we sit idle and pause from hard work, but when we cling to God's word, allowing it to exert its efficacy in us through hearing it proclaimed by the preacher. Believers reap from the preached word the benefits of Christ.

Non-Christians can keep a holiday and enjoy rest and idleness, but the day is not holy for them because of their contempt for God's word. Though many clerics in Luther's time performed diverse religious duties daily in the church, this commandment is not fulfilled in them because they show no reverence for

---

100. "The Large Catechism," *BC*, 397.
101. "The Large Catechism," *BC*, 399.
102. Hans Wiersma, "On Keeping the Sabbath Holy in Martin Luther's Catechisms and Other Writings," *Word & World* 36, no. 3 (2016): 240.
103. "The Large Catechism," *BC*, 400.
104. Carl R. Trueman, *Luther on the Christian Life: Cross and Freedom* (Crossway, 2015), 85.
105. "The Large Catechism," *BC*, 398.

God's word, and live contrary to what they preach. The conceited spirits incur punishment, who, after hearing a sermon or two become indifferent to God's word, feel that they are fully trained in it, and thus see no need for further instructions. They commit the mortal sin of "laziness," which Luther regards as "a malignant, pernicious plague"[106] by which the devil implants in them unbelief and lures them away from the very thing that keeps them holy: God's word.

In *Concerning the Order of Public Worship* (1523), Luther names three serious abuses of true worship:

> First, God's Word has been silenced, and only reading and singing remain in the churches. This is the worst abuse. Second, when God's Word had been silenced, such a host of un-Christian fables and lies in legends, hymns, and sermons were introduced that it is horrible to see. Third, such divine service was performed as a work whereby God's grace and salvation might be won. As a result, faith disappeared and everyone pressed to enter the priesthood, convents, and monasteries, and to build churches and endow them.[107]

Despite these abuses, Luther adamantly aims to restore the office of preaching to its rightful place and use. The third commandment preserves the one thing that is needful—that is, to hear God's word, through which our hearts are kindled to confess his holy name, as taught in the second commandment. The third commandment also recenters us on the first commandment, allowing the Godliness of God to reign in us so that nothing—work and other creaturely pursuits—would be worshipped in God's place.

Public worship is not a meritorious deed that we offer to God but an occasion when God imparts himself and his gifts to believers for the reconstitution of their new self; as Steven D. Paulson writes, "Worship is thus the momentous election, forgiveness, and resurrection of the dead by means of the ear."[108] Sabbath for the Old Testament people and for the Jews means abstaining from work. However, Luther interprets this commandment in a Christian way and puts the emphasis on hearing the word. In his *Treatise on Good Works*, Luther interprets this commandment as God's calling us to "cease from our labor" so that "we let God alone work in us," apart from which we can do nothing of our own.[109] Faith, a passive agent, permits God's word to perform his alien work of killing the old person in order to achieve his proper work of enlivening the new person. Bayer

---

106. "The Large Catechism," *BC*, 400.

107. "The Large Catechism," *BC* (Tappert), 379.

108. Steven D. Paulson, "The Third Commandment: Remember the Sabbath Day to Keep It Holy," in Pless and Vogel, *Luther's Large Catechism*, 205.

109. *LW* 44:72.

expands, "If it is true that we must rest from our work, die to the old self, to let God do his work, faith is primarily neither theory nor practice, neither a speculative life (*vita contemplativa*) nor an active life (*vita activa*), but, to use Luther's term for it, a receptive life (*vita passiva*)."[110] To borrow Sun-young Kim's phrase, "the passive receptivity of faith"[111] underscores God's causative action in such a way that it excludes human merits as part of justification. We stand before God not as an active giver, offering to him sacrifices to appease his wrath, but as a passive recipient of all his benefits that are conveyed through the preached the word and the means of grace; in Vilmos Vajta's formulation:

> Thus Luther's picture of the Sabbath is marked by the passivity of man and the activity of God. And it applies not only to certain holy days on the calendar, but to the Christian life in its entirety, testifying to man's existence as a creature of God who waits by faith for the life to come. Through God's activity in Christ, man is drawn into the death and resurrection of the Redeemer and is so recreated to a new man in Christ. The Third Commandment lays on us no obligation for specific works of any kind (not even spiritual or cultic works) but rather directs us to the work of God. And we do not come into contact with the latter except in the Service, where Christ meets us in the means of grace.[112]

The Fourth Commandment
You Are to Honor Your Parents

The first in the second tablet, the fourth commandment, for Luther, is "the greatest" of the commands for human creatures, as they relate to other people.[113] This commandment safeguards against anarchy and chaos in public life. God created human life with a structure in which he has ordered human creatures to perform various tasks that serve the needs of others and preserve the created order. Specifically, the home must be a place human parents and superiors serve as God's tools and representatives; they are those whom God places before and over us as "the instrument[s] of his power."[114] Peters writes, "On them rests the

---

110. Bayer, *Theology the Lutheran Way*, 93.

111. Sun-young Kim, *Luther on Faith and Love: Christ and the Law in the 1535 Galatians Commentary* (Fortress, 2014), 139.

112. Vilmos Vajta, *Luther on Worship*, trans. U. S. Leupold (Muhlenberg, 1958), 132.

113. "The Large Catechism," *BC*, 400.

114. See Robert Kolb and Carl R. Trueman, *Between Wittenberg and Geneva: Lutheran and Reformed Theology in Conversation* (Baker Academic, 2017), 5, where Kolb uses the phrase "the instrument of his power" to speak of the Word. Here, vocations are God's instruments of power, that through which God accomplishes his purpose.

majesty of God's ordering in creation and by the Word, thereby they share in God's fatherly majesty itself."[115] A linkage occurs between the first and fourth commandments; as Herbert Girgensohn claims, "He who confronts man with his total claim in the First Commandment is facing him with the same claim in the Fourth Commandment."[116] Insofar as we honor our parents as God's representatives, we are truly honoring God. Luther denounces every failure to regard parents highly because of God's will. Godly children will prosper in all things because God, in Luther's words, "treasures [their obedience] so highly, delights so greatly in it, [and] rewards it so richly."[117] To do otherwise is to sin against the creator himself, who imposes strict punishment upon those who transgress the commandment; it too deprives them of a joyful conscience. This commandment is fulfilled by faith, apart from which we would not acknowledge with thanksgiving our parents as God's agents.

Concerning honor and love, Luther sets higher value on the former. We are to love our brothers and sisters and neighbors but honor our parents and truly regard them as high and great; in Luther's words, "Honor includes not only love, but also deference, humility, and modesty directed (so to speak) toward a *majesty concealed within them.* Honor requires us not only to address them affectionately and with high esteem, but above all to show by our actions, both of heart and body, that we respect them very highly, and that next to God, we give them the very highest place."[118] True honoring comprises fearing and loving. Fear that is proper to honor, Luther explains, is filial fear, a kind of "fear mingled with love."[119] This kind of fear effects in us fear of offending the one we honor more than fear of a certain judgment. Fear with love draws us closer to the one we honor rather than causing us to flee from him. On the contrary, for Luther, "fear without love" is abject terror—namely, fear of what we despise, such as a hangman.[120] There is no honor if it were not accompanied by fear with love. "Fear without love," Luther writes, "is a fear mixed with hatred and hostility."[121] God does not will that he be feared or honored with abject terror, as a slave feels before a tyrant, but with filial fear, as a son fears his beloved father. Likewise, God does not will that we honor our parents with fear abstracted from love, but rather with fear united with "love and confidence."[122]

---

115. Peters, *Ten Commandments*, 192–93.
116. Herbert Girgensohn, *Teaching Luther's Catechism*, vol. 1, trans. John Doberstein (Muhlenberg, 1959), 70.
117. "The Large Catechism," *BC*, 405.
118. "The Large Catechism," *BC*, 401, italics added.
119. *LW* 44:81.
120. *LW* 44:81.
121. *LW* 44:81.
122. *LW* 44:81.

Honor is due the parents, not only because of who they are, but because of the responsibilities they exercise on God's behalf for the benefits of their children. Parents and children are created equal in worth but given different roles. Parents govern the home with authority and train the children in obedience. Children first learn obedience at home, which extends to other situations where they abound in all kinds of good works and virtues.[123] Both parents and children work together in the promotion of order and peace.

In connection with this commandment, Luther underscores the kind of obedience in other spheres of authority that develop from parental authority.[124] In addition to biological fathers, Luther introduces three other kinds of fathers whose authority we must obey: household fathers, fathers of the whole country, and spiritual fathers.[125] Household fathers, including masters or guardians, are commissioned to govern in place of parents, expressing their fatherly hearts toward their family. Fathers of the nation—the princes and overlords—have been appointed to rule and ensure peace in civil order. We are to honor them as God-ordained servants through whom God provides goods, homes, protection, and security. Luther adamantly opposes bad governmental practices and promises God's wrath for courtiers and princes who instigate civil disobedience.[126] Finally, spiritual fathers (1 Cor 4:15), who watch over the souls of the common people and govern them by the word of God, even at the risk of losing their lives, deserve to be shown "double honor."[127]

In his *Treatise on Good Works* (1520), Luther proposes that honoring begins with parental authority, is then followed by spiritual authorities, and ends with civil authorities.[128] Luther ranks parents above all walks of life on earth, maintaining that "there is no greater or nobler authority on earth than that of parents over their children, for this authority is both spiritual and temporal."[129] As part of God's design, we are not self-created but dependent upon our parents in whom God hides to sustain and protect us in bodily and spiritual life. Parents are to instruct their children by words and deeds, directing them to worship God in the first three commandments, and to occupy themselves with good works toward

---

123. "The Large Catechism," *BC*, 401; *LW* 45:82.
124. "The Large Catechism," *BC*, 405, 408. This recurs later when Luther deals with the table of callings.
125. "The Large Catechism," *BC*, 408.
126. See discussions in Robert Kolb, "Luther on Peasants and Princes," *Lutheran Quarterly* 23, no. 2 (2009): 125–46, where he analyzes the peasant revolts in the German lands since 1500, especially the great Peasants' Revolt of 1524–25. Luther, like most of his contemporaries, calls for public order and peace. That involves the elimination of feuds among the nobles or those in power.
127. "The Large Catechism," *BC*, 408.
128. *LW* 44:81–95.
129. *LW* 45:46; "The Large Catechism," *BC*, 400.

their neighbors in the last seven.[130] It is through the fourth commandment that the others are upheld and through which we demonstrate a proper relationship both to God, to whom we submit as his obedient children, and to the neighbors whom we serve with love. To produce virtuous and capable citizens for both the civil and spiritual order, parents must undertake painstakingly "the chief duty"[131] of teaching and training their children.[132] Parental responsibility is not a matter of personal preference or whim; it is a strict commandment of God, who holds parents accountable for their actions. God preserves a society through the gift of marriage and family. The entire welfare of a society is contingent upon proper family management that corresponds to God's commands for parents and children and their distinct responsibilities. Luther ends his explanation with a severe warning, that parents will incur sin and divine wrath, thus earning hell, if they fail to raise their children according to God's will.[133]

The Fifth Commandment
You Shall Not Kill

This commandment protects the neighbor's well-being, guarding it against that which may harm and hinder it. The prohibition of killing includes everything that may culminate in murder.[134] But even the hidden desire to kill, though the act itself has not happened, is solemnly condemned. We kill by cursing, wishing death upon others. This commandment, Luther holds, reaches "the root and source" of our bitterness against our neighbor, and like "a mirror" causes us to recognize the sinful passions of resentment, anger, and revenge.[135] Sinful acts that hurt people stem from a failure to fear, love, and trust God above all else. The restoration of peace on earth is a product of trust in God alone, believing that everything good or bad is in God's hands. Instead of retribution, Christians commit their injuries to God. Judgment upon wrongdoers must be restrained, even when they deserve it. We relinquish the prerogative to judge, which belongs solely to God and his appointed agents.[136] Luther teaches us to recall the first commandment, that it is "God's most earnest purpose" to come to our aid, so that we need not harbor bitterness and resort to revenge.[137] We are to treasure life and seek every possible way, as Kolb puts it, "to be the instruments of life-giving,

---

130. *LW* 44:82.
131. "The Large Catechism," *BC*, 410.
132. *LW* 44:82.
133. "The Large Catechism," *BC*, 410.
134. "The Large Catechism," *BC*, 411.
135. "The Large Catechism," *BC*, 411.
136. "The Large Catechism," *BC*, 411.
137. "The Large Catechism," *BC*, 413.

life-preserving, and life-enhancing power."[138] This commandment is fulfilled if we carry out our God-given responsibilities to help and save our neighbors in desperate need. Through personal sacrifices, acts of kindness, and patience, we extend our help to the needy, even as God has showered his mercy on us.

The Sixth Commandment
You Shall Not Commit Adultery

Marriage, for Luther, is "the first" of all institutions.[139] God has established it before all others and sought every possible way to protect it against any violation of this commandment. Marriage is not a human invention but is God's gift, grounded in creation. This gift, when put to its proper use, will fulfill God's purpose for marriage; it will curb all that would defile God's order and promote the peace of society. Luther denies marriage sacramental status but elevates it above celibacy.[140] Marriage is no trivial matter; it is "a glorious institution and an object of God's serious concern."[141] Luther makes use of Paul in 1 Corinthians 7:3–4 to support the equality of partners in a marriage; exploitation has no part in this walk of life. He writes, "Here St. Paul instructs married people in their conduct toward one another with respect to marital duty and speaks of 'conjugal rights.' [Marital intercourse] is a right, yet it should occur voluntarily. . . . For thus the state of matrimony is constituted in the law of love so that no one rules over his own body but must serve his partner, as is the way of love."[142]

Faith enables us to receive marriage as God's gift through which God wills to extend the human family. "For in all nature," Luther says, "there is nothing more excellent and more admirable than procreation. After the proclamation of the name of God it is the most important activity Adam and Eve in the state of innocence could carry on."[143] In the wake of the fall, marriage, like the rest of creation, is subject to the enslaving powers of sin. Despite the fall that has marred sex, procreation remains a God-pleasing activity in his design for humanity.[144]

---

138. Robert Kolb, *Teaching God's Children His Teaching: A Guide for the Study of Luther's Catechism*, new ed. (Concordia Seminary, 2012), 70.
139. "The Large Catechism," *BC*, 414.
140. Carter Lindberg, "The Future of a Tradition: Luther and the Family," in *All Theology is Christology: Essays in Honor of David P. Scaer*, ed. Dean O. Wenthe et al. (Concordia Theological Seminary, 2000), 133: "Luther's application of evangelical theology to marriage and family desacramentalized marriage; desacralized the clergy and resacralized the life of the laity; opposed the maze of canonical impediments to marriage, strove to unravel the skein of canon law, imperial law, and German customs; and joyfully affirmed God's good creation, including sexual relations."
141. "The Large Catechism," *BC*, 414.
142. *LW* 28:13; *WA* 12:101.
143. *LW* 1:117–18; *WA* 42:89.
144. *LW* 1:117–18; *WA* 42:89.

Sex becomes a divine remedy against the lust of the flesh; as Luther writes, "If you look at the main cause (for the existence of marriage), you will see that through it God has established a church, and healed the foul disease of the flesh through marriage and thus closed a road to sin, so that it can no longer seduce you. And you will have to confess that for these reasons marriage must be highly recommended."[145] This commandment secures marriage against its destruction by adultery and every other sexual vice. Luther teaches us how we fear and love God: by conducting a sexually pure life in thought, speech, and actions; and by husband and wife loving and cherishing each other wholeheartedly, binding each other with perfect fidelity. As a result, chastity follows naturally from the heart apart from any external command.[146]

Any perversion of sexuality would threaten the order God ordains for human life. Martin Marty observes three distinct offenses of sexual perversion. First, it is a sin against God when a person misuses what God makes. Second, it is a sin against the other person who is treated no more than a thing for self-gratification; as Marty writes, "The 'I' is related then not to a 'thou'—a free but responsible other person—but to an 'it' which can be used to gratify impulses."[147] Third, it is a sin against myself, as it reduces me to "less than a person who fails to relate responsibly."[148] In his exposition of this commandment in his *Small Catechism*, Luther does not offer a long list of sexual sins, probably because they already abound in society, and because, as Girgensohn claims, "a prohibition depicting sexual sins always acts as a stimulus and therefore provokes the opposite of what the commandment intends."[149]

The Seventh Commandment
You Shall Not Steal

Everything of this world is God's provision and under his lordship so that we look to him and not to our neighbor's possessions for security. This commandment is closely linked with the First Article of the Creed that highlights God as the sole giver of all that is. Faith in God not only abandons all material causes of security but also repudiates all claims to temporal goods. Unbelief disrupts the two kinds of righteous living. First, by trusting in material goods, we sin against God and face God's displeasure; second, by a selfish use of material gifts, we sin against our neighbors, depriving them of their needs. Our confidence is not in

---

145. *WA* 43:19, 28, as quoted in George Wolfgang Forell, *Faith Active in Love: An Investigation of the Principles Underlying Luther's Social Ethics* (Augsburg Publishing House, 1954), 147.
146. "The Large Catechism," *BC*, 415.
147. Martin Marty, *The Hidden Discipline* (Concordia, 1962), 23.
148. Kolb, *Teaching God's Children*, 72.
149. Girgensohn, *Teaching Luther's Catechism*, 1:95.

"this world and its god, the powerless yet omnipotent Mammon," as Peters puts it, but in "the otherworldly and invisible God" from whom alone we seek what we once sought from Mammon.[150] As the sustenance of our well-being, God has supplied us with temporal property and the manifold gifts of daily provision. This commandment thus liberates us from captivity to property that belongs to another, and from every urge to possess what is not ours. As written in the *Large Catechism*, this commandment is far reaching in its scope. People should assume the painstaking duty not to cause harm to their neighbors, not to take advantage of them or defraud them for selfish purposes by any unethical dealings. They should also obligate themselves diligently to protect their well-being and to advance their interests, especially when these acts involve some forms of material transaction.[151] Luther repeatedly stresses that God uses the hangman or jailer to enforce this commandment in the world. The wrath of God must be urged upon the common people, especially knaves and scoundrels, so there is propriety of relationships between individuals, between employer and employee, and between leaders of society and the populace.[152]

Luther beseeches his people to find strength in the generosity of God's character. God lavishes upon us bountiful blessings so that we can happily enjoy much more than we could obtain by ill means. The material gifts provide numerous occasions for the performance of God-pleasing works. God will generously reward us if we put these gifts to proper use, to benefit our neighbor. As support, Luther cites Proverbs 19:17, "Whoever is kind to the poor lends to the Lord, and will be repaid in full."[153] Latent in this commandment is the idea of reciprocal vocation, whereby we minister to each other by giving and receiving, in turn dispelling idolatrous greed and envy. Pless writes aptly, "God has arranged our world in such a way that human beings are daily bread to one another. We both receive our daily bread through others and we are instruments and channels for the giving of daily bread to others. Theft disrupts this giving and receiving."[154]

The Eighth Commandment
False Testimony Against Neighbors

Just as we are not to misuse the name of God, so we must not abuse the name of a human creature, for it cripples them as surely as it causes them pain. Names identify us as the people we really are and thus are not to be taken for granted.

---

150. Peters, *Ten Commandments*, 271.
151. "The Large Catechism," *BC*, 417.
152. "The Large Catechism," *BC*, 416–17.
153. "The Large Catechism," *BC*, 420.
154. John T. Pless, *Praying Luther's Small Catechism: The Pattern of Sound Words* (Concordia Publishing House, 2016), 28.

Our honor and good reputation are as important as our own body, our spouse, and our temporal goods. God "sets a guard over the mouth" and demands that we "keep watch over the doors of our lips" (Ps 141:3), lest we spill lies against our neighbor or twist the truth to deprive him of a good name. We are to refrain from being a lying witness against our neighbor and instead must become his true advocate and defender, even when he admits his faults. In so doing, Peters recognizes that we show ourselves to be children of "the Paraclete who holds up the good word of adoption in Christ against the accusation of Satan and of our own conscience."[155]

God condemns all the sins of the tongue which might harm our neighbor or their peace. In his *Personal Prayer Book*, Luther names those sins that stand under God's judgment: lying, betraying, defaming, flattery, accusation, gossip, deceit, and anything that casts doubt on someone's conduct or speech; failure to defend our neighbor's honor; failure to prevent someone from backbiting; concealing the truth and not defending it; allowing others to speak evil of a neighbor; and failure to speak well of others and defend their reputation.[156] All these things disrupt the order of God's design for human relationships. This commandment forbids all evil speech about the neighbor, whether true or false. But true witness is to be done with proper regard for legal rights, or for the neighbor's benefit.[157] As taught in the fifth commandment, no one can assume the law of the land and judge a neighbor's sin unless appointed to do so by God's command. If he judges without proper authority, he commits a sin greater than that of his neighbor. If those who are in office and possess the right to judge fail to do so, they sin as much as those who condemn without any office. The concern for truth and falsehood has its legitimate place in this commandment, but more crucial for Luther is the preservation of the neighbor's peace and welfare.

The Ninth and Tenth Commandments
You Shall Not Covet

The last two commandments in combination deal with coveting (people or property), the longing to possess that which does not belong to oneself. Luther's exposition of the commandments covers, in Marty's words, "the unspoken, unaccomplished, unenacted desire"[158] to reassign to oneself what God has allotted to the neighbor. The commandments deal with the attitude rather than actions, but in God's sight, the sinful desire is as evil as the act itself. God's command not to covet is closely connected with the seventh commandment not to steal.

---

155. Peters, *Ten Commandments*, 289.
156. *LW* 43:20–21.
157. "The Large Catechism," *BC*, 424.
158. Marty, *The Hidden Discipline*, 31.

Both are directed against the secret desires to acquire what God has not given. "The sinister power of desire," says Girgensohn, "is the hidden source of all sin within us."[159] This evil desire sprouts actions or undertakings that greedily crave after some part of creation, thus endangering the neighbor. Luther mentions several concrete manifestations of evil desires—for example, those who go to court to obtain what is not theirs, or those who use their economic power to gain social ascendancy at the expense of others.[160] To covet is to commit the idolatry prohibited by the first commandment, seeking creaturely things as the basis of security and identity rather than God alone. This commandment curbs envy and covetousness in the hope of preventing casualties and calamities. Contentment arises only from fearing, trusting, and loving God above all else. Only a heart liberated by faith can gladly allow others to enjoy what is theirs and willingly seek to guard another's belongings and promote their interests.

God's last commandment, however, does not address the wicked but the most virtuous, who wish to be treated with high regard for not violating the preceding commandments.[161] Luther again applies to this commandment, as he does to all others, the theological usage of the law, which reaches the recesses of the heart and accuses those who claim uprightness before God.[162] The law kills the old Adam and its false securities. Any misplaced trust, or any desire for other bases of security, is condemned under the law so that God alone remains the ultimate object of trust.

The Appendix to the Conclusion
God's Wrath and God's Mercy

Luther moves from an introduction of the Ten Commandments in the Bible to a concluding synthesis and summary of them. Just as Luther begins his exposition of the first commandment with Exodus 20:5–6, so too he concludes his exposition of the Ten Commandments with the same text as the appendix: "I am the Lord your God, the strong, jealous God, visiting the iniquities of the fathers upon the children to the third and fourth generation of those who hate me, and showing mercy to many thousands who love and keep my commandments." The law and its terrible threats, which God imposes upon his people for a brief period, is set in contrast to the promise and its mighty comfort that assures those who cling to him alone of his mercy for a much longer period, simply because mercy is God's unique nature. We are in the grip of the divine majesty who graciously offers himself to be our beloved Father. We are cordially invited to be God's

---

159. Girgensohn, *Teaching Luther's Catechism*, 1:118.
160. "The Large Catechism," *BC*, 426–27.
161. "The Large Catechism," *BC*, 426.
162. "The Large Catechism," *BC*, 427.

beloved children, richly endowed with his promise, that all that God is and has belongs to those who fear, love, and trust him above all things.[163] And that ought to move us to fix our hearts on God with perfect confidence against the terrifying threat of the law.

God's wrath is a natural outflow of God's jealousy. Human jealousy stems from insecurity or a relentless desire to control, but God's jealousy arises from a pure love that demands exclusive devotion and tolerates no rivalry; as Althaus avers, "This jealousy necessarily becomes wrath in response to sin."[164] God's jealousy does not allow other lords or objects to come between God and us. Neither sin nor wrath is trivialized. Idolatry provokes God's wrath, an alien work, which is not of the essence of God's nature; in Luther's own words, "Wrath is truly God's alien work, which He employs contrary to His Nature [i.e., love] because He is forced into it by the wickedness of man."[165] Philip Watson captures Luther's thought thus: "For the God whose nature is revealed in the Gospel as pure love and grace is no mild sentimentalist, and Luther can actually speak of His 'wrathful love', His *zornige Liebe*."[166] Wrath is nothing but, in Watson's words, "the intensely personal reaction of the Father's all-holy will against sin."[167] God's holy love requires a pure and undefiled relationship. When love meets with sin, it does not stand idly by but reacts with anger. It wrathfully opposes anything that would claim our trust, or anything that supplants God as the ultimate source of identity and security. God's anger against sin is not an unmitigated retribution for the broken law, a wounded pride turned vindictive, or a frustrated love turned vicious. Wrath is God's severe love against evil, an alien work he does to triumph over it, showing that he cares. Hidden in God's vengeful opposition against disobedience, which lasts for a few generations, is God's love for us, which endures over many thousands of generations. This sharp contrast reveals the true nature of God as love, not wrath. Mattes articulates the paradoxical action of God, that "God's 'alien work' of wrath exists for his 'proper work' of mercy. God's alien work is a guise God wears just so to break down proud and idolatrous sinners so that they may be receptive to who he is in himself: love."[168] Luther speaks of the wrath of a loving God but does not reify it. God is most truly God in his sheer goodness, the opposite of wrath, which for Luther is a terrifying, damning work he does not delight in doing but for the sake of his proper work of saving.

---

163. "The Large Catechism," *BC* (Tappert), 370.
164. Althaus, *Theology of Martin Luther*, 169.
165. *LW* 2:134; *WA* 42:356.
166. Philip S. Watson, *Let God be God: An Interpretation of the Theology of Martin Luther* (Fortress, 1947), 158–59. See 182n85 where he quotes WA XXIII.517.2.
167. Watson, *Let God be God*, 159.
168. Mattes, *Luther's Theology of Beauty*, 60.

For Luther, as for Paul, there is a revelation of nothing but damning; as Paul taught, "The wrath of God is revealed against . . . the wickedness of those who by their wickedness suppress the truth" (Rom 1:18). The deepest antithesis, for Luther, is not between our sin and God's grace, but between God's law and God's grace. This antithesis, so offensive to moralists, requires revelation. The bitter truth of nothing but damning—God's wrath against unrighteousness—cannot be known by reason but has to be revealed, lest we moralize or trivialize sin. Viewed in light of the law's absolute demands for perfect righteousness, everyone is worthy of eternal wrath. God is wrathful toward the contraries (law, sin, and death) of justification in order to conquer them for us and make us a people of God's mercy. That God is revealed as wrathful does not constitute wrath as God's being, an ontological attribute which God cannot do without. God's essence is conceived, Kolb aptly writes, "not in terms of the Creator's fair treatment of human creatures according to their actions. Rather, [Luther] confessed that God is truly God at his most Godly when he shows mercy and bestows his love. Even his wrath betrays his desire to show mercy and goodness to those he wants to bring back to faith in himself, for whom he wants to restore truly human life."[169]

Luther admits that there is "no better mirror in which to see your need than the Ten Commandments, in which you will find what you lack and what you should seek."[170] In the same person are two "selves," the old self and the new self that exist in conflict. Confronted by such a heavy obligation to fulfill the Ten Commandments, the old self can do nothing but exclaim with sheer despair, "Alas! I can never fulfill them. I am doomed." Wengert rightly recognizes that "the commandments—all of them—keep their rightful place in Christian theology only when they are in first place—that is, as the Word of death that drives us inexorably to our crucified and risen Lord Jesus."[171] The Creed (gospel) must come to our rescue when we are confronted by the law's annihilating power. In the Ten Commandments, the subject is "you" ("you shall," or "you shall not"). In the Creed, the subject is changed to "God"—more specifically, to the life-giving actions of the triune God in whom we trust. God is actively making us anew so that the new "you" can fear, trust, and love him above all else. The Creed, Luther says, is "the [medicinal] herbs" that supply the power for new obedience to God's command.[172] It is amply furnished with the bounty of God's promises that work for our benefit. It declares God's relation

---

169. Robert Kolb, *Bound Choice, Election, and Wittenberg Theological Method: From Martin Luther to the Formula of Concord* (Fortress, 2017), 34.

170. *LW* 44:63.

171. Timothy J. Wengert, "Martin Luther and the Ten Commandments in the Large Catechism," in *The Pastoral Luther: Essays on Martin Luther's Practical Theology*, ed. Timothy J. Wengert (Eerdmans, 2009), 145–46.

172. *LW* 43:24.

to us *ad extra*: that God provides for us as our creator, that he re-creates us in Christ as our redeemer, and that he sends us his Spirit, the sanctifier. All three persons work together *ex nihilo* as one God to effect a return of the re-created self to Eden, to partake of the eternal bliss of belonging to him, the very purpose for which humanity was originally created. The next three chapters bear this out.

CHAPTER THREE

God's Most Earnest Purpose in Creation

LUTHER GROUNDS HIS entire theology, as Robert Kolb observes, in God's "gracious will and fatherly love."[1] The "most lofty article of faith" in Luther's estimation is not the Second Article but the First Article of the Creed.[2] The First Article declares the grammar about the creator God in relation to us: God the Father is the one who created everything that exists, and all creaturely beings owe their existence to him. The First Article is basically a confession of faith in God who is none other than the God of the first commandment.[3] Paul Hinlicky observes "a deep correspondence" between the first commandment and the First Article; he writes, "We are to have no other gods *because* only the One who is Creator of all that is other than Himself can truly help in every time of need."[4] The creator-creation distinction is maintained. Everything that exists does not emanate from God's being without partition, as he is indivisible. God did not create us or the world autonomous; God is our creator and the Lord of his own creation. The Hebrew word "create," Oswald Bayer writes, is an exclusive attribute of God himself.[5] Creatures do not have life in themselves; they have it outside themselves, in God. "The meaning of this article" is wrapped with two main truths: God the Father Almighty is the giver of all things, and human creatures are the passive recipients. Luther writes:

> It is all that ordinary people need to learn at first, both about what we have and receive from God, and about what we owe God in return. This is knowledge of great significance, but an even greater treasure. For here we see how the Father has given to us himself with all creation and has abundantly provided for us in this life, apart from the fact that he has also showered us with inexpressible eternal blessing through his Son.[6]

---

1. Preface to the Genesis sermons, *WA* 24:18, 26–33, as cited in Robert Kolb, "God and His Human Creatures in Luther's Sermons on Genesis: The Reformer's Early Use of His Distinction of Two Kinds of Righteousness," *Concordia Journal* 33, no. 2 (2007): 170.
2. Preface to the Genesis sermons, *WA* 24:27–28, as cited in Kolb, "His Human Creatures," 170.
3. Henry W. Reimann, "Luther on Creation: A Study in Theocentric Theology," *Concordia Theological Monthly* 24, no. 3 (1953): 26.
4. Paul R. Hinlicky, *Luther for Evangelicals: A Reintroduction* (Baker Academic, 2018), 129. See also Reimann, "Luther on Creation," 26.
5. Oswald Bayer, *Martin Luther's Theology: A Contemporary Interpretation*, trans. Thomas H. Trapp (Eerdmans, 2008), 175.
6. "The Large Catechism," *BC*, 433.

Creation *ex nihilo* not only grounds the origin of all that exists in God, but, as Paul Althaus writes, reflects "an all-inclusive character of God's creating and working."[7] Luther's doctrine of creation is derived from the logic of God's re-creation of sinners. The two doctrines—creation and redemption—parallel each other; both occur *ex nihilo*, purely by grace and apart from human merits or contributions. Confessing faith in the almighty creator means recognizing our own inability to generate our own existence and sustain it; likewise, confessing faith in God the redeemer of the Second Article means acknowledging our inability to liberate ourselves from sin, wrath, and death. Luther moves backward from the Second Article, using it to interpret the First Article; this affirms that God's justifying action informs Luther's understanding of creation. The article of creation is conceived in light of what Christine Helmer calls, "the christologically-accented doctrine of justification."[8] However, the creational language of *ex nihilo* also flows to the justifying language of *sola gratia*. Both creative and re-creative actions are by God's effective word, the instrument of God's power.[9]

Creatures are "masks"[10] in which God's ceaseless activity is hidden. They are instruments through which God continues his creative work in giving and providing. They do not constitute our identity but are where God hides to achieve his purpose. The whole of our existence is predicated upon God's creating us, and we stand in relation to God in the form of trust and contingency. Everything we possess is gifted by God, including the power of, in Risto Saarinen's word, "responsivity."[11] The creature's passive response to God's almighty acts of creation takes on this demeanor: "For all this it is my duty to thank and praise, serve and obey Him."[12] The abundance of all the created gifts God provides effects in us gratitude for him without any reciprocal benefits for him, and motivates free, willing service for neighbors in love without any self-interest.

The Personal Pronoun "Me"
God's Bountiful Provisions

The credal language may seem impersonal and abstract; thus Luther sees the need to instruct each believer in knowing how to relate personally to their creator.

---

7. Paul Althaus, *The Theology of Martin Luther*, trans. Robert C. Schultz (Fortress, 1966), 119.

8. Christine Helmer, "More Difficult to Believe? Luther on Divine Omnipotence," *International Journal of Systematic Theology* 3, no. 1 (2001): 5–6.

9. For a major work on Luther's doctrine of God's Word, see Robert Kolb, *Martin Luther and the Enduring Word of God: The Wittenberg School and Its Scripture-Centered Proclamation* (Baker Academic, 2016).

10. *LW* 14:114.

11. Risto Saarinen, "Communicating the Grace of God in a Pluralistic Society," in *The Gift of Grace: The Future of Lutheran Theology*, ed. Niels Henrik Gregersen et al.(Fortress, 2005), 72.

12. "The Large Catechism," *BC*, 433.

The personal pronoun "me" accentuates us as a passive object of God's creative action and care. Luther's theology of creation, Johannes Schwanke notes, "begins with the concretely created instance of my own person and the world."[13] With Schwanke, Bayer and Niels Henrik Gregersen point out that Luther's exposition of the Creed begins with the subjective, personal aspect of faith—that is, with "me" as an individual rather than with "all the creatures" as a whole.[14] Luther captures this emphasis with his own confession: "I believe that God has made *me* together with the creatures" instead of the general phrase "heaven and earth."[15] God's fatherly care saturates all aspects of our lives, which is, in Gregersen's estimation, summed up in three concentric circles: the personal, the communal, and the wide cosmic sphere.[16] The whole confession ("I believe") of pure goodness ("fatherly, divine goodness and mercy, without any merit or worthiness in me") evinces a proper order, in John T. Pless's formulation,[17] from "the personal" ("has made me"), to "the cosmic/universal" ("all creatures"), to "the communal" ("He also gives me . . . house and home, wife, and children, land, animals and all I have"), to "the providential" ("He defends me against danger and guards and protects me from evil"), to "the doxological" ("for all this it is my duty to thank and praise, serve and obey Him"), all culminating in faith, a fiduciary expression ("This is most certainly true").[18]

The word "create" is an exclusive attribute of God's being, which is not shared with any creaturely beings. The First Article lays the foundation for the first commandment, distinguishing God as one of a kind; as creator, he belongs to an ontologically different category, not to be collapsed into the world of his own creation.[19] Charles P. Arand recognizes in Luther the inclusion of verbs such as "give," "preserve," "provide," "protect," "shield," and "defend" to expand what it means for God to create.[20] This is to stress that our existence is gifted, and we are the beneficiaries of God's manifold gifts: his provision, his preservation, his

---

13. Johannes Schwanke, "Luther on Creation," in *Harvesting Martin Luther's Reflections on Theology, Ethics, and the Church*, ed. Timothy J. Wengert (Eerdmans, 2004), 80.

14. Bayer, *Martin Luther's Theology*, 168–69; Niels Henrik. Gregersen, "Grace in Nature and History: Luther's Doctrine of Creation Revisited," *Dialog: A Journal of Theology* 44, no. 1 (2005): 21; Schwanke, "Luther on Creation," 80.

15. "The Small Catechism," *BC*, 354–55.

16. Neils Henrik Gregersen, "Grace in Nature and History: Luther's Doctrine of Creation Revisited," *Dialog: A Journal of Theology* 44. no. 1 (2005): 21.

17. John T. Pless, *Praying Luther's Small Catechism*: *The Pattern of Sound Words* (Concordia Publishing House, 2016), 40.

18. See Pless, *Praying Luther's Small Catechism*, 38; Bayer, *Martin Luther's Theology*, 163–64.

19. See Charles P. Arand, "Our Stewardship of Creation," in *Luther's Large Catechism with Annotations and Contemporary Applications*, ed. John T. Pless and Larry M. Vogel (Concordia Publishing House, 2022), 346.

20. Charles P. Arand, "Luther on the Creed," in *The Pastoral Luther: Essays on Martin Luther's Practical Theology*, ed. Timothy J. Wengert (Eerdmans, 2009), 152.

protection, his guardianship, and his defense. In Helmer's words: "Created as 'gifted existence' is correlated to the knowledge of God as giver of all temporal goods."[21]

The outpouring of the created mercies in the First Article is a certain proof of God's incessant action and his fatherly love for human life, for God is "the Father of all" (Eph 4:6). The external grace of God is not confined to a few but given to all creaturely spheres. Creation is God's work, and good by nature. It "becomes vain, evil, and harmful from outside, and not by its own fault, namely, because it is perverted."[22] As Henry W. Reimann writes, "It is from man's use of the world, not from God's good creation, that ills and sorrows arise."[23] Contrary to the Neoplatonic and ascetic dualism of the Middle Ages, which taught contempt of physical being, Luther affirms both mind and body as God's gifts. Luther's indignation against reason as "the devil's prostitute"[24] is, as Philip S. Watson rightly notes, precisely because of "the abuse and perversion of what he regards as one of the Creator's best gifts to His creatures."[25] God creates us as a human person, a unity of body and soul. God endows us with human sensation to perceive, and rationality to interpret the empirical world. God weaves us into a network of social relations to provide for us, including house and home, parents, and children. God richly provides all creaturely goods including the civil authority through which God rules and ensures peace and security.[26] God's providential care extends to the cosmic sphere including the rhythms of nature; the life of animals, of plants, of the earth and all that it produces; and the four elements of earth, air, fire, and water.[27] In light of this bounty, Luther acknowledges personally, "[All created things] I have not of myself, that I may not become proud. I cannot either give them to myself or keep them by myself."[28]

Of what good is God as creator unless he is creator to you? God the creator brings into being all things and provides for us so abundantly that we do not suffer any lack in body and soul.[29] The abundance of God's creative gifts serves us. Schwanke says, "The relevance of the Creator is grounded in the relevance of this Creator *to me*";[30] in Luther's own words, "All of the creatures are speaking

---

21. Helmer, "More Difficult to Believe?," 10.
22. *LW* 25:363; *WA* 46:373.
23. Reimann, "Luther on Creation," 32.
24. See *LW* 40:175–76.
25. Philip S. Watson, *Let God be God: An Interpretation of the Theology of Martin Luther* (Fortress, 1947), 87.
26. "The Large Catechism," *BC*, 439.
27. "The Large Catechism," *BC*, 432. See Timothy J. Wengert, *Martin Luther's Catechisms: Forming the Faith* (Fortress, 2009), 54.
28. *LW* 51:163.
29. David A. Brondos, *Fortress Introduction to Salvation and the Cross* (Fortress, 2007), 89.
30. Schwanke, "Luther on Creation," 80.

to us";[31] "God makes all creation help provide the benefits and necessities of life."[32] In his sermon on Genesis 46:19–27, Luther has God say to him: "All that I do in heaven and on earth I direct to the end that it may serve *you*. You are my only concern; I can and will not forget *you*. I attend you with such great care and love."[33] Luther draws from Augustine, who espouses the unity of God's creative and governing grace. Quoting Augustine ("Let him who made you care for you. Since he cared for you before you even existed, how can he fail to care for you now that you are what he willed you to be?"[34]), Luther takes joy in being created and cared for by God. He considers no "sweeter sound" than St. Peter's "He cares for you" (1 Pet 4:19).[35] As it is for us that God creates by his gracious will and goodness without human agency, so also it is for us that God governs over us by his ever-present, providential care without surrendering governing to human agency.[36] God did not create us to leave us but attaches himself to us in his "most gracious will"—as Paul says in 1 Corinthians 12:6, God is he "who works all things in me."

The blessings that God has lavished on us ought to impel us to "commit our care to him in even a small present evil," without doubting that God has forsaken us.[37] Misfortunes and pain are the alien work God does to awaken us from the slumber of ingratitude to thank him for the bountiful mercies that we take for granted. The vision of God's providence must loom large, as it aids in countering the weakness of our faith when visited with life's assaults. We should ponder on the innumerable gifts of God's kindness by which our life's miseries and pain pale into insignificance and thus lose their grip on us. Contradictions and struggles with God are hallowed as God's alien work that strips us of all self-reliance so that we rest on nothing but God alone and his proper work. The former is not the ultimate work, but the latter is. Suffering of all kinds in the creaturely world ought to be seen in light of "God's most gracious will" and the all-encompassing gifts of creation. Luther exults, "If only a man could see his God in such a light! How happy, how calm, how safe he would be! He would then truly have a God from whom he would know with certainty that all his fortunes . . . had come to him and were still coming to him under the guidance of God's most gracious will."[38]

---

31. *WA* 46:494.15ff, 45, as cited in Arand, "Luther on the Creed," 153.
32. "The Large Catechism," *BC*, 432.
33. *LW* 8:90.
34. *LW* 42:153. See Augustine, *Expositions of the Psalms*, trans. Maria Boulding, vol. 2, *Expositions of the Psalms* 33–50, ed. John E. Rotelle (New City, 2000), 220, as cited in *LW* 42:153n33.
35. *LW* 42:154.
36. *LW* 42:152.
37. *LW* 42:153.
38. *LW* 42:154.

Gifted Existence and Passive Response as "Counter-gift"

Creation is God's gift; it is viewed as "the soul's garden of pleasure, along whose paths we enjoy the works of God."[39] God created the earth. "He did not create it a chaos"(Isa 45:18). God did not create the earth like "a desert," which cannot be inhabited; he formed it, like "the Father's house with many rooms" (John 14:2) to be lived in.[40] It is also described as "a ready and equipped home" for our blissful dwelling. In Luther's *Lectures on Genesis* 1:11, he teaches that creation proceeds out of

> the divine solicitude and benevolence toward us, because He provided such an attractive dwelling place for the future human being before the human being was created. Thus afterwards, when man is created, he finds a ready and equipped home into which he is brought by God and commanded to enjoy all the riches of so splendid a home.[41]

The created order is so abundantly furnished that creatures do not need to seek elsewhere for aid. When Luther affirms that God created the world out of his sheer generosity, immediately he qualifies the purpose for which we are created: "And all this generosity is intended to make man recognize the goodness of God and live in the fear of God. This care and solicitude of God for us, even before we were created, may rightly and profitably be considered here."[42] This purpose inheres in the Sabbath observance, that we might acknowledge and revere God. Luther extols the salutary effect of God's created gifts:

> Hence, because everything we possess, and everything in heaven and on earth besides, is daily given, sustained, and protected by God, it inevitably follows that we are in duty bound to love, praise, and thank him without ceasing, and, in short, to devote all these things to his service, as he has required and enjoined in the Ten Commandments.[43]

Just as Luther prefaces his exposition of every commandment with the recurring phrase "we are to fear and love him, and so" as the creature's appropriate response to God's command, so also he inserts this proposition at the end of the First Article as a fitting response to the God whose deity is nothing but extravagant giving: "For all of this I am bound to thank, praise, serve, and obey him."[44] The

---

39. *LW* 43:210.
40. *LW* 17:132–33; *WA* 31.2:365–66.
41. *LW* 1:39; *WA* 42:30.
42. *LW* 1:39; *WA* 42:30.
43. "The Large Catechism," *BC*, 433.
44. "The Large Catechism," *BC*, 433.

word "bound" denotes the passive receptivity of being acted upon by the causative character of God's gift. This understanding is drawn from Luther's teaching on the distinction between the will's "passive capacity" and its "active capacity."[45] Theses 14 and 15 of Luther's *Heidelberg Disputation* bear this out: "Free will, after the fall, has power to do good only in a passive capacity, but it can always do evil in an active capacity."[46] The capacity to reciprocate God's creative grace with gratitude is of a passive nature, that we act causally—not from our own resources, but by God's empowerment. We are endowed with an orientation toward God. This Godward-ness is constitutive of our created nature; it is not ours by merits or rewards but is God's gift of grace. Pless puts it well:

> Through faith, recipients of the Father's good gifts in creation recognize these endowments as flowing not from our merit or as rewards for our worthiness but as gifts given exclusively out of God's fatherly, divine goodness and mercy. On account of such gifts, we have the duty to thank, praise, serve, and obey Him.[47]

God's word, for Luther, was initially framed within the distinction between God's promise and his threat. The promise of life—"you may freely eat" (Gen 2:16)—is safeguarded, Luther writes, by the threat of death: "But of the tree of the knowledge of good and evil you shall not eat, for in the days that you eat of it you shall die" (Gen 2:17). In the pristine state, Adam had the word of God, both in promise and command, which makes responsivity to God a natural orientation. The command of God (law) not to eat of the forbidden tree was given to the righteous Adam in order that he might have "an outward form of worship by which [he would] show his obedience and gratitude toward God."[48] In the prelapsarian state, before the fall, Adam had set this commandment before his posterity. The innocent Adam stands in a righteous relation toward God, rendering to God honor that is rightly his. Created with the gift of "the original righteousness," Luther argues, Adam gladly "loved God and His works with an outstanding and very pure attachment" until Satan deceived him.[49] In Steven D. Paulson's estimation, "Adam 'knew God,' obeying with joy because there was no moment of decision or neutral space to preserve things between the moments of

---

45. *LW* 31:49–50. See Gerhard O. Forde, *On Being a Theologian of the Cross: Reflections on Luther's Heidelberg Disputation, 1518* (Eerdmans, 1997), 55n6, where he discusses the distinction between "active capacity" and "passive capacity."

46. *LW* 31:49.

47. John T. Pless, "Two Kingdoms in Luther's Catechism: A Proposal for Catechization," in *One Lord, Two Hands? Essays on the Theology of the Two Kingdoms*, ed. Matthew C. Harrison and John T. Pless (Concordia Publishing House, 2021), 437.

48. *LW* 1:101; *WA* 42:77.

49. *LW* 1:113; *WA* 42:86.

what God *said* and what he *did*. Adam heard what God said, and 'understood the work' instantly."[50] He was obliged to obey, not to acquire righteousness he originally had, but to express his righteous identity in concrete form; nor did he aim to secure a belonging to him, for he already existed in a "pure attachment" to God. The communion between God who speaks and Adam who hears him in the garden is marked by pure joy, life, freedom, and attachment to God until corruption and distortion overtook it because of Adam's sin. Stephen J. Chester notes, "The discontinuity [of pristine communion] stems from the fact that through sin what was intended for creation was so grievously and entirely lost."[51] In the original state, nature and grace are not antithetical to each other, as they are now due to the fall. Luther declares, "Let us rather maintain that righteousness was not a gift which came from without, separate from man's nature, but that it was truly part of his nature, so that it was Adam's nature to love God, to believe God, to know God, etc."[52] Human creatures are distinctive because they are created for a worshipful response to God's address. The innate ability to worship, Piotr J. Małysz shows, is what Luther means by "original righteousness": that we are created "essentially to fear and trust God, that is, by nature not to be autonomous but to rest in God's goodness and to derive our whole being from the act of worshipping him."[53] Faith, praise, and obedience already existed at the beginning of the created order. The passive, original form that these Godward dispositions assumed includes "utmost joy," "a most sincere desire," "an enlightened reason," "without prompting," and without the "deprivation" the fallen nature now experiences.[54] The proximate relation between the creator and his creatures is God's gift, an unmerited kind that delights the innocent soul.

Passive faith receives what is spoken to us and permits that word to do its own work in us. God's word places human creatures under his authority so that we not only hear him but also are empowered to respond to him in trust, fear, and love. Our created nature is endowed with the gift of responsivity to God. This gift is what Bayer calls a "counter-gift."[55] The power of living for God stems not from the law but from the gospel; not from the works of "active righteousness" but from the gift of "passive righteousness."[56] Righteousness is passive, but it is inherently dynamic to produce works of love. Luther states its prolific

---

50. Steven D. Paulson, *Luther's Outlaw God*, vol. 2, *Hidden in the Cross* (Fortress, 2019), 223, Paulson's italics; cf. *LW* 1:113; *WA* 42:85–86.

51. Stephen J. Chester, "It is No Longer I Who Live: Justification by Faith and Participation in Christ in Martin Luther's Exegesis of Galatians," *New Testament Studies* 55, no. 3 (2009): 329n57.

52. *LW* 1:165; *WA* 42:134.

53. Piotr J. Małysz, "Sin, between Law and Gospel," *Lutheran Quarterly* 28, no. 2 (2014): 169.

54. *LW* 1:53; *WA* 42:47; *LW* 1:113; *WA* 42:86.

55. Oswald Bayer, "The Ethics of Gift," trans. Mark A. Seifrid, *Lutheran Quarterly* 24, no. 4 (2010): 458.

56. *LW* 26:7; *WA* 40.1:45.

nature in the preface to his 1535 *Commentary on Galatians*: "When I have this righteousness within me, I descend from heaven like the rain that makes the earth fertile. That is, I come forth into another kingdom, and I perform good works whenever the opportunity arises."[57] The creative power of God's gift is the ground of the fertility of human hearts. The "bound," backward and passive response to God in fear, trust, and love of God flows from the gift of righteous identity in the pristine state.

Despair and deliverance are opposites, just as law and gospel are. The law creates despair of self, causing us not to turn inward to the self but outward for aid, to take leave of itself and cleave to the gospel for deliverance. The law only demands but never fulfills; the gospel gives freely what is lacking beforehand. In Luther's own estimation:

> Demanding and granting, receiving and offering, are exact opposites and cannot exist together. For that which is granted, I receive; but that which I grant, I do not receive but offer to someone else. Therefore if the Gospel is a gift and offers a gift, it does not demand anything. On the other hand, the Law does not grant anything; it makes demands on us, and impossible ones at that.[58]

The law strips us of all soteriological resources within us; thus it denies the possibility of humans giving to God, in which case it isolates us from the orbit of divine-human intimacy. Bo Kristian Holm argues that "within the realm of the law, it is impossible to understand this counter-gift [passive response] to God positively—or as a gift at all."[59] However, the epistemic perception of the counter-gift as a gift is made possible from the perspective of the gospel. The cheerful heart of a believer freely offers up the sacrifice of praise as a fragrance to God, not out of a deficit, but out of the surplus of God's gifts in creation (and in redemption). Whereas "a theology of deficit itself only serves to isolate the individual," Holm contends, "a theology of surplus" impels the believer

> to give God the only thing God wants, the faith Godself has given, and give the rest to his or her neighbors without destroying the potential for further giving.... This theology of surplus involves a positive integration of the concept of reciprocity. Only by describing the renewed mutual fellowship between God and humanity is it possible to articulate the necessary positive condition behind any further giving.[60]

---

57. *LW* 26:11; *WA* 40.1:51.
58. *LW* 26:208–9; *WA* 40.1:337.
59. Bo Kristian Holm, "Luther's Theology of the Gift," in Gregersen et al., *The Gift of Grace*, 85.
60. Holm, "Luther's Theology of Gift," 85.

The gospel has forgiven the self-incurvature of our nature and gives us the power to begin overcoming it so that all questions of self-interest become insignificant. The nature of this inconceivably extravagant gift is that it does not require anything in return; rather, it "[is granted] freely,"[61] stripped of all forms of conditionality. It possesses its inherent power to evoke responsive praise and love from us. The creature's response in gratitude and obedience is "a passive capacity," that which is wrought in us by the gospel. The gospel does not "demand anything";[62] it simply "commands us to hold our hands and to receive what is being offered."[63] Faith does not bring anything of itself but only receives God's gifts, and in so doing, honors God as God. Thus faith is a human action, a passive kind; it is not a human achievement, but "a divine work in us which changes us" into a new person.[64] God's creative giving makes possible the realization of a counter-gift, a passive response to his extravagant gift that we have received. The receptive character of faith is itself a counter-gift we offer back to God, not as a means to amass merit and earn future grace, but as a gifted response of grace. We stand before the creator God not as an active person but as a passive person, not only receiving from him all his gifts, but also reciprocating his with gratitude. The creator God, in Bayer's formulation, is "the unconditioned and unobligated Giver" whose "categorical giving does not exclude the counter-gift of the creature, but rather empowers the creature to make this counter-gift as a response."[65] The backward, responsive character of gift, Bayer argues, "cannot and need not be understood as a condition attaching to it: it need not be understood as its *causa finalis*."[66] God's gifts are unilaterally given to us, and all human contributions are excluded. A gift, freely given by God, is freely reciprocated by us; the former leads to the latter. Any attempt to offer God something to merit his favor is thereby ruled out; the only thing we can offer him is homage and worship that he rightly deserves. We do not actively earn God's gift but passively receive it by faith; this reception on our part does not isolate us but draws us into the orbit of a renewed communion with God.

God's Word as God's Instrument of Power

God remains God, even without the world; but the world cannot be itself without God. God is God, even without any external relation to his created order. Paulson's formulation captures Luther's doctrine of aseity, affirming that "God is God outside any relation of inside himself through Trinitarian *perichoresis*.

---

61. *LW* 26:208; *WA* 40.1:337.
62. *LW* 26:209; *WA* 40.1:337.
63. *LW* 26:208; *WA* 40.1:337.
64. *LW* 35:370.
65. Bayer, "The Ethics of Gift," 458.
66. Bayer, "The Ethics of Gift," 458.

God *is* in his own nature and majesty—regardless of us and our categories of thought and without any movement or dialectics of God coming out of himself to his creatures and returning again."[67] The triune God's inner life is beyond our grasp, but the triune God's outer relation to the creature is disclosed to us by the eternal Word, the ontic conversation of God's inner life that the Spirit communicates to us. Reimann was right to say that "Luther's religious view of Creation is plainly apparent in what he says about the Word of God. That Word was God's medium and instrument in performing the works of creation."[68] As Luther writes, "From eternity He [the Word] was within God's paternal heart, and through Him God resolved to create heaven and earth."[69] The God who speaks the world into being is, in Hinlicky's phrase, "not the still silence"[70] in himself and external to himself. In order to understand divine things, we must accustom ourselves to the language of the Holy Spirit. Just as a philosopher uses his own language, so the Holy Spirit does the same. The Spirit's language and way of expression is this: that "God, by speaking, created all things and worked through the Word, and that all his works are some words of God, created by the uncreated Word."[71] Denis Kaiser recognizes in Luther a distinction between an unspoken and a spoken word: "The unspoken, uncreated Word was one with God and a separate person, whereas the spoken, created Word created all things. God's spoken words are not merely grammatical words or vocabularies but true and substantial things. Thus, God created all things through the uncreated Word by speaking."[72] When Isaiah implements the prophet's formula "Thus says the Lord," writes Paulson, he is "not describing or explaining the ideal that you aspire to but speaking for God."[73] The word spoken bears its own power to deliver. So, "Israel is saved" (Isa 45:17). Luther's distinction between "name-word" (*heissel wort*) and "action-word" (*thettel wort*) helps clarify what the Bible means by the word of God.[74] David C. Steinmetz explains, "Call-word" only "names all the biblical creatures. He does not create them; he only sorts them out and gives them labels"; but "deed-word . . . not only names but effects what it signifies. Adam looks around and says, 'There is a cow and an owl and a horse and a mosquito.'

---

67. Paulson, *Luther's Outlaw God*, 2:56.

68. Reimann, "Luther on Creation," 28.

69. *LW* 22:9.

70. Paul R. Hinlicky, *Divine Complexity: The Rise of Creedal Christianity* (Fortress, 2011), 225.

71. *LW* 1:47; *WA* 42:35.22–41; also quoted John A. Maxfield, *Luther's Lectures on Genesis and the Formation of Evangelical Identity* (Truman State University Press, 2008), 45.

72. Denis Kaiser, "'He Spake and it was Done': Luther's Creation Theology in His 1535 Lectures on Genesis 1:1–2:4," *Journal of the Adventist Theological Society* 24, no. 2 (2013): 122–23. See *LW* 1:22; *WA* 42:17.

73. Steven D. Paulson, *Luther's Outlaw God*, vol. 1, *Hiddenness, Evil, and Predestination* (Fortress, 2018), 47.

74. *LW* 37:180n32.

But God looks around him and says, 'Let there be light.' And there is light."[75] God's speech is his own act; as Paulson writes, "He speaks rather than waits to be spoken to or about. God acts, but the idol seeks its users to act."[76] When God speaks, he causes something new to happen; God's creative speech effects new realities rather than signifying already actualized realities. The performative power of God's word is the primal origin of all that is outside the immanent Trinity. God creates the world *ex nihilo* without the use of any antecedent material causes except his word and command; in Christoph Schwöbel's words, "We are all God's vocabulary."[77] "The words of God," for Luther, "are realities, not bare words."[78] Commenting on Genesis 1:20, Luther writes, "God speaks a mere word, and immediately the birds are brought forth from the water." When God's word is spoken, realities appear; they are, Luther asserts, "nothing but nouns in the divine language."[79] God's word is not, Jonathan A. Linebaugh writes, "a system of signs that refer to some nonlinguistic *res*." He then cites Psalm 33:9, "God spoke and it was done," to conclude that for Luther, "divine speech does not merely correspond to but actually creates reality."[80] John W. Kleinig compares human speech to divine speech:

> The power of human speech is shown by the way that language works and how we use it. We use descriptive speech honestly to say how things really are, or dishonestly to falsify what is really so. We use imperative speech morally to get others to do what is right, or immorally to urge them to do what is wrong. Most significantly, we use performative speech beneficially to achieve something good, like declaring peace, or detrimentally to do something evil, like declaring an unjust war. Yet, despite its obvious power, the effect of human speech is limited by the limitations of the speaker. It cannot create anything. It seldom achieves all that it sets out to do, and then only for a short while, if at all. It is all too often empty speech.... On the other hand, [God's speech] accomplishes what God wants.... It delivers what it promises to give; ... it is always effective.[81]

---

75. David C. Steinmetz, *Luther in Context*, 2nd ed. (Baker Academic, 2002), 115.
76. Paulson, *Luther's Outlaw God*, 1:47.
77. Christoph Schwöbel, "'We are All God's Vocabulary': The Idea of Creation as a Speech-Act of the Trinitarian God and Its Significance for the Dialogue between Theology and Sciences," in *Knowing Creation: Perspectives from Theology, Philosophy, and Science*, ed. Andrew B. Torrance and Thomas H. McCall (Zondervan, 2018), 47.
78. *LW* 1:22; *WA* 42:17.
79. *LW* 1:49; *WA* 42:37.
80. Jonathan A. Linebaugh, *The Word of the Cross: Reading Paul* (Eerdmans, 2022), 219.
81. John W. Kleinig, *God's Word: A Guide to Holy Scripture* (Lexham, 2022), 22–23.

God's promise is no empty solicitude; it possesses its own efficacy in bringing forth new realities; in Jeffrey G. Silcock's rendering, "[God's Word] is an effective word of promise, a work that bespeaks God's faithfulness—promise. God's Word promises that his word will not return empty and will accomplish what he purposes."[82] Writing on Isaiah 55:10, "For as the rain and the snow come down from heaven and return not thither," Luther resorts to a creaturely analogy to speak of the performative nature of God's word. God's word is like the rain and snow that water the earth and generate life in it. "The rain can achieve everything for the earth. 'So also My Word accomplishes everything.' The effect is the same."[83] Human reason argues that the power to produce life lies not in the rain but the earth. In reply, Luther writes, "But when we experience the absence of rain, we see what the earth produces. So He takes away the glory of the earth and shows that it is not the earth that does it but that it is accomplished by the rain."[84] Though "the Word seems so weak and foolish" that it appears to lack intrinsic power to do anything, Luther teaches that "all the power, victory, and triumph of God" reside in it.[85] This is a consolation for the faint, "lest they be offended at the lowliness of God, who has every victory in His Word."[86]

Creation occurs through the word, which Bayer understands as "speech-act": "It is a working word of address—a work by which God's faithfulness speaks: a promise."[87] Divine speech is "a performative utterance," that which constitutes a reality, not just describes it.[88] God's word is defined, in Luther's formulation, as "the power of God through which He created all things by a method surpassing all reason and understanding." This power assumes as its form the promises that God made with his people; Luther continues, "We must take note of God's power that we may be completely without doubt about the things which God promises in his Word. Here full assurance is given concerning all his promises; nothing is either so difficult or so impossible that he could not bring it about by his Word."[89] According to God's absolute power (*potentia absoluta*), God is free to do anything he pleases; according to his ordained power (*potentia ordinata*), God has acted in a way that is faithful to his covenantal promise. So when "God blesses, the result is the thing itself or that which is said, in accordance with his statement: 'For

---

82. Jeffrey G. Silcock, "The Role of the Spirit in Creation," *Lutheran Theological Journal* 44, no. 1 (2010): 10.
83. *LW* 17:257; *WA* 31.2:460.
84. *LW* 17:257; *WA* 31.2:460.
85. *LW* 17:257; *WA* 31.2:460.
86. *LW* 17:257; *WA* 31.2:460.
87. Bayer, *Martin Luther's Theology*, 102.
88. Bayer, *Martin Luther's Theology*, 102. See 50–51, where he, citing John L. Austin, speaks of God's speech as performative rather than descriptive.
89. *LW* 1:49; *WA* 42:37.

He commanded, and they were created' (Ps 148:5)."[90] God's blessing is not only verbal but actual, for "His Word is the thing itself."[91] Whatever he promises will occur out of "conditional necessity," Alister E. McGrath writes, not of "absolute necessity."[92] Gerhard O. Forde rightly discerns that Luther understands the word primarily, not for its meaning, but for its power to achieve—"what the words do, not merely in what they mean."[93] The believer recognizes, says Luther, that

> it is not all in his hand but only in God's hand. For just as I believe that he created the entire world out of nothing, and that everything has come only from his word and command, so I have to confess, that I am a part of the word and his creation. Therefore, it must follow that in my power there is no ability to raise my hand, but God alone does and effects everything in me.[94]

Commenting on the concept of "rest" in Genesis 2:3, Luther does not intend a physical sense in which we rest to rectify a deficiency in us. Luke T. Johnson offers this insight: "The 'rest' that is God's very being (God's glory) is not disturbed by God's 'working' in the world because all that God does empirically is an outpouring of infinitely rich life rather than an effort to redress a lack."[95] The Sabbath rest does not mean God ceased his activity after having created heaven and earth; rather it means, as Luther contends, "God ceased in such a way that he did not create another heaven and earth."[96] God continues his work in preserving and governing what he has already created. The "rest" refers not to a cessation of divine activity but to the satisfaction God has toward his own handiwork. In Luther's estimation:

> God rested from His work, that is, He was satisfied with the heaven and earth which had then been created by the Word; He did not create a new heaven, a new earth, new stars, new trees. And yet God works till now—if indeed He has not abandoned the world which was once established but governs and preserves it through the effectiveness of His

---

90. *LW* 4:154–55; *WA* 43:247.

91. *LW* 4:155; *WA* 43:247.

92. Alister E. McGrath, *Luther's Theology of the Cross: Martin Luther's Theological Breakthrough* (Wiley-Blackwell, 1985), 56.

93. Gerhard O. Forde, "The Word That Kills and Makes Alive," in *Marks of the Body of Christ*, ed. Carl E. Braaten and Robert W. Jenson (Eerdmans, 1999), 8.

94. Preface to the Genesis sermons, *WA* 24:27–22; cf. On Gen. 1:1, WA 24:21, 31–22:7, as cited in Kolb, "His Human Creatures," 129.

95. Luke T. Johnson, *Hebrews: A Commentary* (Westminster John Knox, 2006), 130, as cited in Mark W. Elliott, *Providence: A Biblical, Historical, and Theological Account* (Baker Academic, 2020), 50.

96. *LW* 1:75; *WA* 42:57.

Word. He has, therefore, ceased to establish; but He has not ceased to govern. . . . Almighty, therefore, is the power and effectiveness of the Word which thus preserves and governs the entire creation.[97]

"Rest" as satisfaction refers to the completion of heaven and earth; "delight" pertains to the continued work of God in the preservation of his creation. Luther connects Genesis 1:18, "And God saw that it was very good," to "the preservation itself, because the creature could not continue in existence unless the Holy Spirit delighted in it and preserved the work through this delight of God in His work."[98]

Against Deism, Luther writes, "God did not create things with the idea of abandoning them after they had been created, but He loves them and expresses His approval of them. Therefore He is altogether with them. He sets in motion, He moves, and He preserves each according to its own manner."[99] God governs and preserves his created order by the power of his word, the instrument by which he also created it. There is in Luther a high doctrine of providence, in which God, after having created us, does not desert us but continues to work and act in the created world. Alberto Bellini's formulation helps elucidate Luther's language about God: "God's being is to act, . . . to give and not receive, so far as God cannot be given anything that is not already his."[100] This language, as Paul O'Callaghan contends, is not so much about a doctrine but "a proclamation of God's action."[101] God, for Luther, is "an energetic power, a continuous activity, that works and operates without ceasing."[102] The created world is "no quiet order" but "an unbroken witness to God's restless creative activity as Almighty Lord."[103] The entire world of creation stands in a creaturely relationship with God, utterly dependent upon God, who is, in Reimann's description, "a restless sort of Mover God,"[104] not the static "unmoved mover" deity of the Greeks.

The Hiddenness of God and Creatures as Masks

For Luther, God is not a deistic deity, nor is he just a primal cause of all creaturely beings; he is my Father who has made me along with all creatures. Creatures are "the masks" in which God hides his activity, reflecting the God whose nature

---

97. *LW* 1:75; *WA* 42:57.
98. *LW* 1:50; *WA* 42:33.
99. *LW* 1:50–51; *WA* 42:38.
100. See Alberto Bellini, "La giustificazione per la sola fede," *Communio* 7 (1978): 34, as quoted in Paul O'Callaghan, *God and Mediation: A Retrospective Appraisal of Luther the Reformer* (Fortress, 2017), 17.
101. O'Callaghan, *God and Mediation*, 17.
102. *LW* 21:328.
103. Reimann, "Luther on Creation," 27.
104. Reimann, "Luther on Creation," 27.

it is to hide himself (cf. Isa 45:14).[105] Gustaf Wingren rightly notes, "A fruit tree... is a disguise for God. The mother who gives her breast to her child is also a disguise, *eine Maske, eine Mumme*. All the way God is giving life, but he does it disguised. All we see are the externals, the *larvae Dei* (masks of God)."[106] Creatures can never create, although they can work with God in the care and stewarding of the created order. Creatures are not the creator; only God himself is. The Hebrew word "create" is exclusively associated with God. As Bayer notes, "Thus the creatures are indeed coworkers, but not those through whom creation is transmitted or co-creators."[107] Bayer's rendering is Luther's—that we are cooperators, not cocreators.[108] God, says Luther, "does not work without us, because it is for this very thing he has recreated and preserves us, that he might work in us and we might cooperate with him. Thus it is through us that he preaches, shows mercy to the poor, comforts the afflicted."[109] Luther maintains the infinite difference between creator and creature as taught in the first commandment. Vítor Westhelle further explains that "by virtue of being endowed with the image of God, what we can do is to produce simulacra of divine artistry by working on a mask that God has given us, even though it is now cracked by sin. Human *poietics* [productivity] is derivative."[110] Creatures are, Luther teaches, "only the hands, channels, and means" through which God provides for us.[111] We come into the world through them—for example, through our parents, whom God constitutes as instruments of his power. This coincides with Luther's explanation of the first commandment where he teaches that we derive our blessings not from creatures but "from" God "through" them.[112] The securing of God's blessings flows from the wealth that is given by God. Luther says, "If you are to have a thread on your skin and a piece of bread in your mouth, the First Commandment has to give it to you, otherwise you will never get anything."[113] Such a perspective reflects the immanence of God and his active involvement in the created order; in Albrecht Peters's estimation, "God, our gracious Creator and good Giver of blessings, is

---

105. The hiddenness of God is his peculiar attribute. I will discuss this in the next chapter, which deals with Luther's various kinds of hiddenness.

106. Gustaf Wingren, "The Doctrine of Creation: Not an Appendix but the First Article," *Word and World* 4, no. 4 (1984): 362.

107. Bayer, *Martin Luther's Theology*, 175–76. See *LW* 33:242–43. Also see Philip Hefner, "Can the Created Co-Creator Be Lutheran? A Response to Svend Andersen," *Dialog: A Journal of Theology* 44, no. 2 (2005): 184–88, for a discussion of Hefner's concept of the "created co-creator," which is not the same as, in Luther's phrase, "co-operators."

108. Bayer, *Martin Luther's Theology*, 176; cf. *WA* 47:857.35.

109. *LW* 33:243.

110. Vítor Westhelle, *The Scandalous God: The Use and Abuse of the Cross* (Fortress, 2006), 105.

111. "The Large Catechism," *BC* (Tappert), 368.

112. "The Large Catechism," *BC*, 389.

113. See *WA* 28:722.20, as cited in Albrecht Peters, *Commentary on Luther's Catechisms: Creed*, trans. Thomas H. Trapp (Concordia Publishing House, 2011), 125.

close to us under the masks (*larvae*) of his creatures and institutions in nature and history. The entire interpretation of the Decalogue looks tirelessly to God's creative commanding as well as commanding creating."[114] All created realities are contingent upon God's creative power, not ours. Therefore, the vocation of the human consists not in creating but in receiving his gifts hidden in our labor as we cooperate with God; as Bayer asserts, "Theological anthropology is an anthropology of responding."[115] The true self, one that is constituted by God's creative power, is not an autonomous self, but a responding self, one that is oriented toward God by faith, born out of God's causative word.

The medieval view of elevating the sacred above the secular no longer governs Luther's thinking. Kolb notes, "His Ockhamist instruction prepared Luther to take the created order seriously and to perceive God's presence in it."[116] Luther does not hesitate to identify worldly orders with creation.[117] God does not encounter us in his naked transcendence but through creaturely forms which vocation assumes. In Edgar M. Carlson's estimation, "It is precisely the created world in all its concreteness and materiality that provides one channel for God's revelation of Himself. The home and family into which one has been born, the school which he attends, the local magistrate, the job which he is assigned in the community, all the instituted authorities by which his activity is governed, these are 'masks of God.'"[118] God imputes value and dignity to the vocation of every Christian and adds his blessing to the ordinary places of human life in which vocational obedience occurs, and through which God's reality is mediated. Our callings in the concrete stations of life—family, church, and civil life—are where God hides his activity to provide the abundance of gifts for body and soul.

The various social positions, such as magistrate, teacher, father, or other vocations and stations, are God's institutions, necessary for this life; they are not to be treated merely as a means for ascent to God. As Watson writes, "God is One who comes down veiled in the *larvae* of His creatures and meets man precisely in the 'material substantial sphere' of the external world."[119] God confronts us in these masks, first as law, exposing our sinful abuse of these creatures; but the eyes of faith enable us to grasp the gospel, that God provides for us so much good through his creatures, which remain good despite being tainted by sin. The

---

114. Albrecht Peters, *Commentary on Luther's Catechisms: Ten Commandments*, trans. Holger K. Sonntag (Concordia Publishing House, 2009), 124–25.

115. Oswald Bayer, "Being in the Image of God," trans. Mark C Mattes and Ken Sundet Jones. *Lutheran Quarterly* 27, no. 1 (2013): 78.

116. Robert Kolb, *Martin Luther: Confessor of the Faith* (Oxford University Press, 2009), 172.

117. *WA* 49:721.10, as cited in Edgar M. Carlson, "Luther's Conception of Government," *Church History* 15 (December 1946): 261.

118. Carlson, "Luther's Conception of Government," 261.

119. Watson, *Let God be God*, 115. See Watson's critique of Troeltsch's interpretation of Luther's religion.

temporal and creaturely things of the world are God's creation, though not to be worshipped as though they are gods. They are, to use Paul's words, "the weak and beggarly"[120] elements, as they, like the negative function of the law, bear neither the power of justifying nor that of creating our identity, which is solely God's. God's divine will and act inhere in his creative masks; but sinners misuse them by attributing divinity to them, thereby putting their trust in them rather in the God of the first commandment.

Our creatureliness thus is not lived out in some spiritualistic sphere separated from this creaturely world in which God dwells and acts. "Apart from a belief that the created world in all its aspects is good because it comes from God and is loved by God," Marc Kolden contends, "it would make little sense to command believers to serve God in earthly things."[121] Believers continue to benefit from God's ongoing creative work in the ordinary activities of a good creation marred by sin. All works that benefit the community are sacred and of equal value, ethically and spiritually; as Luther teaches, "Everyone must benefit and serve every other by means of his own work or office so that in this way many kinds of work may be done for the bodily and spiritual welfare of the community, just as all the members of the body serve one another."[122] Gene Edward Veith Jr. captures Luther's thought well:

> The doctrine of vocation is a theology of the Christian life, having to do with sanctification and good works. It is also a theology of *ordinary life*. Christians do not have to be called to the mission field or the ministry or the work of evangelism to serve God, though many are; nor does the Christian life necessarily involve some kind of constant mystical experience. Rather, the Christian life is to be lived in vocation, in the seemingly ordinary walks of life that take up nearly all of the hours of our day. The Christian life is to be lived out in our family, our work, our community, and our church. Such things seem mundane, but this is because of our blindness. Actually, God is present in them—and in us—in a mighty, hidden, way.[123]

The first commandment repudiates any self-chosen estates and demands that we are faithful in the area where God has located us; in Luther's words, "Be certain

---

120. *LW* 26:403; *WA* 40.1:614. Luther primarily uses the phrase "the weak and beggarly" when speaking of the law's inefficacy to justify us.

121. Marc Kolden, "Earthly Vocation as a Corollary of Justification by Faith," in *By Faith Alone: Essays on Justification in Honor of Gerhard O. Forde*, ed. Joseph A. Burgess and Marc Kolden (Eerdmans, 2004), 269.

122. *LW* 44:129–30.

123. Gene Edward Veith, Jr., *God at Work: Your Christian Vocation in All of Life* (Crossway, 2002), 158, Veith Jr.'s italics).

that your faith, Gospel, and Christ are right and your estate pleases God."[124] All our works to God, Luther describes, are "just such a child's performance" by which God wants to bestow his gifts.[125] The vocations in which God places us, whether at home, in the fields, in the city, government, or anywhere else, are where God hides his gifts, waiting to be received by faith, not achieved by our labor. "These are the masks of God, behind which He wants to remain concealed and do all things."[126] God's presence and acts are concealed in, with, and under, these masks; there God's nearness permeates all creatures, actively performing his "creative commanding" and "commanding creating" apart from which nothing exists, consists, or persists. Luther declares to his congregation: "Everything proceeds out of God's order, and nothing has its own essence of itself; nothing is in charge of its own existence. Rather, everything proceeds from God's hand, counsel, and will, so you should see God in all creatures if we open our eyes or ears and then give thanks."[127] Luther wants us to look beyond creatures to see that God is constantly but hiddenly at work around us. So, he says, "When you see a tree bearing fruit, you will see God the Creator at work."[128] Likewise, when we have butter and cheese on the table, we hear the cow speaking: "Rejoice! We bring you butter and cheese from God. Eat, drink, and share it with others."[129] Whoever disdains creatures scorns the creator, who is hidden in them to accomplish his purpose.

Whoever turns these creatures into idols becomes just like them; as Psalm 135:8 states, "Those who make them and all who trust in them shall become like them." The images and the image makers collapse into each other; in consequence, the image worshippers cannot "hear" God's voice speaking through his creatures. Idolatry blinds them to the truth of God's provision hidden in creatures; it deafens them to the hidden voice of God. They no longer see or hear, as they are idols themselves. Luther concludes, "This is now the citizen, the farmer. They do not serve God but each himself. But they cannot see that the gold, silver, and grain, which they have and which they hold tightly, those things cannot see and hear; such is a dead god. . . . Briefly: As their gods are blind, so are they, for they have ears and cannot hear what God calls out through his creatures."[130]

From the Ockhamist tradition, Luther inherits the insight that even though everything depends on God's power, we should do our part, while knowing that only God can cause things to happen and increase. Luther operates with this

---

124. See *WA* 32:491.38, as cited in Peters, *Ten Commandments*, 126n198.
125. *LW* 14:114.
126. *LW* 14:114.
127. On Gen. 1:14–19, *WA* 24:42.22–25, as cited in Kolb, "His Human Creatures," 134.
128. *WA* 30.2:87.6–9, 10–11 (*Katechismus predigten*, 1528), as cited in Arand, "Luther on the Creed," 153.
129. *WA* 30.1:87ff., 33ff. (*Katechismus predigten*, 1528), as cited in Arand, "Luther on the Creed," 153.
130. See *WA* 46:494.37–495.2, as cited in Bayer, *Martin Luther's Theology*, 110–11.

axiom: "In all our doings He is to work through us, and He alone shall have the glory from it, as Paul says in I Cor. 3:7: 'So neither he who plants nor he who waters is anything, but only God gives the growth.'"[131] Luther proposes the "right balance": "Get busy and work, and yet expect everything from God."[132] God could have done it all by himself and in isolation from us but wants to include us in the production of a certain result. Procreativity, for instance, is a blend of both divine and human work. God could give us children without involving human agency. "But He does not want to do this. Instead, He joins man and woman so that it appears to be the work of man and woman, and yet He does it under the covering of such masks."[133] Our work alone does not produce grain and fruit. We must "plow and plant and then ask His blessing and pray: 'Now let God take over; now grant grain and fruit, dear Lord! Our plowing and planting will not do it. It is Thy gift.'"[134] Our labor does not negate the importance Luther places on the fourth petition ("Give us this day our daily bread") where we pray for God's "left hand" to rule and provide for our physical needs. All human labor is futile without God's blessings accompanying it; it is nothing but "the finding and collecting of God's gifts."[135]

God's inclusion of us in his way of governance provides occasions for the performance of good works taught in the Ten Commandments, and for the reshaping of God's people into the image of Christ. What we obtain from our labor must not be converted into merits; they are fruits of our vocational obedience, subsequent to, and consequent on, God's prior, creative grace.[136] The ability to achieve or acquire all goods is given by God, not to be converted into an idol. Peters states, "God, as our Creator, calls our heart out of clinging to what is created and demands it for himself in an exclusive and undivided way."[137] God includes us in his work but in such a way that our trust is in God, not his creation. God's creation is for us so that we may be for God, praising God the Father Almighty, the giver of all goods. Unless we are annihilated at the foot of the cross, we become puffed up in our works and wisdom, and God is robbed of his glory. Luther holds, "Without the theology of the cross man misuses the best in the worst manner.... He thus misuses and defiles the gifts of God."[138] Creaturely things are good in themselves but can become vain due to unbelief, subjecting them "to a perverted enjoyment."[139] Faith uses created things "not in

---

131. *LW* 14:115.
132. *LW* 14:114.
133. *LW* 14:114.
134. *LW* 14:114.
135. *LW* 45:327.
136. See Risto Saarinen, *Luther and the Gift* (Mohr Siebeck, 2017), 119.
137. Peters, *Ten Commandments*, 118.
138. *LW* 31:55.
139. *LW* 25:363; *WA* 56:373.

a vain way but in a correct way," by not deriving "vain pleasure from them."[140] Luther expands on pious and impious use of God's created goods:

> For if we believed it with our whole heart, we would also act accordingly, and not swagger about and boast and brag as if we had life, riches, power, honor, and such things of ourselves, as if we ourselves were to be feared and served. This is the way the wretched, perverse world acts, drowned in its blindness, misusing all the blessings and gifts of God solely for its own pride, greed, pleasure, and enjoyment, and never once turning to God to thank him or acknowledge him as Lord or Creator.[141]

Luther teaches us "to practice this article, impress it upon our minds, and remember it in everything we see and in every blessing that comes our way. Whenever we escape distress or danger, we should recognize how God gives and does all of this so that we may sense and see in them his fatherly heart and his boundless love toward us."[142] Thus the wonderful knowledge of God's goodness in creation should humble us and kindle in us a desire to use God's gifts in his service. However, this article also terrifies us, as it unveils the hideous truth of our wayward hearts that deny God the doxological praise that is rightly due him.[143] If God is robbed of this praise, says Hans Walter Wolff, a human creature "becomes his own idol, turns into a tyrant; either that, or falling dumb, he loses his freedom."[144] Idolatry results when our hearts cling to the masks of God's providence, thereby collapsing the distinction between the creatures that God employs as instruments of his power and God the creator, the sole provider of all earthly goods. Human activity is not intrinsically its own but arises out of God's hidden activity in our labor. Any flourishing of vocation is not to be attributed to human industry and wit, without any reference to God. "To think that we can provide for ourselves, without at all times relying on him," Lockwood claims, "is an idolatrous deception."[145] When we turn the power to accomplish that God gives us into an idol, we mobilize God's judgment. And when we have other loves including loving ourselves more than the God who calls us to love him above all else, we deviate from the true God and consequently provoke God's

---

140. *LW* 25:363; *WA* 56:373.
141. "The Large Catechism," *BC*, 433.
142. "The Large Catechism," *BC*, 433.
143. Wengert, *Martin Luther's Catechisms*, 48.
144. Hans Walter Wolff, *Anthropology of the Old Testament*, trans. Margaret Kohl (Fortress, 1974), 229; also quoted in John T. Pless, *Luther's Small Catechism: A Manual for Discipleship* (Concordia Publishing House, 2013), 56.
145. Michael A. Lockwood, *The Unholy Trinity: Martin Luther against the Idol of Me, Myself, and I* (Concordia Publishing House, 2016), 45.

wrath. Absolution is withdrawn from those who absolutize themselves, who exalt themselves above God as the ground of their achievements.

We render thanks to God and revere him as the Lord of all gifts. If we love God simply because of these gifts, we do not love him truly but use him for our selfish gain. Luther defines true love as "loving something very dearly and preciously," having regard for the object that is loved—namely, God himself, in spite of these gifts.[146] To love God above all else is "to love Him with a precious love. But to love Him for the sake of His gift, or for some advantage is the lowest kind of love, that is, to love Him with a selfish desire. This is using God, not enjoying Him."[147] To love God for what can be gained from him is to use God, not enjoy him, and that is unacceptable for God.[148] The language of "use" and "enjoy" requires clarification. Luther compares creation to a home fully equipped for our habitation, and we are "commanded to enjoy all the riches of so splendid a home."[149] Here Luther is not denying the pleasure one may find in creatures but rather a distorted kind, a vain pleasure that comes from the sinful misuse of God's gifts. We are commanded to enjoy what God has provided for us in creation; we are not commanded to base our identity on it but on God, the provider. God cannot be used for a selfish purpose; he can be enjoyed or loved for who he is, the unconditional giver of all things. Creaturely gifts are God's means of provision and not to be idolized as though our whole identity is linked to them. The first commandment is fulfilled when the creator alone is enjoyed, loved above all but not with a reciprocal benefit for him. We love God not by giving him anything as if he has any lack in his being but by regarding God with a sense of how dear and precious he is, even though he is already "precious and good in himself."[150] Human partnership with God in God's creative action here on earth is sacred and glorious in its own right; but glory must not be transferred to the creatures or masks, which God uses as his instruments to provide for us; it is reserved for God alone, the generous giver before whom we can do nothing but reciprocate with gratitude, love, and obedience.

Luther's teaching of vocational obedience to God is, in Kolden's phrase, "a corollary of justification by faith."[151] It is indeed an exercise of the relation

---

146. *LW* 25:294; *WA* 56:307.

147. *LW* 25:294–95; *WA* 56:307. See Augustine, *De doctrina Christiana*, in *Patrologiae Cursus Completus: Series Latina*, ed. J. P. Migne, 221 Vols. (Paris, 1844–64), 1:3–5:22, 34:20, 26, as cited in *LW* 25:295n3; *WA* 46:308. The differentiation between "use" and "enjoy" has its root in Augustine. Augustine likens the Christian pilgrim to a traveler, using a certain transport to return home, though not enjoying the journey for its own sake. Likewise, says Augustine, "if we wish to return to our Father's home, this world may be used, not enjoyed. . . . The true objects of enjoyment are the Father and the Son and the Holy Spirit, who are at the same time the Trinity, one Being."

148. *LW* 25:293; *WA* 56:307.

149. *LW* 1:39; *WA* 42:30.

150. *LW* 30:60; *WA* 12:313. See also *LW* 25:294; *WA* 46:307.

151. Kolden, "Earthly Vocation," 267.

between faith and works, the former grounding the latter. As Wingren asserts, "The freedom of faith does not dissolve vocation. On the contrary, it sustains it and gives it new life."[152] Vocational obedience to God's commands (active righteousness) is no cause of human worth; nor is it an occasion for the attainment of our identity. It flows as a result of the gift of identity (passive righteousness).[153] True faith is "an effective and active" kind; it is a causal agent that works through the vehicle of love. Such faith, Luther writes, "motivates good works through love."[154] "Abstract faith"[155]—namely, faith alone—justifies. But a justifying faith is never alone; it must become an "incarnate faith,"[156] a faith accompanied by works of love. Before God, we stand in the same relationship with him, equally righteous by faith; before our neighbor, we stand in a different relationship with them by love, depending on life's stations in which God places us. As Watson notes, "The same neighbourly love, excluding all self-love, is required by all stations and vocations."[157] A living faith does not consist in detachment from the material spheres; it is not to be reduced to the inner psychological or purely spiritual sphere with an exclusive focus on personal salvation. The effective nature of faith does not undercut but impels human actions. Luther exhorts, "Cursed and damned is all life that is lived and sought for its own use and benefit; accursed all works that do not walk in love."[158] Here lies Luther's foundational paradigm of the Christian's twofold existence: they live vertically before God by faith and horizontally before people by love. In Luther's own terms, "The Christian lives not in himself, but in Christ [through faith] and in his neighbor [through love].... By faith he is caught up beyond himself into God. By love he descends beneath himself into his neighbor."[159] Christ-formed faith makes us anew and becomes operative in love. Animated by daily prayer and the word that pronounces us children of God and that cultivates a sense of joy in our new obedience, we are empowered to serve one another in the various situations of God's ordering.

Luther disavows any dualism between the religious office and secular, official obligation. Civil authorities are not necessitated by the fall; they are simply constitutive of the created order that works good in human life.[160] The two

---

152. Gustaf Wingren, *Luther on Vocation*, trans. Carl C. Rasmussen (Muhlenberg, 1957), 66.

153. Robert Kolb, *Bound Choice, Election, and Wittenberg Theological Method: From Martin Luther to the Formula of Concord* (Fortress, 2017), 52.

154. *LW* 26:29–30; *WA* 40.2:36–37.

155. *LW* 26:264; *WA* 40.1:414.

156. *LW* 26:264; *WA* 40.1:414.

157. Watson, *Let God be God*, 115.

158. *WA* 11:272.1, as cited in Peters, *Ten Commandments*, 127n208.

159. *LW* 31:371.

160. For further discussion on whether secular government coexists with spiritual government, see my *Paragon of Excellence: Luther's Sermons on I Peter* (Fortress, 2023), 168–77.

kingdoms—civil and spiritual—are God's, just as law and gospel are both of God. There are two distinct ways in which God governs the world; in Pless's assessment, "The kingdom of Christ is the realm of the ear with faith, but the kingdom of the world is one of the eye, seeing."[161] The law governs the physical realm by the sword, but the gospel governs the spiritual realm by the word. The unity and distinction of the two kingdoms safeguard against a compartmentalization of life; as Anders Nygren argues, "To God there is nothing which is profane, and no place in which God is not at work."[162] To neglect the ordinance of civil office is to permit the malevolent realm of the devil to rise, working chaos and disorder in the created order. Just as the temporal and spiritual spheres are one, Hermann Sasse writes, so also is creation and redemption; both are God's good gifts. In Sasse's formulation:

> It is precisely for the sake of love that the Christian must also carry out these duties within the bounds of his office.... Insofar as he performs his duty within the orders of creation he serves the kingdom of Christ. For the secular and spiritual are indeed to be clearly distinguished and must not be mixed one with the other, but as good gifts of God, as true order given by God, they belong together, just as creation and redemption belong together as works of God. The orders of nature and law, through which God maintains his fallen world, are the presupposition for redemption and the order of redemption for the church and the kingdom of God.[163]

The biblical and Reformation understanding of a generous God sharply contravenes the illusory, self-deceptive, self-actualization of the present age, which desires nothing to be given as gift but everything to be self-achieved. The language of life as a gift is alien to a self-governing or self-defining identity. "The form" of the justified life is, says Saarinen, "a gift, which is not to be won through competition, merit, or achievement, but that which is at hand here and now to be received."[164] The concept of gifted existence safeguards against idolizing our works, dominated by the ceaseless acquisition of goods for the formation of our identity; it too diffuses anxiety and arrogance, thinking that our sustenance is totally of our own rather than the ongoing activity of God. Luther exhorts, "We

---

161. Pless, "Two Kingdoms in Luther," 441.

162. Anders Nygren, "Luther's Doctrine of the Two Kingdoms," *Ecumenical Review* 1, no. 3 (1949): 304.

163. Hermann Sasse, "The Social Doctrine of the Augsburg Confession and Its Significance for the Present" in *The Lonely Way*, trans. Matthew C. Harrison et al., vol. 1 (Concordia, 2001), 95, as cited in Paul T. McCain, "Receiving the Gifts of God in His Two Kingdoms: The Development of Luther's Understanding," in Harrison and Pless, *One Lord, Two Hands*, 344–45.

164. Saarinen, "Communicating the Grace," 72.

should neither worry when we are insecure, nor be proud when we are secure, but in free and true faith ... perform the duties of our calling."[165] Human fecundity has trust as its proper form. Faith, "the root of all good,"[166] produces a calm and cheerful heart; unbelief, "the root of all misfortune,"[167] produces a divided and miserable heart.

Omnipotence and the Father
Law and Gospel

Omnipotence is an ontological attribute, without which God ceases to be God.[168] In his *Bondage of the Will*, Luther writes, "By the omnipotence of God I mean, not the power by which he omits to do many things that he could do, but the active power by which he mightily works all in all."[169] Not simply a power among many, God is the Lord who works all things by his almighty power.[170] Far from being an abstract idea, omnipotence bespeaks God's effective reign and ongoing involvement in the created order. To confess the almightiness of God is to declare that God alone is almighty, and his creative presence is the mystery of all that is in the world. Conversely, this confession acknowledges that humans are not almighty but live by God's creative power.

"Under the general notion of omnipotence," Luther argues, there is no preparation on the part of the human creature for the work of God's creation and preservation.

> Before man is created and is a man, he neither does nor attempts to do anything toward becoming a creature, and after he is created he neither does nor attempts to do anything toward remaining a creature, but both of these things are done by the sole will of the omnipotent power and goodness of God, who creates and preserves us without our help; but he does not work without us, because it is for this he has created and preserved us, that he might work in us and we might cooperate with him.[171]

If God alone works all in all, moving them, and operating on them by his omnipotence, what is there left for humans to do? Here Luther differentiates between "making" and "doing" in speaking of "the works of the LORD" (Ps 77:11–12):

---

165. *LW* 45:330.
166. *LW* 78:207; *WA* 22:77.
167. *LW* 78:207; *WA* 22:77.
168. Oswald Bayer, "God's Omnipotence," *Lutheran Quarterly* 23, no. 1 (2009): 87.
169. *WA* 18:718 (*Bondage of the Will*), 217, as cited in Althaus, *Theology of Martin Luther*, 110.
170. *LW* 33:43.
171. *LW* 33:242–43.

"He first made and then acted and worked with it. For He who made every creature acts with it."[172] Luther teaches this using a nautical metaphor:[173] While God preserves the ship, the sailor navigates it toward the port. The work of preserving is God's, and the work of navigating is the sailor's; both act together toward the same end. The farmer reaps the harvest, but God alone gives it.[174] God alone creates; we do nothing but cooperate with his power. God by his creative power "moves, actuates, and carries along" all creatures so that they "necessarily follow and obey it, each according to its capacity as given it by God; and thus all things, even the ungodly, cooperate with God."[175]

The relevance of God's omnipotence is to be interpreted via the dialectic tension between law and gospel, the two ways in which God encounters us. As law, God's omnipotence is, as Mark C. Mattes notes, an attack on "humanity's presumption of an autonomy."[176] It condemns any human tendency to rise above God and sit in judgment on divine things. As gospel, Mattes continues, "God's omnipotence is precisely His power to rescue sinners from sin, death, the devil, and even His own Law as accusatory."[177] Confessing faith in the Almighty God, Herbert Girgensohn says, curbs "two basic sins, *superbia* and *diffidentia*, pride and despair."[178] It crushes our pride and humbles us so that we recognize God alone is Lord, not us. God's omnipotence causes the despair of self (law) in exchange for the healing of it (gospel). "The logic in the exchange," as Holm suggests, "seems to show that... humility for Luther never can be a human work but has to be a work of God, a humiliation."[179] The knowledge of God as almighty leads to the confession of our inability to create or sustain ourselves. Luther states, "Creatures do not have their essence from themselves, and even though their essence is given to them, they do not have any power of their own."[180] Our power or agency is not intrinsic in that we have it in us but extrinsic in that we have it from outside us; it is causal, in that it is worked in us but not something we work ourselves. The power to act is a borrowed power, not of our own; it is

---

172. *LW* 11:340.
173. *LW* 33:241.
174. *LW* 33:241.
175. *LW* 33:242.
176. Mark C. Mattes, "Properly Distinguishing Law and Gospel as the Pastor's Calling," in *The Necessary Distinction: A Continuing Conversation on Law and Gospel*, ed. Albert B. Collver III et al. (Concordia Publishing House, 2017), 110.
177. Mattes, "Distinguishing Law and Gospel," 110.
178. Herbert Girgensohn, *Teaching Luther's Catechism*, vol. 1, trans. John Doberstein (Muhlenberg, 1959), 134.
179. Holm, "Luther's Theology of Gift," 83.
180. On Gen. 1:9–13, *WA* 24:36.22–24.

bestowed on us out of God's boundless goodness and mercy. Thus, Luther asserts, "the highest article" is not the second but the first.

> This is the highest article of the faith, wherein we say: "I believe in God the Father almighty, creator of heaven and earth." . . . Few are those who come so far as to believe that he really is the God who makes and creates all things. For such a person must be dead to all things, to good and evil, death and life, hell and heaven, and so confess from the heart, that out of his own powers he can do nothing.[181]

The omnipotent acts of creation from nothing effects in us humility before the majestic God and a total abandonment of ourselves to the mercy of God. Leland Mattox explains, "The humble recognition of God as almighty Creator anticipates the interior resignation—'dead to all things.' . . . To believe in the almighty Creator is already to have faith in the one and only God who has the power to save."[182] Those who despair of their failure to fear, trust, and love God above all else become the object of God's almighty action so that they cling to no other lords for remedy than God alone.

The word "creator" communicates creation's origin, that God is the source of all that is; the word "father" communicates the human creature's identity, that we belong to him as his beloved children. Luther preaches to his congregation, saying, "Because you want to know where you and I and all people come from, then listen carefully, for I will tell you: It is God, the Father, the almighty creator of heaven and earth, a single God, who created everything and preserves it."[183] The uniqueness of human beings, Bayer opines, is that they are the objects of God's address, and are given the capacity to respond to God freely in gratitude.[184] Human creatures are they to whom God speaks, as a father speaks to his children, saying, "I created you, I am the one from whom you originated, and you are mine, and you belong to me, even as I belong to you." Human speech is a response to God's speech; for Luther, "there is no mightier or nobler work of the human than speech. For it is by speech, more than by his shape or by any other work, that man is most distinguished from other animals."[185] Thus human creatures alone call God their father, a privilege not given to the animals.

---

181. *WA* 24:18.29–34 (from the preface), as cited in Mickey Leland Mattox, "Faith in Creation: Martin Luther's Sermons on Genesis 1," *Trinity Journal* 39, no. 2 (2018): 217, https://epublications.marquette.edu/theo_fac/782.
182. Mattox, "Faith in Creation," 218.
183. *WA* 45:13.2, as cited in Peters, *Creed*, 78n150.
184. Bayer, *Martin Luther's Theology*, 122.
185. *LW* 35:254.

> Beyond that He teaches us more yet, not only who we are and where we come from, but where we are to be born. That is pointed to us by that little word father, that He wants to be at one and the same time both father and almighty. The animals cannot call him father, but we are to call Him father and are to be known as His children. By means of this word, he shows what He plans to do with us.[186]

The juxtaposition of omnipotence and fatherhood heightens both God's power that works all in all and God's intimacy with us. God's omnipotence, according to Girgensohn, is "determined and defined by his fatherhood."[187] There exists a dynamic interaction between the omnipotence of God and the love of the Father. On the one hand, God's omnipotence preserves us from the power of nothingness and the ongoing possibility of threats to our existence. On the other hand, God's fatherly love is so omnipotent that it draws us to his bosom for security and identity. Girgensohn avers, "The certainty of the love of God is the certainty of this love's omnipotence, which is able to overcome all powers that would stand against it."[188] Thus the Father Almighty is praised as the one who provides for our temporal and spiritual needs and protects us against danger and evil. In tribulation, flesh and blood find it hard to believe, for people judge by what they "see." But people with faith judge by what they "hear"—that is, by God's promise that says, "I am the Creator" by whom "Israel is saved" (Isa 45:17–18).[189] Faith enables us to face the assaults of life, without lapsing into perpetual restlessness. The power of faith lies not in itself but in the promise it grasps. Faith perceives God's promise hidden in the opposite of its appearance. It imparts to afflicted souls the knowledge that they are not beyond the canopy of God's fatherly love, one that is so omnipotent and so divine that it demands their undivided allegiance. Whoever believes in God and thus holds that God is trustworthy fulfills the first commandment. As Luther puts it, it is only by a "living faith" *in* God the creator alone, and not by acquiring historical knowledge, that people receive all God's gifts.[190] Consequently, we must not be impassive but impelled by such "an omnipotent love"[191] of God, as Luther puts it, that we gladly fly to him with love and gratitude. The heart that is seized by the omnipotent, fatherly love of the First Article cleaves to God whose creative actions alone benefit us, and in so doing permits God's most earnest purpose to be our God to be realized in us.

---

186. *WA* 45:16.6, as cited in Peters, *Creed*, 79n151.
187. Girgensohn, *Teaching Luther's Catechism*, 1:133.
188. Girgensohn, *Teaching Luther's Catechism*, 1:134.
189. *LW* 17:133; *WA* 31.2:365.
190. *LW* 43:24.
191. *LW* 42:107.

Creation and Justification
Ex Nihilo (Out of Nothing)

G. Sujin Pak argues that Luther "more precisely identified the *regula fidei* with the rule of justification by faith alone."[192] As an example, she cites Isaiah 44:20 ("a deluded mind has led him astray"), quoting Luther, "Whatever is outside faith, however attractive and toilsome it may be, is idolatry, because the opinion that we are justified by works apart from faith is the source of all idolatry.... This is the rule of faith, that we are justified by the grace and mercy of God."[193] In his Galatians lectures, Luther insists, "Whoever falls from the doctrine of justification is ignorant of God and an idolater."[194] The logic of justification is apparent in his interpretation of the First Article of the Creed, with the use of the phrase "without any merit or worthiness in me." It shows that Luther interprets the doctrine of creation in the First Article in light of "the rule of faith," the central doctrine of justification.

Creation is not an emanation of God's being, nor is it out of a contract God has with his creatures. Creation occurs *ex nihilo*, a free act of God's oceanic grace. The words of Kathryn Tanner echo Luther's thinking: "A single divine intent to give us the grace of God's own life underlies the whole of what happens to and for us, from our beginning in creation to our end in salvation; this intent is entirely gracious in that it has its basis in nothing but God's free love for us. The proper starting point for considering our created nature is therefore grace."[195] Luther is not so much concerned with the mechanics of creation's origin as with the mystery of God's creative grace behind all that is; as Justin Stratis comments, "The inscrutability of the mystery of creation's origin from nothing shares the same mystery as that of the reality of grace."[196] Creation from nothing is not an assertion from nothing to something; rather it is a proclamation of the mystery of *sola gratia*, that all creatures originate with God and owe everything to him, thus stripping them of all boasting. The confession that God the Father is the almighty creator has God's love as the motive behind all that is; in Eberhard Jüngel's estimation, "In the work of creation, God's being not only *acts* as love but *confirms* itself to be love. Therefore, that God is love is the reason that

---

192. G. Sujin Pak, "The Protestant Reformers and the *Analogia Fidei*," in *The Medieval Luther*, ed. Christine Helmer (Mohr Siebeck, 2020), 232.
193. *LW* 17:114, as quoted in Pak, "The Protestant Reformers and the *Analogia Fidei*," 232.
194. *LW* 26:395; *WA* 40.1:602.
195. Kathryn Tanner, *Christ the Key* (Cambridge University Press, 2010), 116.
196. Justin Stratis, "Unconditional Love: *Creatio ex Nihilo* and the Covenant of Grace," in *Theological Theology: Essays in Honour of John B. Webster*, ed. R. David Nelson et al. (Bloomsbury T&T Clark, 2015), 286.

anything exists at all, rather than nothingness."[197] Jüngel draws such a conclusion from Augustine, who holds, "Because God is love, we are";[198] and from Thomas Aquinas, who asserts, "Because He is good, we are."[199] God creates the world, not because of obligation, but purely out of divine freedom and extravagant generosity. Everything proceeds from the overabundance of God's "pure goodness."[200] This can be traced to Augustine, who confesses to God, "You created, not because you have need, but of the abundance of your own goodness."[201] This is evident in Luther's exposition of creation in the *Small Catechism*: "All this He does only out of fatherly, divine goodness and mercy, without any merit or worthiness in me."[202] Thus creation is, in Bayer's words, "an absolute, categorical giving, that finds nothing in its recipients."[203]

In the *Large Catechism*, Gregersen points out, Luther moves backward from the Second Article to the First to highlight the article of creation by the redemptive action of God in Christ.[204] Luther scholars including Paul S. Chung, Oswald Bayer, and Leland Mattox recognize that creation from nothing is predicated upon the logic of justification from nothing.[205] Hidden in the negative language of justification—"without any merit or worthiness in me"—is the positive language of creation—"purely out of fatherly, divine goodness and mercy." William W. Schumacher states, "*Ex nihilo* is the *sola gratia* of the doctrine of creation."[206] The First Article of faith about creation is shaped by the gospel message of the Second Article of faith about redemption. The two doctrines—creation and redemption—accentuate the absolute dependence of all creatures upon God's unconditional

---

197. Eberhard Jüngel, *God as the Mystery of the World: On the Foundation of the Theology of the Crucified One in the Dispute between Theism and Atheism*, trans. Darrell L. Guder (Eerdmans, 1983), 223, Jüngel's italics.

198. See Augustine: "For it is because God is good we exist," *On Christian Doctrine*, in *Augustine: City of God, Christian Doctrine*, ed. Philip Schaff, vol. 2, *The Nicene and Post-Nicene Fathers*, 1st ser., repr. (Hendrickson, 1995), 531, as cited in Jüngel, *God as the Mystery*, 223.

199. The full quote by Thomas Aquinas is as follows: "Hence it does not follow that God is good, because He causes goodness; but rather, on the contrary, He causes goodness in things because He is good; according to what Augustine says (De Doctr. Christ. i, 32), 'Because He is good, we are.'" *The "Summa Theologica" of St. Thomas Aquina, Part I: QQI.–XXVI.*, trans. Fathers of the English Dominican Province, vol. 1 (Burns, Oates, and Washbourne, 1920), 114, as cited in Jüngel, *God as the Mystery*, 223n69.

200. "The Large Catechism," *BC*, 389.

201. Augustine, *Confessions*, trans. R. C. Pine-Coffin (Penguin Books, 1961), 313.

202. "The Small Catechism," *BC*, 354–55.

203. Bayer, "The Ethics of Gift," 452.

204. Gregersen, "Grace in Nature," 22.

205. See Paul S. Chung, "An Ecumenical Legacy of Martin Luther and Asian Spirituality," in Gregersen et al., *The Gift of Grace*, 296; Bayer, "Being in the Image," 77; Bayer, *Martin Luther's Theology*, 96–97; Mattox, "Faith in Creation," 217.

206. William W. Schumacher, *Who Do I Say That You Are? Anthropology and the Theology of Theosis in the Finnish School of Tuomo Mannermaa* (Wipf & Stock, 2010), 151. Also cited in Linebaugh, *Word of the Cross*, 29n24.

love, apart from which nothing creaturely can exist, and no one may be made righteous. As we are saved purely by God's unconditional love and free grace, so the world in its entirety has been created out of nothing as a pure gift from God's sheer goodness. The doctrine of *ex nihilo*, as Kolb and Arand explain, establishes the character of God as "unconditional giver" and the human person as "absolute receiver."[207] Thus *ex nihilo* is *sola gratia*; they mutually interpret each other. Just as *sola gratia* interprets creation *ex nihilo* as "an unconditioned and incongruous gift," Linebaugh suggests, so *ex nihilo* underscores justification *sola gratia* "as a resurrection and as the calling into being of righteousness," making us a new creation.[208]

Creation and justification, Althaus notes, are "part of God's paradoxical creative activity"; he quotes Luther: "God enjoys bringing light out of darkness and making things out of nothing, etc. Thus he has created all things, and thus he helps those who have been abandoned, he justifies the sinners, he gives life to the dead, and he saves the damned."[209] The unconditional gift of Christ sheds light on the fundamental nature of God as giver from whom creation proceeds. However, for Luther, the language of creation as God's gift is also applied to God's justifying action; as Linebaugh contends, "God's incongruous grace is not just a creational or christological past; it is also the pattern of a charismatic present. When, in the Heidelberg Disputation, Luther argues that 'the love of God does not find but creates that which is pleasing to it,' the language is from the doctrine of creation but the context is soteriological."[210] Luther's creational language flows into soteriology, affirming that our created existence is God's gift, just as our justified existence is. Creation and re-creation mutually constitute and interpret each other; both are *ex nihilo*, purely God's gift. Linebaugh rightly discerns:

> The traffic runs both ways.... As the God of the gospel, God is also the God of Genesis; the giver is and acts as the creator. Concerning "the divine work of justification," writes Luther, Romans drives its reader to "say with Paul that we are nothing at all, just as we have been created out of nothing." As the recipient of God's gift, the *homo peccator* is, from this "nothing," "called righteous" and so is, *ex nihilo*, "a new creature."[211]

The article of justification by faith provides proper theological statements about other themes such as human anthropology; it negates what cannot be

---

207. Robert Kolb and Charles P. Arand, *The Genius of Luther's Theology: A Wittenberg Way of Thinking for the Contemporary Church* (Baker Academic, 2008), 37.
208. Jonathan A. Linebaugh, "Incongruous and Creative Gift: Reading *Paul and the Gift* with Martin Luther," *International Journal of Systematic Theology* 22, no. 1 (2020): 55, doi:10.1111/ijst.12388.
209. *WA* 40.3:154, as cited in Althaus, *Theology of Martin Luther*, 120n51.
210. Linebaugh, "Incongruous and Creative Gift," 55.
211. Linebaugh, *Word of the Cross*, 29. See *LW* 34:113, 156, quoted in Linebaugh.

spoken of theologically about the human person. In Gerhard Sauter's assessment, "It is theologically true that no person can achieve self-understanding by self-reference. One cannot examine from this perspective who one is. One also cannot become transparent to oneself but can only exist in a *relationship that God has* created and in which one will be justified (not that justification is, like a goal, attainable through certain steps)."[212] God's justifying action illuminates something fundamental about Luther's anthropology. Only through the knowledge of God's re-creative action in justification do we truly know ourselves as creatures of God. The epistemic perception of our identity flows from God's justifying grace. On that basis, Bayer argues that in his exposition of the First Article, Luther "intensifies" the assertion that true humanity is a derivative of our righteous standing before God, a gift imputed to us in justification apart from any human worthiness or contributions.[213] Creation *ex nihilo* entails a kind of "passive righteousness"[214] that is accrued to humanity as pure gift. Our creatureliness is fundamentally God's gift, not something of our making, just as righteousness is God's gift, not acquired by our efforts. Created humanity is, in Cortez's phrase, "a gifted humanity,"[215] just as our newfound identity in Christ is a gift. Bayer states that "God is categorically the one who gives. His giving nature defines the form that his actions take.... Creation and new creation are both categorical gift."[216] Created nature is endowed with the gift of righteousness, fully alive with God; the fallen nature is restored, given back the righteousness that was lost through Adam's sin, and made alive again. In Luther's terms, the "passive righteousness" that God gave Adam and Eve is the basis of mutual fellowship between God and human creatures in the state of innocence. As love is the external manifestation of the faith alone that justifies, so too the "active righteousness" in the garden is the natural outworking of the gift of passive righteousness.[217] In Kolb's terms, "His love and mercy expressed themselves by forming his creatures as right and righteous in his sight. He formed them with the expectation that they would perform as his children in relationship to the rest of his creation as they trusted in him and showed him their love."[218]

---

212. Gerhard Sauter, "God Creating Faith: The Doctrine of Justification from the Reformation to the Present," *Lutheran Quarterly* 11, no. 1 (1997): 19, Sauter's italics.

213. Bayer, "Being in the Image," 77.

214. See discussion of the two kinds of righteousness in his Galatians commentary; for instance, *LW* 26:4–7; *WA* 40.1:41–43.

215. Marc Cortez, *Christological Anthropology in Historical Perspective: Ancient and Contemporary Approaches to Theological Anthropology* (Zondervan, 2016), 96.

216. Bayer, *Martin Luther's Theology*, 98.

217. For a study of Luther's two kinds of righteousness—passive and active—in his Galatians commentary, see chapter two of my *Grace and Law in Galatians: Justification in Luther and Calvin* (Cascade Books, 2023).

218. Robert Kolb, "Luther on the Two Kinds of Righteousness: Reflections on His Two-Dimensional Definition of Humanity at the Heart of His Theology," *Lutheran Quarterly* 13, no. 4 (1999): 463.

Luther's theological anthropology has largely been negatively caricatured as one that focuses on the corrupted Adamic nature. A corollary to the confession that God Almighty is a person, our creator and Father, is Luther's understanding of who we are—namely, a creature, essentially defined by trust in God. Kolb, in describing the divine-human belonging, says that "Luther could not define God without reference to His relationship to His human creatures; the reformer could not define the human creature without reference to the Creator. Human life centers on and is founded upon trust in the Creator."[219] Human creatures are originally created with a "passive capacity" for divine relationality, defined by a faith that clings to God's gracious and fatherly love. The trust that constitutes human identity arises in conversation, where God addresses them in his speech, and consequently, their identity is created as a result of God's effective word. This reflects a positive valuation of human creatures, whose identity is derived from a loving creator, on whom they are completely dependent. Creaturely gifts in abundance or scarcity do not define our identity; our self-worth is derived from God's creative word.

Luther does not deny the general knowledge of God in creation. In his *Lectures on Genesis* 1:1, Luther writes, "God has reserved his exalted wisdom and the correct understanding of this chapter for Himself alone, although He has left with us this general knowledge that the world had a beginning and that it was created by God out of nothing."[220] Luther affirms the natural knowledge of God in creation but he adamantly insists that only the Christian can "see" God's face—not "the veiled God," but God as he is hidden in the masks. The unregenerate cannot distinguish between the veils and God himself; in Luther's words:

> It is not given to the secular and unregenerate man to see this, but only to the spiritual man. He alone can distinguish the position from the Word, the divine mask from God Himself and the work of God. . . . [In] this life we cannot deal with God face to face. Now the whole creation is a face or mask of God. But here we need the wisdom that distinguishes God from His mask. The world does not have this wisdom. Therefore it cannot distinguish God from His mask. When a greedy man, who worships his belly, hears that "man does not live by bread alone, but by every Word that proceeds from the mouth of God" (Matt. 4:4), he eats the bread but fails to see God in the bread; for he sees, admires, and adores only the mask. He does the same with gold and with other creatures. He puts his trust in them as long as he has them; but when they forsake him, he despairs.[221]

---

219. Kolb, "His Human Creatures," 170.
220. *LW* 1:3; *WA* 42:3.
221. *LW* 26:94–95; *WA* 40.1:173.

Luther exhorts us to keep our eyes on the Son of God through whom we look at everything else. "Permit Christ to be the only image in your heart."[222] Faith conquers unbelief, unveiling the blindness of distorting God's purpose through the misuse of created gifts; it reinstates the original purpose of God's creation, that we devote all gifts to his glory and praise. It enables us to perceive God as the creator of all that is. This is borne out in Luther's exposition of John 3:35, "For the Father loves the Son and has given all things into His hand," where he comments, "Now if I believe in God's Son and bear in mind that He became man, all creatures will appear a hundred times more beautiful to me than before. Then I will properly appreciate the sun, the moon, the stars, trees, apples, and pears, as I reflect that He is Lord over all and the Center of all things."[223] In "the order of being" (*ordo essendi*), creation precedes redemption; in "the order of knowing" (*ordo cognoscendi*), redemption precedes creation. The epistemic perception of God as our creator springs not from rational apologetics but a confession of faith in the redeemer of the Second Article; as Reimann notes, "The soul that trusts in the *revelatio specialis* will be led to the *revelatio generalis*."[224] Knowing the face of God in Christ is prior to, and the presupposition of, knowing God's face in creation or masks. To be seized by the Son of God as our redeemer (special revelation) is to see him as the creator of all the creatures (general revelation), for God has given him everything: "Every creature and whatever there is heaven and on earth, all this gathered into that sum total, into that one Christ, in such a way that He is Mediator, whether we seek spiritual or physical things."[225] When God moves the Son into the center of our vision, we are enabled to perceive the aesthetic beauty of God's glory in nature. Reimann writes succinctly, "Rejoicing in God's goodness in Christ, Luther found joy in the world, in the splendor of the heavens, in the happy singing of the birds, in the majesty of the elements, in the riches of nature."[226] The "incongruous" grace of God in Christ (Second Article) supplies for us a true understanding of who we are (First Article), a creature marked essentially by trust in God who both creates and redeems us. Since God places everything in Christ's hands, there is no need to look elsewhere, as the next chapter will show.

---

222. *LW* 22:499; *WA* 47:206.
223. *LW* 22:496; *WA* 47:203; also quoted in Chung, "An Ecumenical Legacy," 296.
224. Reimann, "Luther on Creation," 34.
225. *LW* 8:275; *WA* 44:781.
226. Reimann, "Luther on Creation," 32.

CHAPTER FOUR

God's Most Earnest Purpose in Redemption

THE SECOND ARTICLE offers a grammar about Christ: "that Jesus Christ, the true Son of God, has become my Lord."[1] God gives himself in his descent into human flesh to reclaim us as his own. Belonging to God "that I may be His"[2] is the soteriological fruit of Christ's work; in Robert Kolb and Timothy J. Wengert's translation, "that I may belong to him";[3] as Christine Helmer writes, "The cross [is] the eternal sermon of the Father,"[4] which the Son receives. The temporal mission of God's Son is already willed eternally in God as "promise" (Rev 13:8); in Paul Althaus's terms, "The gospel and promise are there from the beginning and these include Christ and his work. Thus men of all times who believe the promise, and thereby are blessed, live from the work of Christ—even though this actually first took place on Golgotha."[5] The Son's receptivity of his Father's will is disclosed in history as the obedience he renders to his Father who sends him to death on the cross. Both Father and Son are one being, possessed of a common purpose in bringing sinners to himself. Just as God the Father is the subject of all creative actions, so is God the Son the subject of all redemptive actions—living, speaking, suffering, dying, and rising. Justification in the Second Article consists in a negation of all self-reliance and performance of the law, and a confession of Christ as all-sufficient.

Salvation lies in "no other God than this Man Jesus Christ. Take hold of Him, cling to Him with all your heart, and spurn all speculation about Divine Majesty; for whoever investigates the majesty of God will be consumed by His glory."[6] This is where Scripture begins—namely, with "this man," who is "the lovely picture" of "His majesty sweetened and mitigated to our ability to stand it."[7] Christ has liberated us from these enemies, sin, death, and the devil (the "lords"), so that we might be totally "his and live under him in His kingdom

---

1. *LW* 51:164.
2. "The Small Catechism," *BC* (Tappert), 345.
3. "The Small Catechism," *BC*, 355.
4. Christine Helmer, *The Trinity and Martin Luther: A Study on the Relationship Between Genre, Language and the Trinity in Luther's Works, 1523–1546* (von Zabern, 1999; rev. ed., Lexham, 2017), 235.
5. Paul Althaus, *The Theology of Martin Luther*, trans. Robert C. Schultz (Fortress, 1966), 211.
6. *LW* 26:29; *WA* 40.1:78.
7. *LW* 26:29; *WA* 40.1:78.

and serve him in everlasting righteousness, innocence, and blessedness."[8] Because Christ in his righteous person pleases God, believers who are clothed with his righteousness also please God. In Christ's kingdom, the believer willingly serves him, not as a slave does in servile form, but freely as a child does in filial kind. We no longer serve the devil, death, sin, the flesh, and the world, for they no longer reign over us. These lords do not terrify or condemn us, for we are received to Christ's bosom, where we are sheltered from all contraries. Nothing can harm us, as we are given a new Lord who mightily rules us by his infinite righteousness, sheer life, and unfathomable goodness.[9] We live by the gospel that re-creates us through the perpetual death of the old Adam, the alien work God does, to achieve God's proper work of the resurrection of the new Adam. The new identity created by faith leaves itself behind and cleaves to Christ alone, the sole righteousness. The life we live is an alien life, not in us but outside us, in Christ.

Two Opposing Hidings
The Naked Versus the Clothed God

In his exposition of Psalm 51, Luther uses other terms for the "hidden God" (Isa 45:15) such as the "absolute God" and the "naked" God, and the term the "clothed" God for the "revealed" God.[10] In his *Bondage of the Will*, he sets the God "not preached" against the "God preached."[11] The paradoxical distinction between the hidden God and the revealed God, the naked God and the clothed God, the not-preached and the preached God, does not mean two deities but one. Luther has God say, "From an unrevealed God I will become a revealed God. Nevertheless, I will remain the same God. I will be made flesh, or send My Son. He shall die for your sins and shall rise again from the dead. . . . Behold, this is my Son; listen to him (cf. Matt. 17:5)."[12]

Luther's atonement theology must consider two contrary means of divine hiddenness. Paulson observes, "There are two opposing hidings: one where God refuses to speak and the other where God gives his word in a way that seems contrary to all expectations."[13] God hides in his "unapproachable light" (1 Tim 6:16) and wills not to be found there. This first kind refers to the "absolute"[14] hiddenness, God in his naked majesty before whom we would be crushed by his

---

8. "The Small Catechism," *BC* (Tappert), 345.
9. "The Large Catechism," *BC*, 434.
10. *LW* 12:312.
11. *LW* 33:140.
12. *LW* 5:34; *WA* 43:459.
13. Steven D. Paulson, *Luther's Outlaw God*, vol. 1, *Hiddenness, Evil, and Predestination* (Fortress, 2018), 43; Stephen D. Paulson, *Luther's Outlaw God*, vol. 2, *Hidden in the Cross* (Fortress, 2019), 37.
14. See *LW* 12:312. For Luther, "absolute God" corresponds to "naked God."

glory. In this case, God hides, says Paulson, "to escape discovery,"[15] as it strikes terror, and there is no absolution. The second refers to the specific hiddenness in the incarnate Son through whom we are embraced as God's beloved. In this case, God hides, says Paulson, "to foster discovery,"[16] as it produces comfort and is salvific. It is in this kind of hiddenness that God wills to be found. God wills to belong to us, not in the terrifying hiddenness of the "naked God," but in the redemptive hiddenness of the "clothed God."[17] To deal with the naked God without his word leads to sheer despair, unless we cling to the God clothed in Christ. God's naked majesty will surely annihilate us, and so the foundation of salvation lies in the clothed God; as Luther avows, "This God, clothed in such a kind appearance and, so to speak, in such a pleasant mask, that is to say, dressed in His promises—this God we can grasp and look at with joy and trust."[18] Commenting on Isaiah 65:1, "They sought Me who before did not ask for Me," Luther specifies two opposing ways of seeking God: "first, in His Word and commandment, second, by means of one's own righteousness."[19] By ourselves, we do not seek him but flee him. "God Himself seeks us by means of the Word. Then, after you have been found, then you should seek Him. Therefore God wants to be found, but He does not want to be sought."[20] We seek him only where he wills to be found—namely, in his word. His word effects a divine hiding where God can be discovered, just as it says. As Psalm 33:9 teaches, "He spoke, and it was done." All human attempts at seeking God elsewhere are futile; both seeking and finding are of grace, not of law.

Luther's theology of the cross directs us to the eternal omnipotent deity who hides in human flesh, in weakness, suffering, and death on the cross. The movement to God is, in Althaus's phrase, "from 'below to above'"—that is, from "Christ as a man to Christ as God and thereby to God."[21] The christological basis of justification is made explicit in Luther's exposition of the introduction to the Lord's Prayer, where he states, "In his skin and on his back we too must ascend."[22] Just as God has descended to meet us in Jesus of Nazareth, so we now ascend to him in his humanity. While God comes to us clothed in our humanity with his word, we come to God clothed with Christ's righteousness offered in his word.

With Chalcedon, Luther does not think of Christ as human *in abstracto*, separated from his divinity. "If you separate them, joy is gone. O Thou Boy, lying in the manger, thou art truly God who has created me, and thou wilt not

---

15. Paulson, *Luther's Outlaw God*, 2:111.
16. Paulson, *Luther's Outlaw God*, 2:111.
17. *LW* 12:312.
18. *LW* 12:312.
19. *LW* 17:375; *WA* 31.2:551.
20. *LW* 17:375; *WA* 31.2:551.
21. Althaus, *Theology of Martin Luther*, 186.
22. *LW* 42:23.

be wrathful with me because thou comest to us in this loving way—more loving cannot be imagined."[23] Joy belongs to sinners terrified by their sin through the law, as they will be consoled by "the incarnate, human God" in whom all fatherly gifts are hidden.[24] This is also brought out in Luther's Christmas sermon (1527):

> Reason and will would ascend and seek above, but if you would have joy, bend yourself down to this place. There you will find that boy given for you who is your Creator lying in the manger. I will stay with that boy as He sucks, is washed, and dies. . . . There is no joy but in this boy. Take Him away and you face the Majesty which terrifies. . . . I know of no God but this one in the manger.[25]

With Augustine, Luther acknowledges such a wondrous mystery that the creator should be a creature.[26] In Christ, "this one in the manger," the hostility between God and us is dissipated. The central fact of God's self-humiliation on the cross consisted in that this particular death, that of Christ as God and man in unity, conquers all contraries of justification.

> Christ is God and man in one person. He has neither sinned nor died, and is not condemned, and he cannot sin, die, or be condemned; his righteousness, life, and salvation are unconquerable, eternal, omnipotent. . . . Now since it was such a one who did all this, and death and hell could not swallow him up, these were necessarily swallowed up by him in a mighty duel; for his righteousness is greater than the sins of all men, his life stronger than death, his salvation more invincible than hell.[27]

To permit God's purpose to be our God is to follow the way he designs for us—namely, the economic hiddenness in the cross of Christ alone. A theologian of the cross seeks God in his opposites—that is, in the humility and weakness of the cross that creates faith, not in majesty and power that frighten people away.

Luther does not, in Vítor Westhelle's opinion, opt for an *either-or* but a *both-and* sense of divine hiddenness: "a hiddenness *in* and a hiddenness *behind* the cross."[28] The God who is hidden in the cross is the passible, merciful deity;

---

23. *WA* 23:731.34–733.9, as quoted in Norman E. Nagel, "Martinus: 'Heresy, Doctor Luther, Heresy!' The Person and Work of Christ," in *Seven-Headed Luther: Essays in Commemoration of a Quincentenary, 1483–1983*, ed. Peter Newman Brooks (Clarendon, 1983), 48.
24. *WA* 23:731.34–733.9, as quoted in Nagel, "Martinus," 48.
25. *WA* 23:731.34–733.9, as quoted in Nagel, "Martinus," 48.
26. *WA* 30.2:105.7, as cited in Nagel, "Martinus," 48. See also *WA* 39.2:92–121.
27. *LW* 31:351–52.
28. Vítor Westhelle, *The Scandalous God: The Use and Abuse of the Cross* (Fortress, 2006), 55, Westhelle's italics.

the God who is hidden behind the cross is the inscrutable, impassible, and terrifying deity. The way to conquer the terrifying voice of the apparently inscrutable, impassible, and absolute deity is not through theological or rational efforts, but through grasping the revealed God, "the only true form" in which is hidden the gracious will of God toward us. Luther captures this teaching in the Jonah story, where the sailors, gripped by fear, each cried out to his god (Jonah 1:5). Yet the God they appealed to was one whom they created or imagined for themselves in their hearts. In Luther's diagnosis, "They named the true God, but there was no certainty about form or conception. The only true form of God is for us to grasp Him by faith, namely, to learn that God is always a well-disposed Father and the Father of mercies."[29] God does not wish to be shaped by us, either by speculation or imagination or good works—all this results in idolatry; rather he wills that we be shaped by our knowledge of God and his gracious will toward us. Luther credits Staupitz with leading him to seek God, not in God's naked majesty, but only in Christ's wounds, the form of God's hiddenness where he meets us as a merciful God.[30] The assurance of faith is found in this crucial reversal: not by means of ascent through pious deeds or rational edifice, but by God's descent in human flesh and his efficacious activities. Fear of the dreadful hidden God can only be conquered by the revealed God, the incarnate Son, "the only true form of God," where he becomes graspable by faith. Faith performs its creative function, causing those who suffer under the terrifying hidden God "to flee from and find refuge in God [revealed God] against God [hidden God]."[31] That "God against God" means the distinction between the hidden God and the revealed God reflects an enormous antinomy in Luther's doctrine of God. It is God who, in hiding himself in Christ, overcomes his absolute hiddenness, for those who believe. Gerhard O. Forde clarifies, "Faith is precisely the ever-renewed flight from God to God: from the naked and hidden God to the God clothed and revealed."[32]

Along the same lines, B. A. Gerrish writes, "Faith is not repose, but movement. Hence faith really does take into itself something of the meaning of God's hiddenness even though it is not directed against that hiddenness: rather it is a movement away from the hidden God."[33] Faith perceives God's merciful action that lies hidden in his intolerable wrath. The depth of God's love is most manifest precisely with this distinction in God wherein God battles against himself for

---

29. *LW* 19:11; *WA* 13:246.
30. *LW* 54:97.
31. *WA* 5:204.26 f, as cited in Westhelle, *The Scandalous God*, 59. See also Alister E. McGrath, *Luther's Theology of the Cross: Martin Luther's Theological Breakthrough* (Wiley-Blackwell, 1985), 171–72.
32. Gerhard O. Forde, *Theology is for Proclamation* (Fortress, 1990), 22.
33. B. A. Gerrish, "'To the Unknown God': Luther and Calvin on the Hiddenness of God," in *The Old Protestantism and the New: Essays on the Reformation Heritage* (University of Chicago Press, 1982), 291.

our sake, thereby also revealing himself as suffering against himself to snatch us away from the death-causing powers of the absolute God. To grasp God aright is to begin from below—that is, from God in his human life and suffering action through which the mask of the inscrutable, impassible God is dethroned.

> He who rejects the Son also loses the unrevealed God along with the revealed God. But if you cling to the revealed God with a firm faith, so that your heart is so minded that you will not lose Christ even if you are deprived of everything, then you are most assuredly predestined, and you will understand the hidden God. Indeed, you will understand him even now if you acknowledge the Son and his will, namely, that he wants to reveal himself to you, that he wants to be your Lord and your Savior. Therefore you are sure that God is also your Lord and Father.[34]

The Soteriological Import of the Confessional Title "Jesus Is My Lord"

Just as he does with the First Article, Luther puts the emphasis on the individual "I" in his commentary on the Second Article. The words "in Jesus Christ, our Lord" occupy Luther's exposition of it; in Pless's phrasing:

Faith: "I believe . . ."
Giver: "Jesus Christ, true God . . ."
Gifts: "[My Lord] who has redeemed me . . ."
Response: "so that I may. . . live under Him in His kingdom and serve Him . . ."
Faith: "This is most certainly true."[35]

Luther develops his Christology by his soteriology; as Oswald Bayer comments, "Neither Christology nor soteriology can be understood apart from the other, neither the 'person' nor the action of salvation."[36] In describing Christ's work, Luther accentuates the principle of correspondence: Christ's person is his work, and vice versa. The subject (Jesus Christ) and the predicate (Redeemer) are one. According to Bayer, "He is—in a way that differs from us—identical with that which he does."[37] "My Lord" is not something added to his nature;

---

34. *LW* 5:50; *WA* 43:460.
35. John T. Pless, *Praying Luther's Small Catechism: The Pattern of Sound Words* (Concordia Publishing House, 2016), 43–44; cf. Oswald Bayer, *Martin Luther's Theology: A Contemporary Interpretation*, trans. Thomas H. Trapp (Eerdmans, 2008), 230–31.
36. Bayer, *Martin Luther's Theology*, 234.
37. Bayer, *Martin Luther's Theology*, 232.

rather the nature of his being reflects this title; in Luther's words, "How can one know God better than in the works in which He is most himself? Whoever understands His works correctly cannot fail to know His nature and will, his heart and mind."[38] God is to be found in his coming into the human sphere—specifically, in the efficacious activities of Jesus Christ in which God is most godlike. Any attempt to look for God, Carl E. Braaten says, "in some remote sphere above and beyond the structure of God's operations in and upon the world" is considered false.[39]

The significance of the person is encapsulated in the title "our Lord." The heart of the article is that Christ, by redeeming us from these "lords"—sin, death, and the devil—has become "my Lord."[40] Albrecht Peters claims that Luther is "the first" to "elevate [this title] to the cardinal point for interpretation."[41] Of this title, Luther offers his own interpretation: "Let this be the summary of this article, that the title word 'Lord' simply means the same as Redeemer, that is, he who has brought us back from the devil to God, from death to life, from sin to righteousness, and keeps us there."[42] The rest of the article clarifies "how much it cost Christ and what he paid and risked in order to win us and bring us under his dominion."[43] All that Christ has acquired benefits not himself but us. Luther uses a vivid battlefield image to elaborate the essential meaning of Christ's passion and the benefits we reap from it:

> If you are asked, What do you mean when you say, "I believe in Jesus Christ?" answer: I mean by this that I believe that Jesus Christ, the true Son of God, has become my Lord. How? By freeing us from death, sin, hell, and all evil. For before I had no king and lord; the devil was our lord and king; blindness, death, sin, the flesh, and the world were our lords whom we served. Now they have been driven out and in their stead there has been given to us the Lord Christ, who is the Lord of righteousness, salvation, and all good. And this article you hear preached constantly, especially on Sundays, for example, "Behold, the king is coming to you." Therefore, you must believe in Jesus, that he has become your lord, that is, that he has redeemed you from death and sin and received you into his bosom.... For after we had been created, the devil deceived us and

---

38. *LW* 21:331; *WA* 7:577.26.
39. Carl E. Braaten, "The Problem of God-Language Today," in *Our Naming of God: Problems and Prospects of God-Talk Today*, ed. Carl E. Braaten (Fortress, 1989), 31.
40. "The Large Catechism," *BC*, 435.
41. Albrecht Peters, *Commentary on Luther's Catechisms: Creed*, trans. Thomas H. Trapp (Concordia Publishing House, 2011), 117.
42. "The Large Catechism," *BC*, 434.
43. "The Large Catechism," *BC*, 434.

became our lord. But now Christ frees us from death, the devil, and sin and gives us righteousness, life, faith, power, salvation, and wisdom.[44]

Luther's summary of the first commandment reinforces that no one is without "a lord."[45] Either God alone is Lord, or something else is. Either Christ alone is Lord, or the contraries: sin, death, and the devil. Mark A. Seifrid captures the real meaning behind the confession "Jesus is my Lord," one that is consistent with Luther. He writes, "It is not in our power to choose that Lord. We do not make Christ our Lord. Rather God in grace has given us Christ as our saving Lord: we have been liberated from sin and enslaved to righteousness."[46] While the Father gives himself to us in creation, the Son gives himself to us in redemption. Lordship is understood in terms of gracious self-giving, in which Christ laid down his life in order to reclaim us as God's and place us under his protection. Incarnation occurs so that we learn to know Christ as the Lord or redeemer who helps us, protects us, and saves us. By nature, Christ is God's Son; by the grace of adoption, we are God's sons. Sonship is Christ's by virtue of his eternal relationship with his Father; it is ours by virtue of our relationship with Christ. To confess Jesus as Lord is to declare that the incarnate Son, "the human God,"[47] has conquered all "lords" (including sin, death, the devil, and wrath) that would otherwise bind and annihilate us. Christ does all this "for me" so that "I may be His."[48]

Christ as Lord or redeemer is the chief category Luther employs to instruct people of Christ's life-giving activities. "The glory of Luther's preaching," Pless recognizes, "was its cruciform shape and content";[49] in Luther's terms, "One thing you must preach: the wisdom of the cross."[50] However, to preach the cross alone does not, as Hermann Sasse rightly argues, mean that

> the church year shrinks together into nothing but Good Friday. Rather, it means that Christmas, Easter, and Pentecost cannot be understood without Good Friday. Next to Irenaeus and Athanasius, Luther was the greatest theologian of the incarnation. He was this because in the background of the manger he saw the cross. His understanding of Easter victory was equal to that of any theologian of the Eastern Church. He

---

44. *LW* 51:164. See also *WA* 37:49.16–19.
45. "The Large Catechism," *BC*, 392.
46. Mark A. Seifrid, "Romans 7: The Voice of the Law, the Cry of Lament, and the Shout of Thanksgiving," in *Perspectives on Our Struggle with Sin: Three Views of Romans 7*, ed. Terry L. Wilder (B&H Academic, 2011), 130.
47. *LW* 26:29; *WA* 40.1:78.
48. *BC*, 345; Tappert translates this phrase as "in order that I may be his."
49. John T. Pless, *Martin Luther: Preacher of the Cross; A Study of Luther's Pastoral Theology* (Concordia Publishing House, 2013), 18.
50. *LW* 51:14.

understood it because he understood the victory of the Crucified One. The same can be said of his understanding of the Holy Spirit.[51]

The action by which Christ became Lord is wrapped up in these cycles of the Christian calendar: Christmas, when he became man in order to become our Lord; Good Friday, when he died in order to become our Lord; Easter, when he proved to be Lord over death; and the ascension, when he became the reigning King, assuming dominion at the right hand of the Father. All of this constitutes the content of the entire gospel upon which our salvation rests.[52]

Atonement Motifs in the Creed
Vicarious Satisfaction and Christ as Victor

Since the early church, John Frederick Jansen observes, Christ's redemptive work has been categorized according to the three offices of prophet, priest, and king.[53] However, Luther does not follow the traditional division of Christ's office in instructing people in the faith. Luther, Ian D. Siggins and Marc Lienhard argue, does not espouse any particular theory of the atonement but simply allows the richness of the biblical images of Christ to guide his thinking.[54] Here in the Creed, Luther seems to focus on the priestly work and kingly rule to depict the redemption Christ came to achieve. For the sake of convenience, we will use these familiar terms: vicarious satisfaction and Christ as Victor.

In his exposition of the *Small Catechism*, Luther does not separate the themes of satisfaction and victory. He writes, "And he did all this . . . so that he might make satisfaction for me . . . so that he might become my Lord. . . . He rose again from the dead, swallowed up and devoured death."[55] Luther uses three verbs—"redeemed," "purchased," and "freed"—but the key word is "redeemed," which implies the other two. He writes, "He has redeemed me . . . purchased and freed me."[56] The two concepts of atonement form the substance of the one word "Lord" or "redeemer" as, notes Wengert, "the one who both frees the kidnap

---

51. Hermann Sasse, *We Confess Jesus Christ*, trans. Norman Nagel (Concordia, 1984), 39.
52. *LW* 51:164–65.
53. John Frederick Jansen, *Calvin's Doctrine of the Work of Christ* (James Clarke, 1956), 30–31, where he cites Calvin, Eusebius, Chrysologus, and Aquinas, who adhere to the threefold office of Christ; cf. John Calvin, *The Institutes of the Christian Religion*, ed. John T. McNeil, trans. Ford Lewis Battles (Westminster, 1960), 2.15.1–5.
54. Ian D. Kingston Siggins, *Martin Luther's Doctrine of Christ* (Yale University Press, 1970), 49–51, 109; Marc Lienhard, *Luther: Witness to Jesus Christ*, trans. Edwin H. Robertson (Augsburg Publishing House, 1982), 179.
55. "The Large Catechism," *BC*, 434–35.
56. "The Small Catechism," *BC*, 355.

victim and pays the ransom."⁵⁷ The themes of payment and deliverance, sacrifice and conquest, are part of Luther's doctrine of redemption. The objective aspect of Christ's redemption for us and the subjective effect of his work on us coalesce; they conquer our calloused hearts so that we turn to God.

The satisfaction motif is indicated by the word "purchased,"⁵⁸ which Luther uses to speak of Christ's death as "a satisfaction for me and [payment for] what I owed, not with silver and gold but with his own precious blood."⁵⁹ Luther qualifies Christ's death using the language of vicarious atonement: "his innocent suffering and death."⁶⁰ The victory motif is linked to the phrase "freed me from all sins, from death, and from the power of the devil."⁶¹ It carries the meaning of being freed from every lord or power that holds us captive. Luther expands it by means of the logic of exchange: "Those tyrants and jailers [sin, death, the devil, wrath, and all misfortune] have now been routed, and their place has been taken by Jesus Christ, the Lord of life, righteousness, and every good thing and blessings."⁶² The believer in Christ reaps the effects of Christ's redeeming work "for us": hostility with God is banished, and reconciliation with him is given; the accusing law is ended, and the consoling gospel reigns. In a sermon on Genesis 22:18, Luther exults, "Where there is reference to blessing, there is the gospel, and where the gospel is, there is God with Christ and all his gifts."⁶³

The "Joyous Exchange"
Christ in Our Place

The law reveals the opposite of who we are in Christ; it is encapsulated in two words, "lost" and "condemned," that Luther uses in his *Small Catechism*. Due to Adam's fall, we are alienated from the creator, held captive under the power of the evil one, subject to God's wrath, and merit eternal condemnation. This miserable condition cannot be healed, and there is no comfort or counsel unless the infinite Son of God comes from heaven and bestows his mercy. Luther speaks of sin as an evil agent; it is, in his language, "an omnipotent tyrant" and "no trifle."⁶⁴ "The one word 'sin'" encompasses God's wrath and Satan's kingdom. The magnitude

---

57. Timothy J. Wengert, *Martin Luther's Catechisms: Forming the Faith* (Fortress, 2009), 58.
58. "The Small Catechism," *BC*, 355.
59. "The Large Catechism," *BC*, 434.
60. "The Small Catechism," *BC*, 355.
61. "The Small Catechism," *BC*, 355.
62. "The Large Catechism," *BC*, 434.
63. See Martin Luther: "Wo von segen gesagt wird, da ist Euangelion, wo das Euangelion ist, da ist Gott mit Christo und alien guetern," *In Genesin Declamationes* 55 (1527), *WA* 24:394.4–6 as cited in Niels Henrik Gregersen, "Grace in Nature and History: Luther's Doctrine of Creation Revisited," *Dialog: A Journal of Theology* 44, no. 1 (2005): 20, Gregersen's translation.
64. *LW* 26:33; *WA* 40.1:85–86.

of sin cannot be removed unless by the Son of God. Christ's victory over sin, death, the devil, law, and wrath requires that Christ be God. "For to conquer the sin of the world, death, the curse, and the wrath of God in himself—this is the work, not of any creature but of the divine power. Therefore it was necessary that he who was to conquer these in himself should be true God by nature."[65] The curse of his absolute distance from us (wrath) is canceled by the blessing of his incomparable nearness (mercy) to us. Luther expands on the victory motif:

> For the blessing is divine and eternal, and therefore the curse must yield to it. For if the blessing in Christ could be conquered, then God Himself would be conquered. But this is impossible. Therefore Christ, who is the divine power, Righteousness, Blessings, Grace, and Life, conquers and destroys these monsters—sin, death, and the curse ... in His own body and in Himself, as Paul enjoys saying (Col. 2:15): "He disarmed the principalities and powers, triumphing over them in Him."[66]

That God became human is not his accursedness but a presupposition of it. He assumed a human person so that he might assume our sinful person to give us his righteous person. His becoming a sinner stems from a concord of will between the Father and the Son: "Of his [Christ's] own free will and by the will of the Father he wanted to be the associate of sinners."[67] God the Father, who wills the Son's death and his act of self-humiliation, must not be conceived as an event of discontinuity in the life of God; as Luther asserts, "By the will of the Father, [Christ] has given himself in death for our sins" in order that we may be "drawn and carried directly to the Father."[68] Luther proclaims, "Christ is the image of God's grace against sin, which he assumed and yet overcame by his perfect obedience."[69] The obedience Christ renders to his Father who sends him is passive, as he permits himself to be numbered among transgressors, and in their place bears the judgment of God's holy wrath in his own body. The suffering Christ undergoes is not due to any defect in his person but stems from "his friendly heart [that] beats with such love for you that it impels him to bear with pain your conscience and your sin."[70] The crucified heart of Christ reveals the Father's heart; they are one and the same heart, as they are one being. This is borne out in Luther's *Meditation on Christ's Passion*, where he teaches, "Rise beyond Christ's heart to God's heart."[71] The heart that was historically revealed

---

65. *LW* 26:282; *WA* 40.1:441.
66. *LW* 26:281–82; *WA* 40.1:440.
67. *LW* 26:42; *WA* 40.1:99.
68. *LW* 26:42; *WA* 40.1:99.
69. *LW* 42:197.
70. *LW* 42:13.
71. *LW* 42:13.

in the cross of Christ merely translates "the divine and kind paternal heart" from eternity.[72] Christ is a gift of God's love, and in this God gives not objects but himself to redeem us. The Holy Spirit gives himself by revealing to us God's Son who gives himself by revealing to us the Father's heart that beats with passion for us from eternity.

In incarnation, Christ did not abandon his own divinity, which is his by nature and right, but assumed our humanity into the life of God. Expanding on Philippians 2:6–8, Luther comments, "Although Christ was filled with the form of God and rich in all good things, he was not puffed up by them and did not exalt himself above us and assume power over us."[73] Surrendering his prerogative to be equal to God, Christ "so lived, labored, worked, suffered, and died" just as any human person.[74] The God-forsakenness Christ willed upon himself is not an event where Christ's divinity was separated from his humanity, as in Nestorianism. Instead, Luther writes, "the deity withdrew and hid. . . . The humanity was left alone, the devil had free access to Christ, and the deity withdrew its power and left the humanity to fight alone."[75] Christ as an innocent person has acquired for us the Father's inestimable riches of righteousness, eternal life, and heaven; this he achieves in no other way than "in this form of a servant," in the inexpressible humility of the cross. Christ came concealing his majesty so that we apprehend him in his own act of self-humiliation where God truly was found to be "for us."

Christ in his humiliation achieves satisfaction for us so that mercy and grace become effective in us; in Luther's words, "Christ, the Son of God stands in our place and has taken all our sins upon his shoulders. . . . He is the eternal satisfaction for our sin and reconciles us with God, the Father."[76] Luther changes Paul's rendering of 2 Corinthians 5:21 as follows: "God has made him a sinner for us," not just sin for us. For Luther, there is no separation between sin and sinner, for sin in itself has no reality except in the one who does it. Christ was numbered among transgressors, not just among transgression, so becoming sin is becoming sinner. But this becoming is not to be conceived ontologically, as though there is a change in essence, as though Christ becomes a sinner essentially. Rather, Christ becomes "a sinner" in another—not in himself, but in us. This change is not an ontological change but a relational one. Christ's innocent person as the Son of God knew no sin, but by entering into our place he truly assumed our sinful person and therefore made himself "a sinner." Christ stands in our place before God as "the person of all men, the one who has committed the sins of all

---

72. *LW* 42:13.
73. *LW* 31:366.
74. *LW* 31:366.
75. *WA* 45:239–40, as cited in Althaus, *Theology of Martin Luther*, 198.
76. *LW* 51:92; *WA* 10.3:4.

men," to make satisfaction for them with his own blood.[77] There is a change of place; Christ voluntarily takes our place as "the worst, the greatest, and the only sinner."[78] Christ is guilty, not "in his own person" but in us, bearing "the person of a sinner."[79] In assuming the sin of the world, Christ assumes responsibility for it before God, though he himself is not responsible for it as he commits no sin. Paul R. Hinlicky explains, "Christ's victory is not only a matter of power, God asserting His reign against the evil usurper Death. More importantly, Christ's victory is a matter of *right* as well as might. Christ *rightfully* has won back dominion over sinners who *rightfully* had been held responsible for their sin."[80]

Scriptural language about Christ's death is effective and thus accomplishes its own mission. Commenting on Psalm 63:33, "He will make His voice a mighty voice," Luther extols the peculiar power of God's speech to achieve its own purpose, just as "wine has the power to delight the heart."[81] Guilt and just condemnation are indeed transferred to Christ. Luther says that the death Christ dies is a sinner's death, but it is an "innocent and pure death."[82] God "lays your sin, your death, and your hell on his dearest Son, vanquishes them, and renders them harmless for you."[83] The attribution is not figurative but actual, that Christ truly enters eternal condemnation by the Father on our behalf, just as the word says. God's "dearest Son" enters the realm of God-forsakenness and hell and conquers them to give us God's acceptance and heaven. Luther states, "[Christ] is the heavenly image, the one who was forsaken by God as damned, yet he conquered hell through his omnipotent love, thereby proving that he is the dearest Son, who gives this to us all if we but believe."[84] Christ indeed was "forsaken by God"[85] (*derelictum a deo*) and "carried God's wrath on our behalf" (*portans in seipso iram patris pro nobis*).[86] God's "omnipotent love" suffers the loss of God's "dearest Son" when the Son assumes our sin and God's wrath upon himself to annihilate them in order that he might create a people under God's mercy; as Johannes Zachhuber writes, "After all, the importance of God's presence on the cross was that this particular death led to victory over death, sin, and the devil."[87] Christ obtained

---

77. *LW* 26:280; *WA* 40.1:437.
78. *LW* 26:281; *WA* 40.1:438.
79. *LW* 26:277; *WA* 40.1:434.
80. Paul R. Hinlicky, *Luther for Evangelicals: A Reintroduction* (Baker Academic, 2018), 88, Hinlicky's italics.
81. *LW* 13:35.
82. *WA* 37:59, as cited in Althaus, *Theology of Martin Luther*, 203.
83. *LW* 42:114.
84. *LW* 42:107.
85. *WA* 5:237.38, as cited in Johannes Zachhuber, "Jesus Christ in Martin Luther's Theology," in *Oxford Research Encyclopedia of Religion*, published March 29, 2017, https://doi.org/10.1093/acrefore/9780199340378.013.327.
86. *WA* 5:271.25, as cited in Zachhuber, "Christ in Martin Luther," 5.
87. Zachhuber, "Christ in Martin Luther," 9.

victory over the tyrants of life, not through magnificent miracles, but through the weakness and foolishness of the cross (1 Cor 1:25). The means of payment is not by an economic transaction of material things like gold or silver (cf. 1 Pet 1:8), but through his innocent suffering and death on the cross. God wins us by kindness and love, not by dazzling us with his authority. Comfort and victory lie in the God who hides his mighty grace and mercy, as Kolb graphically puts it, "precisely where the theologians of glory are horrified to find him: as a kid in a crib, as a criminal on a cross, as a corpse in a crypt."[88]

Luther's theology of the cross names reality as it is,[89] that God's wrath against sin is named but also conquered by God himself for those who believe. In Westhelle's estimation, "Jesus suffered because he named the cause of suffering, the law that kills. And in this naming lies the power to overcome it."[90] Knowledge of sin is not naturally known but derived from Christ. Luther avers, "This earnest mirror, Christ, will not lie or trifle, and whatever it points out will come to pass in full measure."[91] To name a thing as it is is to overcome it. Christ named the sins for which he suffered and died, while concurrently naming himself as the remedy for them. Christ interposes himself in the law's path and suffers its alien work of condemnation in order to give us the proper work of consolation. Sinners are so blinded by sin that it requires the forsakenness of God in his Son's cry of dereliction to expose it and to dispose of it as its ultimate end. The terror of God's wrath is most acutely manifest in the cost that is required to absolve it—namely, the death of God's Son as his payment of the grievous penalty for the horror of sin. However dreadful we might be at the knowledge of our sin and God's wrath against us, we are never as frightful as is God the Son. The knowledge of God's wrath through the law, says Luther, "frightened [the Son] so horribly that he experienced greater anguish than any man has ever experienced. This is amply demonstrated by His bloody sweat, the comfort of the angel, His solemn prayer in the garden (Lk. 22:41–44), and finally by that cry of misery on the cross (Matt. 27:46): 'My God, My God, why hast Thou forsaken Me?'"[92] God-forsakenness as the sinner's desert is now transferred to Jesus, as he bore with pain the eternal sentence upon sinners. Luther stresses that God was "unwilling to release sinners even for his only and dearest Son without his payment of the severest penalty for them."[93] In our stead, Christ was "not acting in his own person now. Now he is not the Son of God, born of the virgin. But he is a sinner" who has come

---

88. Robert Kolb, "Luther on the Theology of the Cross," in *The Pastoral Luther: Essays on Martin Luther's Practical Theology*, ed. Timothy J. Wengert (Eerdmans, 2009), 41.
89. *LW* 31:53.
90. Westhelle, *The Scandalous God*, 90.
91. *LW* 42:9.
92. *LW* 26:372; *WA* 40.1:567.
93. *LW* 42:8.

God's Most Earnest Purpose in Redemption

to bear the sins of the world to make satisfaction with his own blood.[94] In a free act of mercy, Christ "placated the wrath of God by his own blood."[95] In Forde's rendering, it is what "God gives and not what God gets,"[96] and this in such a way as to end his wrath "for us," if only we believe this. This is borne out in Luther's teaching on the Lord's Supper:

> The Body of Christ is given and his blood is shed and just so [wrath] is placated. Indeed it is given and shed for you, just as it is said, "for us." Why "for us" except to placate the wrath of God which threatens our sins? Moreover, the wrath of God is placated when sins are forgiven. That is, as it is said, "Given and shed for the remission of sins." For unless it is given and poured out the wrath will be retained. So you see that the work of satisfaction or placation are worth nothing except by faith alone.[97]

Placation of wrath is twofold. Objectively, Christ truly assumed sin, guilt, wrath, condemnation, and death as "his own," says Luther, and if otherwise, these mighty "monsters" would have always remained "in us," and we would be lost forever.[98] Subjectively, faith lays hold of the "highest comfort" hidden in the "fortunate exchange."[99] Lois Malcolm sums up the twofold placation of wrath well: "Christ became a 'curse' for us (Gal. 3:13)—taking upon his Person all sin, death, and the 'curse' of the law, God's holy wrath against sin—in order to free us from them so that, by faith, we might grasp Christ's 'alien righteousness' as our own, becoming heirs of all he possesses: grace, peace, salvation, eternal blessing, and so on."[100] God's propitiation through Christ's blood is God's gift, not humanly earned. This gift is of no use to us unless we appropriate it by faith.

Unity, Not Separation
Cross and Resurrection

Christ's death on the cross and resurrection belong together in Luther's doctrine of justification. On Romans 4:25, "He died for our sins and rose for our justification," Luther explains, "In his suffering Christ makes our sin known and

---

94. *LW* 26:277; *WA* 40.1:434.
95. *LW* 26:355; *WA* 40.1:544.
96. Gerhard O. Forde, "Luther's Theology of the Cross," in *Christian Dogmatics*, vol. 2, ed. Carl E. Braaten and Robert W. Jenson (Fortress, 1984), 51.
97. *WA* 8:442.30, as cited in Forde, "Theology of the Cross," 2:51.
98. *LW* 26:278; *WA* 40.1:434; *LW* 26:292; *WA* 40.1:454.
99. *LW* 26:284; *WA* 40.1:443.
100. Lois Malcolm, "Martin Luther and the Holy Spirit," in *Oxford Research Encyclopedia of Religion*, published March 29, 2017, https://doi.org/10.1093/acrefore/9780199340378.013.328.

thus destroys it, but through his resurrection he justifies us and delivers us from all sin, if we believe this."[101] The cross reveals our sins for which Christ suffered and died; the resurrection conquers sin and confers on us Christ's righteousness; both are inherent realities of Christ's cross and resurrection. Calvary is not to be conceived as a miserable day, followed by Easter, a joyous day. Rather Christ's resurrection is the declaration of what occurs in the marvelous "duel" on the cross, where opposites—"blessing" and "curse"—coincide in Christ, with the former triumphing over the latter.[102] Christ died and buried our sin and rose to restore our righteousness. Good Friday and Easter are one in God's economy of salvation. Their unity points to a celebration of victory over the contraries of sin, death, and wrath. Christ "is the living and immortal image against death, which he suffered, yet by his resurrection from the dead he has vanquished death in his own life."[103] Resurrection renders the cross effectual in that Christ's righteousness swallows up our sin, proving that his victory is nothing other than the victory of the crucified. "For Christ, whom God the Father raised from the dead, is Victor over them [the contraries of sin, death, wrath, and hell], and he is my righteousness."[104] Resurrection, for Luther, "is the most sublime image, for in it ... [we] are set down ... in Christ's righteousness, with which he himself is righteous, because we cling to that righteousness whereby he himself is acceptable to God, intercedes for us as our mediator, and gives himself wholly to us as our high priest and protector."[105]

The "joyous exchange," Randall C. Zachman observes, comprises two aspects.[106] Objectively, the death and resurrection of Christ has achieved for us a joyous exchange of our sin for Christ's victory. Subjectively, this exchange occurs when believers transfer all opposites of justification "from ourselves to Christ" in exchange for Christ's victory, which we transfer from "him to ourselves."[107] The objective exchange is of no avail unless it is appropriated by faith. "Faith alone grasps this victory. To the extent that you believe this, to that extent you have it."[108] This happens not by introspection, looking at sin in us by which we are cast into despair, but by extrospection, looking outside us, to Christ; in Luther's estimation, we "behold [sin] resting in Christ and [see it] overcome by his resurrection and then boldly believe this, even it is dead and nullified."[109] Faith lies

---

101. *LW* 42:13.
102. *LW* 26:282; *WA* 40.1:440.
103. *LW* 42:107.
104. *LW* 26:21–22; *WA* 40.1:65.
105. *LW* 42:165.
106. Randall C. Zachman, *The Assurance of Faith: Conscience in the Theology of Martin Luther and John Calvin* (Augsburg Fortress, 1993), 55–56.
107. *LW* 26:292; *WA* 40.1:454.30–34.
108. *LW* 26:284; *WA* 40.1:443.35–36.
109. *LW* 43:12.

God's Most Earnest Purpose in Redemption

not in "a wooden but in a living Christ, who is Lord over sin and over innocence, who can support and preserve us" against all enemies.[110] Resurrection cements in our hearts that God cannot negate himself and thus cannot abandon us to the terrifying abyss of God's wrath and damnation. We have, John declares, "passed from death to life" (John 5:25). Now faith receives the gift of the life to come; it carries us toward the last day when it gives way to sight. Proclamation must include resurrection and the goods it delivers—namely, the present consolation and the certainty of an eternal hope.

> Thus we see another picture at Easter, that no sin, no curse, no disgrace, no death, but only life, grace, blessedness, and righteousness are in Christ. With such a picture we should lift up our hearts. For it is put before us and presented in such a way, that we should receive nothing else than this, that God has himself awakened us today along with Christ. For just as you see sin, death and the curse in Christ, so you should also believe that God, for Christ's sake, will not see these in you, when you receive his resurrection for yourself and receive its consolation. Such grace faith brings to us. When that day will come, however, one will no longer believe, but see, touch and feel.[111]

Christ's Ascension
The Continual Application

In stressing the work of redemption, Luther does not leave out the significance of Christ's ascension. Siggins notes, "[Christ's] resurrection and ascension are our comfort."[112] The Second Article, "that Christ is our Lord," Luther avows, "is the jewel, the gem, and the golden chain around the neck of the bride, who believes that Christ is true God from eternity, that He descended from heaven and became incarnate of the Virgin Mary, and He, and no other, ascended again into heaven."[113] Through faith's participation in "this Man and the fullness of His ascent and descent,"[114] we no longer remain below but ascend through Christ to where he is above, seated at the Father's right hand. Christ's "going to the Father" (John 16:10) is a gift, not our accomplishment but his for our justification before

---

110. *LW* 43:65.
111. See *WA* 52, *Hauspostille*, 1544: "Erst Predigt am heyligen Ostertag," 250.37–251.6, as cited in Gerald Krispin, "The Consolation of the Resurrection in Luther," *Lutheran Theological Review* 2, no. 1 (1989–90): 44. See the section on eschatology in chap. 5.
112. Siggins, *Luther's Doctrine of Christ*, 166.
113. *LW* 22:334.
114. *LW* 22:336.

God.[115] The ascended Christ takes with him those whom he adorns with his righteousness. His righteousness is lent to us, so that in him we participate in his ascent to God. This borrowed righteousness,[116] which is "outside and beyond us," has become ours through the preached word we hear with faith. It is now hidden from the world but revealed to the believers.

> It is not a thought, a word, or a work in ourselves, as the scholastics fantasized about grace when they said it is something poured into our hearts. No, it is entirely outside and above us; it is Christ's going to the Father, that is, His suffering, resurrection, and ascension. Christ placed this outside the sphere of our senses; we cannot see and feel it. The only way it can be grasped is by faith in the Word preached about him, which tells us that He is our Righteousness. Thus St. Paul says in I Cor. 1:30: "Whom God made our Wisdom, our Righteousness and Sanctification and Redemption," in order that before God we may boast, not of ourselves but solely of our Lord.[117]

Christ's ascension to power in God's right hand is part of his kingly office. The King of glory remains the Lord of grace. Being seated at God's right hand does not mean being impassive or inactive. Luther extols, "Our comfort is that we must not suppose Christ to be an idle king, raised again and glorified for his own sake alone."[118] To reside at the Father's right hand is to preside over all powers. Luther rejoices in the assurance that "as long as Christ remains enthroned there, we will also remain lords and masters over sin, death, devil, and everything. Nothing can undo that."[119] Those who are united to Christ participate in his ascension, and in a joyous exchange his presiding function is transferred to us by faith. Just as Christ is Lord over all enemies of life, we who are in him are also lords over them. Luther expands, "A Christian becomes almighty lord of all, having all things and doing all things, wholly without sin."[120] Christ's redemption has transposed us into his kingdom, in which we live and rule eternally, serving him "in eternal righteousness, innocence, and blessedness."[121]

The devil works ceaselessly to tear Christ down from his ascended throne, yet Christ remains there as the reigning king, though not uninvolved or unaffected by human cries. His ascension does not mean the withdrawal of his effective presence in our lives. From the ascended throne where he sits with the Father, with

---

115. *LW* 24:348; *WA* 46:45.
116. See *LW* 44:24. The goodness we have, for Luther, is "a borrowed goodness."
117. *LW* 24:347; *WA* 46:44.
118. *LW* 12:247.
119. *LW* 43:65.
120. *LW* 42:165.
121. "The Small Catechism," *BC*, 355.

whom he is coeval in power, majesty, and authority, the risen Lord now reigns by continually applying to the believer the joyous exchange of Christ's victory for sin. There Christ continues his intercession, communicating his victory through his Spirit to those whom he appoints as heirs of his kingdom.

Christ's pleading for us before the Father offers relief to those who are burdened with negative thoughts concerning their identity before God. Sinners in themselves and apart from Christ are worthy of nothing but his eternal judgment. Yet God withholds his charge against our residual sin, which still provokes God's wrath. This is because we have "a bishop, namely, Christ, who is without sin and who is our representative, our advocate, until we too become entirely pure like him."[122] Christ's atonement is complete, sufficient, and effective, and is not in need of any supplementation. To add to it is to rob him of glory. In heaven, Christ continues to plead for us, to apply the atoning efficacy of the once-and-for-all sacrifice of Christ; this is contrary to the sacrifice of the Mass in which Christ dies afresh, all over again. We do not offer anything to Christ but receive everything from him; as Scripture states, "From His fullness have all we received" (John 1:16). We remain passive, receiving from him all his gifts, totally unmerited but freely bestowed. Faith waits on God's prior action; as Hans Joachim Iwand writes, "The wonderful deed of faith is persevering in inaction, waiting on the time and manner of divine action. For the Christian faith lives in activity but not from activity."[123]

The Proclamation of Christ "For Us"
Promise and Faith

The emphasis on *pro me, pro nobis* ("for me," "for us") not only reflects Luther's personal experience of Christ but also permeates all Luther's writings.[124] Christ's cross and resurrection happen "for us"; it is not a mere historical event, stripped of all contemporary relevance, but rather bears the power of contemporaneity to identify us as the objects for whom Christ died and rose; as Werner Elert puts it, "The historical indicative becomes a promise by being announced to me." Hearing the "for me," he continues, "makes of the 'historical faith' 'a living faith,' faith which itself is God's doing, God's gift."[125]

---

122. LW 32:28.

123. Hans Joachim Iwand, "The Preaching of the Law," in *Hans Joachim Iwand on Church and Society: Opened by the Kingdom of God*, ed. Benjamin Haupt et al., trans. Christian Einertson (T&T Clark, 2023), 32.

124. See *LW* 42:8n9, where it says that the *pro me* ("for me") reflects "the personal aspect of faith which Luther himself experienced and now expressed in all his writings."

125. Werner Elert, *The Structure of Lutheranism: The Theology and Philosophy of Life of Lutheranism Especially in the Sixteenth and Seventeenth Centuries*, trans. Walter A. Hansen (Concordia Publishing House, 1962), 204–5.

We do not draw God to us by loving him or "by doing what lies within us,"[126] but God draws us to himself by his "omnipotent love" revealed in its opposite, in the sacrifice of his Son.[127] What is bestowed "for us" is God's gift of himself, expressed in the suffering love of the cross. This explains why the Second Article does not present Christ as a model or a teacher, though he is, but as a redeemer "who loved me and gave himself for me" (Gal 2:20). Where faith and Christ are present, sins are no more; the sin that the godly feel is hidden in God. By faith, Christ has now become "Christ for us," a friendly savior, not a terrible judge. The "for us" crucifies all creaturely forms of trust and creates a filial confidence in God, the Father of all mercies. Whoever applies this pronoun "me" to themselves in faith knows for sure that God ceases to be against them, and no enemies of life—law, sin, wrath, and the devil—can separate them from God. Luther feels the force of the Pauline language of God's self-giving love through which we are drawn into Christ's redemptive action so that we can all personally say, "The Son of God loved me and gave himself for me." Luther expressly confesses, "I am revived by this 'giving' of the Son of God unto death, and I apply it to myself. This applying is the true power of faith."[128] Luther exults in the power of the personal pronoun "me," as this "me" includes he himself, along with all saints, as the recipient of the "for us" benefits of Christ's passion.

> Therefore read these words "me" and "for me" with great emphasis and accustom yourself to accepting this "me" with a sure faith and applying it to yourself. Do not doubt that you belong to the number of those who speak this "me." Christ did not love only Peter and Paul and give Himself to them, but the same grace belongs and comes to us as to them; therefore we are included in this "me."[129]

Whoever relies on works for justification is rid of joy and liberty and cannot confess, "It is I, an accursed and damned sinner, who was so beloved by the Son of God that He gave Himself for me" (Gal 2:20).[130] Whoever despairs of themselves and all their actions becomes the very object of christological grace. When the gospel, that Christ was given "for me," is applied to troubled hearts, they will know that Christ is nothing but their "joy and sweetness" and their "Lover," who gives himself to redeem them from all the contraries of life.[131]

---

126. *LW* 31:10, 50.
127. *LW* 42:107.
128. *LW* 26:177; *WA* 40.1:298.
129. *LW* 26:179; *WA* 40.1:299.
130. *LW* 26:176; *WA* 40.1:295.
131. *LW* 26:178; *WA* 40.1:299.

God's Most Earnest Purpose in Redemption

Traditionally defined Christology offers a lens through which we can find God—namely, Jesus Christ; and upon reflection on him and his acts, we derive his relevance to us. As Herbert McCabe once wrote, "I do not reflect on the life of Christ to 'check on the truth of the doctrine' but in order to enter into the immense mystery of the love of God."[132] The story of Christ thus is not merely historical information about him; it is meant "for me" in particular, who, like all others, benefits from the grace of Christ. The Christmas story is not merely about Christ born as God in the flesh (which he is), but that he is born as such "to us"; as the prophet Isaiah proclaims, "For to us a child is born" (Isa 9:6). Of what profit is Christ sweet or good in himself unless he is sweet or good "to me"?

> That is, if I hear the story of Christ and don't think that it all pertains to me, so that it is for me that Christ is born, suffered, and died, then the preaching or knowledge of the story isn't worth a thing. . . . No matter how sweet or good Christ is, he is not recognized, he will not cheer us up, unless I believe that *to me* he is sweet and good—unless I say, "*Mother, this baby is mine.*"[133]

The redemptive action of Christ is set alongside our action of following Christ, but the logical order proceeds from Christ as savior to Christ as example; as Luther states, "It is not the imitation that makes sons; it is sonship that makes imitations."[134] Christ as gift conveys his validity to Christ as example. Not until we are grasped by Christ "as a sacrament which is active in us while we are passive" can we be "active, namely, in the following."[135] Luther highly regards the mystical theology of *Theologica Germanica* in which union with God occurs through self-abasement, and in this, Jesus was hailed as the example of humility. Wolfhart Pannenberg writes, "The mysticism of direct union with God was here combined with the idea of a mystical union with Jesus by way of contemplation of his humility and suffering. But Luther went beyond this model when he conceived of the suffering of Christ not only as an example but as endured for us, in our place, by taking away our sins and their consequences."[136] Luther teaches his people to "grasp Christ at a much higher level"—that is, "before you take Christ as an example, you accept and recognize him as a gift, as a present

---

132. Maurice Wiles and Herbert McCabe, "The Incarnation: An Exchange," *New Blackfriars* 58, no. 691 (1977): 552.

133. See *WA* 9:440, as cited in Phillip Cary, *The Meaning of Protestant Theology: Luther, Augustine, and the Gospel that Gives Us Christ* (Baker Academic, 2019), 178, Luther's italics.

134. *LW* 27:263; *WA* 2:518.

135. *LW* 42:13.

136. Wolfhart Pannenberg, "Luther's Contribution to Christian Spirituality," *Dialog: A Journal of Theology* 40, no. 4 (2001): 286, https://doi.org/10.1111/1540-6385.00088.

that God has given you and that is your own."[137] Proper preaching is not merely instructing people about a biblical story of redemption, as one does in academic institutions; it is to inculcate in the people the promise that Christ was given "for me," that "he has redeemed me." "Christ is not the law,"[138] Luther insists; Christ is gift, given "for me." Christ is the promiser who acts on us effectively, and the pronoun "me" is the one who is acted upon. They are the one to whom Christ's promise is attached, effecting in them new life and salvation. Where the passive pronoun "me" is turned into the active subject "I" (for example, "I have decided to follow Jesus"), we lose joy, for we have converted the gospel into law, turning Christ as a gift into "a new Moses";[139] but passive hearts seized by the fruits of Christ's passion rejoice and become active in imitating Christ. The vocation of Christ's cross now, in a joyous exchange, becomes the believer's vocation for life.

The First Article leads us away from the idolatry of self to the worship of the creator, who is the subject of the verb "he created me"; the Second Article leads us away from the lordship of self to the Lordship of Christ, who is the subject of the verb "he has redeemed me." Phillip Cary intimates that "the grammar itself illustrates how Luther's faith is about being the *object* of divine forgiveness and grace, the one whom God loves, addresses and justifies, rather than the *subject* of faith, the one who believes."[140] In creation and redemption, God is the subject; we are the objects. The proper order of God coming to us is this: the word of Christ addressing us, "I absolve you," is prior to human response, "I believe." The emphasis here is not on anything we do, or desire to do, but on what he does for us or gives us. It is not about what I could offer to God to win his favor, but about what the word of promise ("Christ has redeemed me") does to win us. A believer lives not by the dictate of conscience, which leads us astray, but by the testimony of Christ, which transcends or contradicts empirical verification. Luther declares, "A Christian, however, is not guided by what he sees or feels; he follows what he does not see or feel. He remains with the testimony of Christ; he listens to his words and follows him into the darkness."[141] We hold fast to Christ's words that death, sin, and hell are conquered, although we still feel their terrifying power. Stephen D. Paulson concludes, "Saving faith therefore ceases being a mere psychological reference and refers purely theologically to the word that God gives. A promise justifies apart from law. It does not wait for a human fulfillment of a law. The promise depends only on the one giving it and the promiser's power to bring it about."[142] Justification by faith rests solely

---

137. *LW* 35:119. For a discussion of Christ as gift and as example, see chap. 3 of my *Paragon of Excellence: Luther's Sermons on I Peter* (Fortress, 2023).
138. *LW* 26:137; *WA* 40.1:241.
139. *LW* 35:119.
140. Cary, *Meaning of Protestant Theology*, 156.
141. *LW* 22:306; *WA* 47:35.6–11.
142. Paulson, *Luther's Outlaw God*, 1:91.

on the causative power of God's promise, not on the intensity of our contrition or the strength of faith with which we approach God.

Luther likens faith to an empty vessel for an eternal treasure. Faith's worth lies not in itself, for it is a mere husk, but in the object it grasps—namely, Christ, the kernel. In this regard, all Christians are alike, equally given "the same treasure and the same Christ," irrespective of the quality of their faith. "It is just as if two people have a hundred gulden—one may carry it in a paper bag, the other store and bar it in an iron chest; but they both have the treasure whole and complete. So with Christ. It is the self-same Christ we possess whether you or I believe in him with a strong or a weak faith."[143] Although Luther exhorts his people to grow in faith and exercise their faith, he never wavers in inculcating in them this equality in Christ, faith's treasure.

The justifying fruits of Christ's passion benefit no one except by faith, the means of appropriation. Luther avers that "to preach Christ is to feed the soul, make it righteous, set it free, save it, provided it believes the preaching."[144] The gospel content and faith's appropriation are one, the former conveying its power to the latter. We grasp the word that first grasps us. The distinction between the subjective genitive "the faith of Christ" and the objective genitive "faith in Christ" is brought into view. As David G. Horrell notes, "the noun *pistis* can mean 'faith' in the sense of belief, or (more often) trust (its usual meaning in the Greek of the period), but it can also mean 'faithfulness,' as in Rom 3:3: 'the faithfulness (*pistis*) of God' (KJV has 'the faith of God')."[145] The subjective genitive ("faith of Christ") refers to the efficient causality of the gospel itself, that which renders us righteous, or to the faithfulness of God in giving us his Son for sin; the objective genitive ("faith in Christ") refers to the instrumental causality of faith, that by which we are made righteous. Christ's vicarious obedience to the Father's will acquires the benefits from his Father; our faith acquires the benefits Christ has gained for us.

The word of promise is both faith's object and the means by which faith is created.[146] The promise cannot be without faith, that by which it is received, just as faith cannot be without the promise, that upon which it is based. Just as promise and faith are one, so too are promise and subject. Paulson writes aptly, "Promises from Christ mean nothing in general, they must have the subject, for

---

143. *WA* 33:37.22, as quoted in Siggins, *Luther's Doctrine of Christ*, 147–48.

144. *LW* 31:346.

145. David G. Horrell, *An Introduction to the Study of Paul*, 3rd ed. (Bloomsbury T&T Clark, 2015), 108; also cited in my *Grace and Law in Galatians: Justification in Luther and Calvin* (Cascade Books, 2023), 9.

146. See Graham Tomlin, "Shapers of Protestantism: Martin Luther," in *The Blackwell Companion to Protestantism*, ed. Alister E. McGrath and Darren C. Marks (Blackwell, 2004), 41.

you, with them or they are worse than nothing. A promise not given damns."[147] The promise works effectively through the oral preaching of the "for me" rather than through rational speculation "from me."[148] It is not speaking "about God (theology)" or speaking "to God (prayer)" but speaking "for God (preaching)" that abolishes God's distance from us by effecting God's nearness to us.[149] The ministerial role of preaching consists not in explaining something to hearers but bestowing something to them. Preaching is where the benefits of Christ's passion are conveyed to us; it is where, in Johann Anselm Steiger's assessment, "the *communicatio idiomatum* between God and the human is set in motion in the form of verbal communication."[150] When a word is preached, it is no longer as sign but a reality. The verbal declaration that sinners are made anew is effective, simply because, he continues, "the sermon, like the Word of the Creator himself, is an active Word that does what it says and says what it does."[151] In this regard, Luther does not oppose the forensic or declarative dimension of justification to the effective or performative dimension of it, for the two are one.[152]

The End of the Law and Preaching Repentance

From the Pauline language of "before," "until" and "no longer," Luther derives the concept of the "duration of time" in which the law lasts.[153] Commenting on Galatians 3:23, "kept under restraint until faith should be revealed," Luther conceives of this duration "both in the literal and spiritual sense."[154]

The law lasts until Christ proclaims "what happened historically and temporally" at the bodily advent of Christ—namely, that Christ in his body has overcome the law and its tyranny. This is also what "happens personally and spiritually every day" in a believer who lives in "constant alternation" between two times, "the time of law and the time of grace."[155] In "the time of law," sin is revealed and condemned; in "the time of grace," Christ has acquired liberty

---

147. Steven D. Paulson, "Internal Clarity of Scripture and the Modern World: Luther and Erasmus Revisited," in *Hermeneutica Sacra: Studies of the Interpretation of Holy Scripture in the Sixteenth and Seventeenth Centuries*, ed. Torbjörn Johansson et al., (De Gruyter, 2010), 93.

148. Paulson, "Internal Clarity of Scripture," 93.

149. See Paulson, *Luther's Outlaw God*, 1:5. The prepositions "about," "to," and "for" are Paulson's.

150. Johann Anselm Steiger, "The *communicatio idiomatum* as the Axle and Motor of Luther's Theology," *Lutheran Quarterly* 14, no. 2 (2000): 131.

151. Steiger, "The *communicatio idiomatum*," 131.

152. Mark C. Mattes, "Luther on Justification as Forensic and Effective," in *The Oxford Handbook of Martin Luther's Theology*, ed. Robert Kolb et al., (Oxford University Press, 2014), 266.

153. *LW* 26:317, 340; *WA* 40.1:492, 524. See Jonathan A. Linebaugh, *The Word of the Cross: Reading Paul* (Eerdmans, 2022), 219–20.

154. *LW* 26:317; *WA* 40.1:493.

155. *LW* 26:340; *WA* 40.1:524.

and eternal life for us.[156] We must learn to differentiate between them, Luther clarifies, "not in words but our feelings."[157] The bodily advent of Christ would be of no avail if it were stripped of its contemporary relevance. Christ who was given "once for all at a set time" must be given "every day."[158] Christ cannot be offered except through the word, nor can he be grasped except through faith created by that word. "Christ comes spiritually every day; through the Word of the Gospel faith also comes every day; and when faith is present, our custodian [the law], with his gloomy and grievous work, is also forced to yield."[159] To the extent faith lays hold of the voice of Christ, the voice of the law loses its jurisdiction over us. The simultaneity of the two times in which justified saints live, Jonathan A. Linebaugh notes, "is finally asymmetrical,"[160] as the temporary nature of "the time of the law" gives way to the everlasting character of "the time of grace."[161]

Concerning Romans 10:24, "Christ is the end of the law," Jason D. Lane states, "Necessity is paired with fulfillment. In a real way, Christ fulfills what was necessary under the law. He bears the weight of sin and the law's condemnation and thus silences the law's curse" (Gal 2:20).[162] What is ended is not the law itself but its reign in us. The abolition of the law's reign in us occurs in two ways through the joyous exchange. James Arne Nestingen argues, first, "Christ Jesus takes upon Himself the sinner's sins, the sinner himself or herself, and in a marvelous exchange ... becomes the victim for us so that while He bears our sins and our death, we arise in His righteousness."[163] In Christ, the law's curse is ended in exchange for the gospel's blessing. Where Christ reigns in us by faith, the law's accusatory function ends, and all contraries of justification lose their power. Second, it takes on an eschatological perspective: "The significance of the law is that it points ahead to the shape of life when God completes what he has begun in Christ."[164] God's purpose "that we belong to him" is completed in Christ's redemptive action, yet to be fulfilled in us.[165] Nestingen offers a telling phrase: "The law can only end

---

156. *LW* 26:340–41; *WA* 40.1:524–25.
157. *LW* 26:343; *WA* 40.1:527.
158. *LW* 26:351; *WA* 40.1:538.
159. *LW* 26:351; *WA* 40.1:538.
160. Linebaugh, *Word of the Cross*, 220.
161. *LW* 26:340; *WA* 40.1:526.
162. Jason D. Lane, "That I May Be His Own: The Necessary End of the Law," in *Handing Over the Goods: Determined to Proclaim Nothing but Christ Jesus and Him Crucified; Essays in Honor of James Arne Nestingen*, ed. Steven D. Paulson and Scott L. Keith (1517 Publishing, 2018), 60.
163. James Arne Nestingen, "Speaking of the End to the Law," in *The Necessary Distinction: A Continuing Conversation on Law and Gospel*, ed. Albert B. Collver III et al. (Concordia Publishing House, 2017), 174; also quoted in Lane, "I May Be His," 61.
164. Nestingen, "End to the Law," 174.
165. See *WA* 39.1:349, as cited in Lane, "I May Be His," 60n13: "Cum autem Christus venerit, no solvere, sed implere legem, frustra venit, si nulla sit lex in nobis implenda." I am indebted to Lane's observation.

when it is fulfilled."¹⁶⁶ The law continues its alien work, mortifying the old Adam and his attempts to trust in himself until the final hour. The law reaches, to use Lane's phrase, "its necessary end"¹⁶⁷ in us, in the death of sinful bodies, and the gospel reaches its "necessary end" in us, in the resurrection of bodies. In so far as sin abides, the believer is not beyond law and gospel. So long as we are flesh, we are subject to the deadly—but not dead—ministry of the law that does not save but kills. The law and gospel distinction will cease at the end when sin finally ceases. When this distinction dissolves at death, Christ's joyous exchange of his righteousness for our sin will also dissolve. The righteous identity that faith grasps now will then reach its perfection, where the law's reign is finally ended.

The Christian life on earth is never beyond the law and gospel distinction; its unity can only be spoken of in faith. In the pristine state, law and gospel exist as "a differentiated unity"; they are not opposed to each other. After the fall, the pristine unity of law and gospel is lost. For when the law meets with sin, it is opposed to the gospel. Christ assumes the opposition between the law and the gospel to conquer it for us only if we believe. However, as Bayer writes, "the unity of the law and gospel has not yet been revealed to us."¹⁶⁸ What believers have now is a "paradoxical unity," a predicate of faith; the "original" unity is eschatological and is, to use Jack D. Kilcrease's phrase, "proleptically present"¹⁶⁹ to them by faith. God's purpose to be our God, as disclosed in the first commandment, finds its fulfillment through faith in Christ, partially now but fully then. The "paradoxical" unity gives way to the pristine unity at the end, when all contraries of justification come to an end. Where the "original" unity of the law and the gospel is fully restored, the power of obedience to God is reinstated to its original, pristine state. Althaus elaborates:

> Such faith in the gospel, in spite of the law, fulfills the law in its deepest sense. For the decisive element in the law is the First Commandment. This, however, rests fully on the gospel, that is, in the offer and promise: I am the Lord your God "who both can and will save all who call on him." ... The First Commandment of the law thus demands only that we believe the gospel. ... The First Commandment, when it is fulfilled in faith in Christ, expresses the unity of law and gospel. The original unity is restored by Christ who assumes the distinction between them to overcome it for faith. The opposition between law and gospel in the

---

166. Nestingen, "End to the Law," 174.
167. Lane, "I May Be His," 63.
168. Oswald Bayer, *Theology the Lutheran Way*, ed. and trans. Jeffrey G. Silcock and Mark C. Mattes (Eerdmans, 2007), 192.
169. Jack D. Kilcrease, *Justification by the Word: Restoring "Sola Fide"* (Lexham Academic, 2022), 12.

life of sinful people is only a transitional stage between their original unity and their paradoxical Christian unity in the Christian life. This paradoxical Christian unity consists in the fact that the Christian has not fulfilled God's law and stands under its accusation and condemnation; yet he believes the gospel in spite of it and thus in the midst of his sinful existence fulfills God's First Commandment.[170]

The antinomians derive from Peter's sermon in Acts 2:36–38 the basic premise that repentance ought to be preached from the violation of the Son, not from the violation of the law of Moses, and because of that, they argue, the law in its entirety must be abolished. Luther argues for the contrary, saying, "The law ... always urges and demands perfect fear, love, and trust in God. But no one does this."[171] So God sends his Son, who in our humanity submits himself to the verdict of the law to free us from the curse of the law (Gal 3:13). God commands us to receive Christ, the "Fulfiller of the Law."[172] Yet unbelievers kill and crucify him. "Therefore," Luther adduces, "the Law is not weakened or abrogated by this violation of the Son but is increased and strengthened all the more, for it is written [John 3:18]: 'Whoever does not believe is condemned already.'"[173] The ungodly world, Luther contends, sins in two ways. First, sinful people are disobedient to the law, especially the first commandment, the spring of all the rest. Second, they refuse to apply to themselves Christ's fulfillment of the law. Both amount to the same thing, for the first commandment enjoins us to believe the gospel and place our trust in the Son. The proclamation of Christ's passion and death (*ex violatione filii*) rather than the violation of God's law (*ex violatione legis*) as the basis of repentance, such as we find in antinomianism, opposes the Son to the law, and is a view that Luther himself opposes. Since the Son has been bestowed as a fulfiller of the law, the real violation of the Son is unbelief in him. But rejecting the Son's saving work is indeed a violation of the law, especially considering the first commandment, which demands nothing but faith in Christ, the substance of both Old and New Testaments. Accordingly, it is the law, not Christ, that condemns unbelief. The preaching of repentance based on the rejection of the Son, for Luther, does not constitute preaching of the gospel but of the law.

In rebutting the antinomian thesis, Luther reinforces that "when the unbelief in the Son is emphasized, the law is given double emphasis."

> The violation of the Son—that is, unbelief in the Son—not only fails to fulfill the First Table [of the Ten Commandments] but transgresses

---

170. Althaus, *Theology of Martin Luther*, 265–66.
171. *LW* 73:87; *WA* 39.1:383.
172. *LW* 73:87; *WA* 39.1:384.
173. *LW* 73:87; *WA* 39.1:384.

it doubly: it does not remove the demand of the Law but actually establishes and sharpens it. In the Old Testament what is especially required is the fulfillment of the First Table. In the New Testament what is especially required is belief in the Son. Therefore, those who do not believe in the Son sin doubly: first, against the God who requires perfect obedience to the Law. Now, since no saint was ever able to render this, God sent His own Son to fulfill the Law for them [Rom 8:3–4]. [Second,] those who do not receive this ineffable blessing sin terribly against the One who brings the remedy for the terrors of the Law, for sin and death, and they again crucify the Son of God for themselves (Hebrews 6:6).[174]

The gospel, the antinomians argue, could cause us to recognize sin, as Romans 2:4 declares: "Do you not know that God's kindness is meant to lead you to repentance?"[175] Luther does not deny that repentance can come from the knowledge of the cross of Christ. But this in no wise means that the law is abolished. Luther does not adopt, in Althaus's rendering, the "either-or of repentance, either through the law or through the gospel. On the contrary, the gospel bears the law within itself and the proclamation of the gospel itself is also a proclamation of the law."[176] Here Luther broadens his understanding of the law, affirming that anything that exposes the opposite of justification is law, irrespective of its source, either law or gospel; in Luther's own words:

> But since the law is really whatever performs the office of the law—whatever terrifies, whatever accuses the conscience, whatever exposes ingratitude, lusts, and sin, whether it is in the Gospel or in Moses, it makes no difference in the end where any of these things that convict sins are taken from.[177]

What Althaus says about Luther is substantially correct. However, his phrase "the proclamation of the gospel itself *is* also a proclamation of the law" needs clarification. When repentance arises through the preaching of the gospel, it is really the law itself that is causing this—that is, it is the gospel doing the alien work of the law. In this sense, it is correct to say that the gospel "bears the law within itself and that the proclamation of the gospel itself *can* also be a proclamation of the law," because the proclamation of the gospel *is not* always a proclamation of the law. Most times it is pure gospel, doing its proper work. When

---

174. *LW* 73:88; *WA* 39:1.386.
175. *WA* 39.1:400, 536, as cited in Althaus, *Theology of Martin Luther*, 262.
176. Althaus, *Theology of Martin Luther*, 262.
177. *WA* 39.1:535.2–5; also cited in Jeffrey G. Silcock, "Law, Gospel, and Repentance in Luther's Antinomian Disputations," *Luther-Bulletin* 16 (2007): 49, Silcock's translation.

the gospel, however, brings about contrition, it is its alien work, not its proper work, which is to offer and bestow forgiveness. Law and gospel are inseparably one yet must always be distinguished; the former precedes the latter, not only in God's economy of salvation, but also, and especially in our preaching. The law must first create despair in us in order that we are ready for the gospel to create faith. But the gospel's proper office does not perform two contradictory activities, first creating despair in us in order to create faith in us; rather it always leads to comfort and faith. When Luther does occasionally say that the gospel can lead to repentance, it is not the gospel itself doing this, but the gospel acting in the office of the law. To say that the gospel bears the negative function of the law is not to deny the law but to confirm it even more. This is an important argument that Luther uses against the antinomians, since they held that precisely because the gospel can do the work of the law, the law is not necessary! However, Luther rightly says that even if the gospel can bring about contrition, it is not really the gospel itself that is doing this (because it is not the gospel's proper work) but the law, because the gospel contains the law within itself. The law can be in the gospel, but the gospel cannot be in the law—that is, the law cannot contain the gospel. When that happens, the law functions as gospel and, indeed, becomes the gospel. This leads to what is sometimes called legalism.

The proclamation of Christ as our example performs the law's function of revealing sins. It magnifies sin, urging us to sin more and more,[178] in order to lead us to see just how sinful we really are. In that sense, we can also say that the law reveals sin, though it does not remove it. Likewise, the proclamation of Christ as redeemer can perform the same function as does the law, revealing to us the disease of sin, "which," as Althaus suggests, "precedes it and is presupposed by it"; it also exposes the sin of ingratitude or rebellion against the gracious God of the gospel.[179] The remorse we feel, in Jeffrey G. Silcock's formulation, "is not caused by the gospel [whose proper office is to console] but the gospel functioning as the law."[180] Repentance is not created by the gospel itself but rather by the fact that the good news of Christ's death for us highlights the seriousness of our sins. Unless our ailment is exposed, we will not be able to see the need for its remedy. The office of the gospel presupposes its opposite, the office of the law. Just as the cure is hidden in the diagnosis, so too the gospel is hidden in the law.

God is creative in bringing people to himself through various ways and rhetorical passages such as Romans 2:4. Luther finds support of this in St. Bernard, who teaches, "A hardened heart, which is moved by neither threats nor promises, must be enticed to repentance through divine gifts and promises, and it should be impressed with the Passion and death of Christ, which He took

---

178. See Paul in Romans 7.
179. Althaus, *Theology of Martin Luther*, 263.
180. Silcock, "Law, Gospel, and Repentance," 55.

upon Himself out of sheer love to free the human race from sin and death to which it was subject."[181] Luther cites the story of Korah's rebellion, in which he sins against God by illegitimately assuming the priesthood, in which Korah's sons entreated him with teary eyes to recollect the kindness God manifested to the people of Israel—but all to no avail. Luther does not disavow "the rhetoric of the gospel"[182] to persuade people to repentance, even when the outcome is contrary to its intended goal. For God is not bound by any extraneous factors, and is free to lead us to repentance, either through the law or "the rhetoric of the gospel. . . . It does not matter by what means you come. But we do not abolish the Law because of these."[183] If law is abolished, sin is abolished; "but if sin is abolished, then Christ has also been done away with for there would no longer be any need for him."[184]

Luther concedes that no law moves the heart deeper than this vision of God's kindness. The realization that we have shown disdain and contempt for the promise and grace of God pierces our hearts more deeply than the knowledge that we have violated one of the Ten Commandments. The awareness of sinning against the goodness of God with ingratitude is created by the gospel that does the law's alien work, not by the gospel whose proper office is to console and save. This, Althaus states, "can only be explained in this way: the crucified Christ also bears my sin when I sin against his cross. Or also: The fact that I become and remain guilty of sinning against his love does not change the fact that he has come to save guilty men. Thus the pain of repentance is both preserved and set aside in the joy of faith."[185] The gospel thus makes us guilty (the law's alien function), causing us to feel the negative power of the law, and rescues us from it (the gospel's proper function). The same Jesus Christ against whom we sin with ingratitude does not cease to be our mediator and comforter in times of trials and afflictions. In the light of the gospel, we become ever more aware of the opposite of justification—namely, the horror of sin under the law, and the terror of wrath apart from Christ. Whoever is made aware of this will plunge into despair. Its remedy is, Luther writes, "certainly not from the law, but from the kindness of God, which has become even more painful for him than the law itself."[186]

Where does someone find relief when neither law nor the kindness of God can help, as each in its own way terrifies them increasingly more until they are cast down? The way out of this great distress is not to remain where the law has

---

181. Bernard, *On Consideration*, in *Patrologiae Cursus Completus: Series Latina*, ed. J. P. Migne, 231 vols. (Paris: Garnier Fratres, 1844–64), 1.2.3, 182:730–31; Cistercian Fathers Series (Cistercian Publications, 1970), 37:28, as cited in *LW* 73:102; *WA* 39.1:401.
182. *LW* 73:102; *WA* 39.1:400.
183. *LW* 73:106; *WA* 39.1:406.
184. *WA* 39.1:546, 348f., 317, 535, 546, as cited in Althaus, *Theology of Martin Luther*, 257–58.
185. Althaus, *Theology of Martin Luther*, 265.
186. *LW* 73:192; *WA* 39.1:536.

placed us, which leads us to utter despair. Consolation rather belongs to those who are grasped by the gospel after the law has done its work in leading us to repentance. Such comfort is what the antinomians cannot offer, Silcock explains, "because . . . they have already used the gospel to bring people to repentance. Therefore, they can hardly expect it to also function as a source of comfort. This is why Luther says that their method of preaching will never allow them to console consciences in times of grave spiritual attack."[187] Does it matter how a person arrives at repentance? For Luther, it is crucial—and so he blames the antinomian pastors for the suicide of the jurist Johann Krause because they used the gospel to create in him an awareness of his sins and then had no comfort left to console him when he did finally come to repentance.[188] Consequently, the place where comfort is located now becomes the source of terror. The antinomian logic entails

> a foolish self-contradiction, for using the *violatio filii* instead of the *violatio legis* in preaching repentance, they are making the cross function as law so that it becomes a terrifying accusation. Although they deny the law a role in repentance, they effectively bring it back by holding that the same gospel that forgives also exposes sin and accuses the conscience through presenting it with Christ's suffering and death. However, there are two problems with this. On the one hand, the Decalogue loses its character as instruction; on the other hand the message of the cross is in danger of being changed from the gospel into a new law.[189]

Restored to the Pristine Image
Christ's Identity Is Ours

Luther conceives God's pristine image primarily in terms of our righteous relationship with God: "Man was created in the image of God, in the image of righteousness, of course, of divine holiness and truth, but in such a way that he

---

187. Silcock, "Law, Gospel, and Repentance," 51; cf. *LW* 73:192; *WA* 30.1:537.
188. *LW* 73:192–93; *WA* 30.1:537. "Already in the state of depression after losing his wife and two newborn daughters in a tragic delivery, Kraus finally yielded to the cardinal's pressure and consented to receive the Sacrament under one kind. He then fell into deep despair and terrors of conscience and killed himself with a knife eight days later on the Feast of All Saints" (see 193n.131). See also *LW* 26:195; *WA* 40.1:320, where Luther cites Krause's suicide as an instance of the danger of bad conscience: "This happened in the year 1527 to the pathetic Dr. Krause, in Halle, who said: 'I have denied Christ. Therefore He is now standing in the presence of the Father and accusing me.' Taken captive by the tricks of the devil, he had become so convinced of this notion that he would not permit it to be driven out of him by any exhortation or any divine promises. Thus he despaired and committed suicide most miserably."
189. Silcock, "Law, Gospel, and Repentance," 55.

could lose it."[190] Elsewhere, he writes, "Original sin is the loss of righteousness, or the deprivation of it, just as blindness is the deprivation of sight."[191] The image of God is intrinsically linked to Luther's idea of "passive righteousness," that which establishes our identity as a gift. Humans are "righteous from the beginning"[192] and are capable of divine relationality. Nature and grace interpenetrate in the state of innocence, but not so in the state of the fall. Luther avers, "Righteousness was not a gift which came from without, separate from man's nature, but that it was truly part of his nature, so that it was Adam's nature to love God, believe God, to know God, etc."[193] The pristine "form" of this righteous relationship with God includes "a life that is wholly godly," "content with God's favor," "supreme bliss," and "freedom."[194] These natural endowments constitutive of the image of God are contingent and determined by our response to God. They, Luther avows, are completely lost, without remainder, due to disobedience: "This is My image, by which we are living, just as God lives. But if you sin, you will lose this image, and you will die."[195] Luther concludes that sin has marred everything: "From the image of God, from the knowledge of God, from the knowledge of all the other creatures, and from a very honorable nakedness man has fallen into blasphemies, into hatred, into contempt of God, even more, into enmity against God."[196] The preceding analysis sheds light on the Second Article concerning our fallen human condition, which Luther sums up in two words: lost and condemned. The image lost in Adam but restored in Christ is indeed, Luther teaches, "the image of holiness, righteousness and truth," that of its original state.[197] The lost image can be restored "through the Word and the Holy Spirit,"[198] partially now, but fully at the consummation. Thus, Luther holds that "man in this life is the simple material of God for the form of his future life . . . when the image of God will have been remolded and perfected."[199]

God's work differs from human work; in Luther's terms, "It is God's nature to make something out of nothing; hence one who is not yet nothing, out of him God cannot make anything. Man, however, makes something else out of that which exists; but this has no value whatever." Only those who are reduced to nothing become "God's material" by which God's saving purpose is fulfilled

---

190. *LW* 34:177.
191. *LW* 1:114; *WA* 42:86.
192. *LW* 1:90; *WA* 42:68.
193. *LW* 1:165; *WA* 42:124.
194. *LW* 1:63; *WA* 42:471.
195. *LW* 1:63; *WA* 42:471.
196. *LW* 1:142; *WA* 42:361.
197. *LW* 34:194.
198. *LW* 2:141; *WA* 42:361.
199. *LW* 34:139–40.

in them.[200] Justification occurs *ex nihilo*, purely by grace, not by any preexistent salvific quality we inherit or acquire, but by something outside us (*extra nobis*)—namely, the "alien righteousness" of Christ, which Luther considers as a remedy to "the original righteousness lost in Adam."[201] In Stephen J. Chester's estimation, "Salvation reinstates what creation was intended to be so that we relate to God in the manner first intended [as a righteous person].... The discontinuity stems from the fact that through sin what was intended for creation was so grievously and entirely lost."[202] The justifying love of the cross remakes us perfectly righteous, as is the Son before God; it also reconstitutes us as authentically human, people to whom the true integrity lost in Adam is restored. The "for me" is the application of the efficacy of Christ's cross to the sinful identity, to create a righteous identity via Christ's resurrection.

The death and resurrection of Christ, in Linebaugh's assessment, constitutes two movements in God's economy of salvation: "The movement from the state of creation to the state of fall is the movement from life to death; the movement from sin to salvation, conversely, is the movement from death to life. Within and across these ruptures, salvation is as radical as death and resurrection."[203] Pauline language of dying and rising in Christ, to which Luther appeals, underscores salvation as "a radical discontinuity"[204] with the old creature in exchange for a "reconstitution"[205] of a new creature. God's regenerative action begins with the annihilation of the old creature through the cross, followed by the animation of the new creature through the resurrection. Luther holds, "To be born anew, one must consequently first die and then be raised up with the Son of Man. To die, I say, means to feel death at hand."[206] Justification thus consists of the death of the old identity and resurrection of the new identity, a movement of leaving the self to cleaving to Christ. Chester captures Luther's exposition of Galatians 2:20, "It is no longer I who live but Christ":

> Salvation depends not on perfecting the life that [Paul] already had, but on living an alien life. Thus, the Christian has Christ's righteousness through participation in him, but that participation does not work on

---

200. *LW* 14:163; *WA* 18:497.
201. *LW* 31:298–99.
202. Stephen J. Chester, "It is No Longer I Who Live: Justification by Faith and Participation in Christ in Martin Luther's Exegesis of Galatians," *New Testament Studies* 55, no. 3 (2009): 329n57, https://doi.org/10.1017/S002868850900023X.
203. Jonathan A. Linebaugh, "'The Speech of the Dead': Identifying the No Longer and Now Living 'I' of Galatians 2.20," *New Testament Studies* 66, no. 1 (2020): 87, https://doi.org/10.1017/S0028688519000365.
204. Stephen J. Chester, *Reading Paul with the Reformers: Reconciling Old and New Perspectives* (Eerdmans, 2017), 192n52.
205. John M. G. Barclay, *Paul and the Gift* (Eerdmans, 2017), 568.
206. *LW* 31:55.

the basis of a transformation of the self of the Christian. It works rather on the basis of the leaving behind and abandonment of that self.[207]

The simultaneity of saint and sinner seems to imply that nothing changes in a believer since he remains a sinner, though justified, and Christ's righteousness remains external to himself. Such rendering ignores the Pauline christological phrase "in Christ Jesus," the locus where change occurs. The phrase underscores the new relationship with God under which believers are placed, one that is no longer governed by the old self but by Christ. The relational rather than localized nature of "in" means "next to" or "in close relationship to" Christ. The Christian no longer lives "in himself," but "in Christ Jesus," the new reality from which they acquire a new self, not one that stands by itself, but one that stands outside itself in Christ.

This is what happens to Paul, whose life is hidden not in his person but in Christ. He must abandon his old life ("no longer I"), for to remain in it is despair and death. He must embrace the Christ life ("but Christ"), which is hope and life. Whoever trusts in Christ exists not in himself but in Christ, with whom he is united, thus having "the same righteousness as he."[208] Being transposed to the realm of "in Christ," he no longer sees himself as separate from Christ or Christ as separate from him; they are distinguished but inseparably one. Believers and Christ are one person: "You are so cemented to Christ that He and you are as one person, which cannot be separated but remains attached to Him forever."[209] "Through faith in Christ," Luther affirms, "Christ's righteousness becomes our righteousness and all that he has becomes ours; rather he himself becomes ours."[210] Faith unites us with Christ, in whom we live, not in ourselves but outside ourselves; in Pannenberg's assessment, "*Within ourselves we experience ourselves as sinners, but outside ourselves, in the ecstasis of faith, we participate in Jesus' righteousness, and therefore we are justified.* We are justified outside ourselves in Christ."[211] Pannenberg expands on the power of faith in the reconstitution of our identity through Christ's attachment to us, thereby making him and his righteousness ours:

> Our personal existence gets reconstituted outside ourselves in Christ, and thus the righteousness of Christ remains no longer outside ourselves as Christians. But as Christians we are what we are only in faith, outside ourselves in Christ. . . . In the ecstatic act of faith, Christ is no longer

---

207. Chester, "No Longer I," 329.
208. *LW* 31:156.
209. *LW* 26:168; *WA* 40.1:285.
210. *LW* 31:298.
211. Pannenberg, "Luther's Contribution to Spirituality," 286, Pannenberg's italics.

something alien to us and in that sense outside ourselves. To the contrary, in the act of faith we are one with Christ, and his righteousness and life are ours. We receive a new identity, but we do not possess it separately, in our separate existence apart from Christ, but only "in Christ," which is to say in faith that unites us with Christ, with the Christ "outside ourselves."[212]

Forensic images of justification must be balanced with its affective aspects. Luther's doctrine of justification finds its expression in the affective language of a "royal marriage," a jubilant occasion in which Christ (the groom) fills the bride's (the sinner) heart with overflowing joy.[213] In marriage, the groom (Christ) speaks to the bride (believer), "I am yours" (effective vow), and she responds, "I am yours" (passive faith).[214] The faith response is an effect of the Spirit's effectual calling, not by reason or free will, but by hearing Christ's voice; in Wengert's description, "the true lover's voice."[215] We humbly confess "I believe that I cannot believe, but the Holy Spirit" has rendered effectual the union of faith. "Faith," says Wengert, is "an event, what happens when we hear the lover's voice and fall in love."[216] The gospel announces its forensic truth in such a way that we are truly righteous. What God declares is effective; they are juxtaposed, not opposed. Forensic promise does not denote anticipation of that which is to come. Bayer writes, "The promise is not only an announcement that will only be fulfilled in the future. It is a valid and powerful promise and pledge that takes immediate and present effect."[217] Forensic truth is logically prior to, and subsequently leads to, Christ's union with believers. Faith, created by the promise, unites us with Christ. "In a word," Kilcrease summarizes, "Christ is for believers [forensic] before he is in them [union]."[218] He adds:

> The union of Christ and believers through justification mirrors marriage, where there are both wedding vows (forensic promise) and a consummation (mystical union). Implicit in Luther's marriage analogy, it could be observed that the vows made at the wedding are subsequently guaranteed and made concrete by the bride and groom's physical mutual

---

212. Pannenberg, "Luther's Contribution to Spirituality," 287.
213. *LW* 31:356–57.
214. *LW* 31:300–301.
215. Wengert, *Martin Luther's Catechisms*, 61.
216. Wengert, *Martin Luther's Catechisms*, 61–62.
217. Mark C. Mattes, *The Role of Justification in Contemporary Theology* (Fortress, 2004), 3–4n2, where he quotes Oswald Bayer, *Living by Faith: Justification and Sanctification*, trans. Geoffrey W. Bromiley (Eerdmans, 2003), 51–52.
218. Kilcrease, *Justification by the Word*, 211.

self-gift to one another. To give one's very self to another is to give the ultimate pledge of one's loyalty and trustworthiness to the other.[219]

Faith's object is the Lord Christ who has won for us a joyous exchange of his righteousness for sin, life for death, and heaven for hell. Faith grasps everything Christ is (person) and has achieved in his vicarious humanity (properties). Union with Christ means not only "Christ's righteousness" becomes ours but "he himself becomes ours."[220] Luther does not drive a wedge between the properties or qualities of righteousness Christ possesses and Christ the righteous person, for we cannot have one without the other. We appear before God wrapped in Christ's righteous person, who gives us himself and all that he has. Christ's identity becomes ours so that we who are in him are found pleasing to him, just as he is. Any exclusive focus on the properties in justification suggests a mechanistic and impersonal means of appropriating salvation, a view Luther does not share. Christ's righteousness (the property) through a joyous exchange becomes ours but not abstracted from Christ (the person). Just as faith derives its value from its object (person), so the benefits of Christ receive their virtue from the benefactor (person) who confers it. Faith is bound up not with the proposition about Christ but with the person of Christ who is given "for me." What God gives is God's own self, not merely some objects or signs of his presence. "With Luther," Cary writes aptly, "what the Gospel has always done is give us God in person."[221] He expands, "Faith in the Gospel saves us because the grace signified by the Gospel of Jesus Christ is nothing less that Christ himself, which is to say God in person, with all that he is and all that he has, including salvation, righteousness, holiness, blessing, and eternal life."[222]

The "alien righteousness" swallows up original sin; it is "instilled in us" *ex nihilo*, purely by grace, to enable us to produce "proper righteousness."[223] The instillation does not occur "all at once, but it begins, makes progress, and is finally perfected at the end through death."[224] The second and "proper righteousness" or "actual righteousness" flows from the "first and alien righteousness."[225] We alone cannot work the second; but rather we work with the first kind to work the second.[226] "While the Father inwardly draws us to Christ," says Luther, "Christ [who lives in us] daily drives out the old Adam more and more in accordance

---

219. Kilcrease, *Justification by the Word*, 211.
220. *LW* 31:298.
221. Cary, *Meaning of Protestant Theology*, 334.
222. Cary, *Meaning of Protestant Theology*, 340.
223. *LW* 31:299.
224. *LW* 31:299.
225. *LW* 31:298–99.
226. *LW* 31:299.

God's Most Earnest Purpose in Redemption

with the extent to which faith and knowledge of Christ grow."[227] Victory hinges on whose lordship we have. The old Adam reigns when it is edified by "active righteousness," in which case Christ is no longer the Lord. Where Christ and his righteousness reign as Lord, the old Adam and his works are reduced to naught. The gospel by which we live re-creates us by the fruits of the cross so that "the old Adam, who is especially edified by goods works, is crucified."[228] We are most crucified when our old Adam is most crucified; conversely, our old Adam is most dead when we are most edified. All contraries—sin, death, curse, and hell—die through the Christ who lives in us, communicating to us the fruits of redemption through which we are reconstituted. We are not our authentic selves when we live by the flesh and works of the law; conversely, we are most truly ourselves when we rely on Christ, who lives in us by his righteousness.

The new identity is no longer self-governing; it dies to everything within, but "lives excentrically to himself"[229] by an alien righteousness that is ours by grace alone. Justification does not consist in living the old life but a life of discontinuity with the previous existence. "There is," in Daphne Hampson's assessment, "no linear progress from being a sinner to being justified. It is not that that which is given in creation is transformed through grace. It is only through a discontinuity, through repentance and failure, that in response to the good news of the gospel the human being can come to gain a sense of himself through trusting not in himself but in God."[230] Believers are in the perpetual mode of living out the baptismal identity: dying to sin and rising to righteousness, the two inherent realities of a repentant life. The Pauline antithesis of "no longer I but Christ" means the believer lives in a paradoxical tension between two seemingly contradictory modes of existence, yet the transposition from the old self to the new self is made possible by the promise that faith grasps. This movement entails a break with the former "lords" (sin, law, wrath, and curse) so that the risen Christ alone becomes our Lord. Christ buried the old, sinful identity in his grave, to give us a new, righteous identity in his resurrection. "The Christian life," Mark C. Mattes suggests, "isn't about what I do but what I undergo. It's not about accumulation of merit and development of virtue. Instead, we move from virtue to grace, from progress to mercy, and from self-improvement to resurrection."[231] The "I" of the old nature is dead because it is buried with Christ; the "I" of the new nature is vivified by faith in Christ. The "I" of the fallen self, the object of

---

227. *LW* 31:299.
228. *LW* 31:55.
229. Daphne Hampson, *Christian Contradictions: The Structures of Lutheran and Catholic Thought* (Cambridge University Press, 2001), 12.
230. Hampson, *Christian Contradictions*, 101.
231. Mark C. Mattes, "Theses on the Captivated and Liberated Will," in *Lutheran Preaching? Law and Gospel Proclamation Today*, ed. Matthew C. Harrison and John T. Pless (Concordia Publishing House, 2023), 238.

re-creation, is identical to the "I" of the innocent self, that of the original creation. In justification, God re-creates us, says Marc Cortez, by "*redeeming*, rather than *replacing*, fallen humanity."²³² Christ's redemption has restored fallen humanity to its original shape, stripped of the perversity of self-incurvature, and reinstated to creation's original objective, that of a blissful communion with God, without any deprivation of the power of living for God. The old "I" in the fallen humanity exists in tension with the new "I" in the restored humanity; they are not identical. The sinful self exists "in us," and the righteous self exists "in Christ." The two selves are opposed to each other as nature and grace are due to the fall. But the justified humanity and the created humanity, though distinct, are consubstantial—of one piece. Linebaugh sums up the matter well: "In a sense, the no longer and now living selves are not identical: the 'I' *is* in another as gift. And yet, the 'I' who lives by grace is also the 'I' who was, is, and will be loved by 'the Son of God who loved me and gave himself for me.'"²³³

Human need for validation perdures until we are seized by the knowledge of God's "incongruous" gracious acceptance in the cross. Theologically, the gospel creates our new identity and shields us from the power of nothingness and any negation of our justified status. Any attempt to construct our identity through the performance of law magnifies the lordship of self, and sins against the God of the first commandment. Luther writes, "Whoever holds that our works shape and create us, or that we are the creature of our own work, blasphemes. For it is as blasphemous as saying: I am my own god and I created myself.... Likewise, it is blasphemous to seek one's justification in works."²³⁴ The righteousness of works, in all forms, Luther cautions, is "the source of all idolatry."²³⁵ The new identity in Christ is God's gift, just as the created identity in its pristine form is. It is not discovered by human efforts, but disclosed to us by divine grace, relieving us of the great burden of having to construct our own sense of worth to seek approval from God and others. Bayer writes, "In faith they live outside themselves in God, freed from having to find their own identity or achieve self-fulfillment."²³⁶ However, those who do not possess the sure knowledge of God's approval will seek elsewhere for it. Psychologically, people still seek satisfaction, often in wrong places, and in some extreme cases are in bondage to various voices for recognition. The tension between theological validation and psychological validation still remains and cannot be transcended in this world. However, its force could be reduced, not by reverting inward to the self for aid, but by turning outward and

---

232. Marc Cortez, *Christological Anthropology in Historical Perspective: Ancient and Contemporary Approaches to Theological Anthropology* (Zondervan, 2016), 95, Cortez's italics.

233. Linebaugh, "Speech of the Dead," 87.

234. *WA* 39.1:283.9, as quoted in Hans J. Iwand, *The Righteousness of Faith according to Luther*, ed. Virgil F. Thompson, trans. Randi H. Lundell (Wipf and Stock, 2008), 61–62.

235. *LW* 17:114; *WA* 31.2:351.

236. Bayer, *Living by Faith*, 39.

clinging to the creative power of God's promise, through which the compulsive drive for approval through self-induced or other humanly devised means may subside. Our identity is not definitively determined either by the self or others, by moral transformation, or by emotive piety. As Piotr J. Małysz saliently writes, "Faith, which takes God at his word, is what constitutes human dignity for Luther. To believe is nothing other than to receive oneself from God's justifying act. This faith is what makes one human; it restores one to Paradise and creates one anew."[237] God's judgment by which we live crucifies the old identity and its self-curved attempt to prove its status before God. Assurance of faith comes not by looking for the evidence or fruits of effective justification, but by hearing God's word. "Whoever I am" is answered by God's justifying verdict *extra nos*; as Dietrich Bonhoeffer affirms, "Thou knowest, O God, I am thine."[238] Thus Luther declares:

> And this is our foundation: The Gospel commands us to look, not at our good deeds or perfection but at God Himself as He promises, and at Christ Himself, the Mediator. . . . And this is the reason why our theology is certain: it snatches us away from ourselves and places us outside ourselves, so that we do not depend on our own strength, conscience, experience, person, or works, but depend on that which is outside ourselves, that is, on the promise and truth of God, which cannot deceive.[239]

The certainty of faith lies not in us, but outside us, in God. "The monstrosity of uncertainty"[240] is abolished by the reliability of God's promise to which we cling. Christ's identity as God's Son by nature is ours in a joyous exchange by grace. The effective word of imputation makes us God's children, despite often feeling otherwise due to the old flesh that remains. The gift of identity, that we are God's and in the state of grace, is made certain in our hearts by the Holy Spirit. The next chapter explores this in depth.

---

237. Piotr J. Małysz, "Martin Luther's Trinitarian Hermeneutic of Freedom," in *Oxford Research Encyclopedia of Religion*, published March 29, 2017, https://doi.org/10.1093/acrefore/9780199340378.013.355.

238. See Dietrich Bonhoeffer, "Who Am I?," as quoted in Oswald Bayer, "Justification: Basis and Boundary of Theology," in *By Faith Alone: Essays on Justification in Honor of Gerhard O. Forde*, ed. Joseph A. Burgess and Marc Kolden (Eerdmans, 2004), 85.

239. *LW* 26:387; *WA* 40.1:589.

240. *LW* 26:387; *WA* 40.1:589.

CHAPTER FIVE

God's Most Earnest Purpose in Sanctification

THE THIRD ARTICLE offers the grammar of the Holy Spirit; in Albrecht Peters's terms, "The Holy Spirit is like a poor lute-player who knows how to play but one song"—namely, Christ and what he has done for us.[1] As already stated in chapter 2, there abides in God's inner life a relational dynamism in which the Father gives, the Son receives, and the Holy Spirit reciprocates; all three persons work together as one God in his economy of salvation. God's "omnipotent love" revealed in the Son's suffering of God-forsakenness is, to borrow Christine Helmer's phrase, "the one eternal sermon of the Father" that the Spirit preaches to us;[2] yet there is only one preacher, as they are one God. Christology and pneumatology are basic to soteriology. What Christ acquires for us, an aspect of his receptivity of the Father's will, the Holy Spirit impresses on his own children, constituting them as the beneficiaries of God's fatherly goodness in Christ. Luther avers, "Without the witness of the Holy Spirit it would be hard to believe that a poor human being is destined to be a son of God and a fellow heir with Christ."[3] When theology begins with the Holy Spirit, all that we hold fast to—free will, reason, creaturely achievements, human righteousness—perishes as our foundation. The Third Article indicates a radical shift in subject, from the "I," who confesses that he "cannot believe in Jesus Christ, my Lord," toward the Holy Spirit, who grants the gift of faith. The Holy Spirit is the subject of God's sanctifying actions *ex nihilo* summed up in the verbs "calls," "enlightens," "sanctifies," and "preserves."[4] Unlike the first two articles, the structure of the third is slightly modified. Instead of beginning with faith ("I believe"), it begins with our inability to believe ("I believe that . . . I cannot believe"). John T. Pless and Robert Kolb note that the structure replaces the subjective response with the objective activities of the Holy Spirit, culminating in the eschatological verification of what was begun in

---

1. Albrecht Peters, *Commentary on Luther's Catechisms: Creed*, trans. Thomas H. Trapp (Concordia Publishing House, 2011), 256.
2. Christine Helmer, *The Trinity and Martin Luther: A Study on the Relationship Between Genre, Language and the Trinity in Luther's Works, 1523–1546* (von Zabern, 1999; rev. ed., Lexham, 2017), 237.
3. *LW* 22:88; *WA* 46:612.
4. "The Large Catechism," *BC*, 355.

justification.[5] In Christoph Schwöbel's assessment, "[The Spirit's work] comprises the whole dynamic of God's Trinitarian action. In the Spirit's work the activity of the Father in creation and the work of the Son in reconciliation are actualized, made present and directed towards their future perfection."[6]

The ministry of the Holy Spirit is eschatologically oriented, bringing God's creative and redemptive works to their ultimate consummation.[7] Creation and redemption are accomplished, but the Holy Spirit is incessantly active in his sanctifying work until the last day. Luther states, "For this purpose he has appointed a community on earth, through which he speaks and does all his work."[8] The church, Timothy J. Wengert notes, is the Holy Spirit's "workshop," indicated by the word "gathers."[9] In *Against the Heavenly Prophets*, Luther distinguishes between "salvation achieved and won" and salvation "distributed and given to us."[10] The benefits acquired by the justifying action of the cross are conveyed to us through the created forms in which the word appears. The Spirit "first leads us into his holy community, placing us in the church's lap, where he preaches to us and brings us to Christ."[11] In the church, he begins his work and daily increases holiness through baptism and the Lord's Supper, until perfection is reached at the eschaton. Faith in Christ grants us a righteous status before God (justification), though sin still remains in us; it also gives us "a different, new, clean heart" (sanctification);[12] in Kirsi I Stjerna's formulation, "Holiness, justification, and freedom lend themselves thus as inter-exchangeable words to describe what happens when God encounters the human being in the ways only the Spirit can facilitate."[13] Sanctification defines who we are: set apart by the Holy Spirit to be the temporal object of God's fatherly love in Christ, and the righteous identity restored in Christ reaches its culmination at the eschaton when the Holy Spirit will have wholly sanctified us. Of the Three Articles, Luther considers the Third Article the "most important" one upon which the others rest.[14]

---

5. John T. Pless, *Praying Luther's Small Catechism: The Pattern of Sound Words* (Concordia Publishing House, 2016), 48; Robert Kolb, *Teaching God's Children His Teaching: A Guide for the Study of Luther's Catechism*, new ed. (Concordia Seminary, 2012), 96.

6. Christoph Schwöbel, "The Triune God of Grace: Trinitarian Thinking in the Theology of the Reformers," in *The Christian Understanding of God Today*, ed. James M. Byrne (Columba, 1993), 54.

7. Mickey Leland Mattox, "Luther's Interpretation of Scripture: Biblical Understanding in Trinitarian Shape," in Dennis Bielfeldt et al., *The Substance of the Faith: Luther's Doctrinal Theology for Today*, ed. Paul R. Hinlicky (Fortress, 2008), 21.

8. "The Large Catechism," *BC*, 439.

9. Timothy J. Wengert, *Martin Luther's Catechisms: Forming the Faith* (Fortress, 2009), 63.

10. *LW* 40:213.

11. "The Large Catechism," *BC*, 435–36.

12. "The Smalcald Articles," *BC*, 325.

13. Kirsi I Stjerna, *Lutheran Theology: A Grammar of Faith* (T&T Clark, 2021), 105. See also Naomichi Masaki, "The Church," in *Luther's Large Catechism with Annotations and Contemporary Applications*, ed. John T. Pless and Larry M. Vogel (Concordia Publishing House, 2022), 432.

14. *LW* 43:24.

Faith as the Holy Spirit's Creation
"I Believe That I Cannot Believe"

Like in the first two articles, Luther personalizes his confession of the third. The individual "me" is prior to the "Christian church." The Holy Spirit richly blesses "me," Luther says, "just as" he does all the saints.[15] Pless paraphrases:

> Confession of inability: "I believe that I cannot..."
> Giver: "but the Holy Spirit has called me..."
> Gift: "...enlightened me with His gifts, sanctified and kept me in true faith..."
> Outcome: "On the last day [the Holy Spirit will raise me and all the dead and will give to me and all believers in Christ eternal life]."
> Faith: "This is most certainly true."[16]

The phrase "not by my own reason or strength" from the Third Article corresponds to the phrase "without any merits or worthiness on my part"[17] in the first. "Both phrases," Peters says, "serve as a bridge and are held together by the broad arch that stretches from the creation to the new creation."[18] Creation *ex nihilo* is analogous to new creation *ex nihilo*: both occur by divine agency, independently of any human actions. Just as we do nothing to create or re-create ourselves, so too we do nothing to create faith. This is explicitly borne out, Miikka Ruokanen contends, in Luther's *Bondage of the Will*. He sums up the matter well:

> [There] is a theologically extremely important analogy between Luther's understanding of God's first creation and his "second creation" or "new birth," the justification of the sinner. This analogy strongly unites Luther's Christological and Pneumatological doctrine of grace with the creative work of the first person of the Holy Trinity, the Father. The human being "did nothing to create himself/herself"; in a similar way he/she cannot do anything to "recreate" or "to give birth" to him/herself, to transfer him/herself from the state of unbelief to the state of grace and faith in Christ. It is a sovereign and monergistic decision and power of God.[19]

---

15. "The Small Catechism," *BC*, 355.
16. Pless, *Praying Luther's Small Catechism*, 48. The parenthesis "the Holy Spirit will raise me and all the dead and will give to me and all believers in Christ eternal life" is my addition as an example of the outcome of the Spirit's action. See Oswald Bayer, *Martin Luther's Theology: A Contemporary Interpretation*, trans. Thomas H. Trapp (Eerdmans, 2008), 239–40.
17. "The Small Catechism," *BC* (Tappert), 345.
18. Peters, *Creed*, 235.
19. Miikka Ruokanen, *Trinitarian Grace in Martin Luther's "The Bondage of the Will"* (Oxford University Press, 2021), 112.

"Outside his Kingdom through his general omnipotence,"[20] human creatures do not prepare themselves toward God's work of creation and preservation; likewise, "inside his Kingdom,"[21] the sinner does not prepare himself for God's work of re-creation and preservation. Both are of divine power, not of human power. The fallen will is incapacitated and thus cannot receive God's kingdom unless renewed by the Spirit. "By the notion of his omnipotence," God acts in all without distinction, causing them to respond in a way appropriate to his will and direction; likewise, he acts by the Spirit of grace, particularly on the godly—"that is, in his kingdom, he actuates and moves them," causing those whom he has justified to follow and respond to him.

Here the two kinds of grace are in operation in God's economy of salvation: "For God first gives operative grace" at the beginning of our conversion. God allows it to operate "up to the point where He begins to pour into us a second kind of grace," which is called "cooperative" grace. When this kind is given, "God lets it cooperate, even though when it was first infused it was operative and first grace.... For it is called first grace always with respect to itself, because it operates first, and then in the second place it cooperates."[22] Our created identity is a work of grace; so also is our re-created identity. "God freely and unconditionally gave Adam and Eve their identity," Kolb underscores, "just as he freely and unconditionally restores this identity to those bought into his family by Holy Spirit."[23] No human preparation or predisposition in creation and re-creation is required; it is purely God's gift. In *The Bondage of the Will*, Luther elaborates:

> Before man is changed into a new creature of the Kingdom of the Spirit, he does nothing and attempts nothing to prepare himself for this renewal and this Kingdom, and when he has been recreated he does nothing and attempts nothing toward remaining in his Kingdom, but the Spirit alone does both of these things in us, recreating us without us and preserving us without our help in our recreated state, as also James says: "Of his own will he brought us forth by the word of his power, that we might be a beginning of his creature" (James. 1:18)—speaking of the renewed nature. But he does not work without us, because it is for this very thing he has recreated and preserves us, that he might work in us and we might cooperate with him.... But what is attributed to free choice in all? Or rather, what is there left for it but nothing? And really nothing![24]

---

20. *LW* 33:243.

21. *LW* 33:243.

22. *LW* 25:368–69; *WA* 46:379.

23. Robert Kolb, *Bound Choice, Election, and Wittenberg Theological Method: From Martin Luther to the Formula of Concord* (Fortress, 2017), 49–50.

24. *LW* 33:242–43. See Kolb, *Bound Choice*, 48–52.

The sanctifying work of the Holy Spirit in us is attested in the writings of Paul: "No one can say 'Jesus is Lord,' except in the Holy Spirit" (1 Cor 12:3). Luther does not attribute to the self the ability to turn toward grace. That would be, for Luther, "to exclude the Holy Spirit with all his power, as superfluous and unnecessary."[25] We are created as dependent creatures, endowed with the gift of "responsivity" to God. This gift was lost through Adam's fall but regained through God's prior work in us. The bound will "is not active in sanctification," Marney Fritts notes, but "very active in bondage to sin, actively opposing the Holy Spirit" (Rom 7:18–19).[26] Only the renewed will is active in sanctification; in Paul's passive sense, "they are led by the Spirit" (Rom 8:14). Faith that is oriented to God is not "an active capacity," self-manufactured from within us; it is "a passive capacity," created by the Spirit outside us and through the word;[27] in Piotr J. Małysz's terms, "The will has only a passive capacity to do good in the sense that it first needs to be healed and made good."[28]

The Third Article discloses that we by ourselves "cannot believe in Jesus Christ, my Lord," unless by the Holy Spirit, who causes us to turn to God. This corresponds to the First Article, where Luther teaches that we are not our own lord, creator, or provider. To turn inward to the self or to trust in the self as the basis of justification is to commit idolatry and break the first commandment. Whoever abandons his trust in the "I" and places his confidence in the Holy Spirit has made the transposition from helplessness to hope, from unbelief to faith, from the lordship of self to the Lordship of Christ. Confessing the Third Article means everything in us and in the world dies so that God's justifying action *ex nihilo* becomes operative: making an unbeliever a believer.

In addressing us, the Spirit uses his word of judgment to kill our sinful identity and its old inheritances (vices) and gives us a righteous identity and new inheritances (virtues) through the word of forgiveness. The Holy Spirit ensures that the accusing voice of the commandments reaches its end, and that all contraries of life—sin, wrath, death, and the devil—do not harm us. The Third Article places us under the law by which our ability to believe is reduced to naught so that it leads us to find help in the Holy Spirit. The confession of our inability to believe thus prepares us to receive the grace of the Spirit. Eric Gritsch and Robert W. Jenson capture Luther's point: "Just by your unbelief you prove

---

25. *LW* 33:109.

26. Marney Fritts, "Sanctification is Purely Passive," in *Handing Over the Goods: Determined to Proclaim Nothing but Christ Jesus and Him Crucified; Essays in Honor of James Arne Nestingen*, ed. Steven D. Paulson and Scott L. Keith (1517 Publishing, 2018), 121–22.

27. Gerhard O. Forde, *On Being a Theologian of the Cross: Reflections on Luther's Heidelberg Disputation, 1518* (Eerdmans, 1997), 55; cf. *LW* 31:49.

28. Piotr J. Małysz, "Martin Luther's Trinitarian Hermeneutic of Freedom," in *Oxford Research Encyclopedia of Religion* published March 29, 2017, https://doi.org/10.1093/acrefore/9780199340378.013.355.

yourself the very man whom God loves. He chooses above all the ungodly." That we cannot believe, they assert, becomes the very "reason" for, or the "occasion" of, God's promise.[29]

Luther argues against Erasmus, a humanist who defines free choice as, in Luther's words, "a power of the human will by which a man can apply himself to the good."[30] Scripture comprises so many precepts, laws, threats, and promises, and by implication, Erasmus's diatribe argues that "free choice is proved by the law and cooperates with it to produce righteousness."[31] However, Luther contends that this is contrary to Paul, who teaches that "through the law comes knowledge of sin" (Rom 3:20). Those who are "most devoted" to the law are "farthest" from achieving it, simply "because they lack the Spirit that is the true fulfiller of the law."[32] The law does not promise freedom; only the gospel does. Rather than providing freedom, the law actually removes it. The light of the law "reveals" the opposites of justification—sin, evil, death, hell, and God's wrath—and is "content" with such revelation, though it offers no deliverance.[33] The troubled conscience under such light cannot be healed unless "there is another light to reveal the remedy. This is the voice of the gospel, revealing Christ as the deliverer from all these things."[34] Both ailment and remedy must be disclosed, not discovered by rational or moral efforts. Reason and free choice are no revealing agents, as they cannot grasp the knowledge of the Second Article. Luther insists, "It is not reason or free choice that reveals Christ; how could they when they themselves are in darkness and need the light of the law to reveal their disease, which by their own light they cannot see, but believe themselves to be healthy."[35] Their blindness and ignorance must be lifted by divine revelation.

The Spirit uses the external voice of God's appointed preachers to proclaim Christ "categorically"—that is, through "contrast and antithesis."[36] Using a simple syllogism, Luther further explains, "Moreover since Christ is said to be 'the way, the truth, and the life' (Jn. 14:6) and categorically, so whatever is not Christ is not the way, but error, not the truth but untruth, not life, but death, it follows of necessity that 'free will' inasmuch as it neither is Christ, nor is in Christ, is fast bound in error, and untruth and death."[37] This kind of preaching is

---

29. Eric W. Gritsch and Robert W. Jenson, *Lutheranism: The Theological Movement and Its Confessional Writings* (Fortress, 1976), 44.
30. *LW* 33:112–13.
31. *LW* 33:261.
32. *LW* 33:259–60.
33. *LW* 33:261–62.
34. *LW* 33:262.
35. *LW* 33:262.
36. *LW* 33:287.
37. Martin Luther, *The Bondage of the Will*, trans. J. I. Packer and O. R. Johnston (James Clarke, 1957), 307.

what Gerhard O. Forde calls "categorical preaching,"[38] which is basically exalting the grace of Christ crucified and risen above all else, attributing everything not to us, but to Christ: wisdom, righteousness, sanctification, and redemption (1 Cor 1:30).

> If all the things that are said of Christ and of grace were not said categorically, so that they may be contrasted with their opposites, like this: out of Christ there is nothing but Satan, out of grace nothing but wrath, out of truth nothing but a lie, out of life nothing but death.... If you grant that the Scriptures speak categorically, you can say nothing of "free will" but that which is opposite of Christ: that is, that error, death, Satan, and all evils reign in it. If you do not grant that the Scriptures speak categorically, you so weaken them, that they establish nothing and fail to prove that men need Christ; and in setting up "free will," you set Christ aside, and make havoc of the entire Scripture.[39]

"Categorical preaching" opposes everything that is not Christ, the one, continuous, luminous theme in Scripture. Steven D. Paulson formulates it syllogistically: "Preaching truly sets out Christ, the subject with the proper predicate in this way: Jesus Christ alone justifies. Free will is not Jesus Christ. Therefore, free will does not justify."[40] The distinction between the law and the gospel requires that the subject (Christ) not be changed to law. The law, even as salutary doctrine, traps us in bondage, from which only the gospel can free us.

Luther's position is also contrary to the scholastic theologian Gabriel Biel, who holds[41] "to do what is in us" is the basis of justification. Thesis 13 of the *Heidelberg Disputation* (1518) states Luther's position: "The free will, after the fall into sin, exists only in name."[42] Free will is a divine attribute; by contrast, our will is bound. The fallen will wills nothing but itself, thus succumbs to God's judgment. There is nothing in the fallen creature that prepares or predisposes us for the reception of God's grace. "On the part of man," Luther declares, "nothing precedes grace except indisposition and even rebellion against grace."[43] The fallen will wills its own fallenness, not friendship with God; not conformity to God's purpose, but to its contradiction. Luther affirms, "Man is by nature unable to want God to be God. Indeed, he himself wants to be God, and does

---

38. Gerhard O. Forde, *The Captivation of the Will: Luther vs. Erasmus on Freedom and Bondage*, ed. Steven D. Paulson (Eerdmans, 2005), 78.

39. Luther, *The Bondage of the Will*, 307.

40. Steven D. Paulson, "Categorical Preaching," in *Justification is for Preaching: Essays by Oswald Bayer, Gerhard O. Forde, and Others*, ed. Virgil Thompson (Pickwick, 2012), 129–30.

41. *LW* 31:10.

42. *LW* 31:40.

43. *LW* 31:11.

not want God to be God.... An act of friendship is not the most perfect means for accomplishing that which is in one. Nor is it the most perfect means for obtaining the grace of God or turning toward and approaching God. But it is an act of conversion already perfected, following grace both in time and by nature."[44] Friendship with God is made possible preveniently, by grace preceding conversion. Reason "seeks itself and its own in all things, but not God. This only faith does in love."[45] The bound will is trapped in its own bondage, and only grace can free it; reason is held captive by sin, and only grace can restore its integrity. "I believe that I can believe" is the language of the old Adam, turning inward to the self for soteriological resources; "I believe that I cannot believe" is the language of the new Adam, turning outward and trusting in God alone for salvation. These two kinds of belief are opposed to each other, just as are flesh and spirit. The tendency of self-incurvature exists in tension with the spirit of Godward-ness; they coincide as opposites in the justified existence, just as saint and sinner coinhere in the same person.

The Bound Condition and Freeing Actions
Calling, Enlightening, Sanctifying, and Preserving

The Third Article depicts the various sanctifying activities of one and the same Spirit. They are summed up in four verbs in Luther's exposition: "calling," "enlightening," "sanctifying," and "preserving." These categories do not represent different stages in the temporal process of salvation. Rather they highlight the helplessness of our systemic, bound condition, that "I know that I cannot," and the remedy to that condition, that "by the Holy Spirit," we are called out of bondage to reason and will. Enlightened, no longer trapped in blindness, we are sanctified by grace, not by any self-initiated means, and kept in his power, no longer under the devil's grip. All of this reinforces the relevance of the Holy Spirit, who, as Oswald Bayer notes, "does not work deistically, by merely giving the initial spark; he guides and preserves us" throughout the Christian life.[46]

The Holy Spirit "calls us through the gospel"[47]—that is, through the hearing of the word by which faith is born (cf. Rom 10:17). "First off, before all works and things, one hears the Word of God therein, the Spirit punishes the world because of sin" (John 16:8).[48] In our deafness, God's word comes and opens our ears to hear him with faith. The law only teaches what we ought to do and has no power to justify. "But the Gospel does bring the Holy Spirit, because it

---

44. *LW* 31:10.
45. *LW* 25:234; *WA* 56:355.
46. Bayer, *Martin Luther's Theology*, 241–42.
47. "The Small Catechism," *BC*, 355–56.
48. *LW* 40:73.

teaches what we ought to believe."⁴⁹ In his *Disputation Against Antinomianism*, Luther again puts his emphasis on what the Holy Spirit does; he writes, "When he [Spirit] is 'swaddled' in tongues and spiritual gifts, then he is called 'gift,' then he sanctifies and makes alive. Without this Holy Spirit who is 'gift,' the law points to sin, because the law is not a 'gift,' but the word off the eternal and almighty God, to consciences a consuming fire."⁵⁰ Proclamation bears no fruit unless the Holy Spirit is added. Public worship is a saving event in which the church hears and receives the word of promise conveyed through preachers. The Spirit enlivens us through the preached word so that God himself, not just ideas or memories about him, is fully disclosed to worshippers' hearts. Luther writes, "When you open the book containing the gospels and read or hear how Christ comes here or there, or how someone is brought to him, you should therein perceive the Sermon or the gospel through which he is coming to you, or you are being brought to him. For the preaching of the gospel is nothing else than Christ coming to us, or we being brought to him."⁵¹ God's word is God's speech in action through his appointed agents, drawing us into the inner life of communion with God himself. Schwöbel argues that "the understanding of the Trinity as a conversation grounds the Gospel in the inner life of the triune God. The preaching of the Gospel is therefore never only preaching about the Trinity. Its task to communicate the Gospel can only be fulfilled if it becomes an event for God's Trinitarian self-communication."⁵² Preaching is not a discursive exercise that delivers information about God; it is a saving event that delivers God himself to us. God's presence is truly felt in present times, as certain as it was in the past.

When he enumerates a list of lords that bind us, Luther includes "blindness" as one from whom Christ frees us.⁵³ Unless God shines in us through the word, our blindness remains our own. The Holy Spirit is "the Spirit of truth" (John 14:17); he is God's remedy against all lies and false teachings. His peculiar office is to help us to apprehend the content of Christ's speech and discern all other doctrines; in Luther's words, "Thus He will not only make you warriors and heroes, but He will also confer the doctorate on you and call you doctors and masters who can determine with certainty what is true or false doctrine in Christendom."⁵⁴ The Holy Spirit awakens understanding in our hearts so that we can turn our gaze toward Christ. Whoever "hears" the word, says Luther, "has

---

49. *LW* 26:208; *WA* 40.1:337.
50. See *WA* 39.1:370: 18–371.1, as quoted in Bernhard Lohse, *Martin Luther's Theology: Its Historical and Systematic Development*, trans. and ed. Roy A. Harrisville (Augsburg Fortress, 1999), 238.
51. *LW* 35:121.
52. Christoph Schwöbel, "Martin Luther and the Trinity," in *Oxford Research Encyclopedia of Religion*, published March 29, 2017, https://doi.org/10.1093/acrefore/9780199340378.013.326.
53. *LW* 51:164.
54. *LW* 24:293; *WA* 45:728.

lighted the light and the lamp in our hearts to enable us to see."[55] The word we hear performs an alien work of exposing error and darkness within us to accomplish a proper work—that is, it disposes of error and darkness in exchange for truth and light. Once "enlightened," the old creature is made new and granted the capacity to apprehend the gospel, that Christ has become "my Lord" and has obtained for us the Father's favor. Here Luther recalls the inefficacy of the papacy's preaching, which he attributes to the lack of the Spirit's presence to "reveal this truth and have it preached."[56]

A Christian is "made holy" before God, Luther teaches, "because the Holy Spirit is given to us."[57] The verb "made holy"[58] has no bearing on human performance or fruits following justification. To be "made holy" is to be made by the Spirit the passive beneficiary of the blessings Christ's redemption has wrought, which we could not obtain by ourselves. In us there is nothing but sin and damnation; but in Christ there is nothing but holiness and life. The order of God's justifying action is from person to work, from being to act; in Luther's own words, "No work justifies the person but [the person] must first without any works be justified."[59] Whatever good we might perform springs from God's initial gracious act. We are holy, not because we are without sin, not because we perform good deeds, but because the Spirit communicates Christ's holiness to us through the word. The holiness with which we are clothed is, in Luther's word, "a passive holiness."[60] This holiness possesses so powerful an effect that it blots out all residual sin;[61] as Ian D. Kingston Siggins puts it:

> The progression is precisely the same in sanctification as in justification: to be holy is not to cleanse oneself from sin and live piously, but to believe; this faith sanctifies because its content, Christ's Word and gospel, are holy and unite us to Him; he thus sets us apart for God by washing us and bestowing His Spirit upon us through the priestly sacrifice and offering for which He sanctified Himself. For a highest sanctification is that Christ sanctified Himself for us; indeed, there is no holiness but this. He is to be called the All-holiest, the *sanctus sanctorum*: He alone is the eternal source of all holiness.[62]

---

55. *LW* 30:164; *WA* 14:29.
56. "The Large Catechism," *BC*, 436.
57. *LW* 24:168; *WA* 45:614.
58. "The Small Catechism," *BC*, 355–56.
59. *LW* 75:364; *WA* 10.1.1:325.
60. *LW* 26:25; *WA* 40.1:70.
61. *LW* 69:101; *WA* 28:178.
62. Ian D. Kingston Siggins, *Martin Luther's Doctrine of Christ* (Yale University Press, 1970), 156.

Just as justification is alien to us, so is sanctification alien to us. Christ's righteousness and holiness are extrinsic to us but belong to us perfectly by faith; thus Luther declares, "I cling to the conviction that Christ alone is my righteousness and holiness."[63] We are sinners but are borne by the gift of Christ's righteousness; we are unclean but covered by his holiness, which is given to us.[64] Sanctification is not to be separated from justification; rather it is a continuation of what has been achieved in justification. Both Christ's righteousness and holiness are ours by faith; those whom he has justified he sanctifies. Sanctification defines who we are, setting us apart as the objects for whom Christ died, and to whom Christ's righteousness and holiness are imputed. To be "sanctified," Herbet Girgensohn opines, is equivalent "to be[ing] made a believer,"[65] reckoned with the treasure of salvation won by Christ apart from any human contributions. This treasure must not be "hidden" or "buried";[66] it must be proclaimed so that it may be put to proper use; as Leopold A. Sánchez notes, "The image of unveiled treasure highlights the free generosity of the Spirit, who graciously enlightens us to receive God's promise by faith."[67] Sanctification thus has to do with the Spirit's offer and application to us of the benefits Christ has procured on the cross so that we could make them our own. Luther writes:

> The work is finished and completed: Christ has acquired and won the treasure for us by his sufferings, death, and resurrection, etc. . . . In order that this treasure might not remain buried but be put to use and enjoyed, God has caused the Word to be published and proclaimed, in which he has given the Holy Spirit to offer and apply to us this treasure, this redemption. Therefore being made holy is nothing else than bringing us to the Lord Christ to receive, to which we could not have come by ourselves.[68]

The knowledge of the Father's self-giving, Luther writes, is known in the Son, of whom we have no knowledge unless by the Holy Spirit. "So," Wengert writes aptly, "we have the Trinity in reverse: the Holy Spirit makes known the Son, whom we could not know and who is in turn the mirror of the Father's heart."[69] And the knowledge of Christ's self-giving is of no use unless imparted in

---

63. *WA* 32:329.1.
64. *LW* 42:164.
65. Herbert Girgensohn, *Teaching Luther's Catechism*, vol.1, trans. John Doberstein (Muhlenberg, 1959), 180.
66. "The Large Catechism," *BC*, 436.
67. Leopoldo A. Sánchez M., "The Person and Work of the Holy Spirit," in Pless and Vogel, *Luther's Large Catechism*, 426.
68. "The Large Catechism," *BC*, 436.
69. Wengert, *Martin Luther's Catechisms*, 44. See "The Large Catechism," *BC*, 440.

us by the Holy Spirit. "The ministry of the Holy Spirit," Mickey Leland Mattox explains, "is the starting point of Christian faith and life, for the Spirit brings the Christian to Christ and through Christ reveals the love of the Father."[70] The "that I may be His" of the Second Article becomes real in the believer by the Holy Spirit. The objective work Christ accomplishes on Calvary and at Easter becomes a subjective reality in us through "the self-giving of the Spirit"; Schwöbel notes, "The disclosure of the grace of Christ and its appropriation to believers [enables] believers . . . to receive and to preserve it, use it, communicate it, even increase and extend it. God's Trinitarian action, coming to completion in the self-giving of the Spirit, is the enabling and continuing support of faith apprehending this gift."[71] The Holy Spirit is the perfecting cause of God's threefold self-giving action that restores us to divine favor and results in our reciprocal love for him; in Bayer's estimation:

> The theology of the Holy Spirit, just as the entire theology of the Trinity, is *a theology* of *categorical gift*. God is categorically the one who gives: the Father does not just give some particular things—namely, life and the world; he gives us himself in this creation. In the same way the Son gives himself to us—and at the same time gives us the Father once again in a new way, whose face was obscured from our view because of sin. The Spirit finally is nothing other than the opener and distributor of this self-giving of Christ—and thereby that of the Father as well. We recognize and love God the Father through Jesus Christ in the Holy Spirit.[72]

Luther describes the devil as "a master and an excellent theologian"[73] who seeks to convert us into theologians of glory, causing us to bypass Christ's humanity (as Philip did; John 14:6) and speculate about God as he is in his naked deity. The Holy Spirit leads us to "the man Christ [who has] been given to us as a ladder to the Father."[74] "Christ makes the Holy Spirit a Preacher";[75] he preaches what he receives from the Son, who receives from his Father. The Spirit's sermon is not about unmediated, naked majesty, but about the incarnate Son and his efficacious activities on the cross; in Luther's words, "Christ, God's Son, died for you. He paid for your sins. . . . Christ, your Righteousness, is greater than your sins and those of the whole world; His life and His consolation are stronger and mightier than your death and hell."[76] In ourselves, God is opposed to us, and we

---

70. Mattox, "Luther's Interpretation of Scripture," 20.
71. Schwöbel, "Luther and the Trinity," 4.
72. Bayer, *Martin Luther's Theology*, 254, Bayer's italics.
73. *LW* 24:291; *WA* 45:727.
74. *LW* 43:55.
75. *LW* 24:362; *WA* 46:57.
76. *LW* 24:292; *WA* 45:727.

feel the gnawing of God's wrath at our troubled conscience. The Spirit preaches to us that in Christ, God's blessing has annihilated his curse, and cements in our troubled conscience God's reconciliation with us, despite appearances to the contrary. "For the Holy Spirit must be both the Preacher of this message and the Author who inscribes it in my heart, so that I believe and say: 'I believe in Jesus Christ.'"[77] While the devil tempts us to focus our eyes on only Moses and proclaims God's command by which we are condemned, the Spirit impels us to focus our eyes on Christ and proclaims God's promise by which we are comforted and "kept in true faith."[78] The devil is "a clever accuser" who wants to reduce God's mercy to nothing and convert our sins into mountains.[79] The Spirit, however, is the comforter who assures our hearts that nothing, not even the devil, can sever us from the power of God's "omnipotent love."

"That I May Be His"
Christology and Pneumatology

Christology and pneumatology are basic to soteriology. Luther links christological grace with pneumatologic grace, the former finding completion in us by the latter. The unity of christological and pneumatologic grace is the ground of victory over doubt and anxiety about our justified status. Luther writes:

> Let everyone accustom himself, therefore, to believe for a certainty that he is in a state of grace and that his person with its works is pleasing to God. For if he senses that he is in doubt, let him exercise his faith, struggle against the doubt, and strive for certainty, so that he can say: "I know that I have been accepted and that I have the Holy Spirit, not on account of my worthiness or virtue but on account of Christ, who subjected Himself to the Law on our account and took away the sins of the world (John 1:29). In Him I believe. If I am a sinner, and if I err, He is righteous and cannot err.". . . These things certainly testify that the Holy Spirit is present.[80]

The same grace that descends from the Father through the Son in the Holy Spirit belongs to us. Luther sums up: "For Christ is mine with His suffering, death, and life; the Holy Spirit, with his comfort; and the Father himself, with all his grace."[81] Luther adheres to the patristic paradigm in which the three persons

---

77. *LW* 22:286; *WA* 46:14.4–6.
78. "The Small Catechism," *BC*, 355–56.
79. *WA* 7:788, as quoted in *LW* 42:185n7.
80. *LW* 26:379; *WA* 40.1:577.
81. *LW* 24:292; *WA* 45:728.

work together *ad extra* as "a differentiated unity," communicating to us the triune grace. The mission of God is Trinitarian: the sending Father, the obedient Son, and the effecting Spirit. The Son's passion is an obedience he renders to the Father who sends. The efficacy of the cross of Christ becomes subjectively real in us by the Holy Spirit. Fatherly grace is made known in the Son; Sonly grace becomes operative in us by the grace of the Holy Spirit. The ungodly cannot turn to God, even when presented with an external word, "unless the Father draws and teaches him inwardly" by the Holy Spirit he bestows. "There is another 'drawing' than the one that takes place outwardly; for then Christ is set forth by the light of the Spirit, so that a man is rapt away to Christ with the sweetest rapture, and rather yields passively to God's speaking, teaching, and drawing than seeks and runs himself."[82] Apart from grace, free will "necessarily serves sin" and remains in unbelief. The shift from unbelief to faith is by the *sola gratia* work of the "convincing Spirit."[83] We humbly confess, "I believe that I cannot believe, but the Holy Spirit" has effected the union of faith which grants us a share in the triune life of grace.

The two movements in Luther's Trinitarian theology—in Helmer's categories,[84] the "inside-out" and the "outside-in"—underscore Luther as a theologian of the Holy Spirit. The knowledge of God's eternal love revealed from the inside out of the immanent being in the Son by the Holy Spirit to Christians corresponds to the knowledge of God's fatherly heart communicated from the outside in of the economic being through the Son by the Holy Spirit. The Holy Spirit effects a "joyous exchange" of Christ's righteousness for our sin, assuring us of our justified status before God. Christ's Sonship by nature is credited to us, so that we truly become God's Son by grace, loved as dearly as God's Son by the Father; this is made real in our hearts by the "convincing Spirit." "Christ's ascending and descending," Luther says, "are significant especially for us."[85] The Trinity's double movement of descending and ascending constitutes the substance of the gospel. God descends to our flesh in the Son, revealing his gracious will in history by the Spirit; conversely, by the Holy Spirit we ascend through the Son to the fatherly heart in eternity. In John Thompson's estimation, "The movement of the Son is from the Father by the Holy Spirit and back again, drawing our humanity up into relationship with the Father."[86] We ascend to God by what Wengert calls "the reversed Trinity"[87]—namely, by the Holy Spirit, who effects the justifying action of Christ, through which we are restored to God's fatherly

---

82. *LW* 33:286.
83. *LW* 33:286.
84. Helmer, *The Trinity and Martin Luther*, 216.
85. *LW* 22:332.
86. John Thompson, *Modern Trinitarian Perspectives* (Oxford University Press, 1994), 100.
87. Wengert, *Martin Luther's Catechisms*, 46.

grace in us. Schwöbel writes, "The Spirit makes us co-present to God and that is described as bringing us to Christ and through Christ to the Father by being God's trinitarian co-presence for us."[88] As comforter, the Spirit sends into our hearts "sheer fatherly and cordial love,"[89] revealing to us that God's being is nothing but love—a threefold, self-giving love. Luther imagines Christ saying, "'For I will ask my Father, and as a result of My plea, He will surely give you the Holy Spirit to comfort you. Then you can rest assured that I love you, that the Father loves you, and that the Holy Spirit, who is sent to you, loves you.'"[90] By the "convincing Spirit," the Father's love in his Son is brought to fulfillment in us, thereby completing the whole dynamic of God's Trinitarian love "for us." Thus, Luther asserts, the Third Article is "most important,"[91] one that gathers up all others; as Augustine phrases it, "The Holy Spirit, while being God, should also be called the gift of God. And this gift, surely, is distinctively to be understood as being the charity which brings us through to God, without which no other gift of God at all can bring us through to God."[92]

The Affective Experience of the Holy Spirit
God Alone Is to Be Loved

God places us under the dialectic distinction of law and gospel, exposing to us our inability to love God, and creating in us a hunger for divine help. Luther quotes Augustine favorably: "He commands something which we cannot do in order that we may know what we must ask of him. For this is faith which demands in prayer what the Law demands."[93] The helplessness the law creates in us prepares us to receive God's work done outside us. The law itself is good, but the fallen will is hostile to it. "So grace as a mediator is necessary to reconcile the law with the will."[94] Grace directs "the will," says Luther, "lest it err even in loving God."[95] Sinners are so turned in on themselves that they cannot fulfill what God commands unless by a power external to themselves—that is, by a living, creative, and diffusive grace. The old flesh and its love of itself must perish so that the new self might arise and perform acts of loving God. As Luther sharply puts it: "To

---

88. Schwöbel, "Triune God of Grace," 55.
89. *LW* 24:114; *WA* 45:566.
90. *LW* 24:114; *WA* 45:565.
91. *LW* 43:24.
92. Augustine, *The Works of Saint Augustine: A Translation for the 21st Century*, ed. John E. Rotelle, trans. Edmund Hill, vol. 5, *The Trinity* (New City, 1991), 421.
93. See Augustine, *De gratia et libero arbitrio*, in *Patrologiae Cursus Completus: Series Latina*, ed. J. P. Migne, 221 vols. (Paris, 1844–64), 16:32, 44:900, as cited in *LW* 25:345; *WA* 50:356.
94. *LW* 31:15.
95. *LW* 31:15.

love God is at the same time to hate oneself and to know nothing but God."[96] Luther's formulation is akin to Augustine, who defines pride as "the love of one's own excellence," and humility as "the contempt of one's own excellence."[97] Unless we show contempt of self, the humility God works in us through the alien work of the law, we will not love God. We love God by a "passive capacity" given to us, not by an "active capacity" initiated by us.

Suffering (*tentatio*) causes what lies deep within us—hypocrisy, pride, and impatience—to surface in order to remove it through Christ and his sure promises. Pless writes, "Spiritual attack disables and deconstructs all of our own resources; we are left without anything but Christ and his absolving word."[98] Suffering is, for Luther, "the touchstone"[99] that makes a "real theologian"[100] who knows how to distinguish between law and gospel and move the afflicted from the law's terror to the gospel's comfort. Suffering equips us to be "the instructor of consciences,"[101] leading the afflicted out of themselves to rest on God's promises. Life's assaults are causally useful, as they push us to leave ourselves behind and cleave only to God's word, confident that this will accomplish God's own purpose; thus Luther confesses they have made him "a fairly good theologian."[102]

Suffering strips us naked and leaves us alone; thus in us, we are denuded of love and cannot love God out of our own endowments, but only out of God's prevenient grace. Commenting on Jeremiah 29:13, "You will seek me and find me," Gabriel Biel attributes the first part "seek me" to nature and the latter "find me" to grace. This order, for Luther, amounts to Pelagianism, according to which the natural act of loving God can prepare for grace. Jeremiah 29:13, Theodor Dieter observes, must not be understood apart from Jeremiah 31:18, "Convert me, and I will return, for you are my LORD God," and hence he writes of Luther, "The act of loving God is later in time and order than grace."[103] The grace of God is never "inactive," says Luther, "but it is a living, active, and operative spirit"[104] that causes us to love God above all else, something that is impossible to do by one's own natural power.

---

96. *LW* 31:15.

97. See Augustine: "*Quia qui confitetur peccata sua et accusat peccata sua, iam cum Deo facit.*" *Johannis Evangelium*, in *Patrologia Cursus Completus: Series Latina*, ed. J. P. Migne, 221 vols. (Paris, 1844–64), 12:13, 35:1491, as cited in Franz Posset, *Pater Bernhardus: Martin Luther and Bernard of Clairvaux* (Cistercian Publications, 1999), 226.

98. John T. Pless, "Luther's *Oratio, Meditatio*, and *Tentatio* as the Shape of Pastoral Care for Pastors," *Concordia Theological Quarterly* 80, no. 1 (2016): 43.

99. *LW* 34:286.

100. *LW* 34:287.

101. *LW* 26:10; *WA* 40.1:50.

102. *LW* 34:287.

103. Theodor Dieter, "Martin Luther and Scholasticism," in *Remembering the Reformation: Martin Luther and Catholic Theology*, ed. Declan Marmion et al., (Fortress, 2017), 60.

104. *LW* 31:13.

In ourselves, there is a vacuity of love unless it is wrought in us by the Spirit of grace. Communion with God belongs to those who draw nigh to God, not by a preexistent love within them (which hypocrites imagine they possess), but by a love outside them—that is, by God's love poured into them by the Holy Spirit, who has been given to us, even though we do not deserve him. We do not love God to benefit him, for he does not need anything from us to complete his deity. The Spirit's gift of God's love deposited in us impels us to esteem God "with a precious love,"[105] though he already is "precious and good in himself."[106] The sublime capacity to love God alone is not self-generated but received from God; as Paul writes, "God's love has been poured into us through the Holy Spirit who has been given to us" (Rom 5:5). Following Augustine, Luther renders this text as follows: "It follows that [God's love] is poured into us, not born in us or originated in us. And this takes place through the Holy Spirit; it is not acquired by moral effort and practice, as our moral virtues are."[107] What radically differentiates the children of the eternal kingdom from the children of eternal perdition is their possession of this excellent gift of love. The Spirit, who himself is love, is the causative agency of our love for God and people. Augustine writes, "So it is God the Holy Spirit proceeding from God who fires man to the love of God and neighbor when he has been given to him, and he himself is love. Man has no capacity to love God except from God. That is why he says a little later, *Let us love because he first loved us* (1 Jn 4: 19). The apostle Paul also says, *The love of God has been poured out in our hearts through the Holy Spirit which has been given to us* (Rom 5:5)."[108] "Unless therefore the Spirit is imparted to someone to make him a lover of God and neighbor, he cannot transfer from the left hand to the right."[109] Where the Holy Spirit is present, there the gift of love is. Love is not bestowed unless the Spirit has first been bestowed, spreading love throughout our hearts, and causing us to turn to God, whose face is already turned toward us. Undeniably, "love is superfluous if man by nature is able to do an act of friendship."[110] In ourselves, we hate God and are deprived of friendship with God unless that hatred is banished by God's love; God's wrath, about which we cannot do anything unless it be absolved by God's mercy, remains ours; as Habakkuk 3:2 teaches, "In wrath remember mercy." God's wrath is God's alien work, a judgment to which he was driven by human sin; this he does to achieve his proper work, a restoration of sinners to his mercy.

---

105. *LW* 25:294; *WA* 56:307.
106. *LW* 30:60; *WA* 12:313.
107. *LW* 25:294; *WA* 56:307.
108. Augustine, *The Trinity* 15:5:28, 419, Augustine's italics.
109. Augustine, *The Trinity* 15:5:32, 421.
110. *LW* 31:15.

God's nature is love. In relation to us, wrath is God's alien work, which opposes anything that stands between God and us. Wrath is God's love burning hot in the presence of sin, to move us away from it to dependence upon God's mercy, his proper work. In relation to God, God's love causes God to move toward us, shielding us from that which terrifies us: his own wrath. God's love exposes us to its opposite, God's wrath, to dispose of it, so that we become a people of God's mercy. The Christian now lives paradoxically in twofold existence: in ourselves, and in Christ. In ourselves, God is against us, and we feel the curse of his distance from us. In Christ, God is for us, and we enjoy the benefit of his nearness to us. The God who is "for" us (mercy) is set opposite the God who is "against" us (wrath). The curse of our separation from God is overcome by the blessing of God's reconciliation with us. The antinomy between God's wrath and God's mercy is revealed in Christ but abolished for faith, proving that God's "omnipotent love" has triumphed over God's wrath. The love of God is most "omnipotent" in its opposite—that is, in the self-sacrifice of God's Son, a priestly act that placates God's wrath and procures our reconciliation with God. Omnipotence is revealed in weakness; love is manifested in suffering. The cross does not "necessitate" suffering but "occasion[s] it," revealing the depth of God's being as love; as Abraham J. Heschel holds, "Man's deeds do not necessitate but merely occasion divine *pathos*."[111]

The suffering of God's love must be balanced with the immutability of God's will, lest we attribute to God an ungodly, unbridled passion, which is inapplicable to God. Luther expands, "For this ungodly passion not only gives no one his own, serves no one, is kind to no one, but snatches everything for itself, looks for its own in everything, even in God himself."[112] Not out of "absolute necessity"[113] but in a free act of mercy, God assumes the suffering of the cross upon himself to redeem us. "The indescribable and inestimable mercy and love of God" is established in that "the supreme Majesty cared so much for me, a condemned sinner and a child of wrath (Eph. 2:3) and of eternal death, that He did not spare His own Son, but gave Him up into a most shameful death."[114] God's "omnipotent love" suffers when God's Son undergoes God's wrath against sin, to triumph over it.

The Holy Spirit applies to our hearts the victory of God's "omnipotent love," causing us to boldly approach God the Father and demand from him the inheritance already prepared for us in heaven. The inestimable blessing through Christ's self-sacrifice is given to us, and we are to receive it by faith so that God

---

111. Abraham J. Heschel, *The Prophets* (Harper & Row, 1962), 225.
112. *LW* 14:300.
113. See Alister E. McGrath, *Luther's Theology of the Cross: Martin Luther's Theological Breakthrough* (Wiley-Blackwell, 1985), 55–58, for a discussion of "absolute necessity" and "consequential necessity."
114. *LW* 26:292; *WA* 40.1:455.

alone is esteemed above all. It is in this sense that Luther writes, "God's love is used because only God is loved in this way, not even the neighbor, except for the sake of God, that is, because God so wills, and one loves His will above all things."[115] "God's love is used" to serve not our purpose but his own, that he might constitute a people who love and worship him purely for himself. For this purpose to come to pass is of grace, not of itself; as Augustine teaches, "Because by this grace of God is caused in us, in the reception of good and the persevering hold of it, not only to be able to do what we will, but even to will to do what we are able."[116] We cannot, of our own strength, fulfill his purpose, nor love God at all, much less love God above all else, unless the Spirit causes God's love within us from outside us. Commenting on Romans 5:5, Luther expands on the power of the Spirit's gift of God's uncaused love by which, not only are we loved, but also God alone is loved:

> Therefore "God's love," which is the purest feeling toward God and alone makes us right at heart, alone takes away iniquity, alone extinguishes the enjoyment of our own righteousness. For it loves nothing but God alone, not even His gifts, as the hypocritical self-righteous people do. Therefore, when physical and spiritual blessings flow in, it does not get excited. Again, when they disappear, and physical and spiritual evils deluge us, it is not crushed.[117]

The love we render to God is imperfect, often tainted with selfish desire; even so, God's love covers our iniquities, and places us outside the law and its jurisdiction. The law says, "love God," but it is never accomplished, and we are placed under its curse; grace announces, "believe in" Christ, and it is all done, and we are placed under his blessing. Faith and love parallel each other: "For just as faith is active where it sees nothing, so love should also not see anything and do its work chiefly where nothing lovable but only aversion and hostility is seen."[118] Faith is operative despite appearances to the contrary; likewise, God's love is effective where it meets with its opposite, the unlovable. God's love is incongruous, not determined by the attitude or condition of those on whom love is bestowed. God "proves that he is good by nature," as he "gladly wastes his kindness on the ungrateful."[119]

While God's love for us is uncaused, freely turning toward us with his goods, our love for God is caused in us by the Holy Spirit, effecting a free turning toward

---

115. *LW* 25:295; *WA* 56:307.
116. Augustine, "On Rebuke and Grace," in *Augustine's Anti-Pelagian Writings*, ed. Philip Schaff, vol. 5, *The Nicene and Post-Nicene Fathers*, 1st ser., repr. (Hendrickson, 1995), 32.485.
117. *LW* 25:293; *WA* 56:307.
118. *LW* 30:43; *WA* 12:297.
119. *LW* 14:106.

God. We ascend to God not by anything we inherit or acquire but by God's love that descends on us, radically distinguishing us as God's beloved children (Eph 5:1). "The descending God's love,"[120] which the Holy Spirit pours down on us, the weak, poor, and disgraceful, becomes God's instrument of our ascending, responsive love for God. The love God renders to us is perfect, so lavished on us, without any prior action or merit of ours, that we are moved to action. God's creative love indwells his children to free them from self-incurvature so that they may serve God freely, joyfully, and willingly, without any fear of punishment or desire for reward, but solely to fulfill the Father's will. The Holy Spirit creates in us an affective power to turn to God, to love him above all else. The triadic form of idolatry, "misplaced fear, misplaced love, and misplaced trust"[121] is deactivated by "the affective experience of the Holy Spirit." God's affective grasping of us reactivates the triadic form of true worship so that we may fear, love, and trust in God alone.

Believers experience, in A. Trevor Sutton's apt formulation, "an enigmatic tension: *We may receive the full Gospel yet still long for the fullness of the Gospel*."[122] "The full Gospel" is delivered where the word is preached, heard, and believed. To quote Sutton again: "In the Word, the Holy Spirit brings us to Christ and we receive the *full* Gospel. In the sacraments, Absolution, and 'all kinds of comforting promises' given within the Christian Church we receive the *fullness* of the Gospel."[123] The "full Gospel" reaches beyond the cognitive into the affective, penetrating the heart with uplifting emotions of joy and peace. The gospel's "fullness" includes affective gladness and desire, the embodied fruits of the forensic-effective justification. Luther's doctrine of justification is formulated not in the cold language of the courtroom but in the affective language of a "royal marriage," a happy event in which Christ (the groom) fills the bride's (the sinner) heart with overflowing joy.[124] Where "we feel and experience within ourselves" God's unmerited grace, Luther avows, "there, the hearty love for Him is born. The heart overflows with gladness and goes leaping and dancing for the great pleasure that it has been found in God. There the Holy Spirit is present and has taught us in a moment such exceeding great knowledge and gladness through

---

120. Tuomo Mannermaa, *Two Kinds of Love: Martin Luther's Religious World*, trans. and ed. Kirsi I. Stjerna (Fortress, 2010), 3, 5. Mannermaa labels two kinds of love as "the descending God's Love and the ascending Human Love." He elaborates, "The movement of God's love and Human Love are polar opposites. The direction of Human Love is upwards, that is, turns toward what is grand, wise, alive, beautiful, and good. God's Love, in turn, turns itself or is oriented downward, that is, toward what is lowly, disgraceful, weak, foolish, wicked, and dead."

121. Michael A. Lockwood, *The Unholy Trinity: Martin Luther against the Idol of Me, Myself, and I* (Concordia Publishing House, 2016), 43.

122. A. Trevor Sutton, "Virtual Christianity," in Pless and Vogel, *Luther's Large Catechism*, 454, Sutton's italics; cf. "The Large Catechism," *BC*, 438.

123. Sutton, "Virtual Christianity," 454, Sutton's italics.

124. *LW* 31:356–57.

this experience."[125] Affective joy deluges us, most significantly, through hearing, not seeing. Luther exults, "What man is there whose heart, upon hearing these things [the riches of God's grace], will not rejoice to its depth, and when receiving such comfort will not grow tender so that he will love Christ as he never could by means of any laws or works?"[126] The emphasis on pneumatologic affectivity as the sublime power of creating in us a Godward movement and loving friendship with God, is already apparent in Luther's 1522 *Preface to Romans*:

> But [a kindled] heart is given only by God's Spirit, who fashions a man after the law, so that he acquires a desire for the law in his heart, doing nothing henceforth out of fear and compulsion but out of a willing heart.... How shall a work please God if it proceeds from a reluctant and resisting heart? To fulfill the law, however, is to do its works with pleasure and love, to live a godly and good life of one's own accord, without the compulsion of the law. This pleasure and love for the law is put into the heart by the Holy Spirit, as St. Paul says in [Rom] chapter 5:[5].[127]

The Church as the Locus
The Vehicle of God's Goods

Charles P. Arand recognizes in Luther two concurrent actions of the Holy Spirit's sanctification: faith in Christ and incorporation into the church.[128] The Word is an instrument by which the Spirit creates the church, not vice versa. Luther asserts, "For the church is the daughter born from the Word; she is not the mother of the Word."[129] While the gospel performs a magisterial role in begetting new life, the church performs a ministerial role in conforming us to the image of God. Luther inherits from Cyprian the functional aspect of the church as "the mother that begets and bears every Christian through the word of God, which the Holy Spirit reveals and proclaims."[130] Cyprian once said, "You cannot have God for our Father unless you have the church for our mother."[131]

---

125. *LW* 21:300.

126. *LW* 31:357.

127. *LW* 35:367–68. Also quoted in Simeon Zahl, "The Bondage of the Affections: Willing, Feeling, and Desiring in Luther's Theology, 1513–1525," in *The Spirit, the Affections, and the Christian Tradition*, ed. Dale M. Coulter and Amos Yong (University of Notre Dame Press, 2016), 194.

128. Charles P. Arand, "Luther on the Creed," in *The Pastoral Luther: Essays on Martin Luther's Practical Theology*, ed. Timothy J. Wengert (Eerdmans, 2009), 157.

129. *LW* 2:101; *WA* 42:334.

130. "The Large Catechism," *BC*, 436.

131. Cyprian, "On the Unity of the Catholic Church," in *The Ante-Nicene Fathers: Translations of the Writings of the Fathers Down to A.D. 325*, ed. Alexander Roberts et al., vol. 5, *Hyppolytus, Cyprian, Caius, Novatian, Appendix* (Repr., Hendrickson, 1995), 423.

The maternal care of the church enters Luther's hymn "To Me, She's Dear, the Worthy Maid": "The Mother must be alone, yet God will still protect her and be the true Father."[132]

The enthusiasts of Luther's time claimed to have inner, unmediated illumination apart from the external word. Their confidence rested on something within rather than on the gospel, which is the "one key word" that gathers up the external action of the Holy Spirit.[133] Any search for God within apart from the external forms of God's word, Luther warns, is "of the devil."[134] In *Against the Heavenly Prophets* (1515), Luther insists that God deals with us in two ways: "Outwardly . . . through the oral word of the gospel and through material signs, that is, baptism and the sacrament of the altar. Inwardly . . . through the Holy Spirit, faith, and other gifts."[135] The two actions—inward and outward—are of the same Spirit. "By binding the internal work of the Spirit to the external means of communication," Schwöbel argues, "the relational structure between God's Trinitarian action and the Christian faith is maintained."[136] The order of salvation proceeds from the external to the internal; in Luther's terms, "God has determined to give the inward to no one except through the outward."[137] The triumphalist, Luther chastises, "wants to teach us, not how the Spirit comes to us but how you come to the Holy Spirit."[138] The Holy Spirit comes to us, making us holy through "the Christian church, the forgiveness of sins, the resurrection of the body, and the life everlasting."[139] Bernhard Lohse points out that Luther explicitly adheres to Cyprian's phrase "Outside the church there is no salvation."[140] This is evident in the *Large Catechism*, where Luther writes, "Outside this Christian community, however, where there is no gospel, there is also no forgiveness," and hence "no holiness."[141] For Luther, justification occurs "through" the church but "not outside" it, as the "fanatics" teach.[142] This accounts for the order of the Third Article in which "immediately after the Holy Spirit is placed the Christian Church, in which all his gifts are to be found."[143]

---

132. See the whole song in *LW* 53:292–94, as cited in Peters, *Creed*, 279, Peters's translation.
133. Peters, *Creed*, 241.
134. "The Smalcald Articles," *BC*, 323.
135. *LW* 40:146.
136. Schwöbel, "Luther and the Trinity," 4.
137. *LW* 40:146.
138. *LW* 40:147.
139. "The Large Catechism," *BC*, 436.
140. See Cyprian: "salus extra ecclesiam non est." *The Letters of St. Cyprian of Carthage*, trans. G. W. Clarke (Newman, 1984), 51, as cited in Lohse, *Martin Luther's Theology*, 64n63.
141. "The Large Catechism," *BC*, 438.
142. *LW* 51:168.
143. *LW* 51:168.

Luther's pneumatology, Jeffrey G. Silcock rightly assesses, governs his ecclesiology: "Where the Spirit is, there is the church. But he does not say that where the church is, there is the Spirit. The Spirit is bound to the Word so that the Spirit is present where the Word is preached."[144] The unity of the Spirit and the Word must not be construed as a constriction of God's freedom to act. The activities of God may occur outside the external means of the Holy Spirit. There is no place in which God is not, because of God's simplicity. Niels Henrik Gregersen explains, "There are not two 'gods,' one transcendent, another immanent, nor are there two 'aspects' of God, an immanent plus a transcendent God. Rather, *the transcendent power of God must be wholly and fully present at all places.*"[145] Though God's works are evident in creation, there is no certainty that God is there "for us." Luther asserts, "It is one thing if God is present, and another if he is present for you. He is there for you when he adds his Word and binds himself, saying, 'Here you are to find me.'"[146] The two kinds of divine hiddenness already dealt with in our exposition of the Second Article of faith are relevant here. God does not meet us in his naked transcendence except through a medium. The Holy Spirit leads us away from God in his absolute, naked hiddenness that terrifies us toward God in his specific hiddenness in his word, his covering that consoles us. Luther differentiates between seeing God in heaven and seeing him on earth.

> We see Him as we see the sun through a cloud. For now we cannot bear to see and look at his brilliant Majesty. Therefore He must cover and veil Himself, so to speak, behind a heavy cloud. Thus it has been ordained that he who wants to see and apprehend both the Father and the Son glorified and enthroned in majesty, must apprehend Him through the Word and through the works he performs in Christendom by means of the ministry and other offices.[147]

Only when we seek him where he wills to be found do we possess the assurance that he is there "for us" and not against us. Silcock concludes, "The crucial point is that we do not bind God, but God binds us to the means of the Spirit while remaining free himself. The reason he binds us is that he wants us to seek him where he has promised to be found: in his holy Word and sacraments."[148] God has hidden his promise in the Word and its created forms, which, as Bayer says, "are the concrete way and manner in which Christ is present."[149]

---

144. Jeffrey G. Silcock, "Luther on the Holy Spirit and His Use of God's Word," in *The Oxford Handbook of Martin Luther's Theology*, ed. Robert Kolb et al., (Oxford University Press, 2014), 297.

145. Niels Henrik. Gregersen, "Grace in Nature and History: Luther's Doctrine of Creation Revisited," *Dialog: A Journal of Theology* 44, no. 1 (2005): 23, Gregersen's italics.

146. *LW* 37:68.

147. *LW* 24:67; *WA* 45:522.

148. Silcock, "Luther on the Spirit," 298–99.

149. Bayer, *Martin Luther's Theology*, 53.

Baptism

The Gospel Language

The forgiveness Christ won on the cross was not distributed there but here and now through the proclaimed word and the celebrated sacraments.[150] Luther links baptism to the cross, viewing it not as "a work" but rather "a treasure" that God "gives us and faith grasps."[151] Just as forgiveness accomplished on the cross of Christ is offered and conveyed to us in the sacred word, so it is hidden in baptism and communicated to us in "the Word and received by faith."[152] Despite Luther's huge stress on the "objective sacramental action" of the word and the benefits therein, Carl R. Trueman notes it is "faith in the promise" that ultimately delivers those baptismal benefits to us.[153] Quoting Luther's own words: "Thus it is not baptism that justifies or benefits anyone, but it is faith in that word of promise to which baptism is added. This faith justifies, and fulfills that which baptism signifies."[154] Luther exults in the simple expression "he who believes" (Mark 16:16), which he concedes is efficacious enough to make a person a worthy recipient of forgiveness. Faith, he writes, "trusts this Word of God" we hear in baptism, and renders effectual in us God's promise of grace hidden in it.[155] The justifying word spoken in baptism creates its corresponding reality, that the ungodly, in Luther's own words, "may be righteous and heirs" of eternal life.[156] The justifying verdict becomes, Luther describes superlatively, "surely most certainly true" by means of the faith that simply permits God's word to work in us.[157] Only God can make *ex nihilo* a sinner into a saint, and the reality of being made righteous is established in us by faith, which is, in Gerhard Ebeling's phrase, the "determinative and even decisive" factor.[158] Everything Christ is and all the Holy Spirit's gifts are imputed to the believers.

Luther makes use of Romans 6:4 to affirm baptism as "nothing else than the slaying of the old Adam and the resurrection of the new creature, both of which must continue in us our whole life long."[159] Luther frames baptism within the law-gospel distinction. As law, baptism purges the old creature of its evil inclinations until it finally ends; as gospel, it enlivens the new creature, causing it to

---

150. *LW* 40:213.
151. "The Large Catechism," *BC*, 461.
152. "The Large Catechism," *BC*, 461.
153. Carl R. Trueman, *Luther on the Christian Life: Cross and Freedom* (Crossway, 2015), 141.
154. *LW* 36:66.
155. "The Small Catechism," *BC*, 359.
156. "The Small Catechism," *BC*, 359.
157. "The Small Catechism," *BC*, 359.
158. Gerhard Ebeling, "Luther's Understanding of Reality," trans. Scott A. Celsor, *Lutheran Quarterly* 27, no. 1 (2013): 60.
159. "The Large Catechism," *BC*, 465.

rise in greater vigor. Jonathan Hoglund writes, "The very announcement that one's sins are forgiven in Christ puts one through the experience of faith, that is, through the experience of dying to oneself and living again in God's verdict."[160] The identity of the justified saint is shaped by the cruciform life, where the old Adam is denied free rein, and the new person is made alive and lives again in holiness and righteousness. Luther so highly praises baptism in his *Babylonian Captivity of the Church* that he regards it as "full and complete justification.... This should not be understood allegorically as the death of sin and the life of grace, as many understood it, but as actual death and resurrection. For baptism is not a false sign."[161] In baptism, as in justification, sin is blotted out and righteousness bestowed. Kolb says, "Baptism is gospel language."[162] It not only "announces" new life, says Luther, but actually "produces, begins, and exercises it."[163] As alien work, God's word annihilates the sinful identity; as proper work, it animates life in the righteous identity. It remakes us through the joyous exchange of Christ's righteousness for our sin, conforming us to his image.

Baptism is not merely an initiatory rite but God's continual act of cleansing and renewing throughout the whole Christian life. Jonathan D. Trigg explains, "Progress in the Christian life can never be progress away from the beginning of baptism [when we entered the Christian community], but a repeated return to it."[164] Though baptism is administered only once, its force is not vitiated by postbaptismal sin such as unbelief. The believer must not abandon baptism in favor of some other means to eternal life, such as penance. Luther repudiates Jerome's imagery of penance as "a second plank"[165] that a believer may hold onto for safety once the ship of baptism (a first plank)[166] flounders in the storm of sin. He considers it Jerome's error to see baptism as an act of the past, with no continuing relevance. "Baptism is an eternal covenant which does not lapse when we fall," he maintains, "but raises us up again."[167] Though believers may fall, they never fall outside the promise God has attached to their baptisms. When sins assault him, Luther's defense is baptism; he retorts, "But I am baptized! And if I have been baptized, I have the promise that I shall be saved and have eternal

---

160. Jonathan Hoglund, *Called by Triune Grace: Divine Rhetoric and the Effectual Call* (IVP Academic, 2016), 64.
161. *LW* 36:67.
162. Kolb, *Teaching God's Children*, 121.
163. "The Large Catechism," *BC*, 466.
164. Jonathan D. Trigg, *Baptism in the Theology of Martin Luther* (Brill, 2001), 96.
165. "The Large Catechism," *BC*, 466. See 465n220, which states: "Luther occasionally referred to penance as a sacrament, but in doing so he regarded it as part of baptism, emphasizing the declaration of forgiveness, or absolution, pronounced by the administrator."
166. "The Large Catechism," *BC*, 466n221.
167. *WA* 46:177.12–17, 29–35, as cited in Robert Kolb and Charles P. Arand, *The Genius of Luther's Theology: A Wittenberg Way of Thinking for the Contemporary Church* (Baker Academic, 2008), 192.

life, both in soul and body."[168] God's baptismal word of promise assures us of our identity as God's own. It is, says Luther, "the doorway to all of God's possessions and to the communion of the saints."[169] This "doorway," Stjerna discerns, takes on a Trinitarian shape, providing impetus for sanctification: it is "our Creator who gave and continues to give us life, our Redeemer who cleanses us from our sin and gives us new life again and again, and the Spirit who sustains us and keeps us connected to the Word. We grow in holiness that is not ours but becomes ours, because God wills it so."[170]

Baptismal Action
Confession and Absolution

Though not sacraments themselves, confession and absolution flow from, and are an extension of, the sacrament of baptism. In the *Large Catechism*, Luther adds a practical way in which God's baptismal action is reappropriated in confession and absolution. Against the fanatics or enthusiasts, Luther propounds that God conveys the grace of forgiveness, not through the secret working of the Holy Spirit, but through the physical, external word spoken by human beings: "I absolve you of your sins" (cf. Matt 18:15–19).[171] The whole of a genuinely Christian life, Luther concedes, consists in confession, which is summed up in two things: the acknowledgment of our wretched condition, and the appropriation of God's provision.[172] Luther does not deny private confession to another regarding a particular thing that torments the soul. Though this is not divinely commanded, he encourages the proper use of it to obtain wisdom, strength, and comfort from another.[173] Luther does not confine "the office of the keys"[174] to the professional clergy; rather he regards the absolution spoken by a lay Christian as fully effective as that spoken by the pastor in the stead of Jesus Christ.[175]

In his *Large Catechism*, Luther keeps the distinction between confession and absolution but exalts God's word of absolution.[176] We confess, not relying on the integrity of our confession, but on the efficacy of the word, even when it comes through the lips of a frail person. We express our needs, not for the purpose of impressing God with a splendid work that we perform, but to hear

---

168. "The Large Catechism," *BC*, 462.
169. "The Small Catechism," *BC*, 373.
170. Kirsi I. Stjerna, *No Greater Jewel: Thinking about Baptism with Luther* (Augsburg, 2009), 67.
171. "The Large Catechism," *BC*, 477.
172. "The Large Catechism," *BC*, 477.
173. "The Large Catechism," *BC*, 477.
174. *LW* 41:153–54.
175. *LW* 69:330.
176. "The Large Catechism," *BC*, 478.

God's majestic word by which the contrite heart is healed.[177] Comfort lies in confession only because hidden in it is the gift of absolution.[178] The verbal declaration of forgiveness, Girgensohn writes, is not of a "hypothetical" kind; it truly does what it says.[179] It is no mere sign pointing to a gift hidden elsewhere at a distance; rather it is an effective sign truly delivering the gift of forgiveness, "not at a later time," Bayer notes, "but at the very moment it is uttered."[180] The verbal act of absolution is not simply "declarative," but "performative"; forgiveness is not merely disclosed, but truly delivered.[181]

In the *Small Catechism*,[182] Luther offers a simple instruction on how confession could become, as Ronald K. Rittgers conceives, a "salutary" occasion in which the gospel is conveyed personally to the person in view.[183] Luther places the sinner under the law, the agent exposing sins, which leads him to the gospel, the agent disposing of them. He advises that we should confess our sins against the commandments, and against the Lord's Prayer, acknowledging only those sins we know of, and over which we are troubled. He also suggests using the vocational structure that is laid out in the *Table of Christian Callings* as a guide to expose our sins. For instance, a parent may confess that he has sinned against God for his failure to care for his child. Luther breaks away from the medieval practice of enumerating sins, which had turned confession into a torturous burden. When our consciences are not terribly burdened with guilt, we should neither invent sins nor search within for more, as this only serves to cast us into despair. Instead, we should cite one or two deeds in which we have offended commandments two through ten, through which we become aware of our grievous sin of defiance against the God of the first commandment. When consciences are heavily burdened and cannot be relieved, the confessor should use additional passages of Scripture to comfort them. In a situation where we do not feel any more sins, which for Luther is "(really quite unlikely),"[184] we should then make a general confession and proceed to receive forgiveness for it. The confessor will then bless the penitent and ask him whether he believes the word of forgiveness spoken by him. In response to the penitent's word of faith, "'Yes, dear sir,'" the confessor will pronounce God's verdict: "Let it be done for you according to your faith. And I by the command of our Lord Jesus Christ forgive you in the name

---

177. "The Large Catechism," *BC*, 478.
178. "The Large Catechism," *BC*, 478.
179. Herbert Girgensohn, *Teaching Luther's Catechism*, vol. 2, trans. John Doberstein (Muhlenberg, 1960), 80.
180. Bayer, *Martin Luther's Theology*, 49.
181. Oswald Bayer, *Theology the Lutheran Way*, ed. and trans. Jeffrey G. Silcock and Mark C. Mattes (Eerdmans, 2007), 130.
182. "The Small Catechism," *BC*, 360–61.
183. Ronald K. Rittgers, "Luther on Private Confession," in Wengert, *The Pastoral Luther*, 214.
184. "The Small Catechism," *BC*, 361, Luther's brackets.

of the Father and of the Son and of the Holy Spirit. Amen. Go in peace."[185] A terrified conscience finds relief in the reality of God's promise offered in absolution and leaves the confession with a peaceful conscience. Confession without absolution is fruitless, just as the law by itself works against justification unless it is accompanied by the gospel.

The Lord's Supper
It Benefits Us, Not God

Both baptism and the Lord's Supper share the same gospel "content":[186] the forgiveness of sin. Just as the treasures Christ has purchased through the cross are hidden in the baptismal word, so the benefits he conveys to his own are hidden in the eucharistic word. The Lord's Supper is intrinsically linked to the cross where Christ was crucified for the forgiveness of sin; yet the forgiveness of sin that he acquired is communicated to us, according to Luther, through "the Word."[187] Christ's body and blood are poured out in the Supper; the forgiveness of sin is offered there. Luther elucidates:

> If now I seek the forgiveness of sins, I do not run to the cross, for I will not find it given there. Nor must I hold to the suffering of Christ, as Dr. Karlstadt trifles, in knowledge or remembrance, for I will not find it there either. But I will find it in the sacrament or gospel the word which distributes, presents, offers, and gives to me that forgiveness which was won on the cross.[188]

The justifying word at the banquet bears fruits of itself: it truly delivers forgiveness of sins and creates life, just as it says, and the forgiven saints live on that verdict. The forgiveness of sin is a real gift imparted through the word. "The gift Christ distributes," Girgensohn writes, "is his own body and blood, that is, himself. He is not only the subject but also the object of his action."[189] Christ's body and blood are a "sure pledge and sign" that assure us of it.[190] The sign is no empty sign; nor does it point to a reality in the future; it is that which effects his own action and his real presence at every reenactment of the Supper. The power of the sacrament rests on the strength of the words from Christ's lips, not

---

185. "The Small Catechism," *BC*, 362.
186. *LW* 42:175.
187. "The Large Catechism," *BC*, 469.
188. *LW* 40:214.
189. Girgensohn, *Teaching Luther's Catechism*, 2:94.
190. "The Large Catechism," *BC*, 469.

God's Most Earnest Purpose in Sanctification   179

on human worthiness; it remains valid, "even though a knave should receive or administer it."[191]

Luther conceives the Lord's Supper in terms of a "new and eternal testament" (Gal 3–4) or a "last will and testament" (Heb 9:16–17). Luther writes at length in *The Babylonian Captivity of the Church*:

> A testament . . . is a promise made by one about to die, in which he designates his bequest and appoints his heirs. A testament, therefore, involves, first, the death of the testator, and second, the promise of an inheritance and the naming of the heir. . . . Christ testifies concerning his death when he says: "This is my body, which is given, this is my blood, which is poured out" (Lk. 22:19–20). He names and designates the bequest when he says "for the forgiveness of sins" (Matt. 26:28). But he appoints the heirs when he says "for you (Lk. 22:19–20; 1 Cor. 11:24) and for many" (Matt. 26:28; Mk. 14:24), that is, for those who accept and believe the promise of the testator.[192]

Three things make up a last will: Christ's announcement of his promise of grace, his appointment of the beneficiary of that promise, and the confirmation of his promise by his own death. The Lord's Supper is the reenactment of that will, and the reading of that testament, through which the precious promises of eternal life are now effective, if only we believe. "Hence to seek the efficacy of the sacrament apart from the promise and apart from faith," Luther intimates, "is to labor in vain and to find condemnation."[193] The words of institution with which Christ invites us are so "wonderful" that Luther is motivated to come to the table. There he delights in hearing the last will read again, and receives the distribution of the inheritance, as he lets the words of Christ apply to himself (cf. Luke 1:38).[194] The Supper truly buries sin and bestows life, the corresponding realities not created by bodily eating and drinking, but only by the word itself that underlies faith. Kolb puts it aptly: "The trust which responds to the Word drives our lives, by the power of the Holy Spirit, into Edenic paths and patterns" characterized by righteousness, holiness, and everlasting blessedness.[195]

Like baptism, the Supper is not efficacious in being celebrated but in being believed. "The Lord's Supper is not just a rite guaranteeing grace when correctly performed by a priest (*ex opere operato*)," as Gritsch and Jenson write, "but rather an event celebrating the existential relationship between God's Word and man's

---

191. "The Large Catechism," *BC*, 468.
192. *LW* 36:38.
193. *LW* 36:67.
194. *LW* 42:174.
195. Kolb, *Teaching God's Children*, 129.

faith. The Word creates faith and faith in turn creates the fellowship of those who with grateful hearts celebrate new life with God."[196] A saving relation with God presupposes a correlation of the word of promise and the reception of faith: "For the sacramental form of the word, like the word itself, is present for faith; it depends on faith and contributes nothing to a man's salvation without faith."[197] Both the "content" and "intent," Luther affirms, are inherent in the same words of Christ: "for us, for the remission of sins."[198] Faith grasps both the sacramental content, the bestowal of God's bequests, and the sacramental intent, the reconstitution of the new creature. The passive nature of faith underscores the Supper as God's act, not ours; it is God's gift that we receive. We do not come and benefit the Supper, as though we could give anything to God; rather we receive and benefit from what God gives through the word. The mode of giving and receiving marks the basic difference between eucharistic sacrifice and the sacrament of the Supper.[199] The former is a human work through which we give to God an offering to appease God's wrath. Conversely, the latter is a gift—more precisely, a liturgical enactment of God's grace that we receive and celebrate with gratitude. The key to Luther's theology of atonement, Forde writes, lies in a "great reversal": "not that something is given to God, but that God gives something to us."[200] Such understanding casts light on Luther's view of the Eucharist, that it is not a sacrifice we offer to God, but a gift Christ confers on us. Luther writes:

> We see, then, that the best and greatest part of all sacraments and of the mass is the word of promises of God, without which the sacraments are dead and are nothing at all.... No one gives God anything or does him a service, but instead takes something [from him].... I accept for myself alone the blessing therein offered by God—and here there is no *officium* but *beneficium*, no work or service, but reception and benefit alone.[201]

---

196. Gritsch and Jenson, *Lutheranism*, 76.
197. *LW* 36:38.
198. *LW* 42:175.
199. For a discussion of the distinction between benefit (*beneficium*) and sacrifice (*sacrificium*), see Risto Saarinen, "Luther and *Beneficia*," in *The Reformation as Christianization: Essays on Scott Hendrix's Christianization Thesis*, ed. Anna Marie Johnson and John A. Maxfield (Mohr Siebeck, 2012), 169–88; John T. Pless, "Reflections on the Life of the Royal Priesthood: Vocation and Evangelism," in *Shepherd the Church: Essays in Pastoral Theology Honoring Bishop Roger D. Pittelko*, ed. Frederic W. Baue et al. (Concordia Theological Seminary, 2002), 274–75; Carl F. Wisløff, *The Gift of Communion: Luther's Controversy with Rome on Eucharistic Sacrifice*, trans. Joseph M. Shaw (Augsburg Publishing House, 1964).
200. Gerhard O. Forde, "Luther's Theology of the Cross," in *Christian Dogmatics*, vol. 2, ed. Carl E. Braaten and Robert W. Jenson (Fortress, 1984), 50.
201. *LW* 35:91, 93–94.

God's Most Earnest Purpose in Sanctification

In his Supper, the Lord unites us once again with the body of Christ's death, where the old life of sin dies; he too joins us to his resurrection body, where the new life of grace lives. Like in baptism, God's word performs a double work in us: the alien work of burying "our old skin" and its sins in Christ's tomb where God no longer looks, and the proper work of birthing the new life so that it may grow in holiness as we live on God's justifying word and his gifts.[202] God's word, as Forde puts it, is "the death knell of the old and harbinger of the absolutely new."[203] The eucharistic word is involved in the re-creation of the justified life. It serves as the daily sustenance of our faith so that we are strengthened to combat sins and the vices arising from clinging to the old existence.[204]

The sanctifying work of the Spirit is not restricted to public worship or a "bodily assembly," which Luther distinguishes from a "spiritual assembly."[205] The word "daily" stresses the daily involvement of the Holy Spirit in the life of the righteous: at home, in the workplace, and in the various stations of life. When they gather and pray the Ten Commandments or the psalms and hear the word of absolution from a pastor or others, the Holy Spirit is present in making us holy. Believers are nurtured by the superabundance of God's grace conveyed through these vehicles of divine presence. Luther conceives the church, Michael Richard Laffin discerns, "not in static fashion," but dynamically as "the event of Christ's presence to the community gathered in worship, and therefore understands the church as a creature of the Word, a creature that is both fallible and hidden."[206] The Christian community is so richly furnished that no one is without relief from guilt, forgiveness for residual sins, and strength for weak faith. The church, our mother, may face assaults of this world, but though alone, she is never truly alone, as she remains in the grip of her Father's care. Even when the church fails, she remains our mother, to whom we keep going back for help. The maternal image dispels any element of individualism and independence so characteristic of contemporary churches. The word, and the various forms in which it takes, binds believers in the unity of faith and love, the former being causative of the latter. Love does not justify but is a location in which faith becomes a tangible reality. The life we live before God by faith finds expression in the life we live by love for our neighbors. True faith is never alone; it must become incarnate by its outward works of love. Believers are not only incorporated into Christ but also with each other in him. Participation in the communion of the church, which includes the embodiment of self-sacrificial love, is the incarnate expression of the

---

202. "The Large Catechism," *BC*, 467.
203. Gerhard O. Forde, *Justification by Faith: A Matter of Death and Life* (Sigler, 1990), 37.
204. "The Large Catechism," *BC*, 469.
205. *LW* 11:372; *WA* 4:239.22–24.
206. Michael Richard Laffin, *The Promise of Martin Luther's Political Theology: Freeing Luther from the Modern Political Narrative* (Bloomsbury T&T Clark, 2018), 73.

new creature seized by grace. Justifying faith takes on an ecclesial form so that the Spirit-filled life is never apart from the community through which "there is full forgiveness of sins, both in that God forgives us and that we forgive, bear with, and aid one another."[207] The believer does not exist in solitariness but in solidarity with other believers in a community in which God's grace is mediated. The "communion of saints" benefits all: "Hence, all the prayers and good deeds of all the Christian community benefit, aid, and strengthen me and every other believer at all times, both in life and in death, and that each one bears the other's burden" (Gal 6:2).[208] This steers us away from a purely subjective, unmediated encounter with God apart from the church where the word comes. It safeguards against the reduction of faith to, John M. Barclay rightly describes, "an interior, individual phenomenon" devoid of its social reality.[209]

Justification and Eschatology
Fully Righteous at the End

Luther's emphasis on the individual "me" runs through the First Article ("he created me"), the Second Article ("he redeemed me"), and the Third Article ("he made me holy"). In eschatology, his focus is on the final and complete restoration of the individual to the image of God as found in Christ. Luther ends the Creed with a personal emphasis on the "me," followed by the global "all": the Holy Spirit will "raise me and all the dead, and give to me and all believers eternal life."[210] Sanctification is incomplete without bodily resurrection and eternal life, the remaining two parts of the Third Article summed up by Stjerna in two words: "holiness and hope."[211]

God has yet to complete his work of gathering all believers and communicating his forgiveness. Luther writes, "We remain only halfway pure and holy."[212] This is true of us from the perspective of sanctification. The language of fraction—"halfway"—speaks of the residual sin that still clings to the old Adam, which requires the Spirit's mortification through the law. But at the same time (*simul*), through justification we are perfectly pure and holy and will never become purer or holier than we already are through faith. No work of love turns the justified into persons that they are not already—that is, they are already wholly righteous through faith. Christian emulation of Christ as example is basically the outward expression of Christ as gift. The performance of good deeds

---

207. "The Large Catechism," *BC*, 438.
208. *LW* 43:28.
209. John M. G. Barclay, *Paul and the Gift* (Eerdmans, 2017), 572.
210. "The Small Catechism," *BC*, 355–56.
211. Stjerna, *Lutheran Theology*, 105.
212. "The Large Catechism," *BC*, 438.

is the occasion of actualizing the gift of perfect righteousness that is already possessed by faith, not the occasion of accumulating moral virtues or merits. "The life of the Christian as *partim iustus* and *partim peccator*," Stephen Hultgren writes, "is a struggle for the realization of the total righteousness already given in justification over the human's total fallenness. But this is not to be understood in the sense of the progress of an ethical subject, the Christian's moving forward from an incomplete reality toward a complete ideal. It is rather two complete wholes (complete righteousness and complete fallenness) battling each other."[213] Luther's statement about being "only halfway pure and holy" does not have a temporal and quantitative sense, as Luther is not working with fractions or empirical verification.[214] Luther simply wants to remind us that in sanctification we cooperate with God, under the Spirit's lead, in driving out from us the sin that is clinging so firmly to the old nature. It is like saying we have already been raised in Christ through faith, but the old Adam in us must still be drowned by daily repentance. For Luther, quantitative thinking is not in view; we are both wholly saints and wholly sinners. His language of becoming or fraction ("halfway holy") has to be taken rhetorically and not literally.

Justified existence now is dominated by "coincidental opposites" of saint and sinner; the paradox of faith is, to use Paul Althaus's formulation, "both to have and at the same time not to have, to be and at the same time not yet to be."[215] The imputation of righteousness is "extremely necessary, first because we are not yet purely righteous [in an empirical sense], but sin is still clinging to our flesh during this life."[216] The christological presupposition of justification entails two things: "I am a sinner in and by myself apart from Christ. Apart from myself and in Christ I am not a sinner."[217] In so far as the old flesh remains, we are, in Luther's terms, "sick persons under the care of a physician: they are sick in fact

---

213. Stephen Hultgren, "The Problem of Freedom Today and the Third Use of the Law: Biblical and Theological Considerations," in *The Necessary Distinction: A Continuing Conversation on Law and Gospel*, ed. Albert B. Collver III et al., (Concordia Publishing House, 2017), 204.

214. See *LW* 27:21–22; *WA* 40.2:25, where the language of fraction, that righteousness is becoming and not yet whole and complete, appears in the following passage in his commentary on Galatians. Luther writes, "We have indeed begun to be justified by faith, by which we have also received the first fruits of the Spirit; and the mortification of our flesh has begun. But we are not perfectly righteous. Our being justified perfectly still remains to be seen, and this is what we hope for. Thus our righteousness does not yet exist in fact, but it still exists in hope.... Thus both things are true: that I am righteous here with an incipient righteousness; and that in this hope I am strengthened against sin and look for the consummation of perfect righteousness in heaven." Here is a sample of the language of becoming, as Luther seeks to formulate the *simul* doctrine. In the overall scheme, Luther considers faith as the key concept through which to capture the *simul* of justification, that we are both complete and incomplete at the same time: perfectly holy and still completely sinner—no fractions! This is the paradox of faith.

215. Paul Althaus, *The Theology of Martin Luther*, trans. Robert C. Schultz (Fortress, 1966), 404.
216. *LW* 26:132–33; *WA* 40.1:233.
217. *LW* 38:158.

but healthy in hope and in the fact that they are beginning to be healthy, that is, they are 'being healed.'"[218] Sanctification continues what is accomplished in justification in this life, until it reaches its consummation in future life. The Holy Spirit perfects us through the word, conferring upon us daily forgiveness until the last day when we will be rid of all sin, death, and defects, and become perfectly holy people, fully endowed with infinite righteousness and complete freedom to serve God. In saying this, we must not forget the other side of the equation, and that is we are already perfectly holy people by faith. The difference is that this side of the grave, our perfection and holiness are not empirical realities but must be grasped by faith; but in the resurrection, our new life in Christ will be all there is to see, because the old sinful life will have been destroyed. Luther teaches, "This is as if to say, 'So long as we live on earth, believing in his word, we are a work that God has begun, but not yet completed; but after death we shall be perfect, a divine work without sin or fault.'"[219]

Death, the curse of sin, becomes the cure for it, and in this regard, death is a blessed curse; as Luther stresses, "And that God appointed death to be the destroyer of death can be gathered from the fact that he imposed death on Adam immediately after his sin as a cure for sin" (Gen 3:19).[220] Luther further elaborates that sin, the root, gives rise to death, its fruit. And yet, the root of sin is killed by its own offspring.

> Sin is destroyed by its own fruit and is slain by the death to which it gave birth, as a viper is devoured by its own offspring. It is a glorious spectacle to see how sin is destroyed, not by the work of another, but by its own, and how it is stabbed with its own sword, as Goliath is beheaded by his own sword (1 Sam. 17:51).[221]

For unbelievers, death remains a curse for sin; for believers, death was the agent of God's mercy. "In appearance," says Luther, our sufferings and dying are common to all without distinction; "in reality, our sufferings are the beginning of our freedom as our death is the beginning of life."[222] Death, that which was imposed by God as punishment for sin, ultimately works blessing for believers. Thus those who love life or righteousness must embrace death, which Luther deems as "[God's] servant and workshop."[223] Death itself has no intrinsic value. Yet God deems it a blessing precisely for the work it performs, that it effects a permanent

---

218. *LW* 25:336; *WA* 56:347.
219. *LW* 32:24.
220. *LW* 42:151.
221. *LW* 42:151.
222. *LW* 42:142.
223. *LW* 42:151.

end to the evil of sin, and to all evils. Conceived in this manner, death provides sure comfort; Heinrich Bornkamm writes, "It is not *our* death, since we have a home with the Father; but it is the *death* of our sin, the end of all imperfections. Our incompleteness shall come to an end; death refines us into the purity and perfection of a divine work."[224] God's justifying and sanctifying action are one. God not only begins to make a new creature out of the old, but also continues to re-create the one whom he justifies until he has made him righteous in himself. God justifies believers in the present with an eschatological view of what they will become in the future—completely pure like him. In this, justification cannot be without eschatology.[225] The profound truth here is that the judgment of acquittal that God pronounces over us through faith is the very verdict that God will utter over us at the final judgment. In that sense, the verdict of acquittal that God speaks over us here in baptism and faith is proleptic and anticipates the verdict he will speak over us in the last judgment. The present verdict is identical to the future verdict. The unity of the present verdict and future verdict is a reality at the eschaton, when faith shall be sight; likewise, the "paradoxical" unity of the law and the gospel gives way to the "original" unity of the law and the gospel, when the Spirit will have completed his sanctifying work, and when sin and all its vices are annihilated at the end.

The unity of justification and eschatology points to God as the active subject, working *ex nihilo* all the way from re-creation to consummation. Luther teaches, "We are thus held in God's arms as the beginning of the new creation until we are made perfect in the resurrection of the dead."[226] The "power for obedience," David Löfgren argues, stems "finally not from out of himself or any created thing at all, but rather from faith in the resurrection of the dead, which indeed means the end of dying."[227] Christ's resurrection "has destroyed sin and raised up righteousness, abolished death and restored life, conquered hell and bestowed everlasting glory on us."[228] God is reversing what the first Adam has done amiss, leading us toward this *telos*, that we might be fully righteous like him, and that in paradise, natural endowments—thinking, willing, seeing, fearing, trusting, and loving God—will have reached perfection. Sanctification *ex nihilo* comprises two things: the final termination of sin and every vice, and total restoration of our humanity to its pristine image in Eden. The act of redemption that began

---

224. Heinrich Bornkamm, *Luther's World of Thought*, trans. Martin H. Bertram (Concordia, 1965), 130, Bornkamm's italics.

225. Althaus, *Theology of Martin Luther*, 404: "Luther's theology is thoroughly eschatological in the strict sense of expecting the end of world."

226. *WA* 39.1:83, as cited in Althaus, *Theology of Martin Luther*, 238n69.

227. See David Löfgren, *Die Theologie der Schöpfung bei Luther* (Göttingen, 1969), 301, as quoted in George Wolfgang Forell, "Justification and Eschatology in Luther's Thought," *Church History* 38, no. 2 (1969): 167n15.

228. *LW* 42:164.

in Christ's cross and resurrection points to the eschatological destiny where a full revelation in its glorious future form will occur. Luther expands, "In this life we lay hold of this goal in ever so weak a manner; but in the future life we shall attain it fully."[229] The old, mortal, earthly body of the present gives way to the new, immortal, and glorified body of the future, in which we live eternally with God. What is buried "in dishonor," as Paul says, is raised "in glory" (1 Cor 15:43). This life is confiscated in exchange for the everlasting life.

> On that Day we shall have a better and statelier [life] than the one in Paradise was. For we shall not be placed into a physical life, which by its nature is subject to change, but into a spiritual life, into which Adam, too, would have been translated if he had lived without sin. To this hope we are led by Christ, who has restored our freedom from guilt through the remission of sins and who makes our state better than the state of Adam was in Paradise.[230]

God's judgment crucifies all attempts to depict justification or make it palatable. The believer lives by God's verdict that they are fully innocent via the imputation of Christ's righteousness and are blessed, both now and in the life to come. Faith already receives forgiveness and all graces in the present, awaiting their full revelation in the eschaton. What believers have in this life is a tiny faith that grasps only a small portion of the heavenly inheritances; in Chester's words, "the minute center of an infinite divinely drawn circle that cannot and must not be measured by merely human sense or reason. The only human experience in this life that is of any ultimate significance is the one that points beyond and outside that life, and beyond the world as the realm of human experience, towards eschatological fulfillment."[231] In view of the heavenly inheritance awaiting us, the world and everything in it become vile and pale into insignificance. Luther reflects in contrast, "Whatever the world admires and exalts most, that is foul and worthless. . . . For what is the whole world with its power, wealth, and glory in comparison with God, whose heir and son [we are]? . . . We would not attach our hearts so firmly to physical things that their presence would give us confidence and their removal would produce dejection and even despair."[232] Blessing or bane does not constitute our identity. We neither find security in our abundance nor despair for lack of it. By faith, the merits of Christ are indeed ours, as if we had won them. Our identity as God's

---

229. *LW* 1:131; *WA* 42:98.
230. *LW* 1:100; *WA* 42:76.
231. Stephen J. Chester, "'Abba! Father!' (Gal. 4:6): Justification and Assurance in Martin Luther's Lectures on Galatians (1535)," *Biblical Research: Journal of the Chicago Society of Biblical Research* 63 (2018): 22.
232. *LW* 26:392–93; *WA* 40.1:598–89.

children is given; it is not bound up with the creaturely things we possess, but with the heavenly inheritances won by Christ that are accrued to us, the appointed heirs (Gal 4:7). Whoever is seized by the infinite riches of heavenly inheritance would welcome death (as does Paul in Phil 1:23) as "the most joyous peace for he knows it is the end of all his evils and that through it he comes into his inheritance."[233]

Justification cannot be without eschatology; conversely, eschatology cannot be without justification. The "actual righteousness" or "proper righteousness" we attain on earth can never be the basis of a righteous standing before the judgment seat of Christ. All works of "active righteousness" are sinking sand; Christ's mediatory activity alone is the solid rock. Justification rests on God's judgment, and we bring nothing of our own except the "alien righteousness" that remains hidden in Christ. God's verdict of acquittal is effective now where there is an absence of the demonstrable change or consequence of an effective justification. No change of mind or opinion or renewed morality grounds our assurance except God's justifying verdict. Our trust is not in the proof of our performance, not even in, to use Luther's own phrase, "borrowed goodness,"[234] a goodness created by grace, but solely on the infallible promises offered in the Creed ("Christ has purchased and freed me"; "the Holy Spirit will raise me and all the dead, and give to me and all believers everlasting life"). Original sin results in the movement from life to death; grace reverses the direction, resulting in the movement from death to life. The merits of Christ conquer, to use Hans Joachim Iwand's phrase, "an impossible return to the origin"[235] due to sin and restores to us the righteous identity we originally had in the garden of Eden. On Christ's act of repristination, Mark C. Mattes remarks, "The promise of God is able to intoxicate the soul, making it love God, in a way that is reminiscent of original righteousness. In other words, nature needs not be a self-driven perfection, but liberation. Through such liberation God will bring humans to their fulfillment."[236] On Romans 8:21, "The creation itself will be set free," Luther avers, "Creation will be set free, from vanity, when the ungodly have been condemned and taken away and when the old man has been destroyed. This liberation is now taking place every day in the lives of the saints"; creation "will not only no longer be vain but also it will not subject to corruption in the future."[237] The Spirit's sanctifying work of conforming us to Christ as the object of the Father's love is complete when all opposites of justification are discarded, and we are restored to our original shape and reinstated with the power of new obedience. Every negativity is annihilated: The

---

233. *LW* 26:393; *WA* 40.1:599.
234. *LW* 44:24.
235. Hans Joachim Iwand, "The Preaching of the Law," in *Hans Joachim Iwand on Church and Society: Opened by the Kingdom of God*, ed. Benjamin Haupt et al., trans. Christian Einertson (T&T Clark, 2023), 9.
236. Mark C. Mattes, *Martin Luther's Theology of Beauty: A Reappraisal* (Baker Academic, 2017), 110.
237. *LW* 25:363; *WA* 56:373.

law that holds us in captivity ceases, the old flesh that tempts us dies, the wrath that terrorizes us ends, and the death that frightens us loses its power. We, like the first creatures, live in harmony with God and other creatures, and are again "intoxicated with rejoicing toward God."[238] The beauty of communion with the triune God in perfect bliss, sincere desire, and perfect freedom is given back to "me" and "all believers" *ex nihilo*, ushering us into the eschatological rest. Each "I" must apply to themself this eschatological hope in faith, believing that they, together with "all believers," are given a share in the eternal Sabbath already promised in Christ. The eschatological, eternal rest is "proleptically present" to the righteous identity in time *extra nos* by God's word. Jack D. Kilcrease expands:

> Creatures find their reality suspended between protology and eschatology. On the one hand, creatures find their identity and authenticity in their passive receptivity to the identity bestowed upon them by God's protological word. On the other hand, because creaturely identity necessarily must also anticipate the future, it can repose in the promise of final sabbath rest rather than an identity anxiously established by works performed throughout time. In time, humans can participate in an eschatological fellowship with God's eternal rest, already proleptically present to them in time through God's Word of grace.[239]

The church by the Spirit now lives in the triumphant hope of final victory already begun in Christ, and participates, Peters asserts, in "the eschatological saving work of God and finds [their] true existence in this faith."[240] Despite appearances to the contrary, we are held in the grip of Trinitarian grace from the beginning of faith to its end. Phillip Cary summarizes this well:

> To believe the Gospel is to cling to a kind word of grace in which Christ says "you" and means me, knowing that the word gives every good thing that it promises, because God is true to his word and Christ is God. Our clinging to this word in faith is the work of the Holy Spirit, who by this fact makes us members of Christ's body so that in the end we may stand in the presence of God the Father together with all his holy ones, in perfection and great joy. It is an immense privilege to teach this: the Spirit through the word brings us in Christ to the Father, so that we are partakers in the life of the holy Trinity.[241]

---

238. *LW* 1:94; *WA* 42:71.
239. Jack D. Kilcrease, *Justification by the Word: Restoring "Sola Fide"* (Lexham Academic, 2022), 12.
240. Peters, *Creed*, 278–79.
241. Phillip Cary, *The Meaning of Protestant Theology: Luther, Augustine, and the Gospel that Gives Us Christ* (Baker Academic, 2019), 338.

CHAPTER SIX

God's Most Earnest Purpose in the Lord's Prayer

SINCE IT IS God's nature to give, as the Creed affirms, our position before God is one of receiving, for we cannot give what is not our own. So whether we stand before God as creatures in the First Article, or as sinners in the Second and Third Articles, we remain the passive recipients of God's superabundant grace. The Lord's Prayer causes us to see our helplessness and emptiness so that we do not look within us for help and fulfillment but outside us, to God. It teaches us to receive what the Creed has acquired for us through its fulfillment of the Ten Commandments. Prayer, for Luther, is "a special exercise of faith"[1] by which we grasp the gracious activities of the triune God. "Consequently, nothing is so necessary as to call upon God incessantly and to drum into his ears our prayer that he may give, preserve, and increase in us faith and the fulfillment of the Ten Commandments and remove all that stands in our way and hinders us in this regard."[2] Prayer is our response to God's fatherly invitation to his beloved children to hear Jesus teach and reap from him assurance and consolation. Prayer places us in the passive position of receiving God's grace, not meriting God's favor. Each petition of the Lord's Prayer diagnoses the need that besets us; each is accompanied by a promise of God's mercy as his remedy. Not only do we receive instruction on how and what to pray, but also where to obtain help.[3] The Lord's Prayer, for Luther, is the noblest of prayers, which we should not exchange for the world's riches.[4] It bears powerful witness that God is not only pleased to hear it, but also eager to provide for us.[5] Prayer is not an occasion when we instruct God about our needs; rather it is God instructing us of our needs and of the blessings he lavishly gives. So, Luther stresses, "there is no need for you to persuade Him with your words or to give him detailed instructions. . . . Whatever He gives us will be in excess of our understanding and hopes."[6] Prayer does not cause God to draw nigh; rather in prayer, God causes us to come to him through his own word, as it appears in certain forms:

---

1. *LW* 44:58.
2. "The Large Catechism," *BC*, 440.
3. "The Large Catechism," *BC*, 445.
4. "The Large Catechism," *BC*, 443.
5. "The Large Catechism," *BC*, 443, 445.
6. *LW* 21:144.

his command, his promise, and the words of Christ. All of these are made efficacious by faith, which is summed up in our willingness to close our prayer with the word "Amen." Luther thus hails the Lord's Prayer "the prayer of prayers,"[7] which we should pray for as long as we live.

Just as we by ourselves cannot believe in Christ apart from the Holy Spirit, so too we by ourselves cannot pray to God, especially in circumstances that seemingly contradict God's promise, unless by the Holy Spirit, who draws us to approach God. Our filial confidence on God is the ground of our prayer; it is not achieved by the performance of law; it is solely given by the Holy Spirit. The tiny "sigh" or faith of the Holy Spirit that brings us the Father's comfort and riches is set opposite the "beggarly" function of the law that issues forth fear and impoverishment; the former is the remedy to the latter. Confronted by the internal conflicts between law and gospel, we remain persuaded of the oceanic immensity of God's promise that God is our beloved Father on account of Christ's work by the Holy Spirit, who is imparted to our hearts and causes us to cry "Abba! Father!" (Gal 4.6). Prayer thus takes on a Trinitarian shape, in such a way that "its theological character as promise," Bayer writes, "is central," and is its very "basis and power."[8] An efficacious prayer is not based on its own merit but on the "promise of God whose 'yes,'" Steven D. Paulson says, "is Christ."[9] God's fatherly promises are fully hidden in Christ and are imparted to us through the Holy Spirit. There is nothing for us to do, Luther affirms, except to "accept" his promise of "fatherhood" and "reply with a sigh," saying, "Father"; this guarantees our sonship and our eternal inheritance, including our conversation with God, on account of Christ's mediatorship.[10] All that the Son is and has, including his communion with the Father, belongs to those whom the Spirit "destined to be a son of God and a fellow heir with Christ."[11] His prayer for us and with us is immediate, while ours is mediated through Christ but just as efficacious, for they are one. The fulfillment of prayer presupposes the nothingness of a beggarly heart. What is invoked in prayer is not the preexistent salvific materials in us but the preexistent gifts acquired by the economic action of the Trinity. Prayer that originates from a destitute heart rather than from a self-fortified heart reaches God's ears. A vacuity of heart is the occasion or reason for the reception of God's extravagant gifts by prayer. Not until we are empty of all

---

7. *Table Talk* (1531), no. 88, *WA* TR 1:34.4–5 (n.d.), no. 6288; *WA* TR 5:582.1–2, as cited in John W. Kleinig, "Introduction to the Lord's Prayer," in *Luther's Large Catechism with Annotations and Contemporary Applications*, ed. John T. Pless and Larry M. Vogel (Concordia Publishing House, 2022), 463.

8. Oswald Bayer, *Martin Luther's Theology: A Contemporary Interpretation*, trans. Thomas H. Trapp (Eerdmans, 2008), 346. See 351, where *WA* 17.1:249.15 (*Rogate Sermon*, 1525) is cited.

9. Steven D. Paulson, *Lutheran Theology* (T&T Clark, 2011), 120.

10. *LW* 26:390; *WA* 40.1:593.

11. *LW* 22:88; *WA* 46:612.

human resources through the law's alien work are we ready for a reception of God's creative gracious action in us, including filling our hearts with all his goods by prayer.

The Command to Pray
The Law and Gospel Distinction

The command to pray is to be taken as seriously as any other commandment. As part of his exposition of the second commandment, Luther writes, "God will not have this commandment treated as a jest but will be angry and punish us if we do not pray, just as he punishes all kinds of disobedience. Nor will he allow our prayers to be frustrated or lost, for if he did not intend to answer you, he would not have ordered you to pray and backed it up with such a strict commandment."[12] Just as God imposes on us his command to pray so that we dare not disobey, so also he impresses on us God's promise so that we are motivated to pray all the more. We are drawn to pray, not because we are worthy of it, but because God has commanded it and promised to hear us. Command and promise are bound together; as Luther makes clear, "And just as it is the purpose of Christ's promise and assurance to make us eager and willing, so this command should constrain and compel us. If I want to show you my love of Christ and be obedient to Him, I have an obligation to pray, no matter how unworthy I may be."[13] We pray in obedience to his command, and in holding true to his promise. To do otherwise is to dishonor him and make him a liar or a deceiver.

The command to pray parallels the paradoxical action of God between law as his alien work and the gospel as his proper work. As his alien work, the command to call upon God bears a terrifying threat: "You shall and must obey," or you will incur God's wrath; as his proper work, the command carries a consoling promise that draws us to God. In these contradictory activities, God does his alien work of humbling us via the law so that we may yearn for grace and aid through the promise. God so desires conversation with us that he attaches to the command to pray a terrifying threat on disobedience. To accomplish his most earnest purpose to be our beloved Father, he performs his alien work of judging callous hearts, a work not intrinsic to his nature, so that he might achieve his proper work of embracing us as his very own.

In *An Exposition of the Lord's Prayer for Simple Laymen* (1519), Luther considers the seven petitions as "seven reminders" of our miserable and impoverished condition; it leads "to a knowledge of self" in desperate need for external

---

12. "The Large Catechism," *BC* (Tappert), 422–23.
13. *LW* 24:398; *WA* 46:89.

help.[14] As law, these petitions awaken us from slumber concerning our misery and dire need so that we do not turn to ourselves but to the gospel for aid. Daphne Hampson captures Luther's paradox: "The Law is necessary to the gospel, negatively so."[15] The knowledge of our helpless predicament under the law is causal, as it causes us to find remedy in the gospel. The Lord's Prayer places us under an alien word of terror, as in law, when we do not abide by the seven petitions. Any aversion to praying the Lord's Prayer presents a "great reproach and dishonor to God if we, to whom he offers and pledges so many inexpressible blessings, despise them or lack confidence that we shall receive them and scarcely venture to ask for a morsel of bread."[16] The Lord's Prayer also places us under his proper work of comfort, as in the gospel, when we put the Lord's Prayer into practice, laying hold of God and his infinite riches.

In prayer, as in the Ten Commandments and the Creed, Luther operates with the fundamental assertion that "everything—both the beginning and the end, the willing and doing—must be sought from him and be given by him."[17] Prayer calls for a radical "turn around" from self to God. Luther writes that the purpose of prayer is not to instruct him what he should give us, but to acknowledge him for the manifold blessings that he is "already" bestowing upon us, and to thank God for his promise to give us "still more."[18] Of this, Luther speaks personally: "When my heart is turned to Him and awakened this way [i.e., by acknowledging God as the giver], then I praise Him, thank Him, take refuge with Him in my need and expect help from Him."[19] Prayer is a practical way of exercising the first commandment. By calling upon God, we are declaring the preeminence of God in our lives, allowing God alone to be our God, worthy of trust and praise.

Invoke God by Christ's Mouth
Words to Use in Prayer

In the opening address of the Lord's Prayer in *A Simple Way to Pray* (1535), Luther writes, "Thy dear Son, our Lord Jesus Christ, has taught us both how and what to pray."[20] Based on Matthew 6:9, Luther teaches that we should be

---

14. *LW* 42:27; cf. Bruce G. McNair, "Luther and the Pastoral Theology of the Lord's Prayer," *Logia* 14, no. 4 (2005): 42.

15. Daphne Hampson, *Christian Contradictions: The Structures of Lutheran and Catholic Thought* (Cambridge University Press, 2001), 224.

16. "The Large Catechism," *BC*, 447.

17. *LW* 24:384: *WA* 46:77.

18. *LW* 21:144.

19. *LW* 21:144.

20. *LW* 43:194. For Luther's study of the Lord's Prayer, see Helmut Thielicke, *Our Heavenly Father: Sermons on the Lord's Prayer* (Harper and Row, 1960); James Arne Nestingen, "The Lord's Prayer in Luther's Catechism," *Word and World* 22, no. 1 (2002): 36–48.

impelled to pray because, in addition to God's commandment and promise, "God takes the initiative and puts into our mouths the very words we are to use."[21] Michael Boulton puts it well: "We pray by his mouth."[22] We invoke God by the very words that proceed from the second person of the Trinity; as Helmut Thielicke says, "Prayer is not our action but our reaction. It bases itself on the preceding Word of God which makes it possible."[23] We are to bind ourselves to Christ's mouth, God's word, which by faith becomes the instrument of God's presence. Because this prayer is given by Christ, who taught us to pray, we can rest assured that God is pleased with it when we utter its petitions; in Luther's own words, "God loves to hear it."[24] Prayer has validity not on account of "our person," Luther teaches, but on account of "his Word and the obedience" to it.[25]

Luther's understanding of prayer flows from his doctrine of justification. In justification, we are declared righteous through God's performative nature of God's word, that it accomplishes what it declares; in prayer, we have his effective word that we will be heard, if only we believe. God's word that spoke the world into being now says, "You are justified," and promises that our prayer will be heard. Just as God's creative, justifying, and sanctifying works occur *ex nihilo*, and are pure gift, so also our prayer is granted *ex nihilo*, without any merit or worthiness on our part. Mary Jane Haemig writes aptly, "Just as the new relationship in Christ is pure gift, so also is communication with this God. We are not required to earn a hearing or to merit God's ears."[26]

The word of God is efficacious to deliver what it says. This conviction creates access to the world of God where we commune with him; it too provides an agenda for living out the new life he implants in us. God's word is God turning to us, causing us to turn around from self to God. Prayer is a new reality that is not grounded in the self but in God's re-creative word. For this reason, Luther treats the Lord's Prayer with high regard: "This in short is the way I use the Lord's Prayer when I pray it. To this day I still suckle at the Lord's Prayer like a child and as an old man eat and drink from it and never get my fill. It is the very best of prayers, even better than the Psalter, which is so very dear to me."[27] On the one hand, prayer is our response to God's drawing nigh to us in his word; on the

---

21. "The Large Catechism," *BC* (Tappert), 423.
22. See Michael Boulton, "'We Pray by His Mouth'": Karl Barth, Erving Goffman, and a Theology of Invocation," *Modern Theology* 17, no. 1 (2001): 67–83.
23. Helmut Thielicke, *The Evangelical Faith*, vol. 3, *Theology of the Spirit*, trans. and ed. Geoffrey W. Bromiley (Eerdmans, 1982), 84.
24. "The Large Catechism," *BC*, 443.
25. "The Large Catechism," *BC* (Tappert), 422.
26. Mary Jane Haemig, "Luther on Prayer as Authentic Communication," *Lutheran Quarterly* 30, no. 3 (2016): 308.
27. *LW* 43:200.

other hand, by his word we are drawn to him, casting beneath him our needs and petitions as summed up in the Lord's Prayer. Sufficient time for recitation and thoughtful meditation must be allocated until the heart is kindled toward God. The kindled heart—that is, the one seized by God's speech—will reflect God's voice back to God, trusting in his unmerited goodness for us through his Son. The Godward desire is accomplished not by means of any preexistent disposition toward salvation inherent within us or any good works that we do, but by the word of God addressing us from outside. The Lord's Prayer is a means which God uses, Luther writes, like "flint and steel to kindle a flame in the heart" for him.[28] The word of God begets faith in us and bestirs a desire to pray. We must beware of the devil's tricks and guile to keep us so busy with other duties that we neglect to pray. We should pray the Lord's Prayer before other things occupy us, causing our desire to pray to diminish. "For it is better to pray now, when you are half-ready, than later, when you are not ready at all, and to begin to pray only to spite and vex the devil, even if you find it most difficult and inconvenient to do so."[29]

The Introduction to the Lord's Prayer
"Our Father Who Art in Heaven"

Of all the names there is none that moves God's heart more powerfully than that of "Father." Luther uses various adjectives to describe the word "Father": it is "a friendly, sweet, intimate, and warm-hearted word."[30] By contrast, words like "Lord" or "God" or "Judge" do not comfort us as strongly as the name "Father."[31] Luther draws joy and satisfaction from the name of our God, "Father," whose desire is to hear us, regarding nothing as more lovely than hearing the prayer and praise of his own children.[32] No wonder Luther says, "God loves to hear it."[33] The picture of God Luther paints in his exposition of this prayer is not one of God who dwells in remote and self-contained transcendence, but rather of a beloved father whose very nature it is to speak to us. God speaks through his own word, the Lord's Prayer, to draw us into the orbit of divine-human intimacy.

The phrase "Who art in heaven," for Luther, reveals the miserable and wretched condition of a life totally estranged from the heavenly Father from which none can extricate themselves without God's aid.[34] No one can bridge the gap between heaven, where God is in bliss and abundance, and earth, where

---

28. *LW* 43:209.
29. *LW* 24:387; *WA* 46:79.
30. *LW* 42:22.
31. *LW* 42:22.
32. *LW* 42:22.
33. "The Large Catechism," *BC*, 443.
34. *LW* 42:23.

we are in misery and need. We see the practical outworking of the Trinitarian grammar of faith in prayer. Those who pray "our Father, who art in heaven" and confess their poverty before God, Luther expands, "move God to mercy. This lofty word cannot possibly issue from human nature but must be inspired in man's heart by the Spirit of Christ."[35] Through our rebirth by means of the word, the instrument of the Spirit, we acknowledge that the creator God, in Luther's phrase, is "an immeasurably better Father"[36] than any earthly, mortal father so that we need not be afraid of approaching him. The "Father" language speaks of the immanence of God, whose face is turned toward us with grace and mercy, and whose very heart is easily moved by the prayers of his beloved children, which are the sweetest sound in his ears. Luther extols God's mercy, which bestirs in him "a comforting trust" in God's fatherly love. He prays that God will grant "the experience of the sweet and pleasant savor of a childlike certainty" so that with exuberance we may call him "Father."[37]

The first commandment and the First Article of the Creed inhere in the *Large Catechism*'s introduction to the Lord's Prayer. The God who is to be feared, loved, and trusted above all else is none other than God, the Father Almighty, Maker of heaven and earth, and the Father of our Lord Christ, to whom our prayer is addressed. So, to pray "our Father" is to pray "in the name of our Lord Jesus," in whom the profoundest depth of God's fatherly heart for his own is disclosed. Reconciliation with God, Luther asserts, occurs through "the merit and mediation" of Jesus Christ, as already taught in the Second Article.[38] "Our Father," says Luther, is our "dear heavenly Father," on account of the promise of grace and victory in Christ.[39] Through this revelation, God behooves us to believe that he is our beloved Father, and that we can ascend to him through the incarnate Son "in his skin and on his back."[40] We do not pray to God in his naked majesty, which frightens us away, but as he has come to us in mercy and blessing, which draws us to himself. Because of God's sheer mercy shown to us in Christ's cross, Luther teaches us to pray as a child does to his father.

> O Mighty God . . . now through your mercy implant in our hearts a comforting trust in your fatherly love . . . that we may joyfully call you Father, knowing and loving you and calling on you in every trouble. Watch over us that we may remain your children and never become

---

35. *LW* 42:23.
36. *LW* 43:30.
37. *LW* 43:29.
38. *LW* 43:29.
39. *LW* 43:30.
40. *LW* 42:23.

guilty of making you, dearest Father, our fearful judge, changing ourselves, your children into your foes.[41]

In a Trinitarian sense, the use of the title "My Father" is intrinsically the Son's by nature; it is shared with us by grace. The Lord's Prayer does not focus on "my Father" but on "our Father who art in heaven." Those who pray the Our Father, Luther says, must always hold before their eyes "all mankind."[42] This is intended to lift us out of our self-enclosed life, so that we not only pray for our own needs, but also the needs of all persons as one child might entreat for others. When we pray "our Father," we are not praying alone; all devout Christians are joining us in prayer. We are standing among them with one voice and as one family, for God is the one gracious Father of all. This kind of prayer, Luther is convinced, would empty us of all selfishness, hatred, and strife so that we will love each other with the same affection with which we love God, our common Father.[43]

The question of how our prayer is granted is hidden from us; it lies beyond the scope of our knowledge. Luther advises, "We must not stipulate for God the measure, the term, the manner, the place, or the person. No, we must leave this to His knowledge of what He should give and what is useful to us."[44] Prayer must be done with due respect to the order God has ordained in the Lord's Prayer, giving priority to God's agenda in the first three petitions: that God's name be hallowed, his kingdom come, and his will be done. We pray, trusting that whatever God gives us is the very best, even when it appears the opposite. Though he may withhold what his children ask for, he does this for their own good so that they may learn to feel their Father's heart and be obedient to him. God chastises us, not as a judge does in wrath only, but as a father does in grace through wrath. The discipline God administers in wrath alone is fruitless, but when accompanied by mercy, it makes us pious. God still wants us to present our pleas and needs to him, even though he already knows them in advance. This too, for Luther, is done for our benefit, that through prayer, our hearts may be kindled with an increasing affection for God and a desire for his many gifts.[45]

The First Petition
"Hallowed Be Thy Name"

In his *Exposition of the Lord's Prayer*, Luther regards the first petition as the key to praying the Lord's Prayer: "That is why I just called this first petition an

---

41. *LW* 43:29.
42. *LW* 42:26.
43. *LW* 43:30.
44. *LW* 24:390–91.
45. "The Large Catechism," *BC*, 446.

unlimited one, the foremost one, encompassing the others. If anyone were able to hallow God's name perfectly, he would no longer need to pray the Lord's Prayer."⁴⁶ The first petition connects us back to the second commandment. Just as we are not to misuse the name of God, so we pray that God's name may be kept holy among us. Hidden in the prohibition of the second commandment is its opposite, the hallowing of God's name in the first petition. God's name is holy in itself; it is not holy among us because we are profane, deceptive, and blasphemous. Whoever prays this petition will feel the crushing weight of the law against his wretched life and see the need for repentance; as Thielicke writes, "None can pray who does not pass through the court of judgment, this abyss of extremity."⁴⁷ Just as a bad and unruly child brings disgrace to an earthly father, so those who are called by his name bring dishonor to the heavenly Father by failing to live a life worthy of God.⁴⁸ We pray positively, that God's glory and praise be exalted among us in both doctrine and life, in word and deed; and negatively, that our words and works would be free from blame and not permit God's name to suffer shame.

The Second Petition
"Thy Kingdom Come"

The kingdom of God and the church are not identical, even though the church is intended to be God's agent in extending his dominion. God's kingdom comes by itself, even without our prayer. We can neither bring it in nor banish it. The kingdom of God is already achieved solely through Christ's redeeming work. As taught in the Second Article of the Creed, Christ has trampled underfoot every enemy or lord of life—sin, death, the devil, and wrath—so that he is now my Lord and redeemer.⁴⁹ His triumphant work ushers us into the kingdom, where we live under his reign, serving him in filial obedience and perfect righteousness. To pray this petition is to cling to Christ's victory, in which everything has already been accomplished, and as heirs we possess all that is rightly accrued to us—heaven, righteousness, and life. There is nothing for us to add to God's royal rule, which has already begun. Albrecht Peters writes, "Its eschatological revelation will therefore bring nothing fundamentally new. It will rather cap off the already decided battle through the final overthrow of the enemy."⁵⁰

---

46. *LW* 42:33.
47. Thielicke, *Our Heavenly Father*, 43.
48. "The Large Catechism," *BC*, 445.
49. "The Large Catechism," *BC*, 446.
50. Albrecht Peters, *Commentary on Luther's Catechisms: Lord's Prayer*, trans. Daniel Thies (Concordia Publishing House, 2011), 81.

The second petition not only connects us back to the Second Article but also to the Third Article of the Creed. Robert Kolb comments, "The redeeming power of Jesus and the sanctifying power of the Holy Spirit establish and are the kingdom of God's right hand."[51] Both the Son and the Holy Spirit are involved in this petition. The kingdom is Christ's, God's gift, which comes to us not through any structure of human organization, but through the Holy Spirit, the bearer of Christ. The Holy Spirit, says Luther, "delivers" Christ's kingdom through the word and teaches it to our hearts by his power.[52] The Holy Spirit makes effectual in us the lordship Christ has established over us. We implore God to let his kingdom come to us, and this occurs, Luther writes, in two ways: first, in the present, when our heavenly Father bestows upon us his Holy Spirit, through whom we believe his holy word and live a godly life; and second, in the future through the final consummation of the kingdom.[53] In Jesus's cross and resurrection, the kingdom of God has broken into the satanic domain and conquered it for faith; the Holy Spirit then carries on what Christ has accomplished and continues to renew his reign among us. God's royal reign is already inaugurated, yet it remains invisible and hidden now in the conscience of the justified saint, awaiting its full manifestation at the end of time. Peters highlights Luther's point: "God's rule reaches toward us through the preaching of the Gospel and the Spirit-given obedience of faith. In this the final revelation of the Kingdom is already initiated which culminates in Christ's return."[54]

The Third Petition
"Thy Will Be Done on Earth as It Is in Heaven"

God's will is done even without our prayer. To pray this petition, Walther von Loewenich explains, is not to enter "a little garden of paradise, where the one who is weary of the Word of the cross might take a little rest," but to march onto "the battleground where the sign of the cross has been raised."[55] This petition is a battle cry against the enemies of God within and without. Luther exults in the first two petitions that promise us the "most necessary treasures"—namely, "the Gospel, faith, and the Holy Spirit," which equip us to fight against our enemies.[56] We now pray the third petition, that God would cause his benevolent will to be

---

51. Robert Kolb, *Teaching God's Children His Teaching: A Guide for the Study of Luther's Catechism*, new ed. (Concordia Seminary, 2012), 108.
52. "The Large Catechism," *BC*, 446.
53. "The Large Catechism," *BC*, 447.
54. Peters, *Lord's Prayer*, 79.
55. Walther von Loewenich, *Luther's Theology of the Cross*, trans. Herbert J. A. Bouman (Augsburg Publishing House, 1976), 143.
56. "The Large Catechism," *BC*, 449.

fulfilled in us.⁵⁷ Luther prescribes two ways of praying this petition. Negatively, God's will is done, in so far as God routs every evil counsel and scheme of the devil, the forces of the world, and the prompting of our sinful flesh. All these things stand in contradiction to God's will, as they profane God's holy name and prevent the coming of God's kingdom.⁵⁸ Positively, God's will is done where there is proclamation of the word and its triumph in our daily life; it prevails where God's name is hallowed, and his kingdom comes. The first two petitions are closely linked to the third petition and flow into it. The third receives its content from the first two. So, to pray God's will be done, for Luther, is to pray for the fulfillment of the previous two.⁵⁹ All three petitions extol the efficacy of God's word through which the Holy Spirit teaches and sustains our faith till the end.

This petition is linked programmatically to Luther's theology of the cross, in which the practice of God's will involves the cross and suffering. Where the authentic doctrine of Christ is proclaimed and bears fruit, Luther claims, there "the holy and precious cross will also not be far behind."⁶⁰ Jürgen Moltmann's words echo Luther's: "Participation in the apostolic mission of Christ leads inescapably into tribulation, contradiction and suffering."⁶¹ A life lived under the cross, for Luther, is an essential mark of the church: "The holy Christian people are externally recognized by the holy possession of the sacred cross."⁶² Just as Christ was appointed to the cross as his vocation, so also his followers, in a joyous exchange, assume the cross as their vocation. Hidden under the contrary of God's kingdom are competing forces of this age that seek the heart's allegiance. We pray for God to crush all that hinders the proclamation and performance of God's word. To pray that God's will be done is no sign of "resignation," says Kolb, but "militancy," for we engage in a war against those who oppose the gospel, and suffer attacks and assaults from those whose objective is to obstruct the realization of the first two petitions.⁶³ Thus for our sake we pray that God's will, "which must be done without us," Luther writes, "be done in us" without hindrance so that we endure without compromise, even as we hold fast the precious treasures that are God's glory and salvation.⁶⁴

There is nothing "dearer" to us than our will, and there is no "greater" enemy than the will, which, in Luther's words, is "the greatest and most deep-rooted evil

---

57. "The Large Catechism," *BC*, 357.
58. "The Large Catechism," *BC*, 449.
59. "The Large Catechism," *BC*, 448.
60. "The Large Catechism," *BC*, 449.
61. Jürgen Moltmann, *The Church in the Power of the Holy Spirit: A Contribution to Messianic Ecclesiology*, trans. Margaret Kohl (SCM, 1977), 361.
62. *LW* 41:164.
63. Kolb, *Teaching God's Children*, 110; "The Large Catechism," *BC*, 448.
64. "The Large Catechism," *BC*, 449.

in us."⁶⁵ To pray this petition is to declare war against the self, so that the old Adam together with its evil leaning be subdued. James Arne Nestingen clarifies, "There is a breach, a decisive discontinuity between God and the sinner that requires a break—the sinner must die."⁶⁶ We subject our will to the paradoxical action of God, permitting God to perform his alien work of crushing it in order that he might achieve his proper work of rebuilding it. God must crucify the self-will in order to renew it so that by grace it can choose the good and love God. Luther asserts, "Man must despair utterly of ever having or attaining a good will, opinion, or resolve.... A good will is found only where there is no will [of our own]. Where there is no will, God's will, which is the very best, will be present."⁶⁷ This petition beseeches us to pray against the self-seeking will so that we willingly adopt the cruciform existence that dies to the self and its old allegiances, but lives to God and serves him, in Luther's words, with a "God-fearing will."⁶⁸ "A change of will is demanded," Herbert Girgensohn writes, "but it is also promised and bestowed in the gospel."⁶⁹

The Fourth Petition
"Give Us This Day Our Daily Bread"

In his early writings *An Exposition of the Lord's Prayer* (1519) and the *Personal Prayer Book* (1522), Luther calls Christ and God's word "the daily bread" of the fourth petition.⁷⁰ However, in his *Small Catechism* (1529), Luther abandons the spiritual interpretation of daily bread and adopts a strictly physical understanding of it—namely, the "breadbasket,"⁷¹ as he puts it in the *Large Catechism*. This petition prays for the creaturely gifts already bestowed in the First Article. Luther counts a list of physical blessings: food, drink, clothing, housing, a farm, a healthy body, good weather, good neighbors, faithful family, job security, political peace, and social order. God works through various vocations or spheres including "the civil authorities and the government, for it is chiefly through them that God provides us daily bread and all the comforts of this life."⁷² To pray this

---

65. *LW* 42:48.
66. Nestingen, "Lord's Prayer in Luther," 45.
67. *LW* 42:48.
68. *LW* 42:48.
69. Herbert Girgensohn, *Teaching Luther's Catechism*, vol. 1, trans. John Doberstein (Muhlenberg, 1959), 21.
70. *LW* 42:49–62; *LW* 43:34–35.
71. "The Large Catechism," *BC*, 449. See McNair, "Luther and Pastoral Theology," 44: "This physical interpretation of 'bread' shows a clear break from the medieval and patristic tradition, and dates to (Luther's) translation of the Bible in 1522. No doubt, this interpretation is reinforced by the crop failures of the mid-1520s and the Peasants' War of 1525 and is one he retains throughout his later writings."
72. "The Large Catechism," *BC*, 450.

petition is to inculcate in people that all these things are God's gifts for which we ask; it is also to pray against everything that impedes the enjoyment of them.[73] All we have proceeds not from the merits of our work but solely from God's abundant blessings. This petition is no cause for idleness; it is a call for faithful labor wherein God, says Luther, "is secretly laying his blessing," and through which God provides abundantly for the sustenance of the created world.[74] The word "this day," for Luther, "is a good exercise in faith," praying only for today's needs in order that "we may then trust in a greater God" to supply us with tomorrow's nourishment.[75]

John R. Stephenson recognizes that Luther, in his comment on Psalm 110 (1518), understands the "right hand of God" as the "kingdom (*künigreich*) of Christ, which is a spiritual, hidden *reich*," and "the left hand of God" as the "visible, and bodily *reich*."[76] God's providential care encompasses both temporal and eternal concerns. Of this, Luther writes, "We must carefully distinguish between these two governments. Both are permitted to remain; the one to produce righteousness, the other to bring about external peace and prevent evil deeds. Neither one is sufficient in the world without the other."[77] The political use of the law is imposed upon the secular sphere in which God rules to restrain evil. A distinction between the third and fourth petitions, Kim A. Truebenbach contends, corresponds to the distinction between God's "right hand" and "left hand" rules, the spiritual and civil kingdoms.[78] To pray God's will be done is to pray for God's right hand to govern spiritually, while to pray for daily bread is to pray for God's left hand to provide physically.[79] These two petitions highlight Luther's two kingdoms, in which the "Word" rules by his right hand in the spiritual sphere and the "sword" rules by his left hand in the secular realm.[80] God works in different ways but with the same purpose of resisting Satan's rule and redeeming us from it. Luther uses this petition to pray against the malevolent will of Satan, who seeks every possible way to create in us chaos and despair of God's goodness.[81] By his power, Luther indicates, Satan not only obstructs the spiritual order by instilling in believers lies and unbelief in God's word, but also

---

73. "The Large Catechism," *BC*, 450.
74. *LW* 45:327.
75. *LW* 42:62.
76. *WA* 1:692.8–11, as quoted in John R. Stephenson, "The Two Governments and the Two Kingdoms in Luther's Thought," *Scottish Journal of Theology* 34, no. 4 (1981): 329.
77. *LW* 45:92.
78. Kim A. Truebenbach, "Luther's Two Kingdoms in the Third and Fourth Petitions," *Lutheran Quarterly* 24, no. 4 (2010): 471.
79. Truebenbach, "Luther's Two Kingdoms," 472.
80. *LW* 45:85. For a major study of Luther's two kingdoms, see Heinrich Bornkamm, *Luther's Doctrine of the Two Kingdoms in the Context of His Theology*, trans. Karl H. Herz (Fortress, 1966).
81. "The Large Catechism," *BC*, 451.

disrupts the civil order by hindering any peaceful establishment of social relations and political order, including the daily sustenance for bodily life.[82] Were the devil not restrained by our prayer, we would suffer severe insecurities and physical deprivation.

Just as God's rule comes without our asking, so God's generosity is not dependent upon our prayers. God gives even without our prayer. Although God's creative giving extends to all, even to the godless and wicked, only believers can acknowledge his fatherly goodness with gratitude. Faith enables us to perceive the superabundance of God's mercies in creation and praise God as the outcome.[83] What God demands of us in the First Article ("We owe it to God to thank, praise, serve, and obey") becomes an earnest plea for provision in the fourth petition ("Give us this day our daily bread").[84] The old Adam naturally does not pray; it must die. Unless we are taken out of ourselves, we would not turn to God for all goods; as Nestingen asserts, "Only when we lose ourselves in Him are we simultaneously raised with Him."[85] Not by my own ability ("I believe that I cannot") but by the gospel (the Creed)—that is, by the self-giving love of the triune God—is this petition made effectual. His demand is met by his supply: the obedience imposed upon us by the law is fulfilled by the pure grace of the Creed.

The Fifth Petition
"Forgive Us Our Debt as We Forgive Our Debtors"

This petition presents a theological problem: Is God's forgiveness logically prior to our repentance? If God only forgives when we first forgive others, then God's forgiveness is based on a prior action, which does not conform to justification by faith alone. Repentance then becomes a work necessary for salvation, in which case the *sola gratia* doctrine is destroyed. For Luther, however, repentance puts us in a position to recognize or appropriate our forgiveness; it does not cause it. In the *Large Catechism*, Luther teaches, "Not that he does not forgive us even without and before our prayer; and he gave us the gospel, in which there is nothing but forgiveness, before we prayed or even thought of it. But the point here is for us to recognize and accept this forgiveness."[86] Forgiveness is already in the gospel; all we need to do is receive and accept it. Nonetheless, God's acceptance does not depend upon our accepting his grace, for we are already accepted by God through faith in Jesus Christ, which the Holy Spirit of the

---

82. "The Large Catechism," *BC*, 451.
83. Peters, *Lord's Prayer*, 139–40.
84. Timothy J. Wengert, *Martin Luther's Catechisms: Forming the Faith* (Fortress, 2009), 92.
85. James Arne Nestingen, "The Theology of the Cross in the Lord's Prayer," in Pless and Vogel, *Luther's Large Catechism*, 518.
86. "The Large Catechism," *BC* (Tappert), 432.

Third Article imprints upon our hearts. The sinner is passive—that is, conversion is not self-created but created by the effective word. If our act of accepting God effects a righteous standing before God, then our salvation is not by grace alone. Salvation must be conceived in such a way that the gospel is the only cause that effects a change in us after the law has done its preparatory work of moving us toward repentance and faith. Only the gospel (promise) can change the heart and so bring about faith. The law by itself can never bring about repentance; it must be accompanied by the gospel. Here repentance is the gift of God, which prepares the heart for the proper reception of the word of absolution.

In his *Exposition of the Lord's Prayer*, Luther claims that we sin against God if we refuse to forgive those who sin against us. He writes, "The fact that no one is so pious as not to have in himself some odor and leaven of the old Adam is enough reason for God to justly reject man ... [yet] their sins will not be imputed *if* they denounce their sins, ask for mercy, and forgive their debtors."[87] The "if" question seems to run counter to justification by faith alone. In his *Ten Sermons on the Catechism* (1528), Luther clarifies that in asking God to forgive our sins, it is "not that he does not give it without our prayer, for he has already forgiven us in baptism, and in his kingdom, there is nothing but forgiveness of sins. But we ask [in this petition] that we may acknowledge it."[88] Our forgiveness of others is no cause for God's forgiveness of us but flows from it. God's forgiveness is freely given, Luther states, "out of pure grace," not out of any prior action.[89] Luther elaborates, "Not that you are forgiven on account of your forgiveness, but freely, without your forgiveness, your sins are forgiven. He, however, enjoins it upon you as a sign, that you may be assured that, if you forgive, you too will be forgiven."[90] Forgiveness is not to be sought in good works or in letters of indulgence but in God's unconditional promise. Luther continues, "There you have them both, the promise and the sign, that your heart may rejoice."[91] Therefore we can pray "forgive our sins" with sure confidence, for God has attached to this petition this seal to establish in us the certainty of his promise. Just as the sacraments are instituted signs of God's forgiveness, so forgiveness is a sign which we apply to ourselves, especially at the hour when the troubled conscience needs relief;[92] in Luther's words, "[God] has set this up for our strengthening and assurance as a sign along with the promise that matches this petition in Luke 6[:37], 'forgive, and you will be forgiven.'"[93]

---

87. *LW* 42:70, italics added.
88. *LW* 51:178–79.
89. "The Large Catechism," *BC*, 453.
90. *LW* 51:178–79.
91. *LW* 51:179.
92. "The Large Catechism," *BC*, 453.
93. "The Large Catechism," *BC*, 453.

Luther also advises, "Anyone who feels unable to forgive, let him ask for grace so that he can forgive."⁹⁴ Precisely by the confession that "I know that I cannot" forgive, grace comes to our aid. Luther's paradox applies to praying this petition. The gospel is hidden in the law. Likewise, God's promise of forgiveness is hidden under the sign that we first forgive (law). Law and gospel coincide as an antithetical unity in Luther's exposition of the conditional clause "as we forgive," one that strikes terror that can only be relieved by clinging to God's mercy. As his alien work, God terrifies the conscience by his command ("forgive our debtors") in order that he might console the terrified by his promise ("forgive our sins") as his proper work. Those who are profoundly burdened under the law will be profoundly blessed under the gospel.

The Sixth Petition
"Lead Us Not into Temptation"

Temptation impedes us from fearing, loving, and trusting God above all else. This petition is prayed under the pressure of the assaults that come from the unholy triad of the sinful nature, the world, and the devil. The sinful nature is, for Luther, "the old creature around our necks,"⁹⁵ which remains until we die. Because the old nature abides, he continues, sin still remains in us, though it does not reign over us.⁹⁶ The old Adam continues to work and lure us daily into the many vices that still cling to our old nature. The world with its enticements and empty promises is another source of temptation. It tempts us to resort to vices and injustice for our selfish aims; it drives us away from God, causing us to rest our hearts on creaturely comfort and prestige, which are temporary and fleeting. Luther alerts us that the devil "baits and badgers us on all sides," causing us to scorn God's word, terrifying our conscience with assaults, instilling in us unbelief and despair, and leading us into all kinds of abominable evils.⁹⁷ The devil's aim, Luther asserts, is to destroy our true identity derived from "faith, hope, and love," and to replace it with a false identity marked by "unbelief, false security, and stubbornness."⁹⁸ The outcome is denial, despair, and disdain of God, as well as other deadly vices.

Based on Psalm 91:7, "A thousand may fall at your left side, ten thousand at your right hand," Luther distinguishes between two kinds of temptation.⁹⁹ The first comes from the "left side," which "incites us to anger, hatred, embitterment,

---

94. *LW* 43:197.
95. "The Large Catechism," *BC*, 454.
96. *LW* 22:394; *WA* 47:114.
97. "The Large Catechism," *BC*, 454.
98. "The Large Catechism," *BC*, 454.
99. *LW* 42:73.

aversion, and impatience"; it might include "sickness, poverty, dishonor, and distress of all kinds."[100] This trial is strong in contexts where people stand in our way and oppose our will, plan, and counsel. The second trial comes from the "right hand," which "lures us to unchastity, lust, pride, greed, and vainglory."[101] This temptation is manifested most when people follow our way, honor us, and praise our words, our wisdom, and our achievements. Luther is certain that "this is the most pernicious of all,"[102] for it has caused many downfalls.

To pray this petition is to pray against all the contraries of justification including the law, sin, and death. Like the unholy triad, these enemies work despair and misplaced trust in us. The temptation is to revert to the self for aid or other creaturely means of escape from these woes. Consequently, we are caught in the "idolatrous cycle" of self-reliance, either in the form of introspection or self-chosen crosses, unless we cling to the conquering action of Christ's cross and resurrection. In Nestingen's estimation:

> Exposed, confronted, the self turns inward, seeking within itself the resources and plans necessary to cope. In the inevitable disappointments that follow, it conceives new plans and finds other resources, disappointment feeding on itself until all hope appears to be lost and despair sets its grip. Or the self turns outward, seeking by heroic effort to conquer the forces of the night, embroiling itself with "creatures, saints, and devils" to achieve what only the Creator can bestow. Despair and heroism are two sides of the same coin, the self-seeking self.
>
> Freedom from despair and from the idolatrous cycle of misplaced trust happens only under the sign of Good Friday and Easter, in the death of the self-questing sinner and the resurrection of a new self in Christ's hands. This happens in the praying of the petition. In these words, the Lord Jesus takes on the powers of temptation to overcome them in faith.[103]

Though assaults might come from various sources such as the devil, the world, or the flesh, Luther does not hesitate to attribute them to the work of God. He regards them as part of God's alien work, his instruments to nourish faith. They cast us down and serve the interests of God's proper work: God's final goal of salvation. Luther asserts, "Experience [trials] alone makes a theologian."[104] God lets sin assail us, Luther is certain, so we may know that in ourselves, there is nothing

---

100. *LW* 42:73.
101. *LW* 42:73.
102. *LW* 42:73.
103. Nestingen, "Lord's Prayer in Luther," 47.
104. *LW* 54:7; *WA* TR 1:16.

but weakness and wickedness, and that in God, there is nothing but power and grace.[105] Thus we learn to seek satisfaction not from ourselves but from God alone and praise his mercy. Evil passions can never be extinguished by our own strength but only by God, to whom we pray, "Father, do not lead us into temptation." A frequent usage of this petition, Luther believes, would preserve us from becoming disheartened and weary, lapsing into sin, and giving the devil free rein.[106]

The Seventh Petition
"Deliver Us from Evil"

Luther notes that the Greek translation of this petition reads, "Deliver us... from the Evil One, or the Wicked One."[107] The devil, he says, is "the sum of all evil."[108] All evil comes from the devil, Peters writes, so we now pray to be delivered from him.[109] This petition is directed against all the evils and tragic miseries we encounter in the devil's kingdom; Luther includes here poverty, disgrace, death, insanity, suicide, other dreadful catastrophes, and many heartaches.[110] These evil deeds befit the character of the devil, who is portrayed in John 8:44 as a liar and a murderer.[111] The name of the Father, from whom proceeds all the power of salvation, brings comfort. On the other hand, the name of the devil, from whom flows all the power of destruction, incites terror. Luther makes proper use of this petition, praying for relief from the potency of the devil and his infernal domain. This petition is a celebration of victory, for we are preserved from the evil one and from everything that might do us harm. We pray first that God's name be hallowed, that his kingdom come, and that his will be done, before we can celebrate his triumph over every evil.[112]

In *A Simple Way to Pray* (1535), Luther sees this last petition as referring to death, the last enemy, and teaches us to ask God to help us amid such great evil and embolden us to face the last hour with confidence. He perceives an eschatological edge to this petition, so he prays for the God of mercy to grant us "a blessed departure from this vale of sorrows so that in the face of death we do not become fearful or despondent but in firm faith commit our souls into thy hands."[113] In his *Exposition of the Lord's Prayer* (1519), he advises that this last

---

105. *LW* 42:74.
106. "The Large Catechism," *BC*, 454.
107. "The Large Catechism," *BC*, 455.
108. "The Large Catechism," *BC*, 455.
109. Peters, *Lord's Prayer*, 204.
110. "The Large Catechism," *BC*, 455.
111. "The Large Catechism," *BC*, 455.
112. "The Large Catechism," *BC*, 456.
113. *LW* 43:197–98.

petition should be prayed at "the very last."[114] We should not begin at this petition, asking God for relief from pain and distress, unless it fulfills God's name, his kingdom, and his will. Should it be otherwise, such prayer is no longer "a pleasing and good prayer."[115] Luther again counsels against a self-seeking will and its natural tendency to "reverse the order" of the Lord's Prayer by placing self-interest before and above God's agenda as set forth in the first three petitions.[116]

Prayer as The Voice of Faith
Amen as Justifying God's Word

The Lord's Prayer concludes with a shout of victory: "For thine is the kingdom and the power and the glory forever and ever. Amen." The "Amen," Luther says, "expresses the faith" that goes along with every petition.[117] A sincere "Amen" is a declaration of faith in God; it vindicates God's word as true, that God has pledged himself to grant this prayer to the person who offers it. Faith must be present for the command, promise, and words of Christ to be efficacious. True prayer is, in John T. Pless's words, "the voice of faith,"[118] a bold belief that our cries reach heaven, despite appearances to the contrary. For Luther, prayer and faith are so united that if our prayer concludes "with the word 'Amen' spoken with confidence and strong faith, it is surely sealed and heard."[119] And yet this faith does not originate with the self ("I cannot believe"), but with the Holy Spirit of the Third Article. Faith is God's gift to us, which we exercise in prayer to receive what he lavishly gives. The "Amen" of faith is a true sign of new life. In this regard, Nestingen's formulation "Faith is the contemporary equivalent of the resurrection of the dead" has merit.[120] Luther attaches significance to the word "Amen," for it expresses the faith of the petitioner who does not pray by "chance," but in the knowledge that "God does not lie, because he has promised to grant it."[121] Thus "the efficacy of prayer" lies in that tiny word "Amen," which Luther defines as "an unquestioning word of faith."[122] As taught in the first commandment, faith and God are bound together. The command to pray demands that we hurry to God and cling to him alone as the true God. To pray in faith is to turn our hearts toward no one else but the God of the first commandment from

---

114. *LW* 42:75.
115. *LW* 42:75.
116. *LW* 42:75.
117. *LW* 42:76.
118. John T. Pless, *Praying Luther's Small Catechism: The Pattern of Sound Words* (Concordia Publishing House, 2016), 76.
119. *LW* 42:76.
120. Nestingen, "Lord's Prayer in Luther," 47.
121. "The Large Catechism," *BC*, 456.
122. "The Large Catechism," *BC*, 456.

whom nothing but pure goodness proceeds. Where faith is wanting, prayer is in vain; in Luther's words, "If faith is present, we triumph. Because of faith in Christ our prayer is acceptable and pleasing to God and is also effective. If you believe that this God is your Dwelling place, He is truly a Dwelling place for you. If you do not believe this, He is not."[123] With a strong "Amen," we grasp the true meaning of the fiduciary expression "God's most earnest purpose is to be my God," permitting that reality, the God of the first commandment, to be the basis of our satisfaction and security. Conversely, those who do not pray in faith sin and anger God, supposing that God's ears are closed to them; in consequence, God ceases to be our dwelling place, and his purpose to be ours remains outside us, unrealized in us.

Trinitarian Discourse
The Holy Spirit, Prayer, and the Sigh

The Trinity exists in speech *ad intra* before he speaks to us *ad extra*; the former is hidden from us, while the latter is open to us. For God has stepped out of his own concealment and spoken to us in his Son, through whom we become God's children by faith, as in Galatians 3:26: "You are all sons of God through faith in Christ." By the Spirit, believers are drawn into the inner-Trinitarian discourse; they are given a glorious privilege to commune through the Son with the Father. The Holy Spirit confers on those who are in Christ a filial status, which admits them into the Son's inner conversation with his Father. The majestic deity has condescended and permitted miserable sinners to pray to him. Our participatory discourse with God is given to us, not achieved by us. Luther writes, "To speak with Him means to pray. . . . It is a glorious privilege that the Sublime Majesty in heaven condescends to let us poor worms open our mouths in conversation with Him and gladly listens to us."[124] Grace fosters in us "a twofold conversation: the one which we carry on with God and the one which God carries on with us."[125] Jenson works out the implication of the Trinitarian discourse for prayer:

> Christians dare address God, however others may do it, only because Jesus permits them to join *his* prayer, appropriating his unique filial term of address and relying on his fellowship in the prayer. We pray *to* "our Father." We pray *with* the one who, by uniquely addressing God as "my Father," makes himself the Son, and us as his adoptive siblings children, of his Father. Just so, we enter into the living personal

---

123. *LW* 13:88.
124. *LW* 24:419; *WA* 41:108.
125. *LW* 24:419; *WA* 46:108.

community between them, that is, we pray *to* the Father, *with* the Son, *in* the Spirit.[126]

The Lord's Prayer is more than an instruction of how we may pray to God. It is God's word to us through which we too may converse with God. The Lord's Prayer is Christ's prayer for us *with* his Father; it is also our prayer *with* Jesus to the Father so that our prayer is one with his and just as efficacious.

The Son's communion with the Father is given to those whom God constitutes as his beloved children through faith in Christ, equally loved as is the Son. Only God's children are given the freedom to participate in the inner life of the Trinitarian self-speech and converse with the almighty God, a privilege not given to bond servants. Believers are also granted the honor of being Christ's "brothers," a gift Luther detects in the resurrection account in John's Gospel. There Christ called his disciples "My brothers" (John 20:17), which Luther considers a "friendly, lovely word" that creates peace and calm, especially to those who fail and are terrified by the law.[127] We derive immense comfort from Christ's words that we are his brothers and are bound to retort, in Luther's words:

> Who am I to receive such an honor and be and be called a brother of the Son of God? I am not even worthy that such a great King and Lord of all creatures should call me His creature. So now it is not enough for Him that I should be and be called His creature, but He also wants me to be and to be called His brother. Why should I not rejoice, since the man who calls me His brother is Lord over heaven and earth, over sin and death, over the devil and hell, and over everything that can be named not only in this world but also in the world to come (Eph. 1:21)?[128]

Luther speaks of the glorious consequence of being called Christ's "brothers": "For if I am Christ's brother, just as Christ assuredly promises us in these words, then it irrefutably follows that I am an heir together with Christ of all His possessions and of equal inheritance, possessing in common with Him all the blessings that He has [Rom 8:17]."[129] All that God's Son, our brother, has, belongs to believers whom he reckons as his siblings, and coheirs. Faith has made us equal to God's Son in all things, including his proximity with his Father. Consequently, "His and our prayer must be one," having the same efficacy, except that our

---

126. Robert W. Jenson, *Systematic Theology*, vol. 1, *The Triune God* (Oxford University Press, 1997), 37, Jenson's italics.
127. *LW* 69:306.
128. *LW* 69:306.
129. *LW* 69:306.

prayers must stem from him and be made in his name.[130] Luther's Trinitarian paradigm of prayer in its mature form is succinctly summed up in his *Sermons on John 14–16*:

> I am justified in saying: "I know that my heavenly Father is heartily glad to hear all my prayers, inasmuch as I have Christ, this Savior, in my heart. Christ prayed for me, and for this reason my prayers are acceptable through his." Accordingly, we must weave our praying into His. He is forever the Mediator. Through Him we come to God. In Him we must incorporate and envelop all our prayers and all that we do. As St. Paul declares (Rom. 13:31), we must put on Christ; and everything must be done in Him (1 Cor. 10:31) if it is to be pleasing to God.
>
> But all this is said to Christians for the purpose of giving them boldness and confidence to rely on this Man and to pray with complete assurance; for we hear that in this way He unites us with Himself, really puts us on a par with Him, merges our prayer into His and His into ours. Christians can glory in this great distinction. For if our prayers are included in His, then He says (Ps. 22:22): "I will tell of Thy name to My brethren" and (Rom. 8:16–17) "It is the Spirit Himself bearing witness with our spirit that we are children of God, and if children, then heirs, heirs of God and fellow heirs with Christ." What greater honor could be paid us than this, that our faith in Christ entitles us to be called His brethren and coheirs, that our prayer is to be like His, that there is really no difference except that our prayers must originate in Him and be spoken in His name if they are to be acceptable and if He is to bestow this inheritance and glory on us. Aside from this, He makes us equal to Himself in all things; His and our prayer must be one, just as His body is ours and His members are ours.[131]

The Second Article of the Creed makes us God's new creation, endowed with the right and privilege to pray to God in Christ's "skin and on his back."[132] The knowledge of sin and divine wrath under the law may so terrify the redeemed that they shrink from the gospel, even when they know that Christ has reconciled them to the Father's favor. So, the Holy Spirit of the Third Article comes to embolden terrified sinners to pray with confidence. "For because the awareness of the opposite is so strong in us, that is, because we are more aware of the wrath of God than of his favor toward us, therefore the Holy Spirit is sent into our hearts."[133] The

---

130. *LW* 24:407; *WA* 46:97–98.
131. *LW* 24:407; *WA* 46:97–98.
132. *LW* 42:23.
133. *LW* 26:381; *WA* 40.1:581.

Holy Spirit bears witness with our hearts that the Son's Father is ours, a treasure not won by merit but bestowed by free grace. This is why Luther accentuates the Third Article as the "most important" Article, on which the others rest.

Luther makes use of Pauline texts to expand the intercessory ministry of the Holy Spirit; as Paul writes, "When we do not know how to pray as we ought, the Spirit himself intercedes for us and helps us in our weaknesses" (Rom 8:26); and "God has sent the Spirit of his Son into our hearts, crying: 'Abba! Father!'" (Gal 4:6). By "the Spirit of adoption" (Rom 8:15), we are made heirs with God, and thus are drawn into the Son's proximate relation to the Father, resulting in our crying "Abba! Father!"[134] The Holy Spirit enables us to grasp the truth of the gospel hidden in the appearances that contradict the revealed truth. "The Holy Spirit does this in order that man may remain alive in the midst of death and may be able to keep a good conscience and God's grace even though he is aware of his sins."[135] As comforter, the Holy Spirit intercedes for us, and assures us of our sonship in Christ, despite the trials and afflictions that insinuate doubt concerning our status before God. Paul's word "crying," Luther argues, is intended to expose the weakness of our faith which needs perpetual help.[136] So "to call out in my need," says Charles P. Arand, "is to die, to confess my inability and to seek help from God."[137] Paul identifies this crying as "sighs too deep for words" (Rom 8:26). In temptation, we may not "hear" and "see" these terrible powers, but Luther says, "This feeling is in our hearts."[138] In us, we truly feel the force of innate evil, the enticements of the world, and the assaults of the devil; all this could deter us from praying to God. The godly feel more strongly the contraries of justification—that is, of sin, law, the devil, wrath, judgment, and death. These negative and terrifying forces are overcome, not by the performance of "active righteousness," but by the affective encounter of Holy Spirit, who begins to cry in our hearts "Abba! Father!" The Holy Spirit does not plead for us with "loud" crying, Luther clarifies, but with a "faint" sigh,[139] a tiny "sob and sigh of the heart" that reaches God's ears as "a mighty" cry.[140] This faint cry "Abba! Father!" vanquishes the oppressive cries of the devil, sin, and the law.

---

134. *LW* 26:380; *WA* 40.1:579; cf. *LW* 25:359; *WA* 46:370. For a discussion of the Holy Spirit's sigh, see Stephen J. Chester, "'Abba! Father!' (Gal. 4:6): Justification and Assurance in Martin Luther's Lectures on Galatians (1535)," *Biblical Research: Journal of the Chicago Society of Biblical Research* 63 (2018): 15–22.

135. *LW* 24:360; *WA* 46:56.

136. *LW* 26:380; *WA* 40.1:579.

137. Charles P. Arand, "The Battle Cry of Faith: The Catechisms' Exposition of the Lord's Prayer," *Concordia Journal* 21, no. 1 (1995): 60.

138. *LW* 26:382; *WA* 40.1:583.

139. *LW* 26:381; *WA* 40.1:580.

140. *LW* 26:383, 384; *WA* 40.1:583, 585.

The sigh must not be conceived as a sort of preexistent, salvific material that lies within us preparing us for or predisposing us toward the good; if we do, then we are still operating within the orbit of works-righteousness. For Luther, Heiko A. Oberman argues, "*Gemitus* [sigh] is not another word for *facere quod in se est* [doing what lies in us] or *humilitas* as some kind of condition for justification; rather it characterizes the life of the *sancti*, whose righteousness is hidden. It describes the state of complete identification with Christ."[141] The sigh is not "an affective power,"[142] a residual desire for God; rather, it is a consequence of one's encounter with God. Sigh is the operation of the Holy Spirit, which, as Romans 8:26 teaches, ought not to be attributed to human spirit. Quoting Luther, "The first principle of all good works is faith,"[143] Oberman writes, "*Gemitus* (just as much as *oratio*) presupposes faith and does not refer to a stage of preparation or to a virginal sinproof part in man, but to the life of faith itself: 'Prayer is his desire for Christ; the cry is for Christ to transfigure his wretchedness.'"[144] There is no relief from our misery, unless we sigh to God (as Moses did with "the unexpressed yearning of his heart"[145]), which becomes the locus of God's hidden, merciful work. Moses's sigh marks his total helplessness, which becomes the basis of God's merciful act for him and the people in the Red Sea (Exod 14:15).[146] The sigh is "a true, spiritual longing,"[147] the language of faith that is so oriented to God that it "becomes a great, unbearable cry in God's ears," moving God to respond. The sigh is the form in which a true theologian of the cross waits in hope for God to act mercifully, despite appearances to the contrary. Prayer makes a good theologian out of Luther, as it refers to the absolute nothingness of the one who prays; likewise, the sigh makes a good theologian out of Luther, for it signifies total vacuity in him and utter dependence upon God for deliverance. Like law, sighing is God's alien work, a negation of all that we hold fast. In situations where we are so debilitated by the opposites of justification that we cannot even make a groan, the Holy Spirit does not replace our praying but assists us to pray with "sighs too deep for words" (Rom 8:26)—that is, with a deep longing of our heart that is found pleasing to God. Luther teaches that "when everything is hopeless for us and all things begin to go against our prayers and desires, then

---

141. Heiko A. Oberman, *The Dawn of the Reformation: Essays in Late Medieval and Early Reformation Thought* (T&T Clark, 1986), 151–52. Oberman deliberates, "Whereas in the connection between *gemitus* and true penitence there is a basis for comparison with Abelard, Bernard and Gerson refer to *gemitus* as part of the preparatory stage in the triad 'purgation–illumination–contemplation' or as initiation of the birth of God in the soul" (152).
142. Oberman, *Dawn of the Reformation*, 152.
143. See *WA* 5:119.12–18, in Oberman, *Dawn of the Reformation*, 153.
144. Oberman, *Dawn of the Reformation*, 153; also quoted is *WA* 1:196.25.
145. *LW* 43:248.
146. *LW* 13:114–15.
147. *LW* 43:248.

those unutterable groans begin. And then 'the Spirit helps us in our weaknesses'" (Rom 8:26).[148] Hope begins when we cannot utter a word, at which point the Spirit's grace is most operative. In trials and suffering, we do not recourse to the self, engaging in subjective introspection that might keep us in unbelief, but we are to turn outward to the objective "bare Word"[149] to hear the good news that Christ reigns above all contraries, and sigh by the Spirit, assured of Christ's victory over all terrifying powers. Luther simply states, "Just cling to Christ and sigh."[150] The cries of the law, works, and our feelings and terrified conscience thereby vacate the heart, and their place is taken by the simple saying "Abba! Father!"—"a very short word," Luther says, which contains all that constitutes our identity and well-being.[151]

God hears our prayers and gives us his gifts, but in a way that is contrary to our expectation so that he appears to be more opposed or indifferent to us after our prayers. This is because it is God's nature first to humble us, creating despair of ourselves so that we may leave ourselves behind and cleave to God's mercy. Believers will not lose heart, even though they know fully the opposite of what they have fervently prayed for. They recognize that "the work of God must be hidden and never understood, even when it happens. But it is never hidden in any other way than under that which appears contrary to our conceptions and ideas."[152] "A pleasing and good prayer" must fulfill the first three petitions of the Lord's Prayer—God's name, his kingdom, and his will.[153] What we pray for must conform to God's counsel, just as the material must suit what the artist intends to make.[154] God determines with himself the suitability of our prayer, the form that corresponds to his wise counsel; this Luther illustrates:

> [Just] as in the case of an artist who comes upon some material which is suitable and apt for making into a work of art, the suitableness of the material is in a certain sense an unfelt prayer for the form which the artist understands and heeds, as he gets ready to make what this material calls for through its suitability, so God comes upon our feeling and thinking, seeing what it is praying for, what it is suitable for, and what it desires; then heeding the request. He begins to mold the form which suits His art and His counsel. Then of necessity the form and the model of our thinking is destroyed.[155]

---

148. *LW* 25:365; *WA* 56:376.
149. *LW* 26:380; *WA* 40.1:580.
150. *LW* 26:385; *WA* 40.1:586.
151. *LW* 26:385; *WA* 40.1:586.
152. *LW* 25:366; *WA* 56:376.
153. *LW* 42:75.
154. *LW* 25:366; *WA* 56:377.
155. *LW* 25:367; *WA* 56:378.

The paradoxical action of God consists in that God must first remove from us all that hinders prayer before he fills us with his good gifts by prayer. In removing everything from us, God does not distance himself from us but draws himself near to us, that we might draw nigh to him. Prayer is caused in us through the law's deconstruction of everything we hold fast to move us to dependence upon God's promise. The efficacy of prayer lies in our willingness to undergo the law's "omnipotent" function, God's alien work through which God destroys all human resources and work before we are made ready to receive his works and his gifts. Just as faith is operative despite appearances to the contrary, so also prayer is effective in its opposite, when it comes from the impoverished and lowly, not the rich and proud. The *ex nihilo* doctrine shapes Luther's understanding of prayer, as it does the Three Articles of faith. Not until we are reduced to naught does our prayer reach God's ears. The fulfillment of prayer presupposes a beggarly heart, one that desires the satisfaction of God's boundless grace; only a vacant heart shall be filled with inestimable gifts of God. God's goodness is far removed from those who pray to God, looking at their "active righteousness" as the measure of success. Those who feel secure in their own righteousness remain in the captivity of self-incurvature. Those who feel despair of their own righteousness find themselves in the arms of God's love. For it is not by our working but by resting from it, not by human initiative but by prevenient grace, that we are drawn to pray to God. Prayer is vitiated if it is based on the "active righteousness" with which we fortify ourselves rather than with God's efficacious word which we hear with faith. The theological character of God's effective promise that faith grasps by prayer expels all human merits or action. We do not earn a hearing from God, just as we do not earn a justified status before God; both are purely by unmerited grace, independent of any prior human agency. In justification, we are declared righteous, just as God's word says; in prayer, we are heard, just as God's word says. We pray without doubting the constancy of God's faithful character. God's word in command and promise is made effective in us by faith, expressed in prayer. Luther asserts, "He promised to hear us, yes, he commanded us to pray, for the very reason that we might know and firmly believe that our petition will be heard."[156]

In God's external relation to us, God comes to us with love and acceptance, revealing himself as an extravagant giver of all gifts which we receive by prayer, the means of appropriation. It presupposes an "inside-out" Trinitarian movement from the First Article through the Second to the Third and culminates in the Lord's Prayer. While the Son mediates between God and us to banish God's hostility against us (through which God becomes our Father), the Spirit mediates between the Son and us to communicate to us Christ's triumph over God's wrath against us (through which communion with the Father is possible). While

---

156. *LW* 42:186.

the Holy Spirit effects a subjective reception of the benefits that flow from the suffering love of the cross, prayer acquires a subjective realization of the blessings that proceed from the agency of the triune God.

All three persons work together *ad extra* as one God, bestowing on us manifold gifts *ex nihilo*. The Ten Commandments (law) condemn the scholastic dictum ("do what lies in us") and crucify all soteriological resources—human reason, the will, pious deeds—so that we expect nothing from ourselves but everything from the Creed (promise). All that is needed for identity formation and satisfaction is gathered up in the Creed. In prayer, we do not turn inward to the self to invoke preexistent salvific materials within us (which we do not have), but we turn outward to God to invoke his preexistent gifts stored up in his eternal fountain. So, what is invoked in prayer is the credal benefits, incongruously procured by the triune God. First, we receive the abundance of created gifts the Father bestows on us so that we are without any lack. Second, we acquire the fruits of Christ's passion, that his righteousness and life are ours in exchange for our sin and death. Third, we appropriate through faith all the gifts the Holy Spirit brings to us—righteousness, freedom, sonship, resurrection of the body, and eternal life. Proximate discourse with the triune God, a privilege granted only to God's beloved, marks our life as a receptive kind. The receptive life is beggarly, not measured by a self-fortified, ascending progress we make in faith, but lived by a passive receiving of God's descending, unconditional grace. The passive life, including prayer, is ex-centric, lived not in itself but outside itself and in God. We do not recourse to ourselves for resources, but as beggars, we draw from God's rich life the plenitude of God's Trinitarian grace, the basis of our identity and security.

Conclusion

Let the Gospel Lead the Way

Luther shows us not only what the gospel is, but more importantly, how the gospel does its work so that God's purpose to be ours is realized in us. To believe the gospel is to cling to God's word by faith, leaving the self behind and allowing the triune God to lead the way. That is what Luther means by being a theologian of the cross, one who allows God and his way to form him. To believe God is to believe *in* what each person of the Trinity does or means "to us." God is creator, redeemer, and sanctifier, but these distinctions are of no value unless they relate "to us." Henry W. Reimann puts it well: "The personal God, who is Creator, Redeemer, and Vivifier, is Luther's Lord. Whatever had no relation to this God had no place in his Christian thinking."[1] Unless we grasp the meaning of the personal God, that he is "for us," the gospel is of no use to us. To be a Christian is to be placed outside us and in God, allowing God to be God, and his purpose to shape us. Idolatry is nothing other than demanding God to adjust to human plans, thinking, and the imagination of our hearts. Of this, Isaiah chastised his people: "What likeness will you set for Him?" (Isa 40:18). True worship is thus vitiated because we "want God to be shaped by us, not ourselves to be shaped by God,"[2] which, as Steven D. Paulson discerns, "is a good description of modern religion championed by Feuerbach and Freud."[3] The turn to the self as the orbit of divine things is of the theology of glory (*theologia gloriae*), opposite to the theology of the cross (*theologia crucis*) in which the self is dethroned, and in its place is the God of the first commandment, who is the triune God of the Creed. The gospel underscores the giving nature of God. The gifts God offers are not separated from the person of God, who is by nature self-giving. Paulson writes, "When God gives, he gives sacramentally, not figuratively; he does not give signs of his affection, he gives—Him."[4] We live not by anything we inherit or acquire, but by the gift of Godself in creation, redemption, and sanctification, the three distinct actions in which God is most Godself.

---

1. Henry W. Reimann, "Luther on Creation: A Study in Theocentric Theology," *Concordia Theological Monthly* 24, no. 3 (1953): 26.
2. *LW* 9:54; *WA* 14:589. Also quoted in Steven D. Paulson, *Luther's Outlaw God*, vol. 2, *Hidden in the Cross* (Fortress, 2019), 188.
3. Paulson, *Luther's Outlaw God*, 2:188.
4. Steven D. Paulson, *Lutheran Theology* (T&T Clark, 2011), 53.

The receptive life of faith is not a form of religious consciousness, but as Oswald Bayer notes, it "is in fact completely an act of trust, but it is trust that is grounded and connected. If I do not know the one in whom I place my trust and what I entrust to him, then the faith relationship—no matter how sincere and earnest it may be—remains empty and aimless."[5] "The God with whom we have to do" (Heb 4:12) is not something unknown or someone unnamed but the God who reveals himself as Father, Son, and Holy Spirit. The starting point of Luther's theological task is not God as he is in himself but as he is toward us. The economic actions of the triune God for us stand as the foreground, the immanent relation of the three persons in himself as the background. The God we encounter through his economic relationship to us in Christ and the Holy Spirit is indeed the immanent God we have in eternity. What God does in history does not make God triune; rather it reveals the God who is "beforehand" eternally triune.

For Luther, only through a Trinitarian understanding of the gospel can we truly discern the dynamism of God's salvific relation with us as God's gift. The Trinitarian form of life is *ex nihilo*, without any prior human action or worth; it is, to use Bradley Hanson's phrase, "a graceful life."[6] Graced life is Trinitarian in content: creation by the Father, redemption by the Son, and sanctification by the Holy Spirit—and all occur out of nothing. Gifted life is also Trinitarian in intent: The Father's self-communicative love in the Son through the Holy Spirit achieves a common goal—that is, an effectual return to him, a belonging to him, which was lost through Adam's fall. The gospel of the triune God recenters our lives in God's gratuitous actions "for us" so that we are never without God's creative, justifying, and sanctifying grace, an ascriptive pattern of the Trinity. The life we live is not in us, but outside us. It is grounded in the Trinitarian grammar of faith, that through the Holy Spirit's enablement, we might humbly confess the Son who obtains for us the treasures of redemption, and in whom is hidden the bounty of the Father's goodness in creation for the benefit of our well-being and the constitution of our identity. Miikaa Ruokanen sums up Luther's Trinitarian logic of grace in soteriology, but with an emphasis on the action of *sola Spiritus* "backward" as the basis of our experience of God:

> Luther connects Christology with Pneumatology because it is the task of the Holy Spirit to connect the sinner with Christ. It is the Christological word of God which the Holy Spirit makes vivid and efficient that creates faith and establishes a union between the sinner and the Savior. Without this living connection, Christ and his work would remain historical facts just to be memorized. Luther explains the operation of

---

5. Oswald Bayer, *Martin Luther's Theology: A Contemporary Interpretation*, trans. Thomas H. Trapp (Eerdmans, 2008), 240.

6. Bradley Hanson, *A Graceful Life: Lutheran Spirituality for Today* (Augsburg Fortress, 2000).

saving grace and the creation of faith as the work of the Holy Trinity over against the incapacity and ignorance of free choice outside faith. Liberating the sinner from the bondage of unbelief is exactly the work of the Holy Trinity: the Father draws the sinner to Christ by "pouring out" his Holy Spirit.[7]

The tripartite structure (Ten Commandments–Creed–Lord's Prayer) of Luther's Catechisms locates us outside ourselves so that we do not revert to ourselves for any soteriological materials; it grounds us entirely in God, from whom we derive all that we have. Through the word and its created forms (baptism, the Lord's Supper, absolution), the self-incurvature of the old identity gives way to the ex-centricity of a new identity. The person re-created by the gospel is taken out of themselves so that they cleave to the triune God, from whom proceed all created gifts, more than sufficient for all their needs. Idolatry consists in trusting in our own powers to make something and offer it to God, as though he has needs, to gain his favor. Such action perverts worship by turning it into a sacrifice (*sacrificium*) we offer to God rather than "giving thanks for things received from God; it is being proud and presumptuous concerning offerings to God."[8]

Faith is the causative agency of love. Faith, born of the word, liberates the bound self from every "lord" or enemy of life so that the freed self is "bound"[9] to serve, praise, and thank God. Bayer expands, "The word of faith as the work of God is freedom from the righteousness of the law. . . . In being freed from this burden [that the self lives under both the law and the righteousness demanded by the law], I can take the liberty to separate myself from myself. I am freed to come out of my own shell, to be open toward God, toward others, and toward all creatures."[10] The superabundance of God's goods we have from God by faith, we now give to others in love, shorn of any reciprocal gains. In Phillip Cary's estimation, "The Gospel frees me to live in love, concerned for the good of my neighbor rather than wrapped up in my spiritual anxieties about myself. It is precisely because I am justified by faith alone that I am free to love."[11] Just as Christ empties himself purely for our sake, so too we empty ourselves purely for the interest of our neighbors. All truly good works arise not from "fear of shame and love of honor," but from a gift of identity, marked by trust. The new identity should consider, Luther teaches, "a far higher and nobler incentive, and

---

7. Miikka Ruokanen, *Trinitarian Grace in Martin Luther's "The Bondage of the Will"* (Oxford University Press, 2021), 106–7.

8. *LW* 9:54; *WA* 14:589.

9. "The Small Catechism," *BC* (Tappert), 345.

10. Oswald Bayer, "Justification: Basis and Boundary of Theology," in *By Faith Alone: Essays on Justification in Honor of Gerhard O. Forde*, ed. Joseph A. Burgess and Marc Kolden (Eerdmans, 2004), 84.

11. Phillip Cary, *The Meaning of Protestant Theology: Luther, Augustine, and the Gospel that Gives Us Christ* (Baker Academic, 2019), 204.

that is God's commandment, God's fear, God's approval, and faith and love toward God."[12] Faith as trust in God is the dynamism behind the execution of God's plans for us through the performance of good deeds enjoined by the Ten Commandments. "The growth in love that results from faith in Christ," Cary notes, "is also God's gift to us, but it is not a way to God or a power that draws us near to him. The drawing near must be done by God alone."[13]

As faith and love are one,[14] so also God's gift and the "counter-gift" are one. True faith is truly active in love; likewise, God's gift is truly active, creating in the recipient a passive "responsivity." God's creative self-giving is the efficient cause of our reciprocal giving. As Niels Henrik Gregersen argues, "Life is an unmerited gift, and yet a gift that opens up divine-human interactions. [Hence] the received dichotomy between a purely active God and a purely passive creature" no longer exists.[15] The gift is so creative that it impels the recipient into true giving, bereft of self-interest or any reciprocal benefits; in Bo Kristian Holm's terms, "Justification is the opening of reciprocity, making realized reciprocity itself the gift of grace."[16] God's grace is unconditional, bestowed freely, John M. G. Barclay clarifies, "not to elicit a return or benefit for God, but for our sake alone: this non-selfish love is both in intent and motive non-circular."[17] The fiduciary language of gratitude, love, and obedience, he proposes, "is entirely free of instrumental ends: we love and obey God *only because, not in order that*."[18] The creative nature of grace is the condition of possibility for a passive receptivity, a "counter-gift" we offer back to God who is worthy of our fear, trust, and love.

In the law where there is only demand, giving is impossible, and so is fellowship with God; in the gospel, Holm argues, "the impossibility of giving turns into a possibility of giving."[19] The gospel has so filled our hearts with an abundance of God's gifts that we can reciprocate with gratitude and joy. True freedom is given to the new identity, about which Luther exults with jubilant joy. "Whosoever now believes the Gospel will receive grace and the Holy Spirit. This will cause the heart to rejoice and find delight in God, and will enable the believer to keep the law cheerfully, without expecting reward, without fear of punishment, without seeking compensation, as the heart is perfectly satisfied with God's grace, by

---

12. *LW* 44:44.

13. Cary, *Meaning of Protestant Theology*, 202.

14. For a discussion of the causal link of faith and love in Luther, see my *Paragon of Excellence: Luther's Sermons on I Peter* (Fortress, 2023), chap. 2.

15. Niels Henrik Gregersen, "Introduction: Ten Theses on the Future of Lutheran Theology," in *The Gift of Grace: The Future of Lutheran Theology*, ed. Niels Henrik Gregersen et al. (Fortress, 2005), 13.

16. Bo Kristian Holm, "Luther's Theology of Gift," in Gregersen et al., *The Gift of Grace*, 85.

17. John M. G. Barclay, *Paul and the Gift* (Eerdmans, 2017), 113.

18. Barclay, *Paul and the Gift*, 113, Barclay's italics.

19. Holm, "Luther's Theology of Gift," 83.

Conclusion

which the law has been fulfilled."[20] Whoever has been seized by the efficacy of the cross is moved to proclaim and praise it so that others may also partake of it. Just as faith seeks understanding, so too it seeks proclamation (cf. 2 Cor 14:13). Luther writes, "God has cheered our hearts and minds through his dear Son, whom he gave for us to redeem us from sin, death, and the devil. He who believes this earnestly cannot be quiet about it. But he must gladly and willingly sing and speak about it so that others may come and hear it."[21]

Luther revels in paradox as a way of understanding God's way of relating to us. The first paradox is the distinction between law and gospel, the contradictory activities performed by the one and the same God. Mark C. Mattes contends that "in this distinction, the law is not a manual that presents the steps to travel to eternal life, but is instead a tormentor attacking any self-righteousness one seeks to bring before God. The gospel is not a 'new law' but is instead a gift-word of promise that assures terrified consciences of God's mercy given only to sinners, a word which quickens the dead to new life."[22] The law achieves different ends, depending on the subject administering it. If the subject is the devil, he works in us "demonic terrors,"[23] which lead to "godless despair."[24] If it be God, he works in us "evangelical terrors"[25] that result in "evangelical despair."[26] While "godless despair" is deadly, robbing us of life and hope, "evangelical despair" is salutary, leading us to life and hope. Luther remarks, "In so far as it takes everything away from us, leaves us nothing but God: it cannot take God away from us, and actually brings him closer to us."[27] God creates in us the experience of despair, his alien work, through which we learn to trust only in God, his proper work. It is in this context that Luther calls despair a "delicious despair"[28] that brings God near to us, not a demonic kind that distances God from us. Theologically, the law exposes the disease of sin that only the gospel can dispose of. Luther extols the law, a negative thing, in superlative terms as "the highest and greatest" for the work it does, causing us to leave ourselves behind but cleave to Christ, the "sweetest" mediator.[29] Whoever suffers under the alien work of God's

---

20. See *WA* 10.1.1:158; *The Sermons of Martin Luther*, vol 1 (Baker, 1983), 98, as cited in Holm, "Luther's Theology of Gift," 83n14.
21. *LW* 53:333.
22. Mark C. Mattes, "Luther on Justification as Forensic and Effective," in *The Oxford Handbook of Martin Luther's Theology*, ed. Robert Kolb et al.(Oxford University Press, 2014), 270.
23. Paul Althaus, *The Theology of Martin Luther*, trans. Robert C. Schultz (Fortress, 1966), 259.
24. Althaus, *Theology of Martin Luther*, 259.
25. Althaus, *Theology of Martin Luther*, 259.
26. *LW* 73:124; *WA* 39.1:430. The phrase "evangelical despair" is Luther's. Luther also uses the words "salutary" and "diabolical" despair; cf. *LW* 73:130; *WA* 39.1:440.
27. *WA* 5:165.39–166.1, as cited in Alister E. McGrath, *Luther's Theology of the Cross: Martin Luther's Theological Breakthrough* (Wiley-Blackwell, 1985), 152.
28. *WA* 5:165.39–166.1, as cited in McGrath, *Theology of the Cross*, 152.
29. *LW* 26:329; *WA* 40.1:509.

wrath, Luther avers, "may taste the sweetness of grace, the forgiveness of sins, and deliverance from the Law, sin and death, which are not acquired by works but grasped by faith alone."[30]

The second paradox relates to the dialectic distinction between the hidden or absolute God and the revealed or clothed God. The redemptive hiddenness of the revealed/clothed God is set opposite the annihilation of the absolute hiddenness of the absolute/naked God. In his absolute hiddenness, which terrifies us, God has no salvific relation to us in his naked majesty; in his redemptive hiddenness, which consoles us, God exists in a proximate relationship with us through his incarnate Son. The dread of God's absolute hiddenness in his own dazzling majesty is conquered by the delight of his redemptive hiddenness in his Son, if only we believe this. The distinction between the hidden God and the revealed God is not identical to the distinction between law and gospel, because both law and gospel belong to the revealed God. However, in so far as the hidden God causes us to cling to the revealed God, the distinction between them parallels that of law and gospel, as the law causes us to cling to the gospel. The difference between these distinctions is that the hidden God truly condemns sinners to hell from which there is no escape, while the law truly condemns sinners to hell in order that the gospel can lead them out of it. The alien work of condemning and the proper work of saving are of the revealed God, not the hidden God.

The paradoxical distinction between the terrifying hidden God and the comforting revealed God remained part of Luther's doctrine of God throughout his life. Luther's paradoxical God is one with whom we wrestle, as does he himself, especially when life's horrific cries and painful losses are visited upon us. God's way is hidden, not always transparent or apparent to us. The assault of absolute hiddenness is not to be confused with the accusation of God's law. Those who are afflicted by the law are precisely the objects of God's saving grace. The gracious work of the Holy Spirit is evident when one who suffers the terror of the law is persuaded of the comfort of the gospel. But when we encounter God in his nakedness, "the naked God is *there* with humans in their nakedness."[31] But he is there as our enemy, whom we cannot dislodge were it not for God's descent into human flesh—the Word became flesh—to become our savior. According to Mattes, this explains "why the name of Jesus—God's mercy and compassion—must be at the tip of every preacher's and confessor's tongue."[32] We stand in isolation from God, when we recognize that before the tribunal of a terrifying, wrathful God, we are nothing but a miserable sinner, worthy of

---

30. *LW* 26:338; *WA* 40.1:520.

31. See *WA* 40.2:330, as cited in Oswald Bayer, *Theology the Lutheran Way*, ed. and trans. Jeffrey G. Silcock and Mark C. Mattes (Eerdmans, 2007), 18, Luther's italics.

32. Mark C. Mattes, "Honoring the Pastoral Dimension to Theology," in *Handing Over the Goods: Determined to Proclaim Nothing but Christ Jesus and Him Crucified; Essays in Honor of James Arne Nestingen*, ed. Steven D. Paulson and Scott L. Keith (1517 Publishing, 2018), 141.

eternal damnation. Alister E. McGrath writes, "Through this realization he is moved to flee from God to God (*ad Deum contra Deum*) to receive the mercy hidden in this terrible wrath."[33]

The disconnection between God and humans we lament is real, and at times debilitating. The painful separation we feel would be fatal were it not for the word of promise that we hear through a preacher; in Gerhard O. Forde's terms, "The only solution [to the terror of the absolute God] is the cross itself and the subsequent proclamation of the word of the cross as a divine deed, the work of the Spirit.... Through the preaching of the cross in the living present, not through theological explanations, we are defended from the terror of the divine majesty."[34] The antinomy between wrath and mercy created by the inscrutability of God's "absolute" or "naked"[35] being cannot be resolved except by the credal announcement that in Christ, God's wrath is banished in exchange for his mercy if we believe this. The gospel we proclaim elicits its own power of absolution through which the abyss of the terrifying "absolute God" is conquered; it delivers the good, that Christ died "for me," to redeem me, "a lost and condemned human creature."[36] The speculative words "from me" are too weak and inefficacious to overcome the chasm between God and sinners; only by preaching "for" God can such a breach be overcome. Theological edifice does not lead us to God; only preaching does this, simply because of the performative nature of God's word. In Paulson's estimation:

> Speculation starts with the problem of how weak words are and then tries getting blood from the turnip by peering through these words to what lies beyond words. So, speculation tries seeing through a mirror or looking through the lens of a telescope to see the distant God. Proclamation starts with the power of words—and refuses to see through them. Preaching starts with what words do, such as create, free, grant, give, open—and never goes further than hearing that is faith.[37]

The individual persons of the Trinity, as Wolfhart Pannenberg notes, must not be confused with the majesty and depth of the hidden God,[38] although Luther, as noted by Bernhard Lohse, "later occasionally applies the distinction

---

33. McGrath, *Theology of the Cross*, 173.
34. Gerhard O. Forde, *On Being a Theologian of the Cross: Reflections on Luther's Heidelberg Disputation, 1518* (Eerdmans, 1997), 75.
35. See *LW* 12:312. For Luther, "absolute God" corresponds to "naked God."
36. "The Small Catechism," *BC*, 355.
37. Steven D. Paulson, *Luther's Outlaw God*, vol. 1, *Hiddenness, Evil, and Predestination* (Fortress, 2018), 6.
38. See Wolfhart Pannenberg, *Systematic Theology*, vol. 1, trans. Geoffrey W. Bromiley (Eerdmans, 1991), 339–40.

between the hidden and the revealed God directly to the individual persons [such as the Holy Spirit] of the Trinity."[39] Lohse quotes Luther:

> We distinguish therefore between the Holy Spirit in his nature and substance as God and the Holy Spirit as he is given to us. God in his nature and majesty is our enemy, because he demands that we fulfill the law. . . . This is also true of the Holy Spirit. When his finger writes the law on Moses' tablets of stone, he appears in his majesty, accuses us of sin, and terrifies our hearts. However, when he comes to us in tongues and other spiritual gifts, he himself is "gift" because he makes us holy and gives us life. Without this "gift" of the Holy Spirit, the law condemns our sin, because the law is never "gift," but always is the word of eternal and almighty God.[40]

In the overall scheme of things, Luther focuses on the revealed God in his work, and in his being as the distinct persons of the immanent Trinity. The distinction between the hidden God and the revealed God does not correspond to the distinction between the immanent Trinity and the economic Trinity; as Pannenberg writes, "The Trinity is not part of the hiddenness of God. The Trinitarian God is revealed in Jesus Christ."[41] Luther does not admit a dualism of a revealed and hidden God, though he acknowledges the tension between them abides until the end of history. This leads Pannenberg to argue, "If for Luther the unity of the hidden and revealed God will be definitively manifest only in light of eschatological glory, this means that the unity of the trinitarian God himself is still hidden in the process of history."[42] Faith perceives the unity of the hidden and revealed God despite the contradictions we experience on earth. Toward the end of *The Bondage of the Will*, Luther avows that the antithesis between the hidden and revealed God will disappear at the eschaton: "But the light of glory tells us differently, and it will show us hereafter that the God whose judgment here is one of incomprehensible righteousness is a God of most perfect and manifest righteousness."[43] There, we will recognize a perfect correspondence between the work of the God of the gospel and the work of God's terrible hidden majesty.

---

39. Bernhard Lohse, *Martin Luther: An Introduction to His Life and Work*, trans. Robert C. Schultz (Fortress, 1986),170.

40. *WA* 39.1:370.12–371.1, as cited in Lohse, *Martin Luther: An Introduction*, 170; also quoted in Lois Malcolm, "Martin Luther and the Holy Spirit," in *Oxford Research Encyclopedia of Religion*, published March 29, 2017, https://doi.org/10.1093/acrefore/9780199340378.013.328; Albrecht Peters, *Commentary on Luther's Catechisms: Creed*, trans. Thomas H. Trapp (Concordia Publishing House, 2011), 254. See *LW* 73:76.

41. Pannenberg, *Systematic Theology*, 1:340.

42. Pannenberg, *Systematic Theology*, 1:340.

43. *LW* 33:292.

Conclusion

Only when faith gives way to sight will we grasp fully the perfect mercy and justice of God. In Bayer's formulation:

> The only thing that can be disaffirmed is that this hidden God is for us the Trinitarian God; he is not, not yet. Only when faith's journey is past and we live by sight will this monstrously biting and stinging discrepancy between God's terrible hiddenness and his love, as revealed through the Son in the Holy Spirit, be expunged, overcome, and finally disappear. . . . Unlike the *Deus Revelatus*, finally and fully revealed in the eschaton, the *Deus absconditus* remains for the moment so dark and vague, that he can be mistaken for the devil.[44]

Faith alone enables us to bear God's terrible judgment against our sins, and this is made possible by viewing our condemnation under God's wrath *sub contrario*—namely, through Christ's wounds. Mattes puts it well: "Faith in God's promise allows us to entrust our lives to the care of God as faithful to this promise, even in opposition to God's own accusation against sin, or the terror that can arise from the experience of God's hiddenness."[45] Not a quality, habit, or act of love, but faith, the trust of the heart, perceives the reality of God's justifying action in its opposite: that hidden in the thing that condemns us is the sweet mercy of God. In this regard, Luther avers, "The commandments of God become sweet when they are read not only in books but also in the wounds of the sweetest Savior."[46] When the sinner becomes so cast down by the devil's torment and the law's crushing power that he despairs of God's mercies, he should apply to himself more abundantly the wounds of Christ, to gain complete confidence in God's promise. In his letter to Jerome Weller, Luther writes, "Where the devil attacks and torments us, we must completely set aside the whole Decalogue."[47] The purpose of setting aside the Decalogue and its salutary use is not to deny the commandments but to "make the most of the gospel."[48] Christ as gift, who does not demand but delivers, must be made most use of to defend our faith from "demonic despair." The "coincidental opposites" of judgment and mercy constitute the contradictory activities of God. Paulson portrays this as "a double nearness of God" in relation to us: "God's judgment is not far off, but immanent; likewise, God's mercy was not far off, but impending, so that faith emerged for

---

44. Oswald Bayer, "God's Omnipotence," *Lutheran Quarterly* 23, no. 1 (2009): 91.
45. Mark C. Mattes, *The Role of Justification in Contemporary Theology* (Fortress, 2004), 5.
46. LW 48:66.
47. Theodore Tappert, ed., *Luther: Letters of Spiritual Counsel* (Westminster, 1955), 86.
48. See Commission on Worship of the Lutheran Church—Missouri Synod, *Lutheran Service Book: Pastoral Care Companion* (Concordia Publishing House, 2007), 307: "For the Christian who is driven by the Law to despair of the mercies of God in Christ Jesus, the pastor 'must set aside the whole Decalogue' (Luther's) and make the most of the gospel."

Luther as the one and the only event of salvation that could endure negation and still hold onto positive hope."[49] Faith endures the antinomy between God's judgment and God's mercy and makes the shift from the former to the latter. The faith God works in us is not faith *about* God but faith *in* God—or, as Luther puts it, "a living faith"[50] that fulfills what the first commandment demands ("I am your God. You shall have no other gods"). This kind of faith, born of the gospel (Creed), possesses "everything in richest measure,"[51] even when every visible sign of God's favor is absent. Luther's faith does not consist in a mere assent to propositional truth about God; nor does it depend on the strength or skill of a rational edifice. "The life of faith," Tim Saleska describes, "is clinging like a drowning man to the promise of a future when you are presently experiencing just the opposite. It is finding life and hope in his promise, 'I forgive you,' when God seems to be killing you, and there is death everywhere you look."[52]

Luther's doctrine of God's word as creative has enormous implication for preaching. Oral preaching is a created form of God's word. The word of God spoken is itself God speaking through human language. Luther teaches, "The voice is [the preacher's], but the words he employs are really spoken by my God."[53] Essentially, preaching is God's own speech, which Luther identifies as God's own act. Neither our works nor our thoughts accomplish God's purpose. God's word accomplishes itself, effecting a reality that corresponds to itself—hence Isaiah 55:11, "It shall accomplish what I propose, and prosper in the thing for which I sent it." The word may face opposition and seems to lose its creative power. Yet it will not be "without fruit,"[54] even when it comes from a feeble preacher. The effect of God's word is independent of the preacher's artistry; nor is it dependent on the hearer's ability to apprehend it; it exists solely by the "impressive power"[55] of God's word. The word of God is most effective not in power but in weakness, not in glory but in lowliness. Only those who are in a position of weakness and powerlessness grasp the salutary effect of God's effective word in them. Those who know their inner vacuity and have nothing to offer to God become the very objects of God's effective word. The efficacy of God's word occurs through the dialectic tension of two works: an alien work of crushing self-sufficiency and arrogance in order to perform a proper work of exalting those of low degree. God's work is most causative when our reliance is not on ourselves but solely on

---

49. Paulson, *Luther's Outlaw God*, 2:347.
50. *LW* 42:25.
51. "The Large Catechism," *BC*, 439.
52. Tim Saleska, "The Clarity of Paradox: A Meditation on Exodus 34:6–7," in *Simul: Inquiries into Luther's Experience of the Christian Life*, ed. Robert Kolb et al. (Vandenhoeck and Ruprecht, 2021), 210.
53. *LW* 22:528.
54. *LW* 17:258; *WA* 31.2:460.
55. *LW* 14:94; *WA* 18:370.

Conclusion

the performative speech of God, that which acts efficaciously *ex nihilo*. Just as the creation of the world is by God's word alone, so is the creation of faith in God. Luther says, "Therefore we should give free course to the Word and not add our works to it. We have the *jus verbi* [right to speak] but not the *executio* [power to accomplish]."[56] Preaching the word is ours, but its effect is God's good pleasure.

Luther's emphasis on preaching undergirds the importance of hearing rather than seeing as the receptive mode of apprehension. God's word must be orally spoken so that it be audibly heard, through which communicative relation with God is made effectual. Cary labels Luther's theology as "an epistemology of hearing,"[57] according to which, knowledge of another person "is not an achievement of the knower so much as a gift of the known. We can only know persons if they give themselves to be known, because they have the authority to speak for themselves that we cannot ignore."[58] We come to know the other person through this person's self-disclosure in speech. Such is the "second-hand knowledge" that is gained through hearing what this person says.[59] The emphasis on hearing places us under God and his authority to speak for himself; the knowledge of God stems not from human efforts but from God's free self-giving so that we might know him in his word, the gospel of Jesus Christ. It also locates us in a position of passive receptivity of God's "speech-act" by which the reality of a renewed fellowship between God and us is created. For Luther, hearing defines us, not seeing. This is contrary to Aristotle, Robert W. Jenson argues, for whom

> the paradigm mode of apperception was seeing, so that in Aristotle's doctrine we are what we stare at. The soul—if we may put it so—is a great eye. For Luther the paradigm mode of apperception is hearing, since we are both created and saved by God's speech to us. The soul—we may say—is a great ear, rather than a great eye. We should note also, that in switching from seeing to hearing as the paradigm of apperception, Luther replaces a merely cognitive relation of the soul to its objects with a moral relation. To *hear* the world is to perceive it teleologically, in its adaptation to God's good purpose.[60]

The emphasis on "ears" as the receptor of God's word marks the Christian life as "the passive life" (*vita passiva*)[61]—in Bayer's terms, "passive in the sense that ... it

---

56. *LW* 51:76.
57. Cary, *Meaning of Protestant Theology*, 320.
58. Cary, *Meaning of Protestant Theology*, 321.
59. Cary, *Meaning of Protestant Theology*, 320.
60. Robert W. Jenson, "Luther's Contemporary Theological Significance," in *The Cambridge Companion to Martin Luther*, ed. Donald K. McKim (Cambridge University Press, 2003), 282.
61. The term "*vita passiva*" is found in *WA* 5:165.35ff; 166, II, as cited in Bayer, *Theology the Lutheran Way*, 218n42.

undergoes God's work and so passively receives it."[62] The word as speech-act characterizes us as the passive agent who permits God's word to perform its own work in us. Faith, Paulson notes, "is not inner or subjective," in the sense of "a reference of the self to the self."[63] It is wrought in us by the word addressing us from outside us (*extra nobis*). Faith, which creates solace and rest, springs from hearing the credal announcement of the God who promises to be ours. The passive form in which humans appear before God is faith which, in Forde's estimation, "is the state of being grasped by the unconditional claim and promise of the God who calls into being that which is from that which is not."[64] Such a definition of faith as "being grasped" by God has merit, as it accentuates the prior action of God's effective word, followed by the receptivity of what that word does to us. The gospel—that Christ's redemption has annihilated sin, law, death, and hell—must be preached so that we can "grasp it only with our ears and have it in the Word of God."[65] We are to hear and believe it, and close our eyes to all that seemingly contradicts it.[66] In this regard, the formation of faith is through hearing, not through seeing. It is not through doing the law and good works but through grasping the word with our ears that we become a Christian and are seized by the grace of Christ. Luther asserts,

> Therefore a man becomes a Christian, not by working but by listening. And so anyone who wants to exert himself toward righteousness must first exert himself in listening to the Gospel. Now when he has heard and accepted this, let him joyfully give thanks to God, and then let him exert himself in good works that are commanded in the Law; thus the Law and works will follow hearing with faith.[67]

Luther's pastoral heart shines through his *Large* and *Small Catechisms*. Any section or part of their tripartite structures he could use as a pedagogical tool to lead his congregants into a proper way of Christian meditation. He devises a down-to-earth method of praying according to four distinct types of responses. Luther calls this "a garland of four strands": instruction, or "a school text"; thanksgiving, or a "song book"; confession, or a "penitential book"; and prayer, or

---

62. Bayer, *Theology the Lutheran Way*, 22.
63. Steven D. Paulson, "Internal Clarity of Scripture and the Modern World: Luther and Erasmus Revisited," in *Hermeneutica Sacra: Studies of the Interpretation of Holy Scripture in the Sixteenth and Seventeenth Centuries*, ed. Torbjörn Johansson et al., (De Gruyter, 2010), 93; Paulson, *Luther's Outlaw God*, 1:91.
64. Gerhard O. Forde, *Justification by Faith: A Matter of Death and Life* (Sigler, 1990), 22–23.
65. *LW* 30:164; *WA* 14:28.
66. *LW* 22:498.
67. *LW* 26:214–15; *WA* 40.1:345.

a "prayer book."⁶⁸ All four interwoven create a garland of praise to God, drawing from God his unmerited grace. For example, consider Luther's application of this garland to a fruitful meditation on the First Article, "I believe in God the Father Almighty, maker of heaven and earth":

The First Strand: School Text
Here, first of all, [it teaches] . . . who we are, whence you came, whence came heaven and earth. You are God's creation, his handiwork, his workmanship. That is, of yourself and in yourself you are nothing, can do nothing, know nothing, are capable of nothing. . . . Therefore you have nothing to boast of before God. . . . But here it is declared and faith affirms that God has created everything out of nothing.

The Second Strand: Song Book
Furthermore, we should give thanks to God that in his kindness he created us out of nothing and provides for our daily needs out of nothing.

The Third Strand: Penitential Book
Third, we should confess and lament our lack of faith and gratitude in failing to take this to heart.

The Fourth Strand: Prayer Book
Fourth, we pray for a true and confident faith that sincerely esteems and trusts God to be our Creator, as this article declares.⁶⁹

Luther shows us how to meditate with profit in the Holy Spirit. He counsels against mechanical usage of the four-stranded scheme. He stresses the necessity of a kindled heart for a reception of God's presence. Luther counsels, "It is enough to consider one section or half a section [of The Commandments, the Creed, or the Lord's Prayer] which kindles fire in the heart. This the Spirit will grant us and continually instruct us in when, by God's Word, our hearts have been cleared and freed of outside thoughts and concerns."⁷⁰ He exhorts us to aim at the "rich and enlightened thoughts" that the Holy Spirit inspires in us.⁷¹ Where "thoughts" capture us, he says, "words" are dispensed with, and we are compelled to ponder "the meaning and desires" that words convey.⁷² Once the heart is

---

68. *LW* 43:200, 209.
69. *LW* 43:209–10.
70. *LW* 43:209.
71. *LW* 43:201.
72. *LW* 42:20–21.

rightly inclined toward God, certain words or syllables or prayer formulas must be laid aside to hear the sermon of the Holy Spirit.[73] When the Holy Spirit seizes our hearts, we forgo the rest, honor him there, and listen silently to his sermon. By "one word of his sermon," Luther asserts, we are lifted beyond ourselves into the world of God, to "behold wondrous things of God" (Ps 119:18), which is better than any humanly devised method.[74] The preaching of the Holy Spirit in our hearts is placed above the frequency of prayer itself; as Luther declares, "One word of his sermon is far better than a thousand of our prayers."[75] Pneumatologic sensitivity to when God speaks to us is more crucial than the mastery of the art of prayer. With this, Luther shows himself to be a theologian of the Holy Spirit.

Luther's theology reminds us of how far we as God's beloved children have fallen of the Father's expectations, and yet how much we are sustained by God's unwavering grace by which our hearts leap for joy. It offers a theo-logic of living by the incongruous and prolific grace of the triune God so that we can leave everything behind and cleave to him alone, the giver of all goods. Readers are able to reap sobering and scripturally saturated truths from the Reformer, bestirring in them a reverential fear, and an affective love, of God. And as they read Luther, they too will be trained to thank the triune God for his daily goodness with a joyful heart and vibrant faith, and echo back to him in prayer: "Truly, you are a kind and benevolent God" (Ps 118:1), despite all appearances to the contrary.

---

73. *LW* 43:198.
74. *LW* 43:209.
75. *LW* 43:198.

AFTERWORD

In reflecting on the theme of the book, which the author has masterfully developed, I will highlight some key ways in which God's most earnest purpose comes out in Luther's explanation of the Three Articles of the Creed. In brief, God's purpose begins with the incarnation of the eternal Logos, the birth of the Savior in Bethlehem's manger, by which he conceals his majesty as God, and ends with Christ's cross and resurrection and his exaltation to the right hand of the Father in power and glory.

Although the structure of the Creed is Trinitarian, its beating heart is surely Christ and his atoning work for our salvation. Luther echoes the New Testament witness when he says that God the Father's overwhelming purpose is redemptive: to bring fallen humankind back into fellowship with himself. He does this through Christ's death on the cross, the benefit of which is distributed to all who have faith in the promise through the power of the Spirit.

Even though the Second Article, with its focus on the cross as the apex of God's salvific work, is central in Luther's interpretation, he can still say in his *Personal Prayer Book* that the Third Article on the Spirit is the most important and that the other two are based on it.[1]

The author has commendably given the Spirit his rightful place, which is neither exaggerated nor underestimated. Following Luther, he recognizes that the Spirit's role is not to promote himself but to promote Christ. Jesus himself says of the coming Spirit that whatever he hears the Father telling the Son in their eternal intra-Trinitarian conversation, he will in turn tell us. When Luther says the Third Article is the most important, he is speaking rhetorically to emphasize a point, not dogmatically. There can be no playing of one Article off against another, because all Three Articles are equally important theologically just as all three persons of the Trinity are coequal and coeternal but have different functions. And yet, as we have just seen, he can still single out the Holy Spirit within the unity of the triune God for special mention. This surely can only be because it is the Spirit who mediates and applies to us the work of the Father and the Son.

Luther himself explains God's most earnest purpose very eloquently in the conclusion to the three articles of the faith (Luther's term for the Creed). These words are as memorable as they are profound and deserve to be quoted in full:

---

1. *LW* 43:24; *WA* 10 1.1:388.

> In all three articles God himself has revealed and opened to us the most profound depths of his fatherly heart and his pure, unutterable love. For this very purpose he created us, so that he might redeem us and make us holy, and, moreover, having granted and bestowed upon us everything in heaven and on earth, he has also given us his Son and his Holy Spirit, through whom he brings us to himself. For ... we could never come to recognize the Father's favor and grace were it not for the LORD Christ, who is a mirror of the Father's heart. Apart from him we see nothing but an angry and terrible judge. But neither could we know anything of Christ, had it not been revealed by the Holy Spirit.[2]

Luther elaborates on this, as we have seen, in his explanation of the Creed, which has a tripartite structure corresponding to the Trinitarian shape of God's creative, redemptive, and sanctifying action for us and for our salvation.

The author rightly stresses that God's most earnest purpose is to reunite us in fellowship with himself through Christ in the Spirit, which of course presupposes justification by faith in God's promise of forgiveness, life, and salvation. This is the main theme of the book, which is expressed in different ways. The grammar of faith, which keeps us faithful to the biblical narrative as encapsulated in the Creed, ensures that no matter how this theme is expressed, God's work is always Trinitarian in shape, always christologically oriented, and always pneumatically enacted, and that his work is the effective basis for our work in the Christian life of faith.

The author does a fine job of emphasizing that even if the Christian life, *coram mundo*, is characterized by action, its fundamental orientation *coram Deo* is marked by passivity, for this is consistent with justification by faith and the reception of the Spirit, which form the basis of the active life. Strictly speaking, Christians do not "posses" the Spirit but the Spirit "possesses" them. They "have" the Spirit only insofar as they keep on receiving the Spirit (Eph 5:18). While the Spirit indwells the baptized through faith, the Spirit may be lost through apostasy. We never really have God in our grasp; we never possess the Spirit in a proud or triumphalist way, and we can only ever receive the Spirit as a gift (1 Cor 4:7). Therefore, the *vita passiva* of faith, which allows God to do his work in us, is the only fitting posture for the reception of the Spirit—and thus of the triune God.[3]

The Trinitarian emphasis of the book is a healthy antidote to the imbalance in Trinitarian theology often evident in Protestant circles, especially in the language of prayer, where the triune God is simply addressed generically or reduced to one person, instead of prayer being directed to the Father through

---

2. "The Creed," in *BC* 439–440
3. *LW* 44:72; *WA* 6:244, 3–6.

the Son in the Spirit. The author follows the pattern of the New Testament as well as Luther by highlighting that in prayer, the directionality is from the Spirit through the Son to the Father, which is the opposite direction to the way in which God reveals himself to us in the economy of salvation, which is from the Father through the Son in the Spirit. One way that this Trinitarian relationality can be preserved in the Christian church as it comes under increasing pressure from anti-Christian forces is if we are more deliberate in using Trinitarian language, especially in public prayer, and refrain from the modern tendency to substitute other names for the triune God (such as Mother, Child, and Womb or Rock, Redeemer, and Friend) in place of the biblically warranted Father, Son, and Holy Spirit. In the age of identity politics, we need to remember that God's own identity is bound up with his proper name and that if he is robbed of his name, he is robbed of the particularity of his triune identity, and when that happens, he is no longer the three-personed God whom Christians worship and confess but is turned into an idol of our own making.

If God's most earnest purpose is to reunite us with himself, this can only be because he is generous beyond measure and, as Luther says in his *Great Confession* of 1528, "has given himself to us all wholly and completely, with all that he is and has." But what if God's boundless self-giving is not reciprocated—is not met with faith? Does it have a limit? Luther does not ask this question, which is somewhat akin to the question Paul wrestles with at the end of Romans 11: Does Israel's rejection of God's Messiah mean God's rejection of Israel? When we for our part grapple with the deep mysteries of faith and the inscrutability of God's ways, such as the question of whether in the end all people will be saved and reunited with God, whether God's mercy will prevail over his justice, we too can only do what Paul does after he has gone back and forth wrestling with the question of how God could abandon his covenant people. He recognizes the limits of human reason and simply breaks out into a doxology, a song of praise to the triune God who, according to Luther, is a "glowing furnace of love":[4] "Oh, the depth of the riches and wisdom and knowledge of God! How unsearchable are his judgments and how inscrutable his ways! . . . For from him and through him and to him are all things. To him be glory forever. Amen" (Rom 11:33–6).

Jeffrey G. Silcock

---

4. *LW* 51:95; *WA* 10.3:56, 2–3.

BIBLIOGRAPHY

Primary Sources

Kolb, Robert, and Timothy J. Wengert, eds. *The Book of Concord: The Confessions of the Evangelical Lutheran Church*. Fortress, 2000.
Luther, Martin. *The Annotated Luther*. Edited by Hans J. Hillerbrand, Kirsi I. Stjerna, and Timothy J. Wengert. 6 vols. Fortress, 2015–17.
Luther, Martin. *The Bondage of the Will*. Translated by J. I. Packer and O. R. Johnston. James Clarke, 1957.
Luther, Martin. *D. Martin Luthers Werke: Kritische Gesamtausgabe*. 65 vols. in 127. Weimar: Hermann Böhlau, 1883–1929. Abteilung 1: Schriften vols. 1–56.
Luther, Martin. *D. Martin Luthers Werke: Kritische Gesamtausgabe*. 65 vols. in 127. Weimar: Hermann Böhlau, 1883–1929. Abteilung 2: Tischreden vols. 1–6.
Luther, Martin. *Luther's Works: American Edition*. Edited by Helmut T. Lehman. Vols. 31–55. Fortress, 1957–86.
Luther, Martin. *Luther's Works: American Edition*. Edited by Jaroslav Pelikan. Vols. 1–30. Concordia, 1955–73.
Luther, Martin. *Luther's Works: American Edition*, n.s. Edited by Christopher Boyd Brown, Benjamin T. G. Mayes, and James L. Langebartels. Vols. 56–82. Concordia, 2009–.
Tappert, Theodore G., trans. and ed. *The Book of Concord: The Confessions of the Evangelical Lutheran Church*. Fortress, 1959.

Secondary Sources

Althaus, Paul. *The Theology of Martin Luther*. Translated by Robert C. Shultz. Fortress, 1966.
Althaus, Paul. *Thou Shalt! Sermons on the Ten Commandments*. Translated by John W. Rilling. Chantry Music Press, 1971.
Arand, Charles P. "The Battle Cry of Faith: The Catechisms' Exposition of the Lord's Prayer." *Concordia Journal* 21, no. 1 (1995): 42–65.
Arand, Charles P. "Introduction to the First Article." In Pless and Vogel, *Luther's Large Catechism*.
Arand, Charles P. "Luther on the Creed." In Wengert, *The Pastoral Luther*.
Arand, Charles P. "Our Stewardship of Creation." In Pless and Vogel, *Luther's Large Catechism*.
Athanasius and Didymus. *Works on the Spirit: Athanasius the Great and Didymus the Blind*. Edited by Mark DelCogliano, Andrew Radde-Gallwitz, and Lewis Ayres. St. Vladimir's Seminary Press, 2011.

Augustine. *Confessions*. Translated by R. C. Pine-Coffin. Penguin Books, 1961.
Augustine. "On Rebuke and Grace." In *Augustine: Anti-Pelagian Writings*. Vol. 5, *The Nicene and Post-Nicene Fathers*, 1st ser. Edited by Philip Schaff. Repr. Hendrickson, 1995.
Augustine. *On the Holy Trinity*. In *Augustine: On the Holy Trinity, Doctrinal Treatises, Moral Treatises*. Vol. 3, *The Nicene and Post-Nicene Fathers*, 1st ser. Edited by Philip Schaff. Repr. Hendrickson, 1995.
Augustine. *The Works of Saint Augustine: A Translation for the 21st Century*. Vol 5, *The Trinity*, edited by John E. Rotelle. Translated by Edmund Hill. New City, 1991.
Barclay, John M. G. *Paul and the Gift*. Eerdmans, 2017.
Barth, Karl. *Church Dogmatics*. Vol. 1.1, *The Doctrine of the Word of God*, translated by G. W. Bromiley, edited by G. W. Bromiley and T. F. Torrance. T&T Clark, 1975.
Barth, Karl. *The Theology of John Calvin*. Translated by Geoffrey W. Bromiley. Eerdmans, 1995.
Bayer, Oswald. "Being in the Image of God." Translated by Mark C Mattes and Ken Sundet Jones. *Lutheran Quarterly* 27, no. 1 (2013): 76–88.
Bayer, Oswald. "The Ethics of Gift." Translated by Mark A. Seifrid. *Lutheran Quarterly* 24, no. 4 (2010): 447–68.
Bayer, Oswald. "God's Omnipotence." *Lutheran Quarterly* 23, no. 1 (2009): 85–102.
Bayer, Oswald. *Living by Faith: Justification and Sanctification*. Translated by Geoffrey W. Bromiley. Eerdmans, 2003.
Bayer, Oswald. "Luther's 'Simul Iustus et Peccator.'" In Kolb et al., *Simul*.
Bayer, Oswald. *Martin Luther's Theology: A Contemporary Interpretation*. Translated by Thomas H. Trapp. Eerdmans, 2008.
Bayer, Oswald. *Theology the Lutheran Way*. Edited and translated by Jeffrey G. Silcock and Mark C. Mattes. Eerdmans, 2007.
Bender, Kimlyn J. *Reflections on Reformational Theology: Studies in the Theology of the Reformation, Karl Barth, and the Evangelical Tradition*. T&T Clark, 2021.
Bernard. *On Consideration*. In *Patrologiae Cursus Completus: Series Latina*, edited by J. P. Migne, 231 vols. Paris: Garnier Fratres, 1844–64.
Bielfeldt, Dennis, Mickey L. Mattox, and Paul R. Hinlicky. *The Substance of the Faith: Luther's Doctrinal Theology for Today*. Edited by Paul R. Hinlicky. Fortress, 2008.
Bornkamm, Heinrich. *Luther's Doctrine of the Two Kingdoms in the Context of His Theology*. Translated by Karl H. Herz. Fortress, 1966.
Bornkamm, Heinrich. *Luther's World of Thought*. Translated by Martin H. Bertram. Concordia, 1965.
Boulton, Michael. "'We Pray by His Mouth'": Karl Barth, Erving Goffman, and a Theology of Invocation." *Modern Theology* 17, no. 1 (2001): 67–83.
Braaten, Carl E. "The Problem of God-Language Today." In *Our Naming of God: Problems and Prospects of God-Talk Today*, edited by Carl E. Braaten. Fortress, 1989.
Brecht, Martin. *Martin Luther: Shaping and Refining the Reformation 1521–1532*. Translated by James L. Schaaf. Fortress, 1990.
Brondos, David A. *Fortress Introduction to Salvation and the Cross*. Fortress, 2007.
Burgess, Joseph, and Marc Kolden, eds. *By Faith Alone: Essays on Justification in Honor of Gerhard O. Forde*. Eerdmans, 2004.
Calvin, John. *Institutes of the Christian Religion*. Edited by John T. McNeil and translated by Ford Lewis Battles. Westminster, 1960.

Bibliography

Carlson, Edgar M. "Luther's Conception of Government." *Church History* 15 (December 1946): 261.
Cary, Phillip. *The Meaning of Protestant Theology: Luther, Augustine, and the Gospel that Gives Us Christ*. Baker Academic, 2019.
Chester, Stephen J. "'Abba! Father!' (Gal. 4:6): Justification and Assurance in Martin Luther's Lectures on Galatians (1535)." *Biblical Research: Journal of the Chicago Society of Biblical Research* 63 (2018): 15–22.
Chester, Stephen J. "It is No Longer I Who Live: Justification by Faith and Participation in Christ in Martin Luther's Exegesis of Galatians." *New Testament Studies* 55, no. 3 (2009): 315–37. https://doi.org/10.1017/S002868850900023X.
Chester, Stephen J. *Reading Paul with the Reformers: Reconciling Old and New Perspectives*. Eerdmans, 2017.
Chung, Paul S. "An Ecumenical Legacy of Martin Luther and Asian Spirituality." In Gregersen et al., *The Gift of Grace*.
Collver, Albert B., III, James Arne Nestigen, and John T. Pless eds. *The Necessary Distinction: A Continuing Conversation on Law and Gospel*. Concordia Publishing House, 2017.
Commission on Worship of the Lutheran Church—Missouri Synod. *Lutheran Service Book: Pastoral Care Companion*. Concordia Publishing House, 2007.
Cortez, Marc. *Christological Anthropology in Historical Perspective: Ancient and Contemporary Approaches to Theological Anthropology*. Zondervan, 2016.
Cyprian. "On the Unity of the Catholic Church." In *The Ante-Nicene Fathers: Translations of the Writings of the Fathers Down to A.D. 325*. Vol. 5, *Hyppolytus, Cyprian, Caius, Novatian, Appendix*, edited by Alexander Roberts, James Donaldson, and A. Cleveland Coxe. Reprint, Hendrickson, 1995, 423.
de Margerie, Bertrand. *The Christian Trinity in History*. Translated by Edmund J. Fortman. St. Bede's Publications, 1982.
Dieter, Theodor. "Martin Luther and Scholasticism." In Marmion et al., *Remembering the Reformation*.
Ebeling, Gerhard. "Luther's Understanding of Reality." Translated by Scott A. Celsor. *Lutheran Quarterly* 27, no. 1 (2013): 56–75.
Edwards, Mark U., Jr. *Luther and the False Brethren*. Stanford University Press, 1975.
Elert, Werner. *The Structure of Lutheranism: The Theology and Philosophy of Life of Lutheranism Especially in the Sixteenth and Seventeenth Centuries*. Translated by Walter A. Hansen. Concordia Publishing House, 1962.
Elliott, Mark W. *Providence: A Biblical, Historical, and Theological Account*. Baker Academic, 2020.
Forde, Gerhard O. *The Captivation of the Will: Luther vs. Erasmus on Freedom and Bondage*. Edited by Steven D. Paulson. Eerdmans, 2005.
Forde, Gerhard O. *The Essential Forde: Distinguishing Law and Gospel*. Edited by Nicholas Hopman, Mark C. Mattes, and Steven D. Paulson. Fortress, 2019.
Forde, Gerhard O. *Justification by Faith: A Matter of Death and Life*. Sigler, 1990.
Forde, Gerhard O. "Luther's Theology of the Cross." In *Christian Dogmatics*. Vol. 2, edited by Carl E. Braaten and Robert W. Jenson. Fortress, 1984.
Forde, Gerhard O. *On Being a Theologian of the Cross: Reflections on Luther's Heidelberg Disputation, 1518*. Eerdmans, 1997.
Forde, Gerhard O. *Theology is for Proclamation*. Fortress, 1990.

Forde, Gerhard O. "The Word That Kills and Makes Alive." In *Marks of the Body of Christ*, edited by Carl E. Braaten and Robert W. Jenson. Eerdmans, 1999.
Forell, George Wolfgang. *Faith Active in Love: An Investigation of the Principles Underlying Luther's Social Ethics*. Augsburg Publishing House, 1954.
Forell, George Wolfgang. "Justification and Eschatology in Luther's Thought." *Church History* 38, no. 2 (1969): 164–74.
Fritts, Marney. "Sanctification is Purely Passive." In Paulson and Keith, *Handing Over the Goods*.
George, Timothy. *Reading Scripture with the Reformers*. IVP Academic, 2011.
Gerrish, B. A. "By Faith Alone: Medium and Message in Luther's Gospel." In *The Old Protestantism and the New: Essays on the Reformation Heritage*. University of Chicago Press, 1982.
Gerrish, B. A. "'To the Unknown God': Luther and Calvin on the Hiddenness of God." In *The Old Protestantism and the New: Essays on the Reformation Heritage*. University of Chicago Press, 1982.
Girgensohn, Herbert. *Teaching Luther's Catechism*. Translated by John Doberstein. 2 vols. Muhlenberg, 1959–60.
Gregersen, Niels Henrik. "Grace in Nature and History: Luther's Doctrine of Creation Revisited." *Dialog: A Journal of Theology* 44, no. 1 (2005): 19–29.
Gregersen, Niels Henrik, Bo Kristian Holm, Ted Peters, and Peter Widmann. *The Gift of Grace: The Future of Lutheran Theology*. Fortress, 2005.
Gritsch, Eric W., and Robert W. Jenson. *Lutheranism: The Theological Movement and Its Confessional Writings*. Fortress, 1976.
Haemig, Mary Jane. "Luther on Prayer as Authentic Communication." *Lutheran Quarterly* 30, no. 3 (2016): 307–28.
Hains, Todd R. *Martin Luther and the Rule of Faith: Reading God's Word for God's People*. IVP Academic, 2022.
Hamm, Berndt. *The Early Luther: Stages in a Reformation Reorientation*. Translated by Martin J. Lohrmann. Eerdmans, 2014.
Hampson, Daphne. *Christian Contradictions: The Structures of Lutheran and Catholic Thought*. Cambridge University Press, 2001.
Hanson, Bradley. *A Graceful Life: Lutheran Spirituality for Today*. Augsburg Fortress, 2000.
Harrison, Matthew C., and John T. Pless, eds. *One Lord, Two Hands: Essays on the Theology of the Two Kingdoms*. Concordia, 2021.
Hefner, Philip. "Can the Created Co-Creator Be Lutheran? A Response to Svend Andersen." *Dialog: A Journal of Theology* 44, no. 2 (2005): 184–88.
Helmer, Christine. "More Difficult to Believe? Luther on Divine Omnipotence." *International Journal of Systematic Theology* 3, no. 1 (2001): 2–26.
Helmer, Christine. *The Trinity and Martin Luther: A Study on the Relationship Between Genre, Language and the Trinity in Luther's Works, 1523–1546*. von Zabern, 1999. Rev. ed., Lexham, 2017.
Heschel, Abraham J. *The Prophets*. Harper & Row, 1962.
Hinlicky, Paul R. *Divine Complexity: The Rise of Creedal Christianity*. Fortress, 2011.
Hinlicky, Paul R. *Luther for Evangelicals: A Reintroduction*. Baker Academic, 2018.
Hinlicky, Paul R. "Luther's New Language of the Spirit: Trinitarian Theology as Critical Dogmatics." In Bielfeldt et al., *Substance of the Faith*.

Hoglund, Jonathan. *Called by Triune Grace: Divine Rhetoric and the Effectual Call.* IVP Academics, 2016.
Holm, Bo Kristian. "Luther's Theology of the Gift." In Gregersen et al., *The Gift of Grace.*
Holmes, Christopher R. J. *The Lord is Good: Seeking the God of the Psalter.* IVP Academic, 2018.
Hordern, William. *Experience and Faith: The Significance of Luther for Understanding Today's Experiential Religion.* Augsburg Publishing House, 1983.
Horrell, David G. *An Introduction to the Study of Paul.* 3rd ed. Bloomsbury T&T Clark, 2015.
Hultgren, Stephen. "The Problem of Freedom Today and the Third Use of the Law: Biblical and Theological Considerations." In Collver et al., *Necessary Distinction.*
Iwand, Hans Joachim. "The Preaching of the Law." In *Hans Joachim Iwand on Church and Society: Opened by the Kingdom of God*, edited by Benjamin Haupt, Michael Basse, Gerard den Hertog, and Christian Neddens, translated by Christian Einertson. T&T Clark, 2023.
Iwand, Hans Joachim. *The Righteousness of Faith according to Luther.* Edited by Virgil F. Thompson. Translated by Randi H. Lundell. Wipf and Stock, 2008.
Jansen, John Frederick. *Calvin's Doctrine of the Work of Christ.* James Clarke, 1956.
Jansen, Reiner. *Studien zu Luthers Trinitätslehre.* Lang, 1976.
Jenson, Robert W. "Luther's Contemporary Theological Significance." In *The Cambridge Companion to Martin Luther*, edited by Donald K. McKim. Cambridge University Press, 2003.
Jenson, Robert W. *Systematic Theology.* 2 vols. Oxford University Press, 1997, 1999.
Jenson, Robert W. *The Triune Identity: God According to the Gospel.* Fortress, 1982.
Jenson, Robert W. *Visible Words: The Interpretation and Practice of Christian Sacraments.* Fortress, 1978.
Jüngel, Eberhard. *God as the Mystery of the World: On the Foundation of the Theology of the Crucified One in the Dispute between Theism and Atheism.* Translated by Darrell L. Guder. Eerdmans, 1983.
Kaiser, Denis. "'He Spake and it was Done': Luther's Creation Theology in His 1535 Lectures on Genesis 1:1–2:4." *Journal of the Adventist Theological Society* 24, no. 2 (2013): 116–36.
Kilcrease, Jack D. *Justification by the Word: Restoring "Sola Fide."* Lexham Academic, 2022.
Kim, Sun-young. *Luther on Faith and Love: Christ and the Law in the 1535 Galatians Commentary.* Fortress, 2014.
Kleinig, John W. *God's Word: A Guide to Holy Scripture.* Lexham, 2022.
Kleinig, John W. "Introduction to the Lord's Prayer." In Pless and Vogel, *Luther's Large Catechism.*
Kleinig, John W. "*Oratio, Meditatio, Tentatio*: What Makes a Theologian?" *Concordia Theological Quarterly* 66, no. 3 (2002): 255–67.
Kolb, Robert. *Bound Choice, Election, and Wittenberg Theological Method: From Martin Luther to the Formula of Concord.* Fortress, 2017.
Kolb, Robert. "God and His Human Creatures in Luther's Sermons on Genesis: The Reformer's Early Use of His Distinction of Two Kinds of Righteousness." *Concordia Journal* 33, no. 2 (2007): 166–84.
Kolb, Robert. *Luther and the Stories of God: Biblical Narratives as a Foundation for Christian Living.* Baker Academic, 2012.

Kolb, Robert. "Luther on Peasants and Princes." *Lutheran Quarterly* 23 (2009): 125–46.

Kolb, Robert. "Luther on the Theology of the Cross." In Wengert, *The Pastoral Luther*.

Kolb, Robert. "Luther on the Two Kinds of Righteousness: Reflections on His Two-Dimensional Definition of Humanity at the Heart of His Theology." *Lutheran Quarterly* 13 (1999): 449–66.

Kolb, Robert. *Martin Luther and the Enduring Word of God: The Wittenberg School and Its Scripture-Centered Proclamation*. Baker Academic, 2016.

Kolb, Robert. *Martin Luther: Confessor of the Faith*. Oxford University Press, 2009.

Kolb, Robert. *Teaching God's Children His Teaching: A Guide for the Study of Luther's Catechism*. New ed. Concordia Seminary, 2012.

Kolb, Robert. "Wittenberg Uses of Law and Gospel." *Lutheran Quarterly* 37, no. 3 (2023): 249–67. https://doi.org/10.1353/lut.2023.a905030.

Kolb, Robert, and Carl R. Trueman. *Between Wittenberg and Geneva: Lutheran and Reformed Theology in Conversation*. Baker Academic, 2017.

Kolb, Robert, and Charles P. Arand. *The Genius of Luther's Theology: A Wittenburg Way of Thinking for the Contemporary Church*. Baker Academic, 2008.

Kolb, Robert, Irene Dingel, and L'ubomír Batka, eds. *The Oxford Handbook of Martin Luther's Theology*. Oxford University Press, 2014.

Kolb, Robert, Torbjörn Johansson, and Daniel Johansson, eds. *Simul: Inquiries into Luther's Experience of the Christian Life*. Vandenhoeck and Ruprecht, 2021.

Kolden, Marc. "Earthly Vocation as a Corollary of Justification by Faith." In Burgess and Kolden, *By Faith Alone*.

Krispin, Gerald. "The Consolation of the Resurrection in Luther." *Lutheran Theological Review* 2, no. 1 (1989–90): 37–51.

Laffin, Michael Richard. *The Promise of Martin Luther's Political Theology: Freeing Luther from the Modern Political Narrative*. Bloomsbury T&T Clark, 2018.

Lane, Jason D. "That I May Be His Own: The Necessary End of the Law." In Paulson and Keith, *Handing Over the Goods*.

Lienhard, Marc. *Luther: Witness to Jesus Christ*. Translated by Edwin H. Robertson. Augsburg Publishing House, 1982.

Lindberg, Carter. "The Future of a Tradition: Luther and the Family." In *All Theology is Christology: Essays in Honor of David P. Scaer*, edited by Dean O. Wenthe, William C. Weinrich, Arthur A. Just Jr., Daniel Gard, and Thomas L. Olson, 133–51. Concordia Theological Seminary, 2000.

Linebaugh, Jonathan A. "Incongruous and Creative Gift: Reading *Paul and the Gift* with Martin Luther." *International Journal of Systematic Theology* 22, no. 1 (2020): 47–59. doi:10.1111/ijst.12388.

Linebaugh, Jonathan A. "'The Speech of the Dead': Identifying the No Longer and Now Living 'I' of Galatians 2.20." *New Testament Studies* 66, no. 1 (2020): 87–105. doi:10.1017/S0028688519000365.

Linebaugh, Jonathan A. *The Word of the Cross: Reading Paul*. Eerdmans, 2022.

Lockwood, Michael A. *The Unholy Trinity: Martin Luther against the Idol of Me, Myself, and I*. Concordia Publishing House, 2016.

Loewenich, Walther von. *Luther's Theology of the Cross*. Translated by Herbert J. A. Bouman. Augsburg Publishing House, 1976.

Lohse, Bernhard. *Martin Luther: An Introduction to His Life and Work*. Translated by Robert C. Schultz. Fortress, 1986.
Lohse, Bernhard. *Martin Luther's Theology: Its Historical and Systematic Development*. Translated and edited by Roy A. Harrisville. Augsburg Fortress, 1999.
Malcolm, Lois. "Martin Luther and the Holy Spirit." In *Oxford Research Encyclopedia of Religion*. Article Published March 29, 2017. https://doi.org/10.1093/acrefore/9780199340378.013.328.
Małysz, Piotr J. "Martin Luther's Trinitarian Hermeneutic of Freedom." In *Oxford Research Encyclopedia of Religion*. Article Published March 29, 2017. https://doi.org/10.1093/acrefore/9780199340378.013.355.
Małysz, Piotr J. "Sin, between Law and Gospel." *Lutheran Quarterly* 28, no. 2 (2014): 149–78.
Mannermaa, Tuomo. *Two Kinds of Love: Martin Luther's Religious World*. Translated and edited by Kirsi I. Stjerna. Fortress, 2010.
Marmion, Declan, Salvador Ryan, and Gesa E. Thiessen, eds. *Remembering the Reformation: Martin Luther and Catholic Theology*. Fortress, 2017.
Marty, Martin. *The Hidden Discipline*. Concordia, 1962.
Masaki, Naomichi. "The Church." In Pless and Vogel, *Luther's Large Catechism*.
Mattes, Mark C. "Honoring the Pastoral Dimension to Theology." In Paulson and Keith, *Handing Over the Goods*.
Mattes, Mark C. "Luther on Justification as Forensic and Effective." In Kolb et al., *Oxford Handbook of Theology*.
Mattes, Mark C. *Martin Luther's Theology of Beauty: A Reappraisal*. Baker Academic, 2017.
Mattes, Mark C. "Properly Distinguishing Law and Gospel as the Pastor's Calling." In Collver et al., *Necessary Distinction*.
Mattes, Mark C. *The Role of Justification in Contemporary Theology*. Fortress, 2004.
Mattes, Mark C. "Theses on the Captivated and Liberated Will." In *Lutheran Preaching? Law and Gospel Proclamation Today*, edited by Matthew C. Harrison and John T. Pless. Concordia Publishing House, 2023.
Mattox, Mickey Leland. "Faith in Creation: Martin Luther's Sermons on Genesis 1." *Trinity Journal* 39 (2018): 199–219. https://epublications.marquette.edu/theo_fac/782.
Mattox, Mickey Leland. "Luther's Interpretation of Scripture: Biblical Understanding in Trinitarian Shape." In Bielfeldt et al., *Substance of the Faith*.
Maxfield, John A. *Luther's Lectures on Genesis and the Formation of Evangelical Identity*. Truman State University Press, 2008.
Maxfield, John A. "Martin Luther and Idolatry." In *The Reformation as Christianization: Essays on Scott Hendrix's Christianization Thesis*, edited by Anna Marie Johnson and John A. Maxfield. Mohr Siebeck, 2012.
Mayes, Robert. "St. Hilary's Trinitarian Theology and Luther's Theology of Incarnate Omnipresence." *Logia: A Journal of Lutheran Theology* 14, no. 4 (Reformation 2005): 31–40.
McCain, Paul T. "Receiving the Gifts of God in His Two Kingdoms: The Development of Luther's Understanding." In Harrison and Pless, *One Lord, Two Hands*.
McGrath, Alister E. *Iustitia Dei: A History of the Christian Doctrine of Justification*. 4th ed. Cambridge University Press, 2020.
McGrath, Alister E. *Luther's Theology of the Cross: Martin Luther's Theological Breakthrough*. Wiley-Blackwell, 1985.

McGrath, Alister E. *The Nature of Christian Doctrine: Its Origins, Development, and Function*. Oxford University Press, 2024.

McNair, Bruce G. "Luther and the Pastoral Theology of the Lord's Prayer." *Logia* 14, no. 4 (2005): 41–46.

Nagel, Norman E. "Martinus: 'Heresy, Doctor Luther, Heresy!' The Person and Work of Christ." In *Seven-Headed Luther: Essays in Commemoration of a Quincentenary, 1483–1983*, edited by Peter Newman Brooks. Clarendon, 1983.

Nestingen, James Arne. "The Lord's Prayer in Luther's Catechism." *Word and World* 22, no. 1 (2002): 36–48.

Nestingen, James Arne. "Speaking of the End to the Law." In Collver et al., *Necessary Distinction*.

Nestingen, James Arne. "The Theology of the Cross in the Lord's Prayer." In Pless and Vogel, *Luther's Large Catechism*.

Nestingen, James Arne, and Gerhard O. Forde, *Free to Be: A Handbook to Luther's Small Catechism*. Augsburg Publishing House, 1975.

Nestingen, James Arne, and Gerhard O. Forde. *Martin Luther: A Life*. Rev. ed. Augsburg Books, 2003.

Ngien, Dennis. *Grace and Law in Galatians: Justification in Luther and Calvin*. Cascade Books, 2023.

Ngien, Dennis. *Paragon of Excellence: Luther's Sermons on I Peter*. Fortress, 2023.

Nygren, Anders. "Luther's Doctrine of the Two Kingdoms." *Ecumenical Review* 1, no. 3 (1949): 301–10.

Oberman, Heiko A. *The Dawn of the Reformation: Essays in Late Medieval and Early Reformation Thought*. T&T Clark, 1986.

O'Callaghan, Paul. *God and Mediation: A Retrospective Appraisal of Luther the Reformer*. Fortress, 2017.

Pannenberg, Wolfhart. "God of the Philosophers." *First Things*, June 1, 2007.

Pannenberg, Wolfhart. "Luther's Contribution to Christian Spirituality." *Dialog: A Journal of Theology* 40, no. 4 (2001): 284–89. https://doi.org/10.1111/1540-6385.00088.

Pannenberg, Wolfhart. *Systematic Theology*. Translated by Geoffrey W. Bromiley. 3 vols. Eerdmans, 1991, 1994, 1998.

Pak, G. Sujin. "The Protestant Reformers and the *Analogia Fidei*." In *The Medieval Luther*, edited by Christine Helmer. Mohr Siebeck, 2020.

Pak, G. Sujin. *The Reformation of Prophecy: Early Modern Interpretations of the Prophet and Old Testament Prophecy*. Oxford University Press, 2018.

Paulson, Steven D. "Categorical Preaching." In *Justification is for Preaching: Essays by Oswald Bayer, Gerhard O. Forde, and Others*, edited by Virgil Thompson. Pickwick, 2012.

Paulson, Steven D. "Internal Clarity of Scripture and the Modern World: Luther and Erasmus Revisited." In *Hermeneutica Sacra: Studies of the Interpretation of Holy Scripture in the Sixteenth and Seventeenth Centuries*, edited by Torbjörn Johansson, Robert Kolb, and Johann Anselm Steiger. De Gruyter, 2010.

Paulson, Steven D. *Lutheran Theology*. T&T Clark, 2011.

Paulson, Steven D. *Luther's Outlaw God*. Vol. 1, *Hiddenness, Evil, and Predestination*. Fortress, 2018.

Paulson, Steven D. *Luther's Outlaw God*. Vol. 2, *Hidden in the Cross*. Fortress, 2019.

Paulson, Steven D. *Luther's Outlaw God*. Vol. 3, *Sacraments and God's Attack on the Promise*. Fortress, 2021.

Paulson, Steven D. "The Third Commandment: Remember the Sabbath Day to Keep It Holy." In Pless and Vogel, *Luther's Large Catechism*.

Paulson, Steven D. and Scott L. Keith, eds. *Handing Over the Goods: Determined to Proclaim Nothing but Christ Jesus and Him Crucified; Essays in Honor of James Arne Nestingen*. 1517 Publishing, 2018.

Pelikan, Jaroslav. *The Christian Tradition: A History of the Development of Doctrine*. Vol. 4, *Reformation of Church and Dogma (1300–1700)*. University of Chicago Press, 1984.

Pelikan, Jaroslav. *Credo: Historical and Theological Guide to Creeds and Confessions of Faith in the Christian Tradition*. Yale University Press, 2003.

Pelikan, Jaroslav. *Luther the Expositor: Introduction to the Reformer's Exegetical Writings*. Companion volume to *Luther's Works*. Concordia, 1959.

Peters, Albrecht. *Commentary on Luther's Catechisms: Creed*. Translated by Thomas H. Trapp. Concordia Publishing House, 2009.

Peters, Albrecht. *Commentary on Luther's Catechisms: Lord's Prayer*. Translated by Daniel Thies. Concordia Publishing House, 2011.

Peters, Albrecht. *Commentary on Luther's Catechisms: Ten Commandments*. Translated by Holger K. Sonntag. Concordia Publishing House, 2009.

Pless, John T. "Luther's *Oratio, Meditatio*, and *Tentatio* as the Shape of Pastoral Care for Pastors." *Concordia Theological Quarterly* 80, no. 1 (2016): 37–48.

Pless, John T. *Luther's Small Catechism: A Manual for Discipleship*. Concordia Publishing House, 2013.

Pless, John T. *Martin Luther: Preacher of the Cross; A Study of Luther's Pastoral Theology*. Concordia Publishing House, 2013.

Pless, John T. *Praying Luther's Small Catechism: The Pattern of Sound Words*. Concordia Publishing House, 2016.

Pless, John T. "Reflections on the Life of the Royal Priesthood: Vocation and Evangelism." In *Shepherd the Church: Essays in Pastoral Theology Honoring Bishop Roger D. Pittelko*, edited by Frederic W. Baue, John W. Fenton, Eric C. Forss, Frank J. Pies, and John T. Pless. Concordia Theological Seminary, 2002.

Pless, John T. "Two Kingdoms in Luther's Catechism: A Proposal for Catechization." In Harrison and Pless, *One Lord, Two Hands*.

Pless, John T. and Larry M, Vogel, eds. *Luther's Large Catechism with Annotations and Contemporary Applications*. Concordia Publishing House, 2022.

Posset, Franz. *Pater Bernhardus: Martin Luther and Bernard of Clairvaux*. Cistercian Publications, 1999.

Prenter, Regin. *Spiritus Creator: Luther's Concept of the Holy Spirit*. Fortress, 1953.

Reimann, Henry W. "Luther on Creation: A Study in Theocentric Theology." *Concordia Theological Monthly* 24, no. 3 (1953): 26–40.

Repp, Arthur (Chris). "The Trinity as Gospel." In *Gift and Promise: The Augsburg Confession and the Heart of Christian Theology*, Edward H. Schroeder, edited by Ronald Neustadt and Stephen Hitchcock. Fortress, 2016.

Rieth, Ricardo Willy. "Luther on Greed." In Wengert, *Harvesting Martin Luther's Reflections*.

Rittgers, Ronald K. "Luther on Private Confession." In Wengert, *The Pastoral Luther*.

Ruokanen, Miikka. *Trinitarian Grace in Martin Luther's "The Bondage of the Will."* Oxford University Press, 2021.
Saarinen, Risto. "Communicating the Grace of God in a Pluralistic Society." In Gregersen et al., *The Gift of Grace*.
Saarinen, Risto. *God and the Gift: An Ecumenical Theology of Giving*. Liturgical Press, 2005.
Saarinen, Risto. "*In sinu Patris*: The Merciful Trinity in Luther's Exposition of John 1:18." In *Trinitarian Theology in the Medieval West*, edited by Pekka Kärkkäinen, 280–98. Luther-Agricola-Seura, 2007.
Saarinen, Risto. "Luther and *Beneficia*." In *The Reformation as Christianization: Essays on Scott Hendrix's Christianization Thesis*, edited by Anna Marie Johnson and John A. Maxfield. Mohr Siebeck, 2012.
Saarinen, Risto. *Luther and the Gift*. Mohr Siebeck, 2017.
Saleska, Tim. "The Clarity of Paradox: A Meditation on Exodus 34:6–7." In Kolb et al., *Simul*.
Sánchez M., Leopoldo A. "The Person and Work of the Holy Spirit." In Pless and Vogel, *Luther's Large Catechism*.
Sasse, Hermann. *Here We Stand: Nature and Character of the Lutheran Faith*. Translated by Theodore G. Tappert. Lutheran Publishing House, 1979.
Sasse, Hermann. *We Confess Jesus Christ*. Translated by Norman Nagel. Concordia, 1984.
Sauter, Gerhard. "God Creating Faith: The Doctrine of Justification from the Reformation to the Present." *Lutheran Quarterly* 11, no. 1 (1997): 17–102.
Schumacher, William W. *Who Do I Say That You Are? Anthropology and the Theology of Theosis in the Finnish School of Tuomo Mannermaa*. Wipf & Stock, 2010.
Schwanke, Johannes. "Luther on Creation." In Wengert, *Harvesting Martin Luther's Reflections*.
Schwöbel, Christoph. "Martin Luther and the Trinity." In *Oxford Research Encyclopedia of Religion*. Article Published March 29, 2017. https://doi.org/10.1093/acrefore/9780199340378.013.326.
Schwöbel, Christoph. "The Triune God of Grace: Trinitarian Thinking in the Theology of the Reformers." In *The Christian Understanding of God Today*, edited by James M. Byrne. Columba, 1993.
Schwöbel, Christoph. "'We are All God's Vocabulary': The Idea of Creation as a Speech-Act of the Trinitarian God and Its Significance for the Dialogue between Theology and Sciences." In *Knowing Creation: Perspectives from Theology, Philosophy, and Science*, edited by Andrew B. Torrance and Thomas H. McCall. Zondervan, 2018.
Seifrid, Mark A. "Romans 7: The Voice of the Law, the Cry of Lament, and the Shout of Thanksgiving." In *Perspectives on Our Struggle with Sin: Three Views of Romans 7*, edited by Terry L. Wilder. B&H Academic, 2011.
Siecienski, A. Edward. *The Filioque: History of a Doctrinal Controversy*. Oxford University Press, 2010.
Siggins, Ian D. Kingston. *Martin Luther's Doctrine of Christ*. Yale University Press, 1970.
Silcock, Jeffrey G. "Hearing and Seeing (Eye & Ear): Word and Image in the Bible, Luther, and the Lutheran Tradition." In *Promising Faith for a Ruptured Age: An English-Speaking Appreciation of Oswald Bayer*, edited by John T. Pless, Roland Ziegler, and Joshua C. Miller. Pickwick, 2019.

Silcock, Jeffrey G. "Law, Gospel, and Repentance in Luther's Antinomian Disputations." *Luther-Bulletin* 16 (2007): 41–56.
Silcock, Jeffrey G. "Luther on the Holy Spirit and His Use of God's Word." In Kolb et al., *Oxford Handbook of Theology*.
Silcock, Jeffrey G. "The Role of the Spirit in Creation." *Lutheran Theological Journal* 44, no. 1 (2010): 4–14.
Steiger, Johann Anselm. "The *communicatio idiomatum* as the Axle and Motor of Luther's Theology." *Lutheran Quarterly* 14, no. 2 (2000): 125–58.
Steinmetz, David C. *Calvin in Context*. Oxford University Press, 1995.
Steinmetz, David C. *Luther in Context*. 2nd ed. Baker Academic, 2002.
Stephenson, John R. "The Two Governments and the Two Kingdoms in Luther's Thought." *Scottish Journal of Theology* 34, no. 4 (1981): 321–37.
Stjerna, Kirsi I. *Lutheran Theology: A Grammar of Faith*. T&T Clark, 2021.
Stjerna, Kirsi I. *No Greater Jewel: Thinking about Baptism with Luther*. Augsburg, 2009.
Stratis, Justin. "Unconditional Love: *Creatio ex Nihilo* and the Covenant of Grace." In *Theological Theology: Essays in Honour of John B. Webster*, edited by R. David Nelson, Darren Sarisky, and Justin Stratis. Bloomsbury T&T Clark, 2015.
Sutton, A. Trevor. "Virtual Christianity." In Pless and Vogel, *Luther's Large Catechism*.
Swain, Scott R. *The Trinity: An Introduction*. Crossway, 2020.
Swain, Scott R. *The Trinity and the Bible: On Theological Interpretation*. Lexham Academic, 2021.
Tanner, Kathryn. *Christ the Key*. Cambridge University Press, 2010.
Tappert, Theodore, ed. *Luther: Letters of Spiritual Counsel*. Westminster, 1955.
Thielicke, Helmut. *The Evangelical Faith*. Vol. 3, *Theology of the Spirit*, translated and edited by Geoffrey W. Bromiley. Eerdmans, 1982.
Thielicke, Helmut. *Our Heavenly Father: Sermons on the Lord's Prayer*. Harper and Row, 1960.
Thiessen, Gesa E. "Luther and the Role of Images." In Marmion et al. *Remembering the Reformation*.
Thompson, John. *Modern Trinitarian Perspectives*. Oxford University Press, 1994.
Tomlin, Graham. "Shapers of Protestantism: Martin Luther." In *The Blackwell Companion to Protestantism*, edited by Alister E. McGrath and Darren C. Marks. Blackwell, 2004.
Torrance, Thomas F. *The Trinitarian Faith: The Evangelical Theology of the Ancient Catholic Church*. 2nd ed. Bloomsbury T&T Clark, 2016. https://digitalcommons.augustana.edu/intersections/vol2017/iss46/6.
Tranvik, Mark D. *Martin Luther and the Called Life*. Fortress, 2016.
Trigg, Jonathan D. *Baptism in the Theology of Martin Luther*. Brill, 2001.
Truebenbach, Kim A. "Luther's Two Kingdoms in the Third and Fourth Petitions." *Lutheran Quarterly* 24, no. 4 (2010): 469–73.
Trueman, Carl R. *Luther on the Christian Life: Cross and Freedom*. Crossway, 2015.
Vajta, Vilmos. *Luther on Worship*. Translated by U. S. Leupold. Muhlenberg, 1958.
Veith, Gene Edward, Jr. *God at Work: Your Christian Vocation in All of Life*. Crossway, 2002.
Ward, Benedicta. *The prayers and Meditations of St. Anselm with the Proslogion*. Penguin Books, 1973.

Watson, Philip S. *Let God be God: An Interpretation of the Theology of Martin Luther*. Fortress, 1947.
Wengert, Timothy J., ed. *Harvesting Martin Luther's Reflections on Theology, Ethics, and the Church*. Eerdmans, 2004.
Wengert, Timothy J. "Martin Luther and the Ten Commandments in the Large Catechism." In Wengert, *The Pastoral Luther*.
Wengert, Timothy J. *Martin Luther's Catechisms: Forming the Faith*. Fortress, 2009.
Wengert, Timothy J., ed. *The Pastoral Luther: Essays on Martin Luther's Practical Theology*. Eerdmans, 2009.
Wengert, Timothy J. "The Small Catechism, 1529." In *The Annotated Luther*. Vol. 4, *Pastoral Writings*, edited by Mary Jane Haemig. Fortress, 2016.
Westhelle, Vítor. *The Scandalous God: The Use and Abuse of the Cross*. Fortress, 2006.
Whiteford, Ruth Ang-Onn. "The Second Commandment: Contemporary Christians and Honoring the Name of God." In Pless and Vogel, *Luther's Large Catechism*.
Wiersma, Hans. "On Keeping the Sabbath Holy in Martin Luther's Catechisms and Other Writings." *Word & World* 36, no. 3 (2016): 237–46.
Wiles, Maurice, and Herbert McCabe. "The Incarnation: An Exchange." *New Blackfriars* 58, no. 691 (1977): 542–53.
Wingren, Gustaf. "The Doctrine of Creation: Not an Appendix but the First Article." *Word and World* 4 no. 4 (1984): 353–71.
Wingren, Gustaf. *Luther on Vocation*. Translated by Carl C. Rasmussen. Muhlenberg, 1957.
Wisløff, Carl F. *The Gift of Communion: Luther's Controversy with Rome on Eucharistic Sacrifice*. Translated by Joseph M. Shaw. Augsburg Publishing House, 1964.
Wolff, Hans Walter. *Anthropology of the Old Testament*. Translated by Margaret Kohl. Fortress, 1974.
Wolfson, Henry A. *The Philosophy of the Church Fathers*. Vol. 1, *Faith, Trinity, Incarnation*. Harvard University Press, 1956.
Zachhuber, Johannes. "Jesus Christ in Martin Luther's Theology." In *Oxford Research Encyclopedia of Religion*. Article Published March 29, 2017. https://doi.org/10.1093/acrefore/9780199340378.013.327.
Zachman, Randall C. *The Assurance of Faith: Conscience in the Theology of Martin Luther and John Calvin*. Augsburg Fortress, 1993.
Zahl, Simeon. "The Bondage of the Affections: Willing, Feeling, and Desiring in Luther's Theology, 1513–1525." In *The Spirit, the Affections, and the Christian Tradition*, edited by Dale M. Coulter and Amos Yong. University of Notre Dame Press, 2016.

INDEX

absolution, 176–78, 181, 219, 223
adultery, 69–70
Alber, Erasmus, 23
Althaus, Paul, 32–33, 49, 53, 74, 78, 107, 111, 113, 136–37, 138, 139, 140, 183
antinomians, the, 137–38, 139, 141
Apostles' Creed, the, 2–3, 9, 42, 75, 119–20, 189, 192, 195, 215, 229
Aquinas, Thomas, 106
Arand, Charles P., 79, 107, 171, 211
Aristotle, 227
Arius, 26
Athanasius, 22, 26
atonement, 10–11, 119–25, 129. *See also* cross, the; redemption
  as satisfaction, 119–20, 122–23, 125
Augustine, 5, 8, 22, 26, 27, 33, 34–35, 37, 40, 50, 81, 98n147, 106, 114, 165, 166, 167, 169
authority, 67

baptism, 17, 152, 172, 174–76, 178, 179, 181, 219
Barclay, John, 43, 182, 220
Barth, Karl, 19, 22
Bayer, Oswald, 6, 13, 42, 64–65, 77, 79, 84, 86, 89, 92, 93, 103, 106, 108, 116, 136, 145, 148, 158, 162, 177, 190, 218, 219, 225, 227–28
Bellini, Alberto, 91
Bender, Kimlyn J., 17–18
Bernard of Clairvaux, 50, 139–40
Biel, Gabriel, 11, 157, 166
Bonaventure, 33
Bonhoeffer, Dietrich, 149
Bornkamm, Heinrich, 185
Boulton, Michael, 193

Braaten, Carl E., 12, 117
Brecht, Martin, 56

Calvin, John, 47
Carlson, Edgar M., 93
Cary, Phillip, 132, 146, 188, 219, 220, 227
catechesis, 47
Chester, Stephen J., 84, 143, 186
children, 47, 62, 66, 67, 68, 80, 96
Christ, 38, 63, 111–49, 192–94, 219, 221. *See also* God, the Father; Holy Spirit, the; Trinity, the
  ascension of, 6, 127–29, 164
  "brothers" of, 209–10
  faith in/of, 133
  "for us," 44, 120, 129–34, 143, 223
  as gift, 122, 131–32, 162, 182
  and the Holy Spirit, 41, 43–44, 163–65, 198, 218
  incarnation of, 29, 30–35, 111, 113–14, 115, 118, 121, 122, 164, 222
  intercession of, 129
  as King, 128
  lordship of, 116–19, 155
  passion of, 50, 215
  resurrection of, 125–27, 143, 147, 186, 198
  righteousness of, 14, 16, 39, 44, 112, 125, 126, 136, 143, 144–47, 161, 186, 215
  as *sacramentum*, 5, 131
  as sinner, 122–25
  union with, 145–46
  as Victor, 119–20, 121, 123, 124, 126
Chung, Paul S., 106
church, the, 10, 17–18, 21, 43, 93, 152, 159, 181–82, 197

church year, 118–19
and the Holy Spirit, 17, 171–73
civil order. *See* politics
confession, 176–78
Cortez, Marc, 108, 148
coveting, 72–73
creation, 1, 5, 6–8, 35, 38, 39, 55, 76, 77–110, 152, 217, 218
    as gift, 82–86, 105–10
    goodness of, 80
    and justification, 105–10
creatures as "masks," 9, 78, 91–101, 109–10. *See also* God, hiddenness of; providence
cross, the, 12, 30–35, 39, 40, 96, 113, 114–15, 118, 124, 125–27, 143, 178, 186, 198, 199, 223. *See also* atonement; redemption
Cyprian, 171, 172

death, 184–85, 206–7
Deism, 91
desire, 72–73
devil, the, 162–63, 206–7
Dieter, Theodor, 166

Ebeling, Gerhard, 174
Elert, Werner, 129
Erasmus, 55, 156
eschatology, 135, 136, 151–52, 197, 198, 206–7, 224
    and justification, 16, 182–88
evil, 206–7
exchange, 8, 102, 120, 141–49, 186, 215
    "joyous exchange," 39, 44, 120–27, 128, 129, 132, 135–36, 146, 149, 164, 175, 199
ex nihilo, 1, 7, 8, 15, 38, 78, 88, 105–10, 143, 146, 151–52, 153, 155, 174, 185, 188, 193, 214, 218, 227

faith, 1, 8, 9–10, 12, 15, 18, 19, 36–45, 54, 55–57, 57–58, 64–65, 66, 75, 79, 84, 86, 93, 99, 104, 110, 115, 126–27, 129–34, 139, 144–46, 149, 161, 174, 180, 186, 190, 212, 214, 215, 218, 219–21, 225–26, 228

analogia fidei, 4
    in/of Christ, 133
    and the Holy Spirit, 11, 153–58
    and prayer, 207–8
regula fidei, 4, 105
fall, the, 3, 39, 69, 136, 142, 155
false testimony, 62, 71–72
family, 68, 69, 93
fathers, 67
fear, 66
Feuerbach, Ludwig, 56
Forde, Gerhard O., 13, 17, 18, 47, 83n45, 90, 115, 125, 157, 180, 181, 223, 228
forgiveness, 17, 139, 155, 177, 178, 182, 184, 202–4
free will, 83, 156–58, 164, 165, 199–200. *See also* God, will of
Fritts, Marney, 155

George, Timothy, 18–19
Gerrish, B. A., 56, 115
gift, gifts, 3, 7, 8, 9, 11, 15, 16, 18, 33–35, 36–45, 58, 65, 70–71, 76, 78–86, 95, 96–98, 110, 125, 148, 154, 155, 167, 169, 178, 180, 193, 198, 200–202, 207, 214, 217, 220. *See also* God, self-giving of
    Christ as gift, 122, 131–32, 162, 182
    and counter-gift, 42, 82–86, 220
    creation as gift, 82–86, 105–10
    Holy Spirit as gift, 33–35, 122, 159, 162, 165, 224
Girgensohn, Herbert, 66, 70, 73, 102, 104, 161, 177, 178, 200
God
    actions *ad extra*, 1, 5, 7, 14, 19, 38, 117, 215
    aseity of, 86–87
    character of, 1, 49, 58, 71, 107, 214
    divine freedom, 105–10
    divine speech, 15, 27–30, 35–36, 86–91, 159, 208–15. *See also* word of God
    the Father, 9, 38, 77–110, 111, 121, 190, 194–96. *See also* Christ; Holy Spirit, the; Trinity, the
    "for us," 8–9, 37, 40, 122, 217, 218

Index

hiddenness of, 5, 9–10, 12–13, 35, 37, 78, 91–101, 109–10, 112–16, 173, 213, 222–25. *See also* creatures as "masks"
image of, 18, 32, 141–49, 171, 182
jealousy of, 74
kingdom of, 197–98, 199, 213
mercy of, 11, 51, 53, 57, 73–76, 115, 121, 124, 125, 167–68, 223, 225–26
name of, 60–62, 71, 196–97, 199, 213
power of, 89–90, 101–4, 153–54, 168
provision of. *See* gift, gifts
and revelation, 3, 75, 110, 148
self-giving of, 6–8, 9, 13, 33–35, 38–39, 118, 122, 130, 161–62, 202, 217
self-revelation of, 5, 12, 30, 32, 37, 43, 214, 218, 222, 224, 227
will of, 121, 153, 168, 198–200, 201, 213
wrath of, 5, 11, 51, 53, 57, 68, 71, 73–76, 120, 121, 123, 124, 125, 127, 167–68, 191, 221–22, 223, 225–26
gospel, the, 2, 9, 14, 18, 36, 37, 49–55, 75, 84, 85–86, 101–4, 111, 132, 136, 138–39, 140, 141, 156, 157, 158–59, 166, 170, 171, 174–75, 177, 190, 191–92, 202, 203, 204, 217–30
grace, 3, 8, 12, 36, 40, 41, 44, 75, 83, 84, 107, 110, 124, 142, 143, 149, 163, 166, 169, 179, 187, 189, 202, 215
cooperative, 154
double movement of, 5–6
operative, 154
sola gratia, 8, 78, 105, 106, 107, 164, 202
Gregersen, Niels Henrik, 7, 44, 79, 106, 173, 220
Gritsch, Eric, 155–56, 179–80

Haemig, Mary Jane, 193
Hamm, Berndt, 3, 44
Hampson, Daphne, 147, 192
Hanson, Bradley, 218
Hefner, Philip, 92n107

Helmer, Christine, 5, 6, 22, 31, 32, 78, 80, 111, 151, 164
Heschel, Abraham J., 168
Hilary of Poitiers, 31–32
Hinlicky, Paul, 35, 36, 41, 48, 77, 87, 123
Hoglund, Jonathan, 175
Holm, Bo Kristian, 85, 102, 220
Holy Spirit, the, 38, 43–45, 87, 145, 149, 151–88, 229–30. *See also* Christ; God, the Father; Trinity, the
and "Amen," 190, 207–8
and calling, 151, 158–63
and Christ, 41, 43–44, 163–65, 198, 218
and the church, 17, 171–73
and enlightening, 151, 158–63
and experience, 11–12, 165–71
and faith, 11, 153–58
filioque, 24, 34
as gift, 33–35, 122, 159, 162, 165, 224
and the Lord's Prayer, 208–15
and prayer, 190
as Preacher, 162–63
and preserving, 151, 158–63
and sanctifying, 151, 158–63
sigh of, 211–13
honor, 66–67
Hordern, William, 39
Horrell, David G., 133
household, 80, 93, 181
household, the, 10, 65, 67
Hultgren, Stephen, 183

identity, 3, 7, 8, 10, 13–14, 40, 41, 44, 55, 73, 74, 78, 94, 98, 99, 100, 103–4, 108, 109, 112, 141–49, 152, 154, 155, 161, 175–76, 186–88, 204, 213, 215, 218–20
idolatry, 115, 132, 148, 155
idolatry, idols, 29, 47, 56, 57–60, 73, 74, 94, 95, 97, 98, 205, 217, 219
images, 57–60
imputation, 14, 56, 149, 161, 174, 183, 186
Iwand, Hans Joachim, 50, 129, 187

Jansen, John Frederick, 119
Jansen, Reiner, 5

Jenson, Robert, 28, 29, 35, 155–56, 179–80, 208–9, 227
Johnson, Luke T., 90
judgment, 13, 14, 50, 53, 68, 72, 149, 186, 225
Jüngel, Eberhard, 22, 105–6
justification, 1, 4–5, 6, 7–8, 10, 13–14, 15, 16–17, 44, 49, 51, 52, 65, 75, 98–99, 111, 113, 130, 132–33, 143, 145, 152, 155, 170, 172, 175, 193, 203, 214, 220
   and creation, 105–10
   and eschatology, 16, 182–88
   justifying God, 14–15, 50–51
   and sanctification, 160–61

Kaiser, Denis, 87
Karlstadt, Andreas, 58
Kilcrease, Jack D., 136, 145–46, 188
killing, 68–69
Kim, Sun-young, 65
Kleinig, John W., 3, 88
Kolb, Robert, 9, 10, 54–55, 67n126, 68–69, 75, 77, 93, 107, 108, 109, 111, 124, 151–52, 154, 175, 179, 198, 199
Kolden, Marc, 94, 98
Krause, Johann, 141

Laffin, Michael Richard, 17, 181
Lane, Jason D., 135, 136
law, natural, 47–48, 63
law, the, 2, 3, 5, 14, 18, 47, 49–55, 57, 63, 73, 74, 75, 83, 84, 85, 93, 101–4, 111, 120, 124, 132, 134–41, 156, 157, 158–59, 165, 166, 174–75, 177, 182, 190, 191–92, 202, 203, 204, 214, 220, 221–22, 224, 228. *See also* antinomians, the
Lienhard, Marc, 22, 36n79, 37, 119
Lindberg, Carter, 69n140
Linebaugh, Jonathan A., 7, 38, 88, 107, 135, 143, 148
Lockwood, Michael, 56, 97
Loewenich, Walther von, 198
Löfgren, David, 185
Lohse, Bernhard, 49, 172, 223–24
Lord's Prayer, the, 2, 9, 15, 62, 177, 189–215, 229. *See also* prayer
   "Amen," 190, 207–8
   command to pray, 191–92
   fifth petition, 202–4
   first petition, 196–97, 199, 213
   fourth petition, 200–202
   and the Holy Spirit, 208–15
   introduction to, 194–96
   second petition, 197–98, 199, 213
   seventh petition, 206–7
   sixth petition, 204–6
   third petition, 198–200, 201, 213
Lord's Supper, the, 17, 125, 152, 172, 178–82, 219
Löscher, Valentin, 4n20
love, 11, 29, 34–35, 40–42, 66, 74, 75, 99, 105–6, 107, 123, 165–71, 181, 202, 219, 220
Luther's writings
   The Babylonian Captivity of the Church, 175, 179
   The Bondage of the Will, 101, 112, 153, 154, 224
   Commentary on Galatians, 56, 85
   Concerning the Order of Public Worship, 64
   Confession Concerning Christ's Supper, 21
   Disputation Against Scholasticism, 11
   An Exposition of the Lord's Prayer for Simple Laymen, 191, 196, 200, 203, 206
   First Disputation against the Antinomians, 34, 159
   Against the Heavenly Prophets, 152, 172
   Heidelberg Disputation, 51, 83, 107, 157
   How Christians Should Regard Moses, 47
   Large Catechism, 1, 2, 38, 52, 55, 71, 106, 172, 176, 195, 200, 202, 228
   Lectures on Genesis, 82, 109
   Meditation on Christ's Passion, 8, 31, 121

Index

Personal Prayer Book, 72, 200
Preface to Romans, 171
Sermons on John 14–16, 210
A Simple Way to Pray, 192, 206
Smalcald Articles, 4
Small Catechism, 2, 17, 44, 47, 70, 106, 119, 120, 177, 200, 228
Ten Sermons on the Catechism, 203
Three Symbols, 23
Treatise on Good Works, 64, 67
Treatise on the Last Words of David, 25, 30

Malcolm, Lois, 41–42, 125
Małysz, Piotr J., 84, 149, 155
Mannermaa, Tuomo, 170n120
Margerie, Bertrand de, 39
marriage, 62, 68, 69–70
 as gift, 69
Marty, Martin, 70, 72
Mattes, Mark C., 4–5, 12, 74, 102, 147, 148, 155, 187, 221, 222, 225
Mattox, Mickey Leland, 103, 106, 162
Maxfield, John, 58
McCabe, Herbert, 131
McGrath, Alister E., 5, 22–23, 90, 223
McNair, Bruce G., 200n71
Melanchthon, Philip, 17n90
Moltmann, Jürgen, 199

Nestingen, James Arne, 47, 53, 135–36, 200, 202, 205, 207
Nicene theology, 21–22
Nygren, Anders, 100

oaths, 62
Oberman, Heiko A., 212
O'Callaghan, Paul, 91
ordo cognoscendi, 5, 22–23, 44, 110
ordo essendi, 5, 22–23, 44, 110
Origen, 25

Pak, G. Sujin, 4, 59, 105
Pannenberg, Wolfhart, 30, 40, 131, 144–45, 223, 224

paradox, 49, 51, 53, 63, 74, 107, 112, 136–37, 147, 168, 183, 185, 191, 192, 200, 204, 214, 221–22, 226
parents, 65–68, 80
Paulson, Stephen D., 64, 83, 86–87, 88, 112, 113, 132, 133–34, 157, 190, 217, 223, 225–26, 228
Pelikan, Jaroslav, 3, 28, 36–37
penance, 175
Peters, Albrecht, 2, 12, 18, 61, 65–66, 71, 72, 92–93, 96, 117, 151, 153, 188, 197, 198, 206
Philo, 25
pictures, 60
Pless, John T., 53, 57, 71, 79, 83, 100, 116, 118, 151–52, 153, 166, 207
politics, 9, 10, 52, 67, 80, 93, 200–202
 two kingdoms, the, 99–100, 201
Posset, Franz, 50
prayer, 15–16, 60–62, 189–215, 228–30. *See also* Lord's Prayer, the
 and Christ's intercession, 129
 and faith, 207–8
 and the Holy Spirit, 190
preaching, 63, 64, 65, 118–19, 132, 134–41, 141, 156–57, 159–60, 223, 226–28
predestination, 33
procreation, 69–70, 96
promise, 32–33, 58, 73, 83, 89–90, 111, 129–34, 145, 166, 175–76, 179, 190, 191, 203, 214, 221, 223
providence, 81, 90–104, 189, 201. *See also* creatures as "masks"

reason, 156, 158
redemption, 1, 5, 38, 76, 78, 110, 111–49, 152, 217, 218. *See also* atonement; cross, the
Reimann, Henry W., 80, 87, 91, 110, 217
repentance, 13, 47, 53, 134–41, 197, 202–4
Repp, Arthur, 21
Rieth, Ricardo, 57
righteousness, 10–11, 16, 17, 51, 53, 142, 146–47, 183, 184

active, 10, 51, 54–55, 84–85, 108, 147, 187, 214
alien, 14, 125, 143, 146, 147, 187
original, 83, 84
passive, 10, 51, 54–55, 84–85, 108, 142
by works, 54–55, 148, 212
Rittgers, Ronald K., 177
Ruokanen, Miikka, 153, 218–19

Saarinen, Risto, 37, 38, 40, 78, 100, 180n199
Sabbath, the, 63–65, 82, 90–91, 188
sacraments, 17, 173, 174, 203. *See also* baptism; Christ, as *sacramentum*; Lord's Supper, the
Saleska, Tim, 226
Sánchez, Leopold A., 161
sanctification, 1, 5, 16, 17, 38, 76, 151–88, 217, 218
and justification, 160–61
Sasse, Hermann, 12, 100, 118
Sauter, Gerhard, 8, 14, 108
Schumacher, William W., 106
Schwanke, Johannes, 79, 80
Schwöbel, Christoph, 7, 30, 43, 88, 152, 159, 162, 165, 172
Seifrid, Mark A., 118
Siggins, Ian D. Kingston, 16, 36n79, 119, 127, 160
Silcock, Jeffrey G., 28, 29, 59, 89, 139, 141, 173
sin, 3, 7, 8, 17, 39, 68, 69, 70, 74, 75, 84, 93, 120–21, 122–24, 136, 139–40, 142, 146, 147, 160, 164, 175, 182, 184, 187, 202–4, 204–6, 221
sins, 177, 202–4
sexual, 70
of the tongue, 72
sonship, 15, 112, 118, 164, 190, 208
Staupitz, Johann von, 115
stealing, 70–71, 72
Steiger, Johann Anselm, 134
Steinmetz, David C., 58, 87
Stephenson, John R., 201
Stjerna, Kirsi I., 17, 45, 55, 152, 176, 182
Stratis, Justin, 105

suffering, 81, 166, 168, 213
Sutton, A. Trevor, 170
Swain, Scott, 38

Tanner, Kathryn, 105
temptation, 204–6
Ten Commandments, the, 2, 3, 47–76, 82, 93, 96, 141, 177, 181, 189, 192, 215, 225, 229
eighth commandment, 71–72
fifth commandment, 68–69, 72
first commandment, 1, 9, 12, 48–60, 66, 73, 77, 79, 92, 94, 98, 118, 136–38, 148, 155, 192, 195, 207–8, 226
fourth commandment, 65–68
ninth commandment, 72–73
second commandment, 60–62, 64, 197
seventh commandment, 70–71, 72
sixth commandment, 69–70
tenth commandment, 72–73
third commandment, 63–65

Tertullian, 25
Theologica Germanica, 131
Thielicke, Helmut, 193, 197
Thiessen, Gesa, 59
Thomas Aquinas. *See* Aquinas, Thomas
Thompson, John, 5–6, 164
Torrance, Thomas F., 35
Tranvik, Mark D., 9
Trigg, Jonathan D., 175
Trinity, the, 1, 6–8, 12–13, 15, 18, 21–45, 76, 87, 151–52, 153, 159, 161–62, 163–65, 188, 190, 195, 196, 208–15, 217. *See also* Christ; God, the Father; Holy Spirit, the
economic, 5–6, 22–27, 37, 40, 41–42, 87, 218, 224
and faith, 36–45
immanent, 5–6, 22–27, 37, 40, 41–42, 87, 218, 224
opera trinitatis ad extra sunt indivisa, 25, 38, 215
relations of origin, 23–25
unity and distinction, 5, 22–27, 164

Index

Troeltsch, Ernst, 93n119
Truebenbach, Kim A., 201
Trueman, Carl, 63, 174

Valta, Vilmos, 65
Veith, Gene Edward, Jr., 94
vocation, 9, 10, 71, 93, 94–95, 97, 98–99, 199, 200

Watson, Philip, 43, 74, 80, 93
Weller, Jerome, 225
Wengert, Timothy J., 6, 16, 40, 44–45, 75, 111, 119–20, 145, 152, 161, 164
Westhelle, Vítor, 8, 92, 114, 124
Whiteford, Ruth, 54
Wiersma, Hans, 63
Wingren, Gustaf, 92, 99
Wolff, Hans Walter, 97
word of God, 16–18, 27–35, 35, 43, 57, 58–59, 63–64, 83, 113, 135, 152, 158, 159–60, 171, 172, 173, 174, 178, 179–81, 184, 189–90, 209, 219, 223, 226–28. *See also* God, divine speech; preaching
  as creative/effective, 86–91, 123, 134, 145, 149, 192–94, 203
work
  alien, 18, 51–52, 64, 74, 81, 112, 124, 136, 138–39, 140, 160, 166, 167–68, 175, 181, 191, 200, 204, 205, 212, 214, 221–22, 226
  proper, 18, 51–52, 64, 74, 81, 112, 124, 138–39, 160, 167–68, 175, 181, 191, 192, 200, 204, 205, 221–22, 226
workplace, 10, 181
worship, 59, 60, 64, 84, 85, 86, 110, 132, 159, 181, 202, 219

Zachhuber, Johannes, 123
Zachman, Randall C., 126
Zahl, Simeon, 11

www.ingramcontent.com/pod-product-compliance
Ingram Content Group UK Ltd.
Pitfield, Milton Keynes, MK11 3LW, UK
UKHW010840010326
468475UK00004B/351